From Wounded Knee to Checkpoint Charlie

SUNY series, Tribal Worlds: Critical Studies in American Indian Nation Building

Brian Hosmer and Larry Nesper, editors

From Wounded Knee to Checkpoint Charlie

The Alliance for Sovereignty between American Indians and Central Europeans in the Late Cold War

György Ferenc Tóth

SUNY PRESS

Cover photo courtesy of Dick Bancroft and Claus Biegert; photo archive of the Gesellschaft fur Bedrohte Volker, Gottingen, Germany.

Published by State University of New York Press, Albany

Printed in the United States of America

For information, contact State University of New York Press, Albany, NY
www.sunypress.edu

Production, Diane Ganeles
Marketing, Michael Campochiaro

Library of Congress Cataloging-in-Publication Data

Names: Tóth, György Ferenc, 1976–
Title: From Wounded Knee to Checkpoint Charlie : the alliance for sovereignty between American Indians and Central Europeans in the late Cold War / György Ferenc Tóth.
Description: Albany : State University of New York Press, 2016. | Series: SUNY series, Tribal worlds : critical studies in American Indian nation building | Includes bibliographical references and index.
Identifiers: LCCN 2015027729 | ISBN 9781438461212 (hardcover : alkaline paper) | ISBN 9781438461229 (pbk.: alkaline paper) | ISBN 9781438461236 (e-book)
Subjects: LCSH: Indians of North America—Politics and government—20th century. | Indians of North America—Government relations—History—20th century. | Indians of North America—Civil rights—History—20th century. | Sovereignty—History—20th century. | Anti-imperialist movements—History—20th century. | United States—Relations—Europe, Central. | Europe, Central—Relations—United States. | United States—Politics and government—1945–1989. | Europe, Central—Politics and government—20th century.
Classification: LCC E98.T77 T68 2016 | DDC 323.1197—dc23
LC record available at http://lccn.loc.gov/2015027729

10 9 8 7 6 5 4 3 2 1

In honor of the transatlantic activists for American Indian sovereignty.

Dedicated to my mentors, parents, and grandmother.

Contents

Preface

I was born in 1976—in the year of the U.S. Bicentennial. My parents did not get to attend the anniversary's festivities because we lived on the other side of the iron curtain—in Communist Hungary. We were far away from the official celebrations sponsored by the U.S. government, and from the counter-commemorations and alternative ceremonies staged by dissenting groups and movements, who reflected, reenacted, and challenged the meaning of U.S. national history and identity.

Yet, in spite of Hungary's official anti-U.S. propaganda, we did engage with "American" culture. My grandmother, a Baptist faithful even under the toughest dictatorship, was elated when she heard that Jimmy Carter, a Southern Baptist, was elected president of the United States. As for me, some of my earliest memories are of my mother reading to me at bedtime some of Karl May's novels, in which a young German protagonist goes to the Wild West, strikes up a friendship with an Apache warrior, and together they fight against the "evil" Kiowa Indians and white bandits. When I was a little older, I acted out some of these stories with a friend of mine. Around this time and later, I would go with my parents to the cinema to watch Westerns made in the Eastern Bloc about the nineteenth-century resistance by American Indians to the U.S. Army and land grabs by white capitalists. Their star, Gojko Mitic, was from Yugoslavia, but for us he was an American Indian. Later still, in the early 1990s, I met a Hungarian hobbyist who told me about the people who had been reenacting American Indian cultures in their summer camps in the hills.

However, no one told me about the American Indian Movement's struggles when I was growing up. It was only much later, after long years of learning English at school and at home on TV, after the transition of my country to democracy and capitalism, and once I was majoring in American Studies at university, that I learned about the American Indian radical sovereignty movement. At first I did not make any connections between the Indian fantasies of my childhood and the Native activism on the other side of the Atlantic. As I increasingly used my academic training about the United States to critically examine my own society, I became interested in just what I and millions of other Hungarians (and indeed, Central Europeans) were doing with those fantasies. From recent scholarship I learned to recognize and appreciate the multiplicity of motivations and functions of this "Indian play" among Europeans. However, what kept intriguing me was the possibility that some of the people who engaged in "playing Indian" could also perhaps fight for Indian rights. As I became a Hungarian scholar of the politics of U.S. culture in Cold War Central Europe, I embarked on a project to show that cultural consumption and creative engagement with "America" can lead to not only intercultural encounters, but also to political activism and alliances for social justice across geographical, ideological, and racial divides. Set in the period of my childhood, this is the history of the transatlantic coalition for American Indian sovereignty.

Acknowledgments

This book was written about a select group of people who worked hard for their ideals. As such, the project benefited from the contributions of a select group of people—friends, colleagues, and professionals.

During my research trips I received in-kind logistical assistance from Su Zhang, Carlton Rounds and Michael "Cabbie" Caban, Leslie Holland and Jack Lamb, Carmen Samora, Betsy Loyd and Kol Harvey, Colleen Kelley, Abby Kaiser, and Danielle Dahl.

My research benefited greatly from the assistance of Anna Bánhegyi, Colleen Kelley, Vera Grabitzky, Adrienn Kácsor, Zsuzsanna Horváth, Claus Biegert, Roxanne Dunbar-Ortiz, H. Glenn Penny, Martin Klimke, Trudy Peterson, and anonymous Hungarian hobbyists of American Indian cultures.

During my research trips I relied on the professional services of the staff of the Minnesota Historical Society; Leah Jehan and the staff of the Beinecke Rare Book and Manuscript Library of Yale University; the staff of the National Archives II in College Park, Maryland; the staff of the United Nations Archives in New York City; Donald Burge and the staff of the Center for Southwest Research of the University of New Mexico; the staff of the Library and the Archives Registry Sub-Unit at the United Nations Palace of the Nations in Geneva, Switzerland; the staff of the Federal Archive, Reich and GDR Department, Archive of the Parties and Mass Organizations of the GDR; and the staff of the Federal Commissioner for the files of the State Security Service of the former German Democratic Republic, Berlin, Germany.

My research of the organizational records of the transatlantic sovereignty alliance would not have been possible without the kind help of Alberto Saldamando and the staff of the International Indian Treaty Council, San Francisco; Pirrette Birraux and the staff of the Indigenous People's Documentation Center in Geneva, Switzerland; Helena Nyberg and the staff of INCOMINDIOS in Zürich, Switzerland; and Yvonne Bangert, Tilman Zülch, and the staff at the Gesselschaft für Bedrohte Völker in Göttingen, Germany.

Crucial funding for my research was provided by various offices and departments at the University of Iowa. Finally, my book benefited from the scholarly feedback of Jane Desmond, Virginia Dominguez, Kim Marra, H. Glenn Penny, Joni Kinsey, and Chris Merrill, and from the generous editorial expertise of Bill Lively, and Diane Ganeles and her colleagues at SUNY Press.

Introduction

Indians at Checkpoint Charlie

вы выезжаете из американского сектора.
Vous sortez du secteur Américain.
Sie Verlassen den Amerikanischen Sektor.
You are leaving the American Sector.

"You are leaving the American Sector." As the Cold War was heating up, this sentence was posted in four languages on signs around Checkpoint Charlie and other border crossings in the iron curtain in Berlin, and it stayed there for the duration of the ideological conflict that ordered the world into political blocs and competing realities. To Westerners entering the Eastern Bloc, this sign served as a warning that they were no longer protected by the might of the United States and its NATO allies. Yet for one group of Americans, this sign likely communicated something else. American Indians traveling in Central Europe across the iron curtain in the 1970s and 1980s passed by such signs,[1] and they likely read them differently. For them, this sentence may have been transformed from a warning against the "Evil Empire" of Communism into something empowering, heralding possibilities for a redefinition of their identities as U.S. citizens, American Indians, and members of specific Native peoples—and the promise of a future as sovereign Native nations.

This book is a history of how American Indians got to Checkpoint Charlie and beyond—how they "left the American Sector," and what they accomplished with it. After a number of lethal direct confrontations with police, the Bureau of Indian Affairs, the FBI, and U.S. marshals,[2] the North American Indian sovereignty activists[3] of the 1970s attempted to outflank the U.S. government by seeking support abroad. Through risky and hard work, Native North American sovereignty organizations such as the American Indian Movement (AIM) forged alliances with indigenous groups in the Western hemisphere, national liberation movements, Marxist causes and régimes, solidarity groups in Europe, and used various forums in the United Nations to pressure their countries' governments from the outside for improvements in Indian policy.

In the Central Europe of the late Cold War, older transatlantic images of American Indians had created a pool of potential solidarity activists for the American Indian sovereignty movement. Utilizing the postwar convergence of improvements in news media, telecommunications, and intercontinental travel, the radical Native sovereignty struggle successfully developed contacts and built an alliance with sympathetic Central Europeans on both sides of the iron curtain. This book investigates the ideas involved in this transatlantic sovereignty alliance, the motivations of the actors, the social dynamic between them, the responses of the United States and other national governments to this alliance, and the nature of American Indian access and participation in the United Nations.

This book primarily argues that, in their transnational diplomacy, Native activists performed their ideas of Indianness and Indian sovereignty vis-à-vis the U.S. nation-state. Their diplomatic performances not only critiqued the U.S. nation-state and its Cold War foreign policy. They also earnestly attempted to reconfigure the communities of Native North America into entities with greater independence from the continent's national governments, and into an alliance that cut across the geopolitical blocs of the late Cold War. In its dynamic rise, peak, and legacy, the transatlantic sovereignty alliance was shaped by the composition of the radical American Indian sovereignty movement, by its struggles over the control of the representation of Indians and Indianness, by the responses of the United States and other national governments, by the evolving mechanisms of the United Nations, and by developments in U.S. foreign policy. As an historical analysis of the transatlantic relations of the American Indian radical sovereignty movement of the late Cold War, this book aspires to expand scholarship on the transnational relations of U.S. minorities, the study of Cold War international relations, and the understanding of Indianness, sovereignty and the nation as performed cultural, social, and political categories.

This book makes a number of analytical arguments supported by qualitative historical evidence. First, contrary to the current scholarly consensus, the radical Indian sovereignty movement did not buckle under the U.S. government's legal and clandestine assaults in the mid-1970s.[4]

Both before and while the American Indian Movement was splintering over disagreements about means and representation, a part of their struggle transformed into a transnational alliance and linked up with various national liberation movements, Marxist régimes, and environmentalist and antinuclear groups in Europe. The sovereignty rights movement developed and leveraged its transnational relations to pressure the U.S. government for a more progressive Indian policy. The transatlantic alliance for American Indian sovereignty is an example of the continued transnational relations of U.S. minorities, and of the constructed nature of the U.S. nation-state.

Central Europe served as a social and cultural contact zone for Native American activists and their European allies. In just Switzerland, Austria, West and East Germany, hundreds of volunteers mobilized thousands of people for solidarity concerts, rallies, and demonstrations.[5] In their support for the radical Indian sovereignty movement, Central Europeans were motivated by a sense of identification, romanticized notions of revolution, and a countercultural community. They were also engaging with American culture in alternative ways, and in some cases they were critiquing their own governments' foreign policy toward the U.S. as well as the Cold War global foreign policy of the U.S. government. The transatlantic alliance for American Indian sovereignty is also proof that the attitudes formed by older cultural forms and representations of American Indians in time motivated Central European social groups and connected them across the iron curtain. This is a case of the intra-European use of U.S. culture.

Previous transatlantic cultural forms, representations and "playing Indian" both enabled and constrained the transatlantic alliance. In turn, the radical sovereignty rights movement intervened in old (some transatlantic) forms of "playing Indian" and manipulated them to make political claims. This book is a case study of how cultural representations can inform social movements in the United States and transnationally.

The radical Native sovereignty rights movement that encompassed and even aimed at Native America's full decolonization into independence was channeled at the United Nations into forums of nongovernmental organizations and human rights mechanisms. The transnational relations of the American Indian radical sovereignty movement are an example of the potential and limits of Cold War global alliances for decolonization and a nonaligned course within the Western and Communist Blocs.

As an interdisciplinary history of American Indian transnational diplomacy in the late Cold War, this book makes advances in a number of fields. For scholars of International Relations and more specifically of the history of U.S. foreign policy, it offers a case study of the "foreign relations" of a group traditionally considered a U.S. domestic minority and how they critiqued, contested, and at times even supplanted official U.S. foreign policy. In this, the concept of "diplomacy" is expanded to describe the transnational relations of a non-state actor, and it is also redefined as the performance of the desired status of greater sovereignty, an alternative to the current political status quo. In the field of Transatlantic Studies, this book maps out the extent and dynamics of a political alliance between some of the indigenous communities across the United States and Canada and groups in Central European, primarily Germanic, societies. Both for Performance Studies and American Cultural Studies, my book offers an analysis of U.S.–based social movements as performance forms that denaturalized the social and political hierarchies of the American nation-state and articulated alternatives to it. To Cold War Studies I provide a case study of how the sociopolitical alliance between Indians and Central Europeans straddled the iron curtain, complicating the dichotomy of the Cold War enacted in the international alignment of national governments. This work also shows how "playing Indian," a major subject of American Indian and Indigenous Studies, changed in its politics in Central European societies, and how it influenced the nature and extent of the transatlantic alliance for Native sovereignty. Finally, this book is an effort to open lines of inquiry both in American Indian and Indigenous Studies and Transnational American Studies about indigenous strategies of using Native status vis-à-vis the U.S. nation-state for survival and revival—inside and outside the United States. Here, Transnational American Studies offers American Indian and Indigenous Studies a methodology that expands the field of inquiry to beyond the U.S. national arena. Conversely, American Indian and Indigenous Studies provide Transnational American Studies with a chance to deconstruct the U.S. nation-state from the inside through the traditions and historical agency of one of the very groups who were exploited to construct it. Ultimately, this work contributes to building a case for the importance and value of the ideas and embodied practices of nationally marginalized groups as they work around the nation-state in their international organizing and mobilization of forces for social and political justice.

The chapters of this book will proceed both chronologically and analytically. Chapter 1 sketches out a brief history of American Indians in the transatlantic cultural landscape and specifically highlights how Central European forms of "playing Indian" made for a potential for intercontinental alliances. Chapter 2 redefines the existing scholarly consensus on the American Indian sovereignty struggle as a domestic campaign[6] by recovering the transnational dimensions of Native America and the radical Indian sovereignty movement, and it explains how the struggle posed a transnational challenge to the U.S. nation-state. Chapter 3 traces the rise and functioning of the transatlantic alliance for Indian sovereignty. Chapter 4 probes the fraught intergroup and interpersonal politics of solidarity in the transatlantic coalition, and it analyzes how the older cultural representations of Indians informed these dynamics. In Chapter 5, I investigate the relations between Native activists and Marxist states and movements, and then map out the strategies used by Eastern Bloc national governments to control the transatlantic solidarity movement with Indian sovereignty that they themselves also encouraged. Chapter 6 provides an account of how the movement gained entry to the United Nations, their coalition building there, and how they came to articulate a global indigenous rights régime, much of which is still in place today. In Chapter 7, I offer some case studies of how the U.S. government responded to the transnational diplomacy of the radical Indian sovereignty movement. My conclusion summarizes the arc of the book, and provides a balance of the late Cold War's U.S. record on American Indian sovereignty rights, much of which was made possible by the transatlantic alliance of the radical Indian sovereignty movement.

Theoretical Approaches

The remainder of this introduction defines my topic and terminology, and then lays out the theoretical framework used throughout the book.

The Radical Indian Sovereignty Movement

This is an analytical history of the transatlantic relations of the American Indian radical sovereignty movement. American Indians have always asserted their sovereignty rights in various forms.[7] Native sovereignty evolved as a group of concepts in the history of relations between Native nations and European and North American governments. Between the fifteenth and the mid-twentieth centuries, Indian rights were dramatically curtailed not only in law and federal policy, but also in the actual practices of Indian relations on the ground, which began with trading and treaty making, and lasted through Indian removal, reservations, and boarding schools, and reached their nadir with the Termination Policy of the World War Two era.

The postwar era's Indian leaders and activists developed their ideas about Native sovereignty under fire from their opponents, through their interactions with each other, their understanding of U.S. patriotic anti-Communism,[8] in consultation with their non-Indian allies,[9] and under the influence of the social movements that rocked the long 1960s. For the first few years after its establishment in the Twin Cities of Minnesota in 1968, the American Indian Movement was much like a civil rights community organization in its goals and means: it focused on police brutality and aid and services to Indians in and around Minneapolis.[10] Around the same time, Indians of All Tribes took over Alcatraz and demanded that the island be granted to them as a place for a university, and a cultural center.[11] The decade of the 1960s saw the intensification of Native struggles for international border transit rights in the Northeast,[12] and for fishing rights in the Northwest of the United States.

As in the early 1970s the Native students and city activists of this coalescing radical movement built alliances with the traditionalist families of the Sioux and other reservation communities, their urban concerns soon gave way to a struggle against injustice in reservation border towns, their own tribal governments, and the Bureau of Indian Affairs. In this phase, sovereignty meant legal protection against white racism, and more resources and a greater role for traditionalists in local decisions and policymaking. Simultaneously, it was especially American Indian women who put the fight against involuntary sterilization and the forced enrollment of Native children in white-run boarding schools on the movement's agenda.

Soon, however, more radical ideas of sovereignty emerged from the performances of the new Native rights movement. The dominant notion of Native sovereignty articulated by the leading cohort of the American Indian Movement was no less than full *independence* from the United States. Their vision of full sovereignty ran deeper than the sudden declaration of the "Independent Oglala Nation" at Wounded Knee in the spring of 1973.[13] The following year they launched a sustained and concentrated organizational effort to pursue the decolonization of Native America by seeking admittance to the United Nations and forging alliances with Central European solidarity groups. For one and a half decades—the rest of the Cold War—organizations like the International Indian Treaty Council actively pursued such goals and courses of action. During this period, their ideas of what was desirable, feasible, and realistic in terms of sovereignty changed. It is this period and process that is the focus of my book. Much of what North Americans understand as Indian *self-determination* today—Native or jointly controlled tribal police, courts, educational and cultural institutions, off-reservation hunting and fishing rights, tax-exempt casinos, and greater cultural awareness on the part of non-Native North Americans about Indians—was achieved or strengthened during this period by the Native sovereignty movement. The shortcomings of North American Indian relations and policy—including the abominable public health, poverty, and crime on reservations; the lack of direct funding and jobs in Native communities; the persistent tensions within tribal governments; continuing corporate encroachment on Indian land bases; the abiding myths and prejudices in the mainstream population about Indians—are signs of the failure of those in positions of power more than of those who were relatively powerless to address these issues. In order to fully appreciate the partial successes of the American Indian sovereignty movement, scholars and practitioners need to understand the possibilities of Native sovereignty that were articulated and performed by the radical wing of the movement in the 1970s and 1980s.

This history is concerned with the *radical* sovereignty movement. At the core of this group of Native communities and organizations were a cohort of activists in the American Indian Movement, its offshoot the International American Indian Treaty Council, and its network of Indian councils and international conferences. The bases of AIM included both urban areas like the Twin Cities of Minnesota, the Sioux reservations of the Dakotas, and the Ojibwe/Anishinaabe communities of the U.S. Midwest. The press arm of the radical Indian sovereignty movement was the flagship newspaper *Akwesasne Notes*, based out of the Akwesasne Mohawk Reservation of the Six Nations in Rooseveltown, upstate New York. The Mohawk are part of the Six Nations or Iroquois Confederacy, who call themselves Haudenosaunee, and have a long history of being a transnational group straddling the U.S.–Canadian border. In the course of the 1980s, the Navajo and Hopi of Arizona and New Mexico also engaged in national and transatlantic advocacy in their struggle against relocation from Big Mountain.

While these were the ethnic groups with the strongest representation in the leadership of the radical sovereignty movement, it would be difficult to list all of the Native nations represented at the level of membership and activists. Scholars have called this diversity the "pan-Indianism" of the American Indian Movement and Red Power;[14] their struggle included activists from Native nations throughout the North

American continent. This was also true for the transatlantic wing of the movement. Among the nations of the transatlantic struggle's leaders were the Ojibwa/Anishinaabe (the Bellecourt brothers, Eddie Benton-Banai), the Sioux (the Meanses, Leonard and Mary Crow Dog, John Trudell), the Cherokee (Jimmie Durham), the Cheyenne (Roxanne Dunbar-Ortiz), and the Haudenosaunee (Leon Shenandoah, Oren Lyons, and Wallace "Mad Bear" Anderson). Delegates to the International American Indian Treaty Council conferences came from many Native groups in Canada, the United States, Mexico, and Central and South America. Many of the same indigenous communities also sent delegates to the United Nations. Neck-and-neck with the International Indian Treaty Council, the Canadian-based National Indian Brotherhood also gained non-governmental organization (NGO) status at the United Nations in the mid-1970s. Subsequent Native NGOs at the UN included the Brotherhood's offshoot the World Council of Indigenous Peoples, the Washington, DC–based Indian Law Resource Center, the Indian Council of South America, the Four Directions Council, the Native Circumpolar Conference, and others.

As scholars of the American Indian politics of the Cold War have mapped it out,[15] the Native sovereignty movement had several other organizations. The more moderate ones included the National Congress of American Indians, and the Americans for Indian Opportunity. The more radical ones included the Indians of All Tribes of Alcatraz fame, the National Indian Youth Council, as well as the various local community organizations that spearheaded the struggle for fishing rights in the states of Washington and Wisconsin. All of these, however, differed from the transatlantic wing in their goals, means, or duration. Hence the focus of my book on the group of organizations described above: they pursued a transatlantic alliance for American Indian sovereignty *in a concentrated and sustained way*. My rationale for focusing on the Swiss International Committee for the Indians of the Americas (Incomindios) and the German Society for Endangered Peoples (Gesellschaft für Bedrohte Völker) is similar: while there were many ad hoc solidarity groups, especially in the German-speaking countries of Central Europe,[16] they did not have the longevity or the sustained focus of these two entities. Another and more mundane explanation for my focus on specific groups that developed into nonprofits and nongovernmental organizations is that their office records comprised an identifiable and available source base for my research.

Native Americans as Transnational Actors

This historical analysis of the transatlantic relations of the radical Indian sovereignty movement is also a case study in Transnational American Studies, a scholarly paradigm which probes the limits of the United States as a nation-state, the elasticity of its cultural imaginary abroad, and the circulation of people, ideas, commodities, and cultural forms across and beyond the borders of the United States proper—in my case, across the Atlantic Ocean and the iron curtain. As it was articulated in the early 2000s,[17] Transnational American Studies acknowledges the many forms of domination *and* maps out minority agency along lines of "race," class, ethnicity, gender, sexuality, religion, and region both within and beyond the borders of the United States as a superpower in order to better understand the potential, limitations, and flaws of the American empire. In this, Transnational American Studies has a potential for recovering the alternative practices, visions and agencies of groups marginalized in or excluded from the body of the nation—of which American Indians are a prime example. More recently, Shari Huhndorf has been spearheading a transnationalist paradigm of Native Studies that critiques the North American nation-states as colonial constructions.[18] My analytical framework has been developed unrelated to hers, but we move along parallel lines of inquiry.

The current geographies of Native North America contain traces of a transnational past. The reservations of the Sioux are now in some four different states—North and South Dakota, Nebraska, and Missouri—while the lands of the Navajo/Diné take up northeastern Arizona and extend into Utah and New Mexico, suggesting the extent of Native territories before the U.S. nation-state forced them to give up most of it. The current territory of the Six Nations Mohawk stretches from upstate New York across the U.S.–Canadian border into Ontario and Quebec; and they have been fighting not only for free passage through the national checkpoints, but also for the freedom to travel internationally on their own tribal passports.[19] The Tohono O'odham Nation has likewise been struggling for easier access to their lands straddling the national border between the U.S. state of Arizona and Sonora in Mexico.

Going back far enough in the history of the Western hemisphere, scholarship like this book can demonstrate not only how Indian peoples were *always already* transnational, but that they remain transnational from the inside of the nation-state. On much of the North American continent, the colonizing European powers made treaties with various Native groups—and this practice of intergovernmental diplomacy continued after the American Revolution. Only in 1849 did the U.S. government transfer Indian affairs from the Department of War to the Department of the Interior[20]—an attempt to incorporate Indian relations from U.S. foreign policy into the domestic affairs of the American nation-state. Through the 1860s, the U.S. federal government still continued making treaties with Indian nations—a recurrent recognition of their power and entity as something outside of the U.S. nation-state. Treaty making also constitutes a history of American Indian performances of transnational diplomacy—a window into repeated articulations of alternatives to the U.S. nation-state.[21]

From the 1820s however, legal precedents like the Marshall rulings of the U.S. Supreme Court created a framework for treating Indians as wards of the U.S. government instead of as independent nations. According to what became the dominant legal doctrine, Indians were now seen as "domestic dependent nations" within the United States.[22] Thus, the historical status of American Indians vis-à-vis the U.S. nation-state is arguably transnational from the inside. It was this transnational status that Native activists aimed to reinstate in the 1970s by seeking support and recognition from national governments, liberation movements, and solidarity groups in the Americas, Europe, and the United Nations.

In recent years several scholars have undertaken projects to explicate the complex and layered nature of American Indian status and allegiances. Paul Rosier has identified and traced among American Indian military veterans the sensibility of "hybrid patriotism," which rhetorically articulates their belonging both to the United States and to their Native nations.[23] However, what Rosier sees as "cultural hybridization" or a distinct sensibility,[24] I interpret as one part of a combination of political strategies on the continuum of sovereignty rights. In my framework, U.S. patriotism has been used by American Indians in tandem with a distinct and radical Native nationalism that sought legitimacy beyond the U.S. nation-state.

The scholar who theorized the historical dynamics of Indian relations to its fullest extent is Kevin Bruyneel, who in his 2007 book of the same title claimed that a "third space of sovereignty" is carved out by the political resistance of American Indians to impositions of the colonial settler-state. According to Bruyneel, this Native American " 'third space of sovereignty' [. . .] resides neither simply inside nor outside the American political system but rather exists on [its] very boundaries, exposing both the practices and contingencies of American colonial rule. This is a supplemental space, inassimilable to the institutions and discourse of the modern liberal democratic settler-state and nation."[25]

Examining phenomena located further on the same continuum of Native sovereignty, my book uses a different theoretical and methodological framework from that of Bruyneel's. What he characterizes as a Native agency operating "neither simply inside nor outside," but "across the temporal and spatial boundaries" of the United States as a nation-state I call American Indian *transnationalism*—an Indianness that in performance and embodied practices straddles the U.S. nation-state, and a status that exists beyond it as much as within it. In contrast to Bruyneel's conceptualization, I doubt that such Indian agency "always already" exists, or that any of its third space would be "inassimilable" to the U.S. nation-state. Native agency—whether we call it transnationalism or third-space politics—has to be repeatedly enacted, carved out by human actors *in performance*. Thus, both the stakes of the struggle over American Indian status and the theory and method of Performance Studies compel me to privilege the embodied performances of American Indian activists as they struggled to generate, maintain, and leverage such third spaces for enhanced sovereignty. My book provides a complement to Bruyneel's theorization of the third space of sovereignty by mapping the outer limits of radical Indian activism of the late Cold War that reached beyond the intellectual vision of Vine Deloria, Jr., and the Red Power Movement.

This book also makes an intervention into the more narrowly defined historiography of Native American sovereignty activism in the twentieth century. In their seminal chronicle of the radical Native sovereignty movement, Paul Chaat Smith and Robert Allen Warrior claim that Wounded Knee 1973 was the high point, after which Indian radicalism "faded, disintegrating under the weight of its own internal contradictions and divisions, and a relentless legal assault by federal and state governments."[26] Daniel Cobb's scholarship has correctively expanded the period and concept of Native American activism to include the more moderate organizations that had been lobbying the U.S. government for sovereignty rights in the previous two decades.[27] He has also documented how the young activists who established the radical National Indian Youth Council had already became transnational in their discourse in the 1960s.[28] To correctively advance these lines of inquiry, I contend that rather than imploding and disappearing, by the mid-1970s the radical sovereignty movement actually transformed into a transatlantic advocacy network. Historians do not fully appreciate this dimension of the Native American sovereignty movement because they have regarded the struggle as bounded by U.S. national history, instead of viewing it in terms of a transnational articulation of Native rights, expressed in and further shaped by transnational Native diplomacy. This is all the more surprising because the status that these Native activists aspired to was that of a sovereign *country*. They engaged in diplomacy for *nation building*—for example, they wanted to force the U.S. government to honor its past treaties and resume the practice of treaty-making as international diplomacy with Native nations. This book makes a major contribution to emerging scholarship on American Indians and other indigenous peoples as transnational actors in history and current affairs.[29]

Thus, my study is located at the intersection of the U.S. national paradigm of Indian history on the one hand, and the past of the regional and global reach of indigenous peoples on the other. Compared with the global scope of Ronald Niezen's *The Origins of Indigenism*,[30] this book is rather narrowly concerned with how American Indians attempted to transcend the United States. In his path-breaking work, *The Red Atlantic: American Indigenes and the Making of the Modern World, 1000–1927*, Jace Weaver marks the end of the indigenous shaping of the Atlantic world in the early twentieth century.[31] Taking a cue from him, perhaps I should call the historical period of my book the *red Transatlantic*—an era when, building on the legacy of the red Atlantic, and riding a confluence of improved communications and transportation, the geopolitics of a global ideological struggle, and news reportage, American Indians began to regularly crisscross that ocean to build a "red" transatlantic alliance for Native sovereignty.

The last several decades have also produced scholarship on Central European, and especially German, ideas and representations of American Indians, of which the most intellectually robust is H. Glenn Penny's *Kindred by Choice: Germans and American Indians since 1800*, a (trans) cultural history of over a century of German affinities with American Indians. While Penny's scholarship carefully traces the sociocultural underpinnings of the German fascination with American Indians over the *longue durée*, my book relates its visual and performance dimensions to the rather brief peak of the radical Indian sovereignty struggle of the 1970s and '80s, and reconstructs how they made for a transatlantic alliance in a variety of causes. In some ways, this works zooms in on a period of twenty years, aiming to demonstrate how, in Penny's words, "the meanings of these encounters [. . .] were scripted decades earlier and drew on the revision of persistent tropes that retained their strength and salience across a broad span of years and stark political divisions."[32]

Transnational Relations

As an academic field, the study of International Relations traditionally considered its primary object the relations between nation-states, including state-controlled cultural and foreign policy. As it will be used here, the term "transnational relations" denotes communication between both state and nongovernmental actors in the United States and in Central Europe on both sides of the iron curtain. As an analytical concept, *transnational relations* complicates academic and diplomatic frameworks that privilege the nation-state as international actor, and the national government as the exclusive source and executor of foreign relations.

Under "relations" I mean both social and political relations, especially as they were expressed in personal communication, demonstrations, meetings, and conferences; their attendant media coverage; and private and governmental diplomatic correspondence. Using earlier case studies of the Atlantic black diaspora as a model,[33] my study demonstrates that a cohort of the American Indian sovereignty activists not only had an awareness of the promise of transnational relations, but that they actively engaged in building transnational and transatlantic alliances. In its consideration of the transatlantic relations of a U.S. group in "the long 1960s," my project is part of ongoing research to map the networks of the movements of "the global sixties."[34] Following investigations of American race relations in the early Cold War,[35] this study will also document how the U.S. federal government tried to control Native transnational diplomatic efforts, managed the overseas image of U.S. Indian relations, and attempted to exploit Central European interest in American Indian history and identity for its own purposes.

In the last three decades, historians have produced a spate of scholarship on the outlook and role of American minorities and marginalized groups in U.S. foreign policy—including those of African Americans and women.[36] Complementing these, this study makes the case that American Indian sovereignty activists practiced a kind of diplomacy—negotiations and the building of alliances—in order to press the United States government to address Native claims and needs. Such diplomacy was part of a long tradition of indigenous negotiations and treaty-making with the colonizing European powers and the U.S. federal government,[37] as well as of Native self-representation abroad. I deliberately call the program of the radical Indian sovereignty movement *diplomacy* and not "advocacy," "lobbying," or something else, for several reasons. For one, this stage of the American Indian sovereignty struggle resembled a national liberation movement in its goals: the activists of the American Indian Movement and its organization the International Indian Treaty Council actually wanted to achieve independence for various Native North American communities. Therefore, their efforts aimed at a profoundly diplomatic goal: a fully sovereign Indian country. Accordingly, their strategies included approaching the U.S. State Department, demonstrating and lobbying at the United Nations, building relations with European politicians and governments, Marxist régimes, and national liberation movements. These Native activists claimed to represent an all-Indian entity—with the ideology that scholars have called "pan-Indianism"[38]—as they conducted relations with the U.S. government, foreign governments, and other transnational movements. Also, their transnational program was diplomacy because it reasserted Native nations' prerogative to make treaties—an international diplomatic activity—and also because it concerned maintaining peaceful relations, and making peace is reserved by the U.S. Constitution for the federal government, thus it is a governmental diplomatic power. Finally, the radical Native sovereignty movement sought the recognition of treaty and sovereignty rights as valid international law—another major object of diplomatic relations.

To use a term from Postcolonial Studies, this kind of Native statecraft was the diplomacy of the "contact zone:"[39] negotiations between a group in a marginal position and groups in relative positions of power. Such diplomacy requires the kind of creativity and flair for action that radical activists exhibited in the U.S. Civil Rights Movement as well as in Europe in the 1960s and '70s. This modern-age diplomacy of the contact zone served to assert Native rights to a status at the governmental level—as an international state actor.

I conceptualize the region of Central Europe, divided by the iron curtain between West and East Germany, and Switzerland, Austria, and Hungary, as a contact zone in Mary Louise Pratt's definition: "the space of colonial encounters, the space in which peoples geographically and historically separated come into contact with each other and establish ongoing relations, usually involving conditions of coercion, radical inequality, and intractable conflict [. . .] often within radically asymmetrical relations of power."[40] In the framework of the Cold War, the colonial powers were the United States and the Soviet Union. Groups living in their satellite societies—which in contemporary geopolitical terms were also termed "buffer countries" or a "buffer zone"—were the inhabitants of what became in-between spaces, constituting a cultural and political contact zone. American Indian activists made incursions into this Central European contact zone to use its heightened political significance to pressure the U.S. government to address their claims and needs. In these attempts, they tried to build alliances on both sides of the iron curtain with governmental and nongovernmental actors.

Performances of Indian Sovereignty

In its investigation this book uses a major premise of Nationalism Studies and Performance Studies: the claim that the category of nation is not natural but *performed* in cultural representations, government policy, and international diplomacy. Diplomacy is the performance of the nation through "representation"—the standing in of an individual or a team for the interests and positions of a larger "imagined community."[41] Diplomacy performs the imagined community through the metonymy of the "diplomat" representing the whole of their country. In their diplomatic efforts to build transatlantic relations, Native American sovereignty activists performed their own alternatives to the status of Indians as "domestic dependent nations"[42] within the United States—they articulated their visions of "inherently limited and sovereign"[43] Native American nations in the past, present, and future.

American Indian activists' articulations of their pan-Indian nationhood were a combination of performances of social protest and performances of diplomacy for recognition of Native nations as government-level sovereign actors. The concept of social protest as performance was developed by Richard Schechner in the 1970s. In analyzing the 1960 civil rights sit-ins in Greensboro, North Carolina, as "staged events," Rebekah J. Kowal concurs with Schechner that performances for social protest are communicative events, and are often designed as such.[44] Kowal convincingly argues that the Greensboro student activists exercised a kind of "scenographic oversight" over their actions, taking into account their visual and verbal rhetorical impact.[45] Thus, their "[alternative] reality was enacted as a scripted if improvised performance."[46] Scholarship about the American Indian sovereignty movement's major events confirms that AIM and other activists likewise understood their performance interventions as public events by which they could communicate their messages and champion their causes through television and printed media—and that their scripts were often complemented by on-the-spot improvisation and impulsive decision making.[47] The fact that national commemorations and historic sites generally rely on spectacle likewise conditioned the social protest events staged by AIM and other groups.

In her 2003 book *The Archive and the Repertoire*, Diana Taylor theorizes the categories and relationship between forms of knowledge fixed in objects, and embodied practices. Taylor defines the archive as containing "documents, maps, literary texts, letters, archeological remains, bones, videos, films, CDs, all those items supposedly resistant to change." On the other hand, the repertoire "enacts embodied memory: performances, gestures, orality, movement, dance, singing—in short, all those acts usually thought of as ephemeral, nonreproducible knowledge."[48] Taylor is careful to point out that while the archive is often privileged over the repertoire, these two forms of knowledge work in complementary ways, and she observes that materials from the archive can shape performance practices.[49] In this book I will interpret historical documents as "scripts" for such embodied performances, but also as their imprints in the historical record. These documents were always mediated by both the editorial decisions of those who created them, and by the nature of the medium (such as the technology of photography) itself. In turn, such archival documents can motivate future performances, thus forming a feedback loop that itself is conditioned by selective retrieval. In this, I am acutely aware that historians cannot access the "original" event; they can study only the traces and versions of the embodied experiences through archival research, oral histories, and the observation of practices genealogically linked to the historical experience.[50]

In their social protest and diplomatic performances, radical Indian sovereignty activists intervened in what cultural historian Philip Deloria has called "playing Indian." In his 1998 book of the same title,[51] Deloria traces the centuries-old tradition of Euro-Americans impersonating natives as a way to articulate their colonial and U.S. American identities. Deloria's work conceptualized the surprising elasticity of Indian impersonation and fantasies for whites both in the United States and abroad. In my framework, "playing Indian" refers to the transatlantic representations of Native North Americans in a wide variety of cultural forms. The social protest and diplomatic performances of the American Indian sovereignty struggle were a subset of "playing Indian."

What makes Deloria's book more than a study of exclusively white representations of American Indians—the kind of Americanist scholarship that has been scathingly criticized by native scholars of American Indian and Indigenous Studies[52]—is the author's consistent attention to

Native American agency. Deloria carefully documents how, "[t]hroughout a long history of Indian play, native people have been present at the margins, insinuating their way into Euro-American discourse, often attempting to nudge notions of Indianness in directions they found useful. As the nineteenth and twentieth centuries unfolded, increasing numbers of Indians participated in white people's Indian play, assisting, confirming, co-opting, challenging, and legitimating the performative tradition of aboriginal American identity."[53] The social protest and diplomatic performances of the radical Indian sovereignty movement are examples of such interventions into the transatlantic practices of playing Indian. Thus in this book playing Indian is understood as a sociopolitical performance practice which, even as it was practiced primarily by non-Indians, has nevertheless afforded Native North Americans to mount interventions for social justice. Calling protest performances by Native Americans playing Indian does not trivialize the gravity of their struggle. It does the opposite: it recovers Native agency in creatively leveraging white imaginaries about Indians for a pressing political cause—the struggle for Native sovereignty in its full potential.

The term playing Indian also denotes the scholarly paradigm in which social and political categories like "race," ethnicity, and nationality are enacted through performance—and it is also through performance that they can be challenged.[54] The terms *performative* and *performativity* are rather expansive theoretical notions referring to acts or practices "as" performance—speech acts or performative writing, for example.[55] I apply the concepts of performativity and performance to discrete events such as demonstrations, counter-commemorations, personal meetings, concerts, and rallies for the specific political purposes for building transnational alliances and advancing American Indian sovereignty rights.

A Note on the Use of Sources

As a transnational history of a U.S. sociopolitical movement, this book reflects a number of challenges to projects of its kind. It is my belief that scholars should be smart enough to identify the sources that can answer their questions or test their hypotheses. However, sometimes such sources or even whole source bases have been thinned out or destroyed—this was the case with the Indigenous Peoples' Documentation Center, the office of which went up in a fire in the 1980s; or the International Indian Treaty Council, which lost several boxes of its records during its relocation of its offices within the United States, and subsequently to culling for space—or are simply not accessible—like the personal papers of East German author Liselotte Welskopf-Henrich, which were closed for research due to construction during my visit to Berlin in 2011; or much of the post-1976 records of the U.S. State Department, which are still classified and can be pried open only with lengthy and costly Freedom of Information Act requests. Hence, while some of the research for this book may have been path-breaking, its archival dimension is not as complete as it could be.

One obvious weakness of this book is its dearth of oral interviews with veteran activists and UN and U.S State Department officials. Without making excuses for the author, this is due to several factors. One side effect of the rigor of research ethics regulations at U.S. universities is that they tend to "discipline" interdisciplinary scholars out of Social Science research methods. The intricacies and demands of institutional ethics review boards presented this author with hard choices between postponing oral interviews and thereby the whole research process, and abandoning this component altogether.

The way I have tried to compensate for the lack of personal interviews and oral histories is to attempt to recover the voices of activists from the archival record, and do personal walk-throughs of the sites where they performed their interventions for sovereignty rights. I was also helped by the fact that several of the leading members of the movement have published their memoirs, which they intended to be definitive accounts of their involvement in a variety of causes in the late Cold War. The oral histories of some other key figures have been recorded and I accessed them in various archives. Some veterans, like Roxanne Dunbar-Ortiz, have continued to actively publish on this and related topics, and I have used their writings as well.

1

"Playing Indian" Revisited

American Indians in the Transatlantic Cultural Landscape

> *Archie Fire Lame Deer:* So if you talk about the respect for our people in East Germany, when you walk there, I have to thank this man called Karl May, even though it was a world of fantasy that he had written about, never seen Lakotas, and made ridiculous things as Navajos with Mohawk haircuts [*Richard Erdoes*: I can tell you all about that!] but he still raised the consciousness of the people of the Indian people.
>
> *Erdoes:* We were all born and raised pro-Indian, all the German, and Austrian, and the Swiss and French kids clapped when they see the Indian—going "Boo!" when the cavalry come. [. . .][1]

Painting, Playing, Printing: Karl Bodmer and George Catlin

The Central European forms and traditions of "playing Indian" were transatlantic in their production and circulation. In the long line of representations that spanned the previous centuries since European contact,[2] especially influential were the Indian paintings of Swiss artist Karl Bodmer, who in the early 1830s traveled to the Upper Missouri Valley with German Prince Maximilian of Wied-Neuwied. While wintering at Fort Clark, present-day North Dakota in 1833–34, Bodmer created many likenesses of the Mandan and Hidatsa people. After his return to Europe,

Bodmer used his sketches to make scores of paintings, which were then published in the prince's travel account in German in 1839, and subsequently in French and in abridged form in English.[3] Among them were his most famous ones, the 1834 *Mató-Tópe (Four Bears), Mandan Chief*, and his 1835 *Pehriska-Ruhpa of the Dog Society of the Hidatsa tribe*. Bodmer is usually credited with highly accurate ethnographic detail and is known as a visual artist who documented Plains Indians in the early stages of European contact.[4] Over time these prints became so popular and ubiquitous that by the middle of the twentieth century they had been circulating in various reproductions on the Old Continent. Thus, Bodmer's visual representations of Plains Indians have become a part of the transatlantic cultural landscape, serving as "raw material" or "props" for playing Indian in Central Europe.

U.S. painter George Catlin spent much of the same decade visiting and painting some of the same Native communities in the same region. Catlin and Bodmer overlapped to the extent that, for example, both painted the Mandan leader Four Bears (who is credited with alternative spelling by Catlin in his 1832 *Máh-to-tóh-pa, Four Bears, Second Chief, in Full Dress*). Much more than Bodmer, Catlin's enterprise ran the gamut of "playing Indian" in its variety of media. After spending years on the Missouri River, Catlin published his travel account as *The Manners, Customs, and Condition of the North American Indians* in 1841, then lectured and exhibited his Indian Gallery in a variety of U.S. cities before he took it to Europe.[5] There, Catlin complemented his collection with *tableau vivants* of Europeans dressed up as Indians, himself masqueraded as a Sac warrior, and he staged live performances with groups of Ojibwa and Iowa Indians, which drew large audiences. Complete with an open air encampment and horses,[6] Catlin soon operated a veritable proto-Wild West Show, which he took to Brussels, Dublin, London, and Paris. In London in 1848, he published a companion book to his American West travel account, this one titled *Catlin's Notes of Eight Years' Travels and Residence in Europe, with his North American Indian Collection. With Anecdotes and Incidents of the Travels and Adventures of Three Different Parties of American Indians Whom He Introduced to the Courts of England, France and Belgium.*[7]

In his writings, Catlin deployed the figure of the American Indian as a foil for celebrating U.S. democracy and critiquing European Christian practice and industrial society. According to his account, the Iowa and Ojibwa in his service repeatedly wondered about the great wealth and dire poverty coexisting in European cities, and even berated Christian missionaries for attempting to convert them instead of tending to the poor.[8] At best, actual Native agency was buried in Catlin's rendering of the cultural and literary trope of the *noble savage* of the Enlightenment and Romanticism. A report likely closer to the actual experience of these Indians was published in 1848 by Maungwudaus (The Great Hero), a member of Catlin's second Ojibwa group, titled *An Account of the Chippewa Indians, Who Have Been Travelling Among the Whites, in the United States, England, Ireland, Scotland, France and Belgium*.[9] Another Indian critique of European and American society is provided by the very context of these encounters: as observed by Christopher Mulvey, the Iowa and Ojibwa crossed the Atlantic because of white encroachment on their land and way of life—but during their European tour, some eleven of them died of smallpox and other causes.[10]

The "Wild West" Tours Europe: Buffalo Bill Cody

While Catlin's Indian gallery met early success in Western Europe, the U.S. pioneer who turned playing Indian into a long-term show business on both continents was Buffalo Bill Cody. L. G. Moses documented how some of the members of the Great Plains ghost dance movement, deemed to be too rebellious to live on the reservations, were allowed by the U.S. government to be hired as performers for Buffalo Bill's European tours.[11] This was a characteristic transfer between Indian revitalization movements, government policy, and playing Indian in popular culture. When a number of Native tribes engaged in the spiritual practice of ghost dancing, the U.S. government perceived this as a real threat to the status quo of Indian relations, and responded with repressive measures that culminated in the killing of Big Foot's band at Wounded Knee. As part of the crackdown on the ghost dancers, the U.S. government then partnered with Buffalo Bill Cody to remove the troublemakers and channeled them into performing nostalgic and exotic reenactments of "the Indian Wars" in the United States and abroad. Moses argues that considering the circumstances, these Plains Sioux performers exercised some agency in representing their own history, and benefited financially from the arrangement.[12] As performances of colonial rule, Buffalo Bill's successful tours of Europe were akin to the fin-de-siècle *Völkerschau* (live exhibitions of "exotic" Native people from far-flung European colonies) by Carl Hagenbeck, and they spawned imitators in content or form, among them the Sarrasani circus of early twentieth-century Germany.[13]

Pressed in Pulp: Dime Novels and the World of Karl May

While James Fenimore Cooper's *Leatherstocking Tales* were published in German as early as 1845,[14] it was the advent of the dime novel that truly accelerated the diffusion of Indian imaginaries across the Atlantic. With advances in printing and transportation technology, publishers perfected the production and mass dissemination of popular literature at low prices. In the United States, the firm of Beadle and Adams are credited with publishing the first dime novel series in 1860. Their first dime story, *Malaeska, the Indian Wife of the White Hunter*, established a major theme in the genre: pioneer and Wild West stories that featured American Indian characters. With the onset of the Civil War, the publishers established their transatlantic arm, Beadle's American Library, which for five years reprinted some of their runs for the British market.[15] This was one of the early instances of the transatlantic publishing of U.S. dime novels[16]—a practice that not only provided Europeans with a steady fare of Western fantasies but also inspired "native" European literature about American Indians, and thus helped provide the "script" for Europeans playing Indian.

The foremost and most influential example of homegrown Central European stories about American Indians remains the *Winnetou* cycle of novels written by German author Karl May around the turn of the twentieth century.[17] Karl May's formula of positioning a German hero in an alliance with "noble" Natives against greedy and evil whites and "bloodthirsty" Indians proved to be immensely successful in Central Europe. Over time, the author's oeuvre developed into veritable "culture industry," with between eighty and one hundred million copies sold in twenty-eight languages.[18] May's works served as "script," or at the least as inspiration, to whole generations of Central Europeans for playing Indian in a variety of cultural forms, from stage performances to feature films and hobbyist reenactment.

While his novels were set in the Southern Plains region of the United States in the second half of the nineteenth century,[19] both scholars and ordinary Germans point out that Karl May's stories are purely fictional and not based on much (if any) personal experience with American Indians.[20] May was more likely influenced by the popular accounts of the Wild West and "the Indian Wars" of the late nineteenth century, and their renderings in the transatlantically circulating dime novels. This allowed him the liberty to "play Indian" as a German in more than one way. May deliberately blended his own personality with that of his narrator and his protagonist when he masqueraded as the hero of his own Wild West adventure stories; he even commissioned replicas of the rifles that his hero wielded on the frontier and posed for photographs in costume as Karl/Sharlee/Old Shatterhand.[21]

In his stories, Karl May positions his German hero in a peculiar alliance with his fictional American Indian characters. The inherent skills, strong body, and character of Karl/Charlie, a German immigrant to the U.S. West, soon allow him to outperform the Americans in frontier skills, and his feat of knocking out a man with his bare first earns him the nickname of "Old Shatterhand." After his early encounters with good and evil frontiersman and Indians, Shatterhand soon chooses sides and strikes up a friendship with the Apache warrior Winnetou. With his Indian "blood brother," Old Shatterhand lives through a series of adventures in which he battles white bandits and the hostile Kiowa and Oglala Sioux.

May's literary partnership between German frontiersmen and American Indians has a peculiar politics that I argue would later inform the transatlantic alliance for Native American sovereignty. Scholars have observed that in the process of Karl's (almost overnight) transformation into Old Shatterhand, the frontiersmen who are key allies to him and the Apache all turn out to be German immigrants.[22] In an especially emotional scene of the first story, the white Klekih-petra, who had spent decades with the Apache and had taught their chiefs the tenets of Christianity, is fatally wounded by the bullet of a drunken white surveyor. Dying in the arms of his beloved pupil Winnetou, Klekih-petra turns to Karl/Old Shatterhand, whom he had met only hours before, but whose German origins he shares. Speaking in German, which the Apache do not understand, Klekih-petra asks Karl/Shatterhand to take his place and be a friend and teacher to Winnetou. Karl vows to fulfill this role.[23] Through this and subsequent scenes,[24] May positions Germanness as a commitment to an alliance with American Indians, in particular with the Apache.[25] This, however, is not a commitment to mass and violent resistance: after the Apache warrior's father and sister are shot dead by another white outlaw, Old Shatterhand successfully talks Winnetou out of convening all the Indian tribes and waging war on the whites.[26]

At the core of Old Shatterhand's alliance with the Apache is attraction. Karl is immediately drawn the "noble" appearance and behavior of Winnetou, and he later finds that the feeling is mutual.[27] However, the fulfillment of the two men's secret hopes for friendship is delayed for a long time by the fact that the Apache consider Karl an enemy not only because he surveys their land for the white railroad, but also because one of his fellow surveyors has killed Klekih-petra. What follows is a series of adventures in which Karl and white hunter Sam Hawkens successfully manipulate the Apache and a band of Kiowa marauders in order to survive and punish the evildoers. These adventures are rich in reversals and successively feature Winnetou and Karl as each other's prisoner and jailor. Throughout, a combination of pride, cunning, and misperceptions keeps the two men from disclosing their strong sympathy for each other. Only after Karl/Old Shatterhand fights a series of duels—including one against Winnetou that leaves him severely wounded—is his allegiance adequately proven, and is he reconciled with the Apache leaders. Now Old Shatterhand and Winnetou swear blood brotherhood and, in the words of Apache chief Intshu-tshuna, become, "[a] single person and warrior with two bodies, howgh!"[28] Meanwhile, Old Shatterhand also admires the beauty of Winnetou's sister Nsho-tshi, whose love for the German hero is nipped in the bud by her untimely death of a white bandit's bullet.[29] Thus, May's German hero experiences attraction for and becomes the subject of desire by both an Indian man and an Indian woman. As I will show in subsequent chapters, this trope of attraction and desire would inform not only successive forms of Europeans playing Indian, but also the transatlantic alliance of the Indian sovereignty movement.

Staging Indians: The Karl May Festivals

Besides their mass marketing in dozens of languages, Karl May's novels have also been adapted in a variety of other media and cultural forms. One of the most remarkable of these is the dozen or so Karl May stage festivals scattered throughout Germany and Austria.[30] Mostly established in the post-World War Two period, these venues usually feature a Wild West theme park with vendors, merchandise, an Indian "village" or "reservation," and other attractions. The main event, however, is invariably the performances of the adaptations of the *Winnetou* stories on a "natural" stage, with horses, amplifiers, stuntmen, and pyrotechnics. Held in amphitheaters that can seat up to thousands, these performances are always carefully choreographed for spectacular visual effect and action. According to Katrin Sieg, over time the stage plays have used Karl May's novels to amplify or advocate a variety of successive and sometimes contradictory attitudes, which include imperialism and anti-imperialism, racism and multiculturalism, anti-materialism and commodity fetishism.[31] Commodifying a peculiar German fantasy of American frontiersmen and

Indians, these stage performances and the surrounding industry[32] have entertained and shaped the attitudes of generations of German-speaking Central Europeans toward the history of Native Americans.

Into the Woods: The Central European Reenactment Hobby

Parallel to the more business-oriented cultural forms, playing Indian in Central Europe[33] also developed into a "grassroots" movement. The fans of dime novels, Wild West shows, and Karl May books became cultural producers and authors/performers in their own right by organizing Western and Indian clubs, circulating newsletters and journals, and holding conventions and performances. While these societies ran the gamut from literary to social, the German and Central European hobbyist reenactment of American Indian cultures received some scholarly attention in the last twenty years.[34] Here I will use some of these sources and my own research to briefly sketch out the history and characteristics of these groups through the late Cold War.

Some of Central European Indian hobbyism dates back to the 1910s, but by the early twenty-first century their groups numbered in the hundreds.[35] One Central European tradition of reenacting Indian cultures initially existed within the German Wild West clubs: established in 1913, the members of the Cowboy-Club München Süd studied the history of the American West, collected books and artifacts, and learned Indian songs and dances, as well as the cowboy skills of riding and lassoing—to prepare for the Wild West shows staged by themselves and other clubs.[36] German clubs founded in the 1930s included one named Manitou (likely after Winnetou's designation of the Great Spirit), and the Indianerklub Frankfurt West.[37] Inspired by the popular literature sent by his brother Raul from the United States, in the 1930s Hungarian Orientalist Ervin Baktay created a "saloon," held "meetings" in cowboy regalia, annually reenacted the Battle of the Little Big Horn, camped out on the Danube near Budapest, and posed both as a sheriff and as Plains Indian "Chief Buffalo Lying Down."[38] Another example of the transatlantic circulation of ideas and forms of performance, one of the influences of the Czech and Slovak hobbyist groups was the Woodcraft Indian movement launched by Ernest Thompson Seton's books for boys published in the first two decades of the twentieth century.[39]

After a hiatus imposed by World War Two (although the Hungarians held a camp as late as in 1943), Central European Indian hobbyism picked up again. In the postwar period the Hungarian Danube group saw increased attendance at their events.[40] Old Manitou, the first Indianist club of East Germany, was founded near Radebeul in 1956; it was followed in 1958 by a group of Mandan reenactors who called themselves Hiawatha and lived near Leipzig. The town of Meißen saw the emergence of The Dakota in 1961; and the Sieben Ratsfeuer [Seven Council Fires] established their own club in Magdeburg in the year 1963.[41] Inspired by the *Leatherstocking Tales* and the *Winnetou* stories, Hungarian singer-songwriter Tamás Cseh and his friends started playing Indian shortly after they graduated from high school, and by the mid- to late-1960s had launched the second Hungarian hobbyist group, known for their annual camps in the Bakony hills.[42]

In his seminal treatment of embodied representations of Indians by white Americans, Philip Deloria explains how, as the result of a new discourse of cultural relativism and a crisis of individual identity, Cold War white hobbyists began engaging Native American cultures by dancing and singing with real Indians.[43] Here Deloria distinguished between two groups of hobbyists. "Object hobbyists" replicated Indian artifacts as their objects of desire without engaging living Indians, who they considered part of the past and racially other. "People hobbyists" engaged in intercultural contact with live Indians on the powwow circuit, and negotiated the differences between Native agency and Euro-American imagination.[44] It is important to point out that while postwar Germany underwent a suppression of racialist discourse of identity that was more forceful than the one in the United States,[45] German hobbyists did not have access to living Native people the way Euro-Americans did. In other words, their desire for true cross-cultural interaction and experiences had very few venues, which were also highly mediated. One of these was the rare appearance of actual Indians at German Wild West festivals[46] and hobbyist encampments. Another venue would be the correspondence and eventual collaboration with Native Americans in the transatlantic sovereignty movement.

With the dearth of opportunities for interaction with live Indians, the Germans reenactors became "object hobbyists" by default. Like the Hungarians,[47] many German Indian hobbyist groups self-admittedly transitioned from rather crudely acting out popular culture fantasies of American Indians to a kind of Native impersonation that was based on what they regarded as rigorous research.[48] The Indianerklub Hunkpapa e.V. emphasized the authenticity they gleaned from scholarly publications and visits to museums and saw themselves as an "ethnological club for the tradition and culture of the North American Indians [. . .] striving to preserve Indian customs, songs, and dances."[49] In the early 1980s, Peter Bolz reported that German reenactors of the Hunkpapa Lakota "[would] use drawings and paintings by Karl Bodmer as reference and try to reproduce the articles depicted there as accurately as possible. Their productions are actual replicas consciously made as an effort to bring elements of a past culture back to life again."[50] The Bakony group of Hungarian hobbyists were proud to be listed in the 1972–73 *Smithsonian Bulletin* as an organization that reenacted American Indian warfare.[51] For the members of the four different groups who Katrin Sieg interviewed in the early 2000s, being "serious" about their hobby meant having respect for Native Americans, commitment to scholarly accuracy and hard work in handicrafts, and engagement with substance beyond the surface.[52] The German hobbyists emphasized the authenticity and ethnographic detail[53] of their activities to set themselves apart both from their less rigorous fellow hobbyists and from the general public, who they aimed to educate about false stereotypes and the "real" cultures of American Indians.[54] These discursive and embodied practices of "authenticity" conferred authority and legitimacy, but they could also disrupt the hobbyist movement. As their chief measure of acceptance and esteem, the authenticity of hobbyists' bead- and quillwork and dancing and singing were often subject to dispute, and such policing in the hobbyist movement sometimes led to the splintering of groups.[55]

Among the venues of testing a group's authenticity were the annual regional meetings of the hobbyists. In West Germany, where the first so-called "Indian Council" was held in 1951, the number of the Western and Indian hobbyists who gathered over the Pentecost weekend on a club's property could reach the thousands. These conventions and encampments featured campfire activities, discussions and presentations, trading, contests, exhibitions, and historical reenactments such as the treaty ceremony between General Terry and Sitting Bull. By the mid-1980s, the West German clubs had bought some property near Koblenz specifically for annual meetings, which attracted up to 3,000 participants, and had up to 350 teepees.[56] Beginning in 1958, the hobbyists of East Germany also held an annual council of their clubs, which rotated from place to place.[57]

In the Performance Studies terminology of Katrin Sieg, the West German Indian hobbyists progressed from self-admittedly amateurish play acting or *masquerade* to what they considered masterful and accurate replication, reenactment, or *mimesis*.[58] We have seen that this origin narrative was professed by other Central European hobbyist groups as well. Their discourse and performances of authenticity made them an authority on historical Indian cultures to the extent that, in some cases, they fed back into the popular cultural representations of American Indians: the headband of the Sioux chief in the 1966 East German Western film *Die Söhne der Großen Bärin* [*The Sons of the Great Mother Bear*] was made by the Old Manitou Indianist club in Radebeul.[59] Thus, as Katrin Sieg observed, Central European hobbyists positioned themselves as *the* heirs and guardians of American Indian history and cultures. I agree with her assessment that this kind of positioning in effect supplanted live Indians and their living traditions with a German identification with and authority over the Native past.[60] This is indeed a colonialist practice. However, Sieg's theoretical conclusion needs to be qualified in the context of early Cold War Central Europe, where the Native American presence was small at best. To use Diana Taylor's analytical framework: without access to the embodied repertoire of living Native Americans, the Central European (object) hobbyists utilized white-made popular and artistic representations and ethnographic scholarship as the archive for their own performances of Indian authenticity. Without challenges to their practices by Native Americans, the Central European hobbyists of the early- to mid-Cold War did what they thought was a service to American Indians, the Western world, and their own societies. The emerging transatlantic alliance for American Indian sovereignty would increasingly challenge the often colonialist cultural practices of Central European Indianist hobbyism with the ethno-political repertoire of real American Indian activists.

As the Cold War intensified and expanded into the realm of cultural production and consumption, Wild West and Indian fandom first became subject to state control, then they were turned into a battleground of ideologies. The government-controlled *Kulturbund* association of the German Democratic Republic seized on the figure of the American Indian as a tool of anti-American propaganda.[61] At the same time as it elevated American Indians, the East German state proceeded to "purge" Western fandom in the country. Cowboys, white pioneers, and frontiers people were designated as the historical "henchmen" of U.S. imperialism. Originally opened in 1928, the Karl May Museum of Radebeul was renamed the "Indian Museum" in 1956, and references to Indians killing General George Custer or playing in Buffalo Bill's show were removed from the exhibits. Finally, the Museum was moved to Bamberg one year before the Berlin Wall was completed.[62] As part of the ideologically correct realignment of popular culture, East German and Hungarian authorities also made sure to remove any firearms from Wild West fan communities,[63] and the former also suppressed cowboy fandom. In response, some reenactors pretended to impersonate Indians in public and indulged in playing cowboys in private.[64] Clandestine cowboy life largely came to an end after some clubs were shut down and others reorganized into Indianist fan circles.[65]

Indians as Ideology

The Cold War's reevaluation of the ideological elements of culture extended to the realm of publishing. After the war, the *Winnetou* novels had become suspicious because Hitler and his Nazi youth movement had admired Karl May's oeuvre; now people in East Germany were discouraged from reading them.[66] A potential candidate for elevation, Fritz Steuben's 1930s cycle of novels about the life of early nineteenth-century Shawnee Confederacy leader Tecumseh, was likewise reviled for being proto-fascist.[67] The author who became East Germany's literary spokesperson for the historical experience of American Indians was Liselotte Welskopf-Henrich, professor of ancient history at Humboldt University, Berlin, and subsequently a member of the German Academy of Sciences. Beginning in 1951, Welskopf-Henrich wrote a six-book series of historical novels titled *The Sons of the Great Mother Bear*[68] about the odyssey of the Teton Sioux during the gold rush in the Black Hills. Buttressed by her day-job as a scholar and professor, Welskopf-Henrich's novels were regarded as "historically accurate"[69]—for example, the Sioux chief at the beginning of her story bore the name *Mattotaupa* or "four bears"—obviously taken from Bodmer and Catlin's 1830s paintings of the Mandan chief Mah-to-toh-pe/Mató-Tópe (Four Bears). With her books translated into several other Central European languages,[70] Welskopf-Henrich "self-consciously created a socialist tradition of Indian literature,"[71] and distinguished it from the "clichéic" stories of Karl May, J. F. Cooper, and Fritz Steuben.[72] Starting in the early 1960s, Welskopf-Henrich also paid visits to reservations in the United States, and in the 1970s she became a node in the transatlantic alliance for American Indian sovereignty.

Katrin Sieg has observed that, in postwar Germany, Wild West fandom redefined the German position from conquered oppressor to a friend to the resistance to oppression.[73] At first, Karl May's novels may have worked analogously, reflecting the new political and economic alliance: Winnetou's blood brotherhood with Karl/Old Shatterhand may have recast official German–U.S. relations from an adversarial relationship into a new alliance sealed with pledges and in-kind assistance. This may have well been a reason why West Germany upheld the esteem of Karl May. With the East German state rejecting the same tradition, it was only a matter of time before the two sides would start using such popular culture for ideological propaganda.

Screen Indians: The *Winnetou* Movies and the *Indianerfilme*

With the increasing availability of audiovisual technology, by the early to mid-1960s the cultural front of the Cold War had moved into cinema and television. Beginning in 1962 and through most of the decade, West German studios produced a dozen or so movies based on Karl May's Winnetou stories.[74] Made in West German, Italian, and Yugoslav co-production, these movies starred an athletic, blond and blue-eyed Lex Barker as Old Shatterhand opposite a genteel and graceful Pierre Brice as Winnetou—both dressed in fringed buckskin.[75] From the mid-1960s through the early 1980s, East Germany's government-owned DEFA studios responded by releasing a dozen of their own so-called *Indianerfilme*, which they co-produced with fellow Communist and non-aligned countries like the Soviet Union and Romania.[76] The lead in these films was Serbian physical education student-turned actor Gojko Mitic.[77] Through partial nudity, Mitic's manly physique was emphasized in almost all of the *Indianerfilme*, and his physicality and facial features made for a more erotic and exotic Indian warrior than Brice's Winnetou.[78]

These two sets of Central European Westerns competed over their shared German-based identification with American Indians. Many of both sets of movies were shot on location in Yugoslavia, thus both sharing and contesting the very landscape of their setting. In the person of Gojko Mitic, who had been an extra in some of the early *Winnetou* movies before becoming the perennial star of the *Indianerfilme*,[79] these movies also shared a technical expertise and screen presence that literally migrated across the iron curtain.

The lines of battle over the two Germanies' shared professional savvy and popular cultural heritage of playing Indian were now drawn with ideology. If the *Winnetou* movies rehearsed the cultural equivalent of the postwar West German–U.S. geopolitical alliance, the *Indianerfilme* were a socialist cultural assault on U.S. imperialism and capitalism, including its product the clichéic Western,[80] as well as a claim of a more "just" and "authentic" German identification with Indians. Through portraying the Indians' heroic but ultimately doomed resistance to white Americans' ruthless encroachment on their land for gold, the socialist Westerns used historical materialism to critique the genre of the classic American Western, and to condemn not only U.S. colonialism, but also to indict American capitalist expansion[81] in the past, and, by implication, in the present. As Gerd Gemünden pointed out, these screen Indians stood in for contemporary East German and other socialist responses to American imperialism.[82] In the 1973 East German movie *Apachen* [*The Apaches*], Indian resistance raises class consciousness: from the Native example, the Mexican miners gradually come to question the wisdom of the white American company, and the relations of production in which they participate. Likewise, in the 1971 *Osceola*, the Seminole leader negotiates decent wages for all plantation workers. As Gemünden observed, Osceola's rallying cry "Indians of all countries, unite!" is at the same time a banner for socialist solidarity against American imperialism.[83] In the 1975 *Blood Brothers*, the interracial friendship of Winnetou and Old Shatterhand is replayed in the alliance between Gojko Mitic's Indian warrior Hard Rock and disillusioned American soldier Harmonika, played by U.S. singer-turned-Marxist actor Dean Reed, himself recently repatriated to East Germany. Here, the historical call for an all-Indian ethnic coalition (espoused by other figures like the Shawnee leader Tecumseh and later by the actual sovereignty movement) is made "red" in a different sense—by a Marxist class-based movement. In the absence of Native critiques, the *Indianerfilme* assimilated historical American Indians into the struggle of the international working class against capitalist exploitation.[84] This ideologically motivated identification with Indians and the resulting openness for cooperation would in time become a component in the transatlantic alliance for American Indian sovereignty.

Conclusion

By the late 1960s, a longstanding Central European cultural fascination with American Indians had converged with a variety of commercialized forms of popular culture, and the use by national governments of the figure of the American Indian for ideological propaganda. Importantly, the above variety of transatlantic cultural forms and their consumption had made for a curious specificity in playing Indian in Central Europe.

The Indian tribes played for and by Central Europeans were overwhelmingly either the Apache of the Southern Plains or the Sioux peoples of the Northern Plains—in the middle and second half of the nineteenth century.[85] Whether it was Tecumseh, Mató-Tópe, Sitting Bull, Winnetou, Osceola, or Ulzana, the specific figure available for direct or indirect identification was invariably a male warrior or chief. Karl Bodmer's 1835 painting of *Pehriska-Ruhpa of the Dog Society of the Hidatsa tribe* was admired and reenacted by Central European hobbyists enamored with the Indian warrior ethos.[86] Different from most U.S. and British white representations, the Central European figure of "the" American Indian was stereotyped positively as an exotic noble savage[87] and a subject of desire and identification. In general, this figure came to stand for a "beleaguered yet defiant" heroic resistance to overwhelming forces, whatever they be.[88]

The identification of Central Europeans with these historical Indians articulated the potential for a variety of alliances. Karl May's novels positioned their German-American hero in a latently Christian alliance with the Apache that he had earned through the performance of frontier feats, and which was based on mutual sympathy and a blood brotherhood that practically meant adoption into the tribe. This alliance, however, precluded mass, organized, ethnic, and violent resistance to colonialism. The Central European hobbyists asserted their guardianship and authority over North American Indian cultures (again, primarily the Plains Sioux in the late nineteenth century) through their "research-based" replication and performances of "authentic" representations of these societies. In their turn, the popular *Indianerfilme* portrayed American Indians as a group in a potential class-based international coalition against U.S. imperialism in the past and present. At the same time as they opened up possibilities for collaboration between live Indians and Central Europeans, these tropes of playing Indian made for attitudes that both enabled and frustrated the building of a transatlantic network for Native sovereignty.

By the late 1960s, the transatlantic cultural landscape had become fertile and ready for an alliance between Central Europeans and live American Indians. The next chapter investigates the actors on the North American side of this alliance and how the radical Indian sovereignty movement came to pose a transnational challenge to the U.S. nation-state.

2

There Ain't No Red in the American Flag[1]

The Indian Sovereignty Movement as a Transnational Challenge to the U.S. Nation-State

> We're gonna have the power. Same level as the white race government. We're one of the government[s]. Whatever they call us. Right now today we gonna have power, before God.
>
> —Oglala Lakota elder, Wounded Knee, spring 1973[2]

In May of 1973, an American Indian was standing in New York City's UN Plaza. His was an imposing figure not only because of the long black hair, which evoked centuries of Indian imagery. This human body was also striking because it was wrapped in the flag of the United States—upside down. Leaning against the wooden rails of the "Police Line" separating his rally from the United Nations compound, this Native demonstrator stood still even as his fellow protestors were waving signs and marching up and down the street to the beating of the AIM drum.[3] Immobile but radiating tension amid the swirling demonstration, this Indian activist was poised for "leaving the American Sector," issuing a transnational challenge to the U.S. nation-state.

Transnational Discourse and the Radical Native Press of the Early 1970s

Movement lawyers and scholars have made the argument that since Indian treaties were originally considered intergovernmental agreements, and American Indians never relinquished the rights enshrined in them, treaties should continue to be recognized and enforced as international law.[4] In its historical context, this argument provides a window into the transnational dimension of Native America. Over the course of its whole post-revolutionary history, the United States government used its full power to gradually subsume Native communities under the American nation-state. Especially during the "twilight" or assimilationist era of Native America between the 1890s and World War Two, Indian transnationalism was suppressed. However, as the United States government assumed a global role and adopted a discourse to fit its self-image in postwar domestic and foreign policy, several groups traditionally considered domestic minorities now reasserted their transnational relations and visions. Penny Von Eschen has investigated how African Americans attempted to link their civil rights struggle to global anticolonial movements between the 1930s and 1950s.[5]

American Indians were not far behind. Daniel Cobb has shown how, coming out of the University of Chicago and the University of Colorado–Boulder's workshops on American Indian affairs, the generation of activists who founded the National Indian Youth Council saw the sovereignty struggle less in the context of Western democracy's struggle against Communism than as part of a global anticolonial movement.[6] As the 1960s drew to a close, this old-new vision of American Indians as nations in the decolonizing world carried over into the transnational discourse of the radical Native press. This globalized focus would influence the next generation of activists—including the leaders of the American Indian Movement—in effect providing scripts for their transnational diplomatic performances.

A survey of the coverage of *Akwesasne Notes* shows that the foremost radical American Indian newspaper of the early 1970s exhibited a transnationalist Native discourse that disseminated information about other indigenous, anticolonial, and national liberation struggles in the United States, the Western Hemisphere, and beyond. Inspired by a transnational event itself, the paper's assembly and production happened across borders.[7] In its reports on Native conscientious objectors against the draft as well as it coverage of the atrocities of the war in Vietnam,[8] the paper recorded and provided scripts for performances that critiqued U.S. foreign policy. Finally, and most importantly, the *Notes* reported on Native efforts to build transnational alliances by traveling to other countries.[9] In this, the paper was documenting, informing about, and inspiring, performances of transnational diplomacy for Native sovereignty.

Predictably, the potential of *Akwesasne Notes* to mobilize transnationally incurred the attention and wrath of both the U.S. and the Canadian governments. By the early 1970s, the paper was edited by non-Native Jerry Gambill, who had earned his tribal name Rarihokwats ("he uncovers facts") by working with and on behalf of the traditionalist Longhouse faction of the Mohawk. Originally a U.S. citizen, in the mid- to late-1960s Gambill had worked for the Canadian government's Department of Indian Affairs in the area, and in the process had acquired Canadian citizenship. The Department of Indian Affairs first reprimanded, then fired Gambill for associating with the Mohawk traditionalists. The Longhouse people took him in and put him up on Cornwall Island, on the Canadian side of the tribal territory, and he spearheaded the creation and subsequent expansion of the *Akwesasne Notes*. As the paper self-admittedly became an organ of the Longhouse faction that was opposed to the Mohawk tribal trustees and the Department of Indian Affairs, the latter two institutions attempted to silence or at least disrupt the paper by going after Rarihokwats. In 1971 and 1972, Rarihokwats was arrested, briefly jailed, and subjected to an investigation and interrogation by U.S. immigration agents and state troopers.[10] In this, both nation-states attempted to quash the editor of a transnationalist Indian newspaper.

Turning the Nation Inside Out: Wounded Knee, 1973

One of the most dramatic event of the American Indian rights movement was the February 1973 takeover of the village of Wounded Knee by Oglala Sioux traditionalists and the militant activists of the American Indian Movement (AIM). During the ensuing three-month-long standoff, the occupiers held their ground in the face of overwhelming pressure—and firepower—from the Pine Ridge Reservation tribal police, South Dakota state troopers, the FBI, federal marshals, and the American military—the full force of the United States government. The demands of the occupiers—a federal investigation into the wrongdoings of tribal chairman Dick Wilson, the reinstatement of the 1868 Fort Laramie Treaty as the basis of relations between the U.S. government and the Sioux Indians, and amnesty for all in the village—were at best partially met by a government that stalled, negotiated, hedged its bets, and tried to wear out those in the Knee by sealing the roads, imposing a media blackout, and keeping the village under withering gunfire that cost the lives of two Indians. Nevertheless, the occupation proved to be a momentous event that galvanized Native activism, and garnered national and international solidarity; and it was a milestone on the road to further U.S. and international legislation on indigenous rights. Scholars have discussed the siege as a major event in the Native sovereignty struggle as a domestic social movement.[11] The following analysis is a reinterpretation of the spring 1973 occupation of the village of Wounded Knee as a transnational challenge to the U.S. nation-state.

Wounded Knee as Vietnam: Challenges to Cold War U.S. Imperialism

One way in which Wounded Knee 1973 posed a discursive and embodied challenge to the U.S. as a nation-state consisted of how those involved in the standoff connected it to the military involvement of the United States in Vietnam. By 1973 the antiwar movement in the United States was in full swing, and the federal government was being forced to respond to it. By linking Wounded Knee to Vietnam, the Native activists both critiqued current U.S. foreign policy and linked their cause to the mainstream social movement against the war—thus broadening their coalition for Native sovereignty.

According to participants and scholars, the embodied experience of Wounded Knee 1973 had strong parallels with the war in Vietnam. In this scenario, a village—or military base?—was defended by a few hundred people, among them the elderly, women, and children, who could be considered civilian noncombatants—and was besieged by a government with superior firepower and technology. Even as they smuggled weapons and supplies into the village, the defenders had mostly hunting rifles and shotguns, and several of them later disclosed that what outsiders judged to be more advanced weaponry were often mere sticks disguised as machine guns mounted in bunkers and trenches. U.S. government forces, on the other hand, used M-16s, large-caliber machine guns, armed personnel carriers, and even the Air Force—the kind of weaponry that they had just stopped using in Vietnam—in their well-coordinated operations against the village.[12] The ensuing prolonged, albeit one-sided, firefights would have only further reinforced the stakes and parallels involved in this standoff. Like the perimeter battles and search-and-destroy missions of Vietnam, Wounded Knee 1973 was about life and death, a high-tech and regular military versus a popular uprisings' guerilla army, and the profound uncertainty about the status, value, and fate of the civilians involved.

While its critics—including some local whites, tribal chairman Dick Wilson, and some in the U.S. government—charged that the occupation was inspired, supported, or committed by Communists,[13] what is striking is how consistently the activists and their sympathizers linked Wounded Knee 1973 to the American war in Vietnam. For years before Wounded Knee 1973, the radical Native American press had carried articles that bitterly observed that "The Frontier Moves West: The U.S. Has Got Itself Some New Indians" in Indochina, elaborated on the shared characteristics of historical "Indian fighter" Kit Carson and the My Lai massacre's perpetrator Lieutenant William Calley, or pointed out that the world-famous photo of naked Vietnamese children running from a napalm attack "could be Cheyenne, Lakota, or Pomo country, a century or less ago."[14] During the actual event, radical and outspoken figures such as Angela Davis characterized the siege of Wounded Knee as "It's just like a Vietnam battlefield out there."[15] Memoirs and scholars point out that several of the Native occupiers were veterans of the Vietnam War[16]—Bobby Onco and his (presumably originally Communist-made) "souvenir" AK-47 rifle[17] provided a sense of the embodied connection between the American Indian struggle and the American intervention in Southeast Asia. Another veteran, Woody Kipp, in his memoir—tellingly titled *Viet Cong at Wounded Knee*—explains that during the siege he identified with the Vietnamese guerillas against the U.S. government.[18] AIM occupiers sarcastically designated the no-man's-land used for negotiations as the "DMZ,"[19] while federal forces called the secret routes into the village "AIM's Ho Chi Minh road."[20] Thus, participants discursively transferred Wounded Knee 1973 out of U.S. domestic policy into the foreign policy of the U.S. superpower in Cold War geopolitics. In this, the standoff tested the outlines and behavior of the United States as a nation-state on (what had been presumed to be) its own soil. Such a discursive maneuver further connected the American Indian rights struggle to a global anticolonialist project in the minds of the occupiers and the mainstream antiwar movement.

Re-Territorializing Wounded Knee as a Performance of Native Sovereignty

The occupation of Wounded Knee was a discursive and embodied transnational challenge to the U.S. as a nation-state because it was an experiment in the re-territorialization and building a Native nation within, but at the same time outside, of the United States. Pan-Indian nationalism, or the idea that Indian communities in the United States should be treated by the government as individual nations sovereign in their own right, was not new to the American Indian rights movement—in fact, it had been called variously "sovereignty" or "self-determination." Nor was Wounded Knee the first event where Indian activists took action to make their nationalistic demands heard: during the 1972 "Trail of Broken Treaties" to Washington, DC, the American Indian Movement (AIM) issued its "Twenty Points" declaration, which included the demand to abolish the Bureau of Indian Affairs (BIA), the government agency in the Department of the Interior that had conducted Indian relations since the early nineteenth century. At the end of the journey, activists, furious over the lack of governmental responsiveness, took over the headquarters of the BIA in the U.S. capital, and they renamed the building "The American Indian Embassy."[21] As in the 1969–70 takeover of Alcatraz Island and the 1972 occupation, the activists holding Wounded Knee furthered the project of such nation-building—but considering the possible consequences, not only on the symbolic level.

During the seventy-one-day standoff, Oglala traditionalists and AIM activists physically took and held the village of Wounded Knee—this slightly over one-square-mile piece of land—and in effect placed it outside of the legal jurisdiction of the U.S. government and its sanctioned tribal police of the Pine Ridge Reservation. U.S. federal, state, and reservation laws were not enforceable in Wounded Knee as long as AIM and the Oglala held the village. However small the area and however brief the occupation, the activists captured space and time from the United States as a nation-state and opened them up to implement their vision of an alternative sovereign country made up of Indians and their allies. Accordingly, they early on declared that "Wounded Knee will be a corporate state under the Independent Oglala Nation,"[22] and soon appointed a "provisional government"[23] with committees on housing, defense, immigration, internal security, public health, and information.[24] According to AIM leader Russell Means, this "symbolic Indian government" needed help from all over the country so that Native people could demonstrate to everyone that they were fit to rule themselves.[25]

After this initial declaration, the new Indian government of the occupiers quickly set about defining its population and delimiting the nation. The leaders offered citizenship to those in the village, and they issued passports and visas to the press and those they deemed "foreigners."[26] For some, the ritual of declaring the birth of a new, sovereign nation seemed to be transformational: after Russell Means warned that "if any foreign official representing a foreign power, specifically the United States, comes in here without permission, that will be treated as an act of war and dealt with accordingly," two U.S. postal inspectors were apprehended and held for a few hours until they were cleared of charges of spying for the American government.[27]

It was not only the urban activists who advanced the project of re-territorializing Wounded Knee and establishing a new nation-state on an equal footing with the U.S. government. In the ensuing negotiations with U.S. officials, one Oglala elder insisted that "We're gonna have the power. Same level as the white race government. We're one of the government[s]. Whatever they call us. Right now today we gonna have power, before God." The occupiers applauded.[28] After the declaration of the independent Oglala Nation, newly appointed defense minister Stan Holder told U.S. government officials, "Since we are an independent nation now we no longer recognize your authority and I have no authority on behalf of our country to negotiate with you. Any agreements made until now were made by me as an American citizen and are no longer in effect."[29] Some key leaders of the occupiers thus attempted to reset, or define a new beginning for, relations between the Oglala and the U.S. nation-state.

Pressure from Without: Indian Rights as U.S. Foreign Relations

The transnational challenge of Wounded Knee 1973 to the United States government went beyond the level of rhetoric. American Indian activists actively attempted to forge alliances with sympathizers outside of the nation-state, and sought out transnational institutions to put pressure on the American government to meet their demands and recognize their rights. Some did this by accommodating the foreign media at Wounded Knee. According to Carol Sullivan, "international press coverage was remarkable considering the remoteness of the village. One of the most controversial accounts was an article published in several languages in the Soviet weekly paper *Новое время* [*New Times*], featuring as its front cover a photo of an Oglala with a rifle. [. . .] A group of Dutch journalists put an advertisement in the *New York Times*, [titled] "The Dutch at Wounded Knee," calling for a sense of proportion and a writing campaign to the [U.S.] Department of Interior asking for a "lowered voice and reasonable conversation."[30] For its own part, the federal government considerably impeded media coverage: as he was escorting a funeral caravan out of the village, Pine Ridge police and the FBI apprehended Danish author and filmmaker Jacob Holdt, stripped him of his press credentials, and kicked him off the reservation.[31] A European reporter who had played hide-and-seek with the FBI had to talk his way out of a reservation jail cell—just to go back to smuggling weapons and ammunition into the village.[32]

The defenders of Wounded Knee also had their own representatives overseas. According to memoirs, during the siege AIM member Vernon Bellecourt served as the occupiers' "roving ambassador," traveling outside of the United States, holding press conferences, creating phrases for sound bites, lecturing on television, and making speeches in countries like Italy.[33] The communication and personal interaction between Native envoys and Europeans and the resulting transatlantic alliance for sovereignty will be discussed in chapters 3 and 4.

The most remarkable effort of the defenders of Wounded Knee to challenge the United States government as a nation-state came with their sympathy rallies and petitions to the United Nations and the U.S. State Department. For several years before Wounded Knee, several U.S. and Canadian Native organizations had been trying to get the United Nations involved in indigenous issues.[35] Now, the siege of the village generated a flurry of activities by American Indians and their sympathizers that aimed to use the attention of the UN as leverage against the U.S. government. As early as a week into the occupation, the Oglala petitioned the United Nations to send observers to Wounded Knee and allow an Indian leader to address its General Assembly. Their plea was rebuffed by Secretary-General Kurt Waldheim, who explained that the UN "cannot interfere in matter of domestic jurisdiction," because it "has to deal with 132 member states and cannot deal with those who contend they are nations within nations." Waldheim advised the petitioners to find a UN member state to sponsor their delegate, which would thus enable them to speak to the Assembly.[36] This early exchange is telling about how the United Nations, an international institution, was very much governed by the ideology of the nation-state, and was hard pressed to accommodate transnational issues such as indigenous rights in North America. Chapter 6 discusses in more detail how the United Nations eventually channeled the radical Indian sovereignty movement into creating a global indigenous rights régime.

During the siege, in a move that can itself be considered transnational pan-Indianism, the Oglala at Wounded Knee requested help from the Onondaga of the Six Nations to resolve the standoff. The Six Nations, whose territories straddle the U.S.–Canadian border, had been fighting for a status that would allow them to issue their own passports and travel internationally as members of their own nation.[37] On March 19, 1973, the Iroquois Confederacy's delegation called on the U.S. government to withdraw its federal agents and grant amnesty to those in the village.[38]

After several agreements were brokered and then fell through, the occupiers decided to increase pressure on the national government from without. Native, white, and black sympathizers organized benefits and rallies to support the struggle in several cities of the United States, the most remarkable of which was a demonstration in UN Plaza in New York City on May 4, 1973. Richard Erdoes's photographs of the event show Native activists, among them Clyde Bellecourt, Mad Bear Anderson, and Eddie Benton Banai, variously dressed in tribal regalia, Western wear, or wrapping themselves in the U.S. flag, giving interviews and marching with signs demanding a resolution to the siege.[39]

At the demonstration before the UN, a delegation of the Six Nations delivered a petition both to the chair of the UN Human Rights Commission and to the United States mission to the UN, offering their services in resolving the dispute at Wounded Knee, and requesting that the UN provide free access for the media, food, medicine, and spiritual and legal counsel to those in the village. In a face-to-face meeting, an official explained to the delegates that "USUN has no responsibilities for Indian affairs." The Six Nations then asked that their petition be conveyed to the appropriate government agency in Washington. The U.S. mission promptly forwarded the petition to the State Department, along with a document written by the Oglala leaders, which authorized the Six Nations to seek peacekeepers from the United Nations.[40]

The fact that such petitions and messages of solidarity arrived at the U.S. State Department shows that Native activists and their sympathizers consciously chose to bypass the Bureau of Indian Affairs and its home, the U.S. Department of the Interior, in order to put pressure directly on the U.S. government's foreign policy arm. In this, they reframed Indian rights as U.S. foreign relations. On March 16, 1973, the American Embassy in Mexico City received a letter from the Inter-American Indian Institute, offering to mediate in the Wounded Knee standoff. The Embassy cabled the State Department for instructions on how to respond to the offer.[41] In its response, the Department directed the Embassy to politely decline the offer, and remind the Institute that the legitimate authority at the village was the elected tribal government, and the occupiers were not tribal officials, therefore the U.S. government would continue to negotiate and prevent armed crimes in the area.[42] At some point during the siege, the State Department cabled several of its embassies with instructions on how to respond to demonstrations and questions regarding the oppression of American Indians. As the United States Information Agency observed, "If Indians are killed, we can surely expect sharp and widespread foreign condemnation of this U.S. government action. It would come at a particularly unpropitious time, giving Arab governments an excuse to fog up the terrorist issue."[43] This was an internal recognition that the outcome of Wounded Knee 1973 would reflect on American foreign policy and would be used for propaganda. Quietly, the State Department also sent to Wounded Knee a journalist from the Voice of America, one of the U.S. government's media organs overseas.[44]

Perhaps the most telling single document about how Wounded Knee 1973 challenged the hegemony of the U.S. nation-state is a five-page referral from the State Department to the Department of the Interior. On May 4, 1973, Alicia Castillo of Madison, Wisconsin, sent a telegram addressed to President Nixon. In her message, Castillo asked Nixon to "please guarantee the rights of the Indians at Wounded Knee, since they were promised those rights in good faith in 1868" (a reference to the original Treaty of Fort Laramie). Because the letter was written in Spanish, it was first forwarded to the office of the Secretary of State "for translation and appropriate handling." Once it was translated, State Department officials were puzzled about how to handle a request concerning the traditionally "domestic" issue of Indian relations at the foreign policy arm of the United States government. One State official wrote in hand on the document's "routing slip," "Shouldn't this have gone to Interior?" to which another responded, "Yes—Julie—ask them how we send these back."[45] As Castillo's Spanish letter demanding rights for Indians at and beyond Wounded Knee bounced back and forth between U.S. government agencies, it traced the external and internal fault lines of the American nation-state.

Going beyond the confines of a domestic social movement, the occupiers of Wounded Knee 1973 and their sympathizers issued a transnational challenge to the United States as a nation-state in a number of ways. By physically occupying the village and holding it against the forces of the federal government, the Native activists re-territorialized Wounded Knee from being part of the United States into being the domain of the Independent Oglala Nation. From the archives of Native historical memory and U.S. legal history, the occupiers used the 1868 Fort Laramie Treaty to make their case for the reinstatement of Native rights as U.S. foreign relations. In their embodied performances and their rhetoric, the defenders of Wounded Knee 1973 argued that the U.S. government was using the same violence in South Dakota as it was in Vietnam, and that this violence was the means by which whites had colonized Native America centuries before. Finally, American Indian activists and their allies tried to put pressure on the U.S. government from without by taking their grievances to the United Nations and addressing them to the State Department, the foreign policy arm of Uncle Sam. In these, Wounded Knee 1973 briefly became a tear at the seams of the U.S. nation-state—a tear that had to be mended by turning the nation inside out.

"Inside-Outside" U.S.–UN

The Wounded Knee delegation had at least one other meeting at the United Nations on May 4, 1973. "Apparently, as byproduct of demonstrations at UN Plaza, Chief Leon Shenandoah of 'Six Nations,' accompanied by Six Nations's [sic] lawyer Omar Ghobashy, asked to call at USUN and were received by Polcouns mid-afternoon May 4."[46] In their visit to the United States Mission at the United Nations, this Native delegation used the petition that they had just presented to UN officials as a script for a carefully constructed performance of sovereignty in the interstices of the U.S. nation-state and the international forum of the UN.

In contrast with the repeated and emphatic assertions of sovereignty earlier that day at the United Nations, the language of this performance was conciliatory to the U.S. government.

> After describing Six Nations leadership as *conservative, intensely loyal Americans with long record of good relations with Washington authorities*, Ghobashy provided text of petition by Six Nations (on behalf of Oglalas) which he said had just been presented to [the UN Secretary-General] and chairman of Human Rights Commission [. . .]. He emphasized that *this step had been taken reluctantly,* at request of Oglalas, *not as a disloyal act,* but as a matter of representing the case to the international community, "particularly the US public," in context of rumors of alleged federal ultimatum to Wounded Knee Indians.[47]

This performative framing of the petition clearly aimed to play on the Indian militancy expressed in the siege, some of the demonstrations, and the attendant press coverage. The Six Nations delegation knew that the implications of demonstrating at and petitioning the United Nations were not lost on U.S. authorities, and that these maneuvers amounted to a transnational challenge of the U.S. nation-state. In their meeting they aimed to assuage fears from Native American separatism by playing to U.S. nationalism. Emphasizing the American patriotism of the Iroquois was also meant to reassure U.S. officials that the Six Nations mediation team would be on their side in the negotiations. Their explanation presented the Six Nations as taking this measure to rein in extreme "rumors" that were threatening to lead to the further escalation of the standoff.

After such reassuring overtures, Ghobashy explained that at the request of the Oglala, the Six Nations were now making an official offer to mediate in the conflict between the U.S. government and the Oglala defenders of Wounded Knee. Most specifically, the Iroquois were offering to help interpret the agreement of April 5, 1973, "which each side asserts the other has failed to adhere to." While waiting for the response of the U.S. government to the offer, the Haudenosaunee wished to reiterate the request of the Oglala for free access to Wounded Knee for humanitarian aid, lawyers and the media, as outlined in the original petition. They further advocated for unrestricted publicity to combat the rumors that the government had issued an ultimatum and was preparing to move in with military force, and persecute Native Americans beyond Wounded Knee. "Indians are afraid that 'repressive measures' may be byproduct of Wounded Knee. They fear such things as arrests, illegal searches, harassment, retardation of legislation. Callers said they were now reasonably convinced rumors of ultimatum, which had included references to tanks and crop burning, were false."[48]

"Callers conducted themselves with dignity and courtesy throughout interview." In their performance at the U.S. Mission to the UN, Chief Shenandoah and Omar Ghobashy carefully positioned the Six Nations, an historically and geographically transnational Indian people, as a politically moderate, patriotic, squarely domestic(ated) force of American citizens offering to help the U.S. government in brokering a stand down with the separatist Oglala and AIM militants holed up in Wounded Knee. Whether they were doing this because the Six Nations leadership were genuinely more conservative, or because they wanted to manipulate the U.S. government, in effect they were playing a kind of "inside-outside" game that American Indian activists had engaged in during the previous decade.

The "inside-outside" approach was originally identified by historian John Lewis Gaddis as a Cold War political strategy of the nonaligned countries, which would manipulate the United States and the Soviet Union "by laying on flattery, pledging solidarity, feigning indifference, threatening defection, or even raising the specter of their own collapse and the disastrous results that might flow from it," all to further their own projects.[49] Applied to Native activism by historian Daniel Cobb, the Indian "inside-outside strategy" exploited the rivalry between various agencies of the U.S. government, such as the Bureau of Indian Affairs and the Office of Economic Opportunity under the Lyndon B. Johnson Administration—as Standing Rock Sioux activist Vine Deloria, Jr., put it, "praising one agency while kicking the ass of another."[50] To be distinguished from a passive aggressive obstructionism, the "inside-outside" game plan is a servant-of-two-masters scenario in which an actor of little power has to navigate and productively manipulate two forces, each of which would easily overwhelm him or her in a direct confrontation. In negotiating from asymmetrical power relations, the Native inside-outside strategy was part of the kind of contact zone diplomacy which I elucidate later in this chapter.

In their inside-outside game with the United Nations and the U.S. State Department, the Wounded Knee delegation was performatively positioning the Six Nations inside the body of the U.S. nation-state, juxtaposing it with their more radical assertions of expanded sovereignty that were at times reaching for full independence outside of the U.S. nation-state. Even as they were demonstrating and petitioning the United Nations to intervene at Wounded Knee and thereby implicitly recognize Native sovereignty rights as a transnational issue, some of the very same American Indian activists were reassuring the U.S. nation-state of their patriotism and loyalty as they were offering to mediate in the dispute. In this, the American Indian rights movement of the late Cold War not only discursively identified with nonaligned and decolonizing countries, but they also used some nonaligned models in the embodied practices of Native political activism, lobbying and diplomacy. The threat of a UN intervention in the matters of the U.S. nation-state was calculated to induce the U.S. government to address American Indian demands.

These Native performances likely hit home. Whether as a direct result or a coincidence in timeline, just a few days after the first Oglala petition to the UN Secretary-General, the U.S. government forces removed the roadblocks and opened access to Wounded Knee, which promptly filled with Indians and allies from all over the country. Later, in addition to reporting their meeting with the Wounded Knee delegation, the U.S. Mission to the United Nations also cabled the State Department both the resolution of the Oglala to authorize the Six Nations to be their broker, and the Six Nations petition to the UN Secretary-General and Human Rights Commission. The U.S. UN Mission also recommended State to forward the documents to the Justice Department.[51] While their subsequent route is not clear, these performances and their document imprints may well have contributed to the restraint on the part of the U.S. government at Wounded Knee. Paul Chaat Smith and Robert Allen Warrior have shown how government negotiators wanted above all else to avoid repeating the massacre of 1890 at Wounded Knee in 1973.[52] For the Nixon Administration, the mere knowledge that the United Nations had been alerted and requested by American Indians to intervene in the standoff likely added an argument against a resolution by the kind of repressive measures the Indians feared.

Performing Indian Treaties as International Law

While it is beyond the scope of this study to make a legal case for the continued validity of American Indian treaties, it is certain that the American Indian radical sovereignty movement led a sustained attempt at reinstating Native treaties as domestic and international law, and thereby expanded American Indian rights. Congress had ended treaty-making as a part of Indian relations in 1871, and subsequent federal policy was applied to supersede the nineteenth-century treaties. Charles Wilkinson has shown how the sovereignty movement brought Native America back from the brink of Termination through their treaty litigation in the post-World War Two period.[53] The occupations of the radical sovereignty movement—among them Alcatraz, Mount Rushmore, and Wounded Knee—were often carried out on the grounds of past U.S. treaties granting specific land to the Indians, and they also demanded the recognition of these treaties. In this, they were Native embodied enactments of agreements that were originally meant to be binding, but were subsequently disregarded or unilaterally modified by the U.S. government. The protest form of the takeover thus performed what Indians considered to be the original meaning of the treaty, and re-territorialized the ground on which it happened.

The Native occupations of the early 1970s paralleled nineteenth-century treaty-making in yet another aspect. In her seminal 1992 book on colonialism and literature, Mary Louise Pratt defined the *contact zone* as "the space in which peoples geographically and historically separated come into contact with each other and establish ongoing relations, usually involving conditions of coercion, radical inequality, and intractable conflict [. . .] often within radically asymmetrical relations of power."[54] The radical Native activists and traditionalists of the 1969–70 occupation of Alcatraz Island, the 1970 campout on Mount Rushmore, the 1972 takeover of the BIA building in Washington, DC, and the spring 1973 siege of Wounded Knee, South Dakota, negotiated from a position of relative power. Their power came from the presence and coverage of the media, the international attention generated by the more prolonged occupations, as well as from the U.S. government's reluctance to resolve the conflict with violence—to repeat the Wounded Knee of 1890 at the Wounded Knee of 1973.[55] This power meant that the radical Indian sovereignty movement had more leverage than during the "assimilationist era" between the late nineteenth century and World War Two. Their power position enabled groups in the radical sovereignty movement to negotiate as a unit outside of the nation-state—the transnational diplomacy of the contact zone. This contact zone was recreated in the no-man's-land on the perimeter of Wounded Knee, where the occupiers and the U.S. government met in a tepee, much like at the signing of the 1868 Treaty of Fort Laramie.[56] In this, the negotiations of Wounded Knee 1973 were also a commemorative reenactment of the treaty-making of the nineteenth century.

The ethno-political repertoire of the radical Native sovereignty movement relied on both the idea and the actual archival documents of nineteenth-century Indian treaties. Created after the siege to defend the activists against the U.S. government's relentless prosecution, the Wounded Knee Legal Defense/Offense Committee (WKLD/OC) regularly introduced the 1868 Fort Laramie Treaty in court as historical evidence that could exonerate the defendants.[57] Whether referring to the treaty as international or as U.S. law, the lawyers of the movement argued that the occupiers were within the jurisdiction of the original treaty. Against the full legal apparatus of the U.S. government, WKLD/OC achieved an acquittal rate of over 92 percent.[58]

As seen above, a cornerstone of the transnational program of the radical sovereignty movement became the quest for the recognition of Indian treaties as international law. Accordingly, the International Indian

Treaty Council—the name of which clearly reflected this focus—not only submitted, but persistently discussed Native treaties in world bodies. While references to and texts of treaties were a recurrent part of Native submissions to the United Nations (including at its breakthrough 1977 conference on discrimination against Indians in the Americas), not until 1989 did that body commission a study on treaties between indigenous populations and national governments.[59]

Finally, the radical sovereignty movement made the recognition of Indian treaties part and parcel of its transnational relations with national liberation movements and national governments. During its fact-finding missions to Nicaragua in the early 1980s, the International Indian Treaty Council studied the provisions of the 1860 Treaty of Managua.[60] In this treaty, Great Britain recognized the sovereignty of Nicaragua but reserved autonomy for its Miskito Indians based on historical precedents. American Indian Movement leader Russell Means attempted to leverage his organization's support of Nicaragua's Sandinista government for their recognition of U.S. Indian sovereignty rights. In March 1982, he pressed Commandante Jaime Wheelock to endorse the 1868 Fort Laramie Treaty as an international agreement in return for the continuing support of the Sandinista régime by the International Indian Treaty Council.[61] While this particular meeting did not result in a ringing endorsement of either party, the Treaty Council nevertheless had a long, if troubled, alliance with Nicaragua's Miskitos and its Sandinista government.[62]

The Transnational Program of the Indian Sovereignty Movement

By early 1974, the radical sovereignty movement was at a crossroads. Groups like the National Indian Youth Council, Indians of All Tribes, and the American Indian Movement had distinguished themselves from the moderate old guard represented by the National Congress of American Indians both in their transnational anticolonialist ideology and their more confrontational methods.[63] The forms of activism that this radical cohort had been employing ranged from teach-ins, marches and demonstrations patterned after the Civil Rights Movement to counter-commemorations and similar performative interventions in U.S. historical memory with dramatic elements of confrontation, infusing these with forms from Native cultures like drumming, singing, and dancing. The resulting ethno-political performances drew media attention and raised national awareness of the sovereignty rights struggle.

However, demonstrations, occupations, and standoffs such as the ones at Alcatraz, the BIA building in Washington, DC, and Wounded Knee also required much in the way of resources and prolonged efforts to maintain supply lines and media interest. The resulting national media coverage was also often ambiguous if not sensationalist and rehashing Indian stereotypes. At the same time, these prolonged events also generated international media coverage, foreign interest in Indian demands, and expressions of support and solidarity.[64]

The Native attempts to exploit such interest beyond the nation-state, to use the United Nations as leverage, and to rely on the expertise of practitioners of U.S. and international law all provided an experiential basis for discussions among sovereignty activists about pursuing a distinct transnational strategy. In their seminal chronicle of the radical Native sovereignty movement, Paul Chaat Smith and Robert Allen Warrior claim that Wounded Knee was the high point, after which Indian radicalism "faded, disintegrating under the weight of its own internal contradictions and divisions, and a relentless legal assault by federal and state governments."[65] I contend that, even as it was struggling to protect its activists and to legitimately represent its constituencies, the sovereignty movement actually transformed into a transnational advocacy network. This transformation was inaugurated by a conference.

Visions at Standing Rock: The First International Indian Treaty Council Conference

One year on the heels of the siege of Wounded Knee, the American Indian Movement and its allies held the First International Indian Treaty Council at Mobridge, the Standing Rock Sioux reservation on June 8–16, 1974. Dubbed "the largest intertribal gathering of Indian people ever,"[66] estimates of the number of its delegates ranged from "thousands" to over 5,000.[67] Some ninety-seven Native communities were represented from the Americas,[68] and all fourteen Sioux reservations in the U.S. and Canada sent traditional leaders to the gathering.[69] The first in a long series of International Indian Treaty Council conferences, the gathering laid down plans for a program of transnational diplomacy of the American Indian rights movement. The conference institutionalized the "international work" of sovereignty rights[70] by establishing the

International Indian Treaty Council, one of the few organizations which not only spearheaded North American Indian participation in the United Nations, but during the next four decades also helped inaugurate a global indigenous rights régime.

Declaring American Indian Independence

Most of the suggestions, motions, and resolutions made by the activists in the breakout meetings were eventually included in the final document of the conference, thus making for a declaration of the transnational program of the radical Indian sovereignty movement. Likely drafted during the conference and typed on organization letterhead only afterward, the *Declaration of Continuing Independence* for the first time featured the logo of the International Indian Treaty Council—the geographical silhouette of North and South America, their isthmus crossed by a smoking peace pipe adorned with feathers on each end.[71] At odds with the absence of Latin American indigenous peoples in the conference meeting records, the new logo depicted a red Western Hemisphere connected by the pipe, a symbol of treaty-making amongst and between North American Indian tribes and European powers, and subsequently the national governments of the Americas. This graphic suggested that the indigenous communities of the hemisphere were linked by this performative form of diplomacy, a relationship which the new Treaty Council was created to revive.

The document's title likewise suggests a struggle for expression to underpin the embodied struggle for full sovereignty. *The Declaration of Continuing Independence by the First International Indian Treaty Council at Standing Rock Indian Country June 1974*[72] replaced the word "reservation" with the phrase "Indian Country." This deliberate titling of the document rejected one Euro-American word and concept at the same time as it appropriated another previously derogatory phrase, now deploying it to assert the full sovereignty of an independent "Indian *country*."

Even as it relied on the concept and form of one of the founding documents of the U.S. nation-state, the *Declaration*'s "Preamble" both indicted the U.S. government for violating its own founding principles, and reasserted Native independence.

> The United States of America has continually violated the independent Native Peoples of this continent by Executive action, Legislative fiat and Judicial decision. By its actions, the U.S. has denied all Native people their International Treaty

> rights, Treaty lands and basic human rights of freedom and sovereignty. This same U.S. government which fought to throw off the yoke of oppression and gain its own independence, has now reversed its role and become the oppressor of sovereign Native people.
>
> [. . .]
>
> The International Indian Treaty Conference hereby adopts this Declaration of Continuing Independence of the Sovereign Native American Indian Nations. In the course of these human events, we call upon the people of the world to support this struggle for our sovereign rights and our treaty rights. We pledge our assistance to all other sovereign people who seek their own independence.[73]

In addition to using some of its phrases (such as "in the course of human events"), the Treaty Council conference's *Declaration* borrowed the conceptual move of affirming the "independence" (full sovereignty) of Native nations—and appealing to world opinion—from the document created by the "Founding Fathers" of the United States. The Indian sovereignty activists likewise shared with the American Revolution the very precariousness of their project. Similar to the U.S. *Declaration of Independence*, the Indian sovereignty movement's document cited certain rights existing prior to as well as during the status quo of colonial rule. For the writers, full sovereignty was rooted in the "basic human rights" of freedom and sovereignty, the right to live in harmony with the environment, and the treaty rights to land. Their *Declaration* was a response to the U.S. government's (in all its three branches) transformation into its own antithesis—from freedom fighter to oppressor. Both in its force and its title, the document asserted that Indian nations continued to be independent of the U.S. government, thus they were outside of the American nation-state even as their lands were on U.S. soil.

The *Declaration* early on established that "[t]reaties between sovereign nations explicitly entail agreements which represent "the supreme law of the land" binding each party to an inviolate international relationship." According to the authors, all the lands belonging to Indians within the boundaries of the United States had been recognized by treaties between Native nations and the U.S. government. "We the sovereign Native Peoples charge the United States with gross violations of our International Treaties"—exemplified by the case of the Black Hills having been taken from the Sioux despite the Fort Laramie Treaty's provisions, and the forced relocation of the Cherokee from Georgia to Oklahoma on the "Trail of Tears," the Supreme Court's protections notwithstanding. Since the U.S. Constitution itself recognized treaties as part of the rule of law, the authors "will peacefully pursue all legal and political avenues to demand United States recognition of its own Constitution in this regard, and thus to honor its treaties with the Native Nations."[74]

Although not fully articulated by the body proper of the *Declaration*, one of the most powerful legal arguments for sovereignty rights concerned the continuity of the status of Native American communities. The *Declaration* insisted that "[a]ll treaties between the Sovereign Native Nations and the United States Government must be interpreted according to the traditional and spiritual ways of the signatory Native Nations."[75] The document's "Glossary" defined the concept of "sovereign" in a way that provides a key to this notion of continuity.

> SOVEREIGN—"independent of, and unlimited by, any other; possessing, or entitled to, original and independent authority or jurisdiction." Only a state or sovereign can enter into a treaty. The U.S. government made 371 treaties with Native American nations, all of which considered themselves sovereign and fully capable of making treaties. They still so consider themselves and are desirous of claiming the authority and jurisdiction thereof.[76]

In arguing that the Native Nations never ceded their sovereignty rights, the *Declaration* does not give birth to a new concept. In fact, it reaches back in Indian historical memory to the traditional Native interpretation of treaties, and asserts that Indian independence continues, if now championed by the newly minted International Indian Treaty Council.

Conceptually, the renewed recognition of treaty rights as the basis of Indian relations would entail a repeal of all major post-treaty legislation. As a first step of treaty enforcement, the *Declaration* both recognized and called on the U.S. government to recognize, the "Provisional Government of the Independent Oglala Nation," established on March 11, 1973, during the siege of Wounded Knee.[77] Next, as Greg Zephier, Michael Haney, and Eddie Benton (Banai) had urged in the meetings,

> We reject all executive orders, legislative acts and judicial decisions of the United States related to Native Nations since

> 1871, when the United States unilaterally suspended treaty-making relations with the Native Nations. This includes, but is not limited to, the Major Crimes Act, the General Allotment Act, the Citizenship Act of 1924, the Indian Reorganization Act of 1934, the Indian Claims Commission Act, Public Law 280 and the Termination Act.[78]

In order to secure the U.S. government's recognition of treaty rights, the new organization "will seek the support of all world communities in the struggle for the continuing independence of Native Nations."[79] More specifically,

> The International Indian Treaty Council will establish offices in Washington, D.C. and New York City to approach the international forces necessary to obtain the recognition of our treaties. These offices will establish an initial system of communication among Native Nations to disseminate information, getting a general consensus of concerning issues, developments and any legislative attempt affecting Native Nations by the United States of America.
>
> [. . .]
>
> The International Indian Treaty Council established by this conference is directed to make the application to the United Nations for recognition and membership of the sovereign Native Nations. We pledge our support to any similar application by an aboriginal people.
>
> This conference directs the Treaty Council to open negotiations with the government of the United States through its Department of State. We seek these negotiations in order to establish diplomatic relations with the United States. When these diplomatic relations have been established, the first order of business shall be to deal with US violations of treaties with Native Nations, and violations of the rights of those Native Nations who have refused to sign treaties with the United States.[80]

The plan to launch permanent Treaty Council posts in these two cities articulated a strategy to approach the U.S. government from the outside. The IITC staff in Washington, DC, would attempt to perform Native independence through diplomacy with the U.S. government. This same office could potentially also bypass the government and visit foreign diplomatic missions, like Deskaheh and the Wounded Knee delegation had. The Treaty Council post in New York City would permanently lobby the United Nations for Native membership as well as report back on the proceedings of that supra-national body.

Much of the transnational solidarity advocated by Russell Means and Jimmie Durham also came to be expressed by the *Declaration.* In addition to proclaiming support for the Puerto Rican independence movement (without a specific party affiliation), "The International Indian Treaty Council recognizes the sovereignty of all Native Nations and will stand in unity to support our Native and international brothers and sisters in their respective and collective struggles concerning international treaties and agreements violated by the United States and other governments." This was a call for an alliance that would transcend nation-states—between Native groups across various countries and societies—but in relation to national governments. This transnational coalition was to be marshaled for a specific purpose. "We call on the conscionable nations of the world to join us in charging and prosecuting the United States of America for its genocidal practices against the Sovereign Native Nations; most recently illustrated by Wounded Knee 1973 and the continued refusal to sign the United Nations 1948 Treaty on Genocide."[81] In addition to direct diplomacy, one other means of advocacy for Indian sovereignty rights would be the court of world opinion.

The map illustrating the claims of the *Declaration of Continued Independence* is not unlike the maps of the Amerindianist American Redman's Party (NAARP) sent to the Secretary-General of the United Nations the previous summer.[82] Both maps re-territorialize a part of U.S. soil according to the full sovereignty of the Sioux Nation in the area. The map of the *Declaration* reaches back to the geography of the past, using the 1868 Fort Laramie Treaty to reassert the older boundaries of the Sioux Nation, which used to take up much of the territories of Montana, Wyoming, North and South Dakota, and Nebraska.[83] In this, the *Declaration* again used Native historical memory to reassert full territorial sovereignty.

The International Indian Treaty Council of the *Declaration* seemed to recognize Native diversity in its wider, goal-based transnational coalition, and focused on only one step of possible nation-building: the recognition of treaty rights. There is some indication that at this point the Treaty Council conference participants thought of the Fort Laramie Treaty and treaty rights as a model of independence replicable across

Native communities in North America,[84] and possibly in the Western Hemisphere. In this, the approach of the radical Indian sovereignty movement fits Benedict Anderson's definition of nationalism as a framework replicable across societies.[85] Even as they searched for a form of political organization that could transcend or at least demarcate itself from the U.S. nation-state, the activists of the radical Indian sovereignty movement nevertheless resorted to using similar trappings of the nation-state.

Refining the Transnational Program

The next several years proved to be a defining time for the International Indian Treaty Council and the kind of diplomacy they engaged in on behalf of the radical Indian sovereignty movement. It was during this period that the leading members of the Treaty Council refined their conceptual tools, made contacts beyond the United States and Canada, and were officially granted entry to the United Nations. In these years, the IITC gained transnational status in more than one sense.

Even with some of its relevant internal records no longer available,[86] it is clear that during the mid-1970s the activists of the Treaty Council honed their notions of sovereignty further. Roxanne Dunbar-Ortiz, who joined AIM in 1974 and was active in the Treaty Council during its early years,[87] credits the organization with "produc[ing] a more or less conscious strategy" of lobbying even under the pressures of scarce funding and the ongoing crises in Native communities. Dunbar-Ortiz recalled that between 1974 and 1982, "[i]nternal discussions among IITC activists revolved around the question of self-determination, generally called '*sovereignty*.' Clearly, the already existing model of independent nations emerging from colonialism did not neatly fit the situations of Indian peoples in the Americas." Nevertheless, she pointed out that reservation-size island countries had gained UN membership—and that the territory of the Navajo was larger than most of these.[88]

Recognizing the diversity of Indian communities, their circumstances, and selecting appropriate measures for political activism beyond North America was a challenge that required conceptual adjustment. At a February 1975 meeting between Treaty Council activists and international lawyers,[89] "[d]iscussions of independence centred on the Indian people under U.S. and Canadian jurisdiction, with little comparative analysis of other areas of the Americas, although *the assumption was that independence was the ideal goal.* The principal barrier to pursuing the course of independence was identified as the U.S. government."[90] The

Treaty Council would have to learn to bridge differences within as well as between indigenous groups in the United States, Canada, and Central and South American countries.

In the same meeting, international lawyers expressed doubts that Indian communities could be successful in gaining status as independent nations. "One international lawyer suggested that a distinction be made between *external* sovereignty, which relates to foreign relations, and *internal* sovereignty, which relates to governing the territory and the people within it." He suggested that external sovereignty may not be as important to many Indian groups as internal sovereignty. He recommended that the Treaty Council be a "political status land rights" organization.[91] "Other international experts envisaged a confederation of Indian peoples which could collectively seek a seat as an observer at the UN, with a transfer of trusteeship administration from individual states to the UN Trusteeship Council."[92] Still, most advisors supported the original goal of the IITC. It was hoped that their pursuit of independent nation status in the UN for the Sioux Nation based on the Fort Laramie Treaty of 1868 would set a precedent for other Indian nations, like the Navajo, whose leadership at that point was reluctant to pursue this strategy.[93]

The few surviving documents from these years testify to an urgency in the movement under the overwhelming pressure of the U.S. government. The *Red Paper* of the Second International Indian Treaty Conference at the Yankton Lakota Sioux Nation of South Dakota on June 13–20, 1976, shows that the radical Indian sovereignty movement was responding to the U.S. government's crushing police and legal offensives with renewed attempts to outflank the American nation-state by approaching the United Nations and appealing for international support. In addition to historical grievances such as treaty violations, forced white education and sterilization, imposing "puppet" tribal governments, and current statistics about demographics and health, the document also listed not only the government's use of military might at Wounded Knee in 1973, but also "[t]he recent invasion (July 1976) of the Pine Ridge Lakota Reservation by 200 FBI men armed with M-16 rifles and dressed in military fatigues;"[94] the trials of Indian leaders Russell Means, Dennis Banks, Lakota spiritual leader Leonard Crow Dog, Dino Butler, and Bob Robideau; Ponca Carter Camp's imprisonment; the warrant for Pawnee Stan Holder; and Anna Mae Aquash's botched murder investigation.[95] The document placed these events in the context of a longer history of U.S. colonialism and indicted them together as "the most flagrant violations of international law, human rights, and self-determination principles."[96] In this, the participants of the conference were using the discourse of human rights to assimilate their most recent grievances into the historical memory of U.S. Indian policy held by the Sioux and other Native nations, thereby bolstering their case for social and political change.

While the *Red Paper*—the titling of which suggests both a reclaiming of an Indian ethnic identity and an awareness of the radicalness of the Native position—reveals an abandonment or failure of the first treaty conference's plans to establish relations with the U.S. State Department and congressional committees on foreign relations, it evidences a renewed pursuit of the United Nations strategy. As yardsticks for the above rights violations, the document cites the "United Nations Charter (Preamble, Ch. 1 Art. (1), (2), (3), Art. 2 (4), Art. 55, 56), and the Declaration on the Granting of Independence to Colonial Countries and Peoples (Resolution 1514 (XV) 14 December 1960)."[97] In addition to a violation of its pledge to using peaceful international conflict resolution mechanisms, as well as to create equitable and safe social and economic conditions for human rights and self-determination, the writers of the *Red Paper* also accused the U.S. government of committing genocide both against the movement and against Indians as "an ethnic national group." Without crediting it, they quoted the criteria of genocide established in the United Nations General Assembly's 1948 Convention on the Prevention and Punishment of the Crime of Genocide:

> a) deliberately inflicting on the group conditions of life calculated to bring about its physical destruction in whole or in part;
>
> b) imposing measures intended to births within the group;
>
> c) forcibly transferring children of American Indians to non-Indians [. . .].[98]

For the writers of the *Red Paper*, "international work" continued to be an integral component of their program of activism for sovereignty rights. They identified the exploitation of Native natural resources by non-Indians as an urgent crisis, and aimed to

> [. . .] c. Bring international pressure to bear in our efforts to maintain all of our resources.

> d. Expose corporate and government collusion in the theft of our resources, especially by the large multinational corporations, by exchanging data and information by other Third World countries which have been exploited by these corporations and the United States government.[99]

The American Indian radical sovereignty movement's first programmatic recognition of the transnational corporation as an adverse force in cooperation with, but also beyond the U.S. government, is at once also a statement of identification with communities in "developing" or non-aligned countries in opposition to the West headed by the U.S. nation-state. Beyond the further refinement of their worldview and expression, this phrasing also signals an ethno-political self-identification more completely divorced from the United States as an imagined community than either the conservative patriotism of some of the earlier generation of activists,[100] or the middle ground of a measured "internal" sovereignty earlier suggested by one of their legal advisors.

At the first IITC gathering two years before, San Jose, California, attorney John Thorne's suggestion that in addition to the World Court they also lobby the "UN Colonial Commission"[101] was not incorporated into the conference's final declaration. Those authoring the *Red Paper* now seem to have seized on this latter strategy. First quoting the relevant passages of the UN General Assembly's declaration and establishment of a Special Committee for "the Granting of Independence to Colonial Countries and Peoples,"[102] the authors now accused the U.S. government of violating provisions for the transfer of all power to the people under colonial domination, and the cessation of measures disrupting their national unity and territorial integrity. They claimed that with its denial of independence to Indian nations, the United States continued to endanger international peace and security. In addition to these, the *Red Paper* argued, the U.S. government had violated both the "principles and purposes" of the United Nations Charter.

The drafters of the document of the second International Indian Treaty Conference defined "[s]overeignty [as] an expression of national consciousness of identity, of tradition, and of the spirit. Despite massive assault our Indian Nations remain sovereign." Similar to the Enlightenment idea of God-given natural rights enshrined by the U.S. *Declaration of Independence,* the *Red Paper* seems to define sovereignty rights as something essential to human communities. In this, it approximates the discourse of human rights, which sovereignty activists began deploying with increasing readiness in this period, especially once Jimmy Carter made human rights a cornerstone of his U.S. foreign policy.

The *Red Paper*'s program[103] is evidence not only of visionary grand schemes but of careful transnational thinking. For the authors of the *Red Paper*, membership in OPEC, the WHO, and the Food and Agriculture Organization likely offered hopes not only of learning to leverage Native natural resources for more profit and the recognition of sovereignty rights, but also of receiving moral and material support for economic development. Successfully approaching the Non-Aligned Movement could bring a chance of joining a major geopolitical alliance that was playing the two great powers against each other. Status in the International (World) Court of Justice could give the radical sovereignty movement the moral high ground against the U.S. government. The Native strategy concerning the United Nations involved taking the Fort Laramie Treaty, until now regarded as a historical document of U.S. domestic policy, and filing it with UN agencies as a currently valid international treaty. Here, a document from the historical archives of the U.S. nation-state would be recovered and, redefined by Native historical memory, be placed in the archives of international legal instruments. Finally, the conference leaders hoped to trigger an investigation of U.S. Indian human rights abuses by the United Nations Commission on Human Rights—which would have been a major foreign policy embarrassment for the incoming president of the United States of America.

Conclusion

This chapter recovered the transnational dimensions of the early radical Native sovereignty movement. In its early years, the radical Native newspaper *Akwesasne Notes* placed the American Indian sovereignty struggle in an international context, critiqued U.S. foreign policy in Southeast Asia, and covered attempts and suggested strategies for transnational alliance building for Native sovereignty. The spring 1973 takeover and siege of Wounded Knee, South Dakota, by AIM and Oglala traditionalists posed a transnational challenge to the U.S. nation-state. Both the occupiers and the U.S. government discursively and performatively placed the village outside of the United States and likened the conflict to that going on in Vietnam, thereby critiquing U.S. foreign policy. AIM and its allies also performed full Indian sovereignty—independence—as an alternative to the current Native status of "domestic dependent nations" within the body of the United States. Negotiating with the U.S. government from a position of relative power due to media coverage and the international attention of the Cold War, the Native activists practiced a kind of contact zone diplomacy that initially gave them a tactical advantage.

The siege of Wounded Knee also catalyzed Native overtures to the U.S. State Department in order to reinstate Indian policy as foreign relations, and it redoubled Indian appeals to the United Nations, one of which literally transcended the American nation-state in May 1973. One year after the siege, the first International Indian Treaty Council conference laid down a program of transnational diplomacy, which was further refined in subsequent IITC conferences. Accordingly, the legal and diplomatic efforts of the radical Indian sovereignty movement focused on achieving recognition of Indian treaties as domestic and international law.

Just how did these Indian activists get from Wounded Knee to Checkpoint Charlie and beyond? How did their movement benefit from "leaving the American Sector"? The next chapter traces the rise of the transatlantic alliance for Native sovereignty.

3

The Rise of the Transatlantic Sovereignty Alliance

> Wounded Knee provided a very important victory [. . .] For the first time we have shown internationally that Indian people exist as a living society, that we are not only in cowboy-and-Indian movies, in literature, and in museums throughout the world where the bones of our ancestors are put on display.
>
> I am here to try to form committees, such as the newly-formed American Indian Committee in France and the one in Italy. We are in the process of forming such an organization in Switzerland among our supporters here.
>
> —AIM leader Vernon Bellecourt at a press conference in Geneva, Switzerland, June 1973[1]

After Wounded Knee 1973, the radical Indian sovereignty movement did not buckle under the U.S. government's legal and clandestine assaults—it morphed into a transnational alliance and linked up with various national liberation movements, Marxist régimes, and the environmentalist and antinuclear movements in Europe. In her 1997 book *Race Against Empire*, Penny von Eschen mapped out how African Americans struggling for U.S. civil rights connected their cause to the circum-Atlantic black diaspora's decolonization project.[2] In his 2010 tome titled *The Other Alliance*, Martin Klimke showed how the student movements of what he calls "the global sixties" formed a grassroots coalition between the United States and West Germany, and that this transatlantic network influenced the official U.S. foreign policy partnership between the two countries that was a bedrock of Cold War international relations.[3] Taking Klimke's and von Eschen's scholarship as models, this chapter discusses the emergence and the functioning of the transatlantic alliance for Indian sovereignty in the late Cold War.

The history of the transatlantic sovereignty coalition that I am reconstructing here shows that in the late Cold War the region of Central Europe served as a social and cultural contact zone for Native American activists and their European allies. Here, previous transatlantic cultural representations and forms of "playing Indian" both enabled and constrained the transatlantic alliance. The sovereignty rights movement intervened in these older transatlantic forms of "playing Indian" and manipulated them to make political claims. By engaging with the radical Indian sovereignty movement, Central Europeans were not only transforming their own ideas about Native Americans that were rooted in older transatlantic Indian imagery. Through their indigenous rights activism, environmentalism and antinuclear struggle, Central Europeans were also critiquing their own governments' foreign policy towards the United States as well as the Cold War global foreign policy of the U.S. government. The transatlantic alliance for American Indian sovereignty is proof of the continued engagement with U.S. popular culture and social movements by Central European societies through what other scholars have termed "grassroots Americanization."[4] The transatlantic alliance for American Indian sovereignty also shows that the attitudes toward American Indians formed by older cultural forms and representations motivated Central European social groups and connected them across the iron curtain. This is a case of an intra-European use of U.S. culture.

An Austrian Accent in the Indian Sovereignty Movement: Richard Erdoes and AIM

In his book on Native American activism before the Indian radical sovereignty movement, Daniel Cobb discusses American Indian involvement in Martin Luther King, Jr.'s spring 1968 Poor People's Campaign in Washington, D.C. One of these marches took the Indians and their allies to the State Department, where they forcefully expressed their views on current U.S. foreign policy.[5] The Poor People's Campaign was the same protest event that brought together the Indian delegation with Richard Erdoes, an Austro-Hungarian-German émigré who would serve as a chronicler of the radical sovereignty movement, and would also shape that struggle in subtle ways. The case of Richard Erdoes is one instance when age-old transatlantic white fantasies about finding a home among American Indians and being "adopted" into their communities were meaningfully translated into a joint struggle for social justice.

Richard Erdoes was born in Vienna in 1912 to an Austrian mother and a Hungarian opera singer father with the family name Erdős. The boy grew up in Central European cities like Vienna, Berlin, and Frankfurt, where his family periodically moved for stage performances. An avid young journalist and cartoonist, Erdoes incurred the wrath of the Nazis in the early 1930s and had to move to Austria, where he continued his studies in art and worked for antifascist newspapers. After the Anschluss of 1938, Erdoes fled to Paris, London, and eventually to New York, where he lived in the city's exile German community and worked as an illustrator and photographer for magazines like *National Geographic* and *Life*. The latter magazine sent him to Washington, DC, to cover the Poor People's Campaign in 1968. It was there that Erdoes met the Lame Deers, a traditionalist family of the Pine Ridge Lakota Sioux Reservation of South Dakota. Through the Lame Deers, Erdoes befriended both Dennis Banks and the Crow Dogs, prominent political and spiritual leaders of the American Indian Movement. In the following four decades, Erdoes co-authored a total of five book memoirs with Banks, the Lame Deers, and the Crow Dogs, shaping the perception of the radical Indian sovereignty movement.[6]

While all the ways of Erdoes's involvement in the movement could only be mapped out with more extensive research, some of them are obvious enough to point out here. Growing up in Central Europe in the 1920s and '30s, Erdoes was almost certainly familiar with the transatlantic visual, literary, and performance forms of "playing Indian," including the Western dime novels, the Wild West Show spinoffs, the Völkerschau ethnic exhibitions, and Karl May's *Winnetou* stories. After his first career in the United States, Erdoes may have channeled this naïve European fascination with American Indians into his publications of Native American folklore, myths, and stories.[7] His photographs of his early involvement with the Crow Dog and Lame Deer families suggest a shift from classical white Euro-American depictions of American Indians to a more overt acknowledgment of Native agency and participation in U.S. modern urban life. During the Lakota medicine man's visit to New York City in 1969, Erdoes posed Henry Crow Dog wrapped in a blanket, sporting traditional head gear, and holding a fan and pipe—studio poses reminiscent of the classical Anglo-American portraiture of Indian headmen and delegations by George Catlin, Charles Bird King, and Edward Sheriff Curtis. Of the ten shots, Erdoes selected for publication a half profile with an expression of gravity on Crow Dog's face.[8] In contrast, Erdoes's photos taken a year later show John Fire Lame Deer "on tour"—getting on a plane, sitting in a city park and in a newspaper office, smoking a cigarette, giving an interview, and looking out the window over the skyline of a metropolis.[9] Even in their ambiguity—Erdoes produced a classical Indian profile in the window shot—the photographs recognize both the subject's idiosyncrasy (Crow Dog's cowboy hat and cigarette) and the agency suggested by the appearance of "Indians in unexpected places."[10] Taken together, these images are visual evidence of Erdoes's transformation as portraitist and photojournalist, and clues of his attitude toward his Native collaborators. His photographs attest that Erdoes was both shaping and documenting the ways of "playing Indian" by traditionalist Indians.

The peculiarity of the urban setting notwithstanding, Erdoes initially acted on his white and Central European sensibilities when he sought out American Indians from the reservations. As it circulated across the Atlantic, the age-old trope of the "vanishing native" located Indians on the reservations, and not in contemporary urban relocation programs, or in other settings where their presence and activities contradicted this cultural and social prophesy. During the years when the urban militant American Indian Movement was emerging in Minneapolis and Saint Paul, Richard Erdoes was building relationships with the families of the traditionalist factions of the Lakota Sioux reservations. This also positioned him in a peculiar way in the politics of Native America. His friends, the Lame Deers and Crow Dogs, had been marginalized and become part of the opposition to reservation tribal governments established after the passage of the 1934 Indian Reorganization Act, which imposed a U.S. democratic model on Indian governance, and at the same time further divided Native communities into haves and have-nots in terms of economic and political power.

After participating in the protest takeovers of Mount Rushmore in 1971 and the Bureau of Indian Affairs Building in 1972,[11] Erdoes and his wife Jean (née Sternbergh) opened their home in New York City to their Native friends and provided members of the radical Indian sovereignty movement with a logistical base during their visits to the East Coast.[12] Some of his most intense involvement with the American Indian Movement was during the period when Erdoes served as head of the legal committee for the defense of Lakota AIM medicine man Leonard Crow

Dog and others charged with crimes committed at Wounded Knee in 1973. Between 1975 and 1977, Richard and Jean Erdoes raised funds, oversaw the trials' defense coordination, and comforted and hosted in their home for extended periods of time Leonard's wife Mary Crow Dog and others.[13]

Erdoes's role in shaping the perception and historical record of the radical Indian sovereignty movement would deserve a study in itself, and is only possible through a careful examination of his research and writing process as co-author. Until this is undertaken, two examples will have to suffice. As interviewer and co-author, Erdoes's subtle presence shaped both the telling of oral histories and the final product. The oral history of Lakota medicine man Archie Fire Lame Deer's experiences and teachings, recorded on audio tapes for their book together, is punctuated by Erdoes's thick Austro-Hungarian-German accent. Pronouncing "th" as "z" and either dropping or nasalizing his r's, Erdoes occasionally asks some questions or comments on the story, at one point taking center stage as he relates how he had to spend one of his book advances on a lawyer after being arrested on drug charges because Pennsylvania police had found in his car a Lakota gift pipe, herbs, and tobacco.[14] In both of her books co-authored with Erdoes, Mary Crow Dog first explains that the boarding school she attended was run by *German* nuns who cut off the braids of Indian girls and rubbed them in medical alcohol, but then "for the sake of objectivity" she expresses her respect for the *German* priest who had earlier written Lakota dictionaries and grammars.[15] Erdoes's mere presence influenced his subjects and co-authors to be mindful of certain topics, and his role in their memories and lives. Even as he comes across as unassuming and hands-off, Richard Erdoes was a player in the politics of authorship and exerted some influence in the performances of the memory of the radical Indian sovereignty movement.

While he devoted much of his life to the members of AIM and their cause, Erdoes did not make a special effort to build a transatlantic alliance. While he hosted and traveled with Germans in the United States,[16] they were not necessarily in the solidarity movement. However, the fact that his papers contain newsletters and publications from German solidarity organizations suggests that he at least followed the work of the transatlantic alliance for Indian sovereignty. Most importantly, in 1974 Richard Erdoes hosted author Liselotte Welskopf-Henrich, who had become a literary spokesperson for Indian issues in East Germany.[17] In this, Erdoes served as an important node in the transatlantic alliance in the making.

A Native Flagship Crosses the Atlantic: The Press and the Central European Readership of the Radical Sovereignty Movement

The transatlantic alliance first developed out of the dramatic media performances of the radical Indian sovereignty movement, and it was enabled by the press and facilitated by activists on both sides of the Atlantic. The West German press covered the events of the sovereignty struggle, including the expansion of the coalition to Central Europe. Remarkably, copies and content of the radical Native press also circulated over the Atlantic, and elicited strong responses from Central European readers, which further fueled the movement.

"Playing Indian" for Sovereignty in the West German Press

Aribert Schroeder's contemporary survey of newspaper articles on Indian issues provides a snapshot of West German coverage of the radical sovereignty movement from the late 1960s through the early 1980s. National dailies like the *Frankfurter Allgemeine*, the *Süddeutsche Zeitung*, *Die Welt*, the tabloid *Bild*, national weeklies like *Die Zeit*, and regional dailies from all parts of West Germany covered the major events of the sovereignty struggle. Articles in the largest and most prestigious papers were sometimes carried in other press, thus multiplying their circulation in number and geography.[18] The Cold War division of Germany notwithstanding, it can be reasonably assumed that, because it was in the same language, this coverage to some extent also circulated in Switzerland and Austria, and in East Germany, in addition to the German-speaking populations of other Central European nations, thus magnifying the prominence of Indians issues by informing readers in these four countries and beyond.

In spite of the remoteness of the village and the tribal and federal government's efforts to minimize access, the spring 1973 siege of Wounded Knee, South Dakota, received media coverage both within and beyond the United States. West German newspapers reported on both the early and less noted demonstrations for Indian sovereignty;[19] however, the most press attention focused on the events at Wounded Knee. As with the other events, West German articles drew on U.S. reportage, international press services like the *United Press International*, *Associated Press*, *Reuters*, and German and other European agencies, but they also received articles from West German correspondents out of Washington, DC, New York, and San Francisco, some of whom they also sent out into the field to procure material. A combination of these sources in writing the West German copy also presumably allowed for more objective reporting about events the participants of which could be very subjective and biassed.[20]

As Schroeder's analysis shows, despite their ideal of objective reporting, West German writers only partially met the challenge of filtering out biases in their articles about the radical sovereignty movement in general and Wounded Knee 1973 in particular. Drawing from U.S. coverage, West German editors omitted certain passages they considered opinion rather than fact. They also employed the strategy of quoting directly from representatives of the U.S. federal government, white farmers and businessmen, and Indian groups including AIM. Accordingly, loaded and opinionated phrasing from some of these sources found its way into the language of the West German reportage. The U.S. government's designations "rebel Indians," "insurgent Sioux," and "Indian War" were adopted by writers into German as "rebellische Indianer," "aufrührerische Sioux," and "Indianerkrieg." On the other side, some articles also internalized the discourse of AIM activists who drew parallels with Vietnam by referring to the "Demilitarized Zone" and My Lai, or claiming they were "warriors" ready to die for their cause.[21] The first set of phrases fit neatly into the old transatlantic imaginary of American Indians, while the second cluster would have communicated the movement's self-image and political urgency to those West Germans and Central Europeans who had been critically thinking about contemporary U.S. foreign policy in the Third World.[22]

Even as they were rehearsing some of them, West German writers were careful to position themselves *against* the German stereotypes of American Indians. In fact, Schroeder points out that they cautioned against this so frequently that their repeated caveat became a cliché in its own right.[23] This practice was a part of the discursive search for "Indian" authenticity in German public culture mapped out by Glenn Penny.[24] An added function of such maneuvers was to shore up the authority of the journalist by setting them apart from "popular" culture and positioning them as informed cultural arbiters, regardless of how familiar they really were with American Indian issues and communities.

In spite of their professed struggle against stereotyping, some West German articles about the radical Indian sovereignty movement nevertheless reinforced transatlantic clichés. As Schroeder observes, the authors' use of phrases like "redskins," the indiscriminate use of "chief" ("Häuptling") to designate any and all Native leaders regardless of their actual position and title, and the frequent inclusion of imagery from historical photographs or artwork showing Indian headmen (including Geronimo and Sitting Bull) in regalia may have been calculated more to grab the readers' attention then to provide complementary information.[25] However, these also undercut and potentially questioned the gravity and vitality of Native activists and their struggle for sovereignty by flattening out the contemporary complexity and urgency of their actions and arguments, and portraying them as another "gasp" of the "vanishing noble savage." Using Swiss artist Karl Bodmer's paintings of Indian leaders and rituals from Prince Maximilian Neuwied's 1830s expedition to the U.S. West to illustrate the 1977 United Nations NGO conference on the Indians of the Americas[26] relegated the breakthrough interventions of the Indian sovereignty struggle to the ethnographically colorful but politically inert past. While photos of European actor Pierre Brice in the title role of the *Winnetou* movies were used to illustrate some articles, the crudest and most unapologetic example of this move came from the Hungarian Communist Party's *Youth Magazine*, which in an op-ed titled "The Last of the Last of the Mohicans" predicted the "failure" of the 1973 occupation of Wounded Knee as foreordained due to popular apathy, and, even as it expressed solidarity with them, called on the Indian activists to return to their place once again on the pages of juvenile literature and the displays of museums—and in the minds of children who still believe in humanity. Predictably, the article was illustrated by an uncaptioned, undated and uncredited photograph of Indians wearing feathered headdresses.[27]

Subtly or in more obvious ways, the West German coverage of the radical Indian sovereignty movement attempted to fit the new, "unexpected" Native protest performances—Indians "playing Indian" for sovereignty—into the transatlantic and homegrown Central European forms and imagery of "playing Indian." The articles' focus on clichéic 'Indianness' certainly demonstrates this. Schroeder observes that the photographs selected by writers and editors showed either traditionalist Indians, or radical "Indian activists who were dressed in traditional costumes, wore their hair in braids, or at least sported items of garment or ornaments considered 'Indian,'" like blankets, pipes, or the buffalo skull.[28] While U.S. domestic media stereotypes of the new activists included the Indian militant, the peyote-tripping visionary, and the environmentalist "natural' "native,[29] according to Bernd C. Peyer, the transatlantic reportage of the early 1970s "transformed the contemporary Indian into a primitivistic symbol of resistance against the system, in this case U.S. capitalism." In the rooms of European leftist students "[i]mages of Geronimo and Sitting

Bull were posted up alongside of Ché Guevara's, and the AIM 'Warrior' became their immediate reincarnation."[30]

It is obvious that in their performances, the activists of the radical Indian sovereignty movement were aware of the need to engage United States and transatlantic stereotypes and white ways of "playing Indian." In some of their earliest demonstrations, AIM activists intervened in the dominant white imaginary and memory of American Indians by protesting against the screening of the movie *The Man Called Horse*, taking over national historic sites like Mount Rushmore in the Black Hills of South Dakota, crashing national holidays and celebrations like the 1970 Thanksgiving at Plymouth, Massachusetts, occupying Alcatraz in 1969–71, the BIA building in Washington, DC, in 1972, and Wounded Knee in 1973.

The activists manipulated the media and its audiences not only in their choice of place and form, but also in their own appearance. Paul Chaat Smith and Robert Warrior observed that in its early years the Red Power movement was influenced by a quasi-Indian hippy fashion originating in the urban centers.[31] However, during the early years of the American Indian Movement, veteran activist Hank Adams advised Russell Means to look to American Indian history and culture for models of leadership and economic, social, and educational resources.[32] The subsequent adoption by the male AIM leadership of the "Indian warrior" ethos not only gave them renewed pride and a sense of once again fulfilling their traditional political and gender roles,[33] but it also manipulated white fantasies and imagined Indian identities—and resonated not only in the United States but also across the Atlantic. In the photographs used in West German coverage of Wounded Knee, their trial in Minnesota, and the 1977 UN Geneva conference, Dennis Banks and Russell Means are wearing berets, headbands and braids, feathers, and other AIM insignia.[34] The photos most reproduced in the West German media were Oscar Bear Runner's pose with a rifle across his chest with a finger on the trigger (five times), the image of an Indian man and woman on horseback (four times), and Wounded Knee occupiers posing with firearms in trenches, on roofs, on horseback, and at entrances. These pictures were used repeatedly in later years (1975, 1977) to illustrate other events of the radical sovereignty movement.[35] In these instances, the subjects of the photos likely "played Indian" for the transatlantic media as well as for the radical sovereignty movement and for their immediate purposes at the events.

European Response in the Radical Native Press

> Here in Germany we have had a small meeting, including people from Switzerland and a student from Haiti. We talked about your problems and came to the conclusion that you are doing a very important work. [. . .] We consider the *Akwesasne Notes* as the most informative and all-embracing Indian publication. Our press here relates Indian problems only from white sources. This is understandable because it fits into the schemes of integration, progress, and development dear to our people here. We are all trying to open minds and hearts of more people to your way of life, and we will acquaint different people with your paper to enlarge the circle of your readers.[36]
>
> What do you call it when a foreign power with great military forces comes into your country, surrounds you, sets up a government, forms a nation and tells you: "Now you are no longer a nation"?[37]
>
> —Letters from German readers,
> *Akwesasne Notes*, September 1970

In addition to their national presses, Europeans also had some information about the sovereignty struggle from North American Indian printed sources. There is evidence in the historical record that some of the radical Native press also circulated in Central Europe. It can be assumed that some Native American G.I.s stationed in Western European countries would have subscribed to and received issues of the *Akwesasne Notes* and passed them on to family members or German civilians.[38] What is evident from the letters section of the paper is that Europeans[39] were responding to what they read and heard about the radical Indian sovereignty movement. At the very least, in writing to the paper, these Europeans were seeking a way to join a discussion of the goals and means of the movement, and to address Indians in North America. In turn, the selection of European letters for publication in the *Akwesasne Notes* suggests an editorial desire to bolster the paper's stature and sense of mission for its readers by showing that people as far as Europe and Australia followed and supported the Native sovereignty struggle.

European readers of the *Akwesasne Notes* expressed frustration with the dearth of information about Indian issues in their own societies, and they often condemned those as misleading stereotypes of popular culture, or propaganda by the U.S. government.[40] Their letters reveal that publications of the radical Native press like the *Akwesasne Notes* circulated in Europe as they were both sent there by relatives and friends living in the United States,[41] and also by readers who became subscribers and distributors themselves.[42] In their engagement with the Native press, European readers not only tried to better understand the needs, goals, and worldview of Native nations;[43] they also attempted to use the history of U.S. colonialism and Native resistance to understand their own recent past.[44]

Analyses of the West German press and the letters published in the *Akwesasne Notes* show not only that Europeans were interested in learning about, identified with, and responded to the events of the radical Indian sovereignty movement taking place in the United States.[45] They demonstrate that the European press and readers struggled to understand these performances of "Indians playing Indians in unexpected places"[46] by using some ideas from the transatlantic cultural forms that they had been familiar with. Finally, the press coverage and readers' letters indicate that even before Wounded Knee 1973, not only did some Europeans follow the radical sovereignty struggle, but some had also started organizing groups and doing solidarity work such as corresponding with Native activists, educating people in their own societies, and collecting signatures and sending letters and petitions to North American governments.[47]

Openings, Breakthroughs and Corridors: The U.S. Heartland–Mitteleuropa Axis

Even with the interest strong and some of the connections already made, the event that truly catalyzed the transatlantic alliance for Native sovereignty was the spring 1973 siege of Wounded Knee. The occupiers catered to the press in their performances,[48] and the length of the standoff allowed for the media to build up a presence in and around the village. As shown earlier, the European response to the press coverage was strong.[49]

The champions of Wounded Knee also crossed the Atlantic. In June 1973, just weeks after the final stand down at Wounded Knee, AIM leader Vernon Bellecourt informed the press in Geneva, Switzerland, that "I am here to try to form committees, such as the newly-formed American Indian Committee in France and the one in Italy. We are in the process of forming such an organization in Switzerland among our supporters here."[50] The proximity of Switzerland to France and Italy had allowed Bellecourt to cover a number of European countries on his tour. The most enduring of his support groups would be the Swiss-based

International Committee for the Indians of the Americas (Incomindios). One of their first publications was a 1974 English and French booklet which, in addition to Bellecourt's above statement, contained "A Letter to Europeans" by Cherokee activist Jimmie Durham—a plea for financial support:

> The trials of the brave men and women who, at Wounded Knee in 1973 tried to reason with and speak to the U.S. government, begin soon. The U.S. government uses money as a weapon against us. We cannot gain justice by ourselves. [. . .] If each person who reads these words sends us ten francs, five francs, something like that, and then passes the book on to a friend it would help us very much. Don't you think we deserve to live our lives? Thank you very much for your solidarity with us.[51]

In addition to the Sioux Falls address of WKLD/OC, the text also gives the readers the bank account information of the "Swiss Wounded Knee Defense Committee."[52]

While Jimmie Durham certainly had a hand in the formation of Incomindios and the Swiss post of WKLD/OC, he would soon be departing from Switzerland. According to Claus Biegert, as a student of art in Geneva, Durham was walking in a park one day in 1973 when he had a vision of a dead badger telling him to return to the United States.[53] By the summer of 1974 Durham was back in the United States, where he attended the first International Indian Treaty Conference at Standing Rock, and then became the chief administrator of the International Indian Treaty Council, to embark on an enduring program of transnational Indian diplomacy in the United Nations. The fact that both the Swiss Incomindios and the International Indian Treaty Council letterhead soon came to use one and the same logo—the geographical silhouette of North and South America, their isthmus joined together by a peace pipe—is itself proof of the institutionalization of the transatlantic alliance for Indian sovereignty.

That same year another group of radical sovereignty activists visited Central Europe. In 1973, East Berlin hosted the 10th World Festival of Students and Youth, and among the participants was a delegation from the American Indian Movement. Some of them were veterans of the siege of Wounded Knee. These AIM activists were hailed in the Eastern

Bloc as the heroes of a shared resistance against imperialism, and the German Socialist state capitalized on this, which I discuss in Chapter 4.

Openings: "A.I.M.—Europe Bureau Berlin–West," 1975

The immediate and personal European response to these Indian calls for support must have given hope to Native sovereignty activists. It certainly spurred efforts within AIM to strengthen and make more permanent the existing transatlantic relations as well as to build new ones. At the invitation of the World Council of Churches, AIM leader Clyde Bellecourt toured Europe in 1974,[54] and the following year Dennis Banks and Vernon Bellecourt visited author Liselotte Welskopf-Henrich in East Berlin. This was an important development. As a university professor and popular author of Indian-themed novels, Welskopf-Henrich had been recognized by the East German government as a sort of literary spokesperson for American Indians, and commanded a wide following in the GDR and the Eastern Bloc. Moving away from her earlier historical treatments even as she continued consulting for the Marxist historical adventure *Indianerfilme*, by the mid-1970s Welskopf-Henrich had been writing a fiction pentalogy, titled *The Blood of Eagles*, focusing on current Indian issues.[55] By late 1974, Welskopf-Henrich herself had visited the United States, where she had met Richard Erdoes, an Austro-Hungarian émigré illustrator turned writer closely involved with the radical sovereignty movement. In her letters written to Erdoes in November 1974 and April 1975, Welskopf-Henrich thanked him and his family for their hospitality, shared her hopes that she would be able to publish Erdoes's latest book in German, and reported that she had asked her readers to send petitions to the United States on behalf of Russell Means, currently in custody on charges stemming from a shooting.[56] As Glenn Penny has documented, by the time of her death in 1979 the East German author had been using her full stature and range of resources spanning the iron curtain to promote German solidarity with American Indians, including the circulation of information, connecting activists, petition writing, and material support.[57] Through their visits and correspondence, the AIM leaders, Erdoes, and Welskopf-Henrich were building a Rapid City–New York–Berlin axis for the transatlantic sovereignty alliance.

These Native American–German encounters proved to be so promising that on their 1975 visit, Dennis Banks and Vernon Bellecourt authorized the opening of an AIM office in West Berlin.[58] In a February

1975 letter to Richard Erdoes, German volunteer Regina Mayer gave an update of the activities of the office.

The letter's purple-pink letterhead forms a psychedelic hippie-style wave of the words "American Indian Movement A.I.M. Bureau Berlin West." Over the inscription is the AIM logo—an Indian profile with the peace sign, the two fingers of which form two feathers at the back of the Indian head. The logo is inscribed "Remember Wounded Knee 1890 1973." Next to the logo is the image of a phoenix-like creature, perhaps representing the European or German members of the transatlantic sovereignty alliance, inscribed "Freedom and Justice for All Indian Nations."[59] Aware of the strangeness of this iconography of the transatlantic sovereignty movement, Mayer playfully commented on the product,

> Personally I think it looks a little too pop art like, but it was real cheap. Also the paper was supposed to be blood-red, so just use your imagination and you will see a real good design on real red-power paper.[60]

More importlantly, Regina Mayer described the activists' work at the office.

> After Clyde [Bellecourt] left, many people came up to us and showed their interest in the situation of the native Americans today. So we started giving radio-interviews, we are having speaking-engagements all the time in schools, universities not only in Berlin but also in West-Germany, we do many benefit-concerts, but we still hardly get any money in. The universities don't pay for those speaking-engagements. Also we have a 14-day thing going in the University of Erlangen, showing films, give speeches, discussion-groups, a photo-exhibition, etc.
>
> [. . .]
>
> So there is really something happening in Germany concerning Indians. I really think that if we get even better organized we can get half of the German population to support native Americans. That's no show-off, the only thing is, we need money and more time and more good people. We need the money to buy equipment to work faster with the media, we need full-time people to work for AIM, we need

> a truck to travel around and so on . . . I want you to tell everybody about this!!![61]

At this stage, the AIM Berlin office was experiencing high demand for their activities; it had an audience and potential pool of volunteers, but no steady income and monetary infrastructure. It is obvious from Mayer's words and tone that she and her fellow activists were still riding the high on the enthusiasm and interest generated by Bellecourt's recent visit.

Besides the author, the letter was signed by "Brigit," Alex White Plume, Robert Red Eagle, and Pete "Wyoming" Bender. The latter was the same West German performer who back in 1971 had sent *Akwesasne Notes* a call for Native musicians to put together a production of Indian poetry.[62] A photograph most likely from this same year (1975) shows Bender with Vernon Bellecourt and Dennis Banks in front of a wall plaque with the words "AIM Berlin American Indian Movement e.V."[63] Since "e.V." is the abbreviation of an officially registered and authorized German civic association or club ("Verein"), the sign was an indication that the radical sovereignty movement was already becoming institutionalized in Central Europe.

AIM's West Berlin office proved to be short-lived—it does not appear in the historical record after 1975. What these early Native tours, the establishment of the Swiss Incomindios, and the Berlin office accomplished, however, soon proved vital for the radical sovereignty movement, which was struggling just to survive in the U.S. heartland.

From Karl Marx Stadt[64] to Sioux Falls: European Support in the Wounded Knee Trials

> Dear Mr. Schulze-Thulin,
>
> I can't express how gratifying it was for us to receive your generous contribution just now, when funds have withered and we are plagued with unpaid bills. The response to our need, which is now desperate, from people in Europe, and Germany in particular is a constant source of hope and courage to us.
>
> I suspect you know much more about the progress of the trials than most people here in our own country, as the media coverage here has been deplorable. But even though by now you may have heard of the acquittals [of] Lania Ackerman, Lorelei Means, and

> Madonna Gilbert, I take pleas[ure] in repeating it to you here. No defense witnesses were called; the judge heard the prosecution's case and promptly granted a motion for acquittal.
>
> Of course, the bulk of the cases have yet to be tried, and even though we hope for and expect many more favorable outcomes, the drain on our resources is enormous and is daily growing. It is only though the continued support of people like you that we will be able to carry on this work. Again, thank you, from all of us here.
>
> In solidarity, Bonnie Fultz
> Wounded Knee Legal Defense/Offense Committee[65]

Scholars and witnesses have established that after the 1973 siege of Wounded Knee, the U.S. government embarked on a large-scale legal campaign against the American Indian Movement. Their strategy was to prosecute the leaders, members, and allies of the movement regardless of the expected outcome, simply to deplete their coffers with the court costs, tie up their human resources, and wear down their energy and spirit. The federal and state governments charged hundreds of sovereignty activists and the trials were held in several locations around the Midwest, which necessitated the creation and moving around of offices by the Wounded Knee Legal Defense/Offense Committee (WKLD/OC), a group of lawyers and volunteers dedicated to the defense of AIM and their allies. As AIM was founding support groups in Europe and opening an office in West Berlin, WKLD/OC was struggling to keep up with trial expenses and other bills. These years proved to be a supreme test for the resilience and resourcefulness of the radical Indian sovereignty movement in the face of overwhelming pressure from the U.S. government. It was during this period that European solidarity groups came to play a crucial role in the survival of the radical Indian sovereignty movement.

WKLD/OC correspondence bears witness to the difficulty experienced by the organization, AIM, and the whole radical Indian sovereignty movement.[66] Financial donations soon became an important part of the international support for the Wounded Knee AIM trials.[67] In light of the figures in the group's correspondence, it is reasonable to assume that even as they were refining their ways of raising money internationally, WKLD/OC and AIM received thousands of dollars in European support over several years.[68]

The Native activists' immediate response to the trickle of financial donations was relief.[69] In return for their generosity, European supporters asked WKLD/OC for up-to-date information on the trial proceedings.[70] In response, WKLD/OC sent European support groups trial updates in their letters, as well as the current and recent issues of their newsletter and press materials.[71] European organizations like the Irish Committee for the Defense of Wounded Knee, the "KIVA group, Friends of the North American Indians in the Netherlands," and the "Comité francais de soutien á AIM" of Paris, France, then incorporated these materials into their own newsletters and public relations kits, some of which they also sent back to WKLD/OC.[72] Thus, European financial donations incentivized the exchange of information about the radical Indian sovereignty struggle, which circulated across the Atlantic.

While material support was crucial, WKLD/OC and European support groups were communicating on another level—that of solidarity. In response to AIM's calls for support, letters of solidarity, resolutions of protest, and petitions were drafted across Europe, and sent to WKLD/OC.[73] Some European expressions of solidarity made common cause with American Indian activists by asserting shared goals and enemies.[74] Other European writers placed the Indian sovereignty movement into a larger international class struggle against capitalism.[75] Whether using it as compulsory rhetoric or an abiding internationalist commitment, national liberation organizations and Marxists on both sides of the iron curtain claimed common cause with American Indians in fighting for freedom from a dominant Western power.

In their messages of solidarity, European supporters urged Indian sovereignty activists to keep fighting.[76] By far the most messages of solidarity with the Wounded Knee defendants and the movement arrived from the German Democratic Republic. While many of these were plain letters from students,[77] others were more formally constructed petitions from clubs and associations sanctioned under East German cultural policy.[78] In their letters, German writers often assured Native sovereignty activists of the broad-based support in their countries.[79] For East Germans, writing such messages of solidarity meant doing their duty to a Communist state that aggressively positioned itself as a champion of an international class struggle including colonized peoples. For both Germans and Indians, these assurances served as encouragement and expression of solidarity. Yet for Germans, these letters likely also maintained a self-image of Germanness that latently spanned the iron curtain.

In turn, WKLD/OC's activists responded to such messages of solidarity with surprised gratitude and sharing a renewed commitment to the cause.[80] WKLD/OC's responses to German donations and solidarity messages soon developed a remarkable trope.[81] Even more than with other European support groups, WKLD/OC's activists felt a kinship with Germans, because these groups and individuals seemed to know about the Indian past and to care about the current struggle disproportionately more than most Americans or other European nationality groups. For WKLD/OC volunteers, who saw themselves as a lone island struggling against the government's assaults in a sea of uncaring white people, such financial and moral support from overseas meant a spiritual and social boost, an infusion of faith that they were not alone in their struggle.

European supporters of the radical Indian sovereignty movement derived satisfaction from the successes of WKLD/OC, which also likely reinforced their self-image as individuals, groups and societies actively contributing to the survival of American Indians. Their donations, messages of solidarity, and petitions[82] seemed to bear fruit with the acquittal of AIM Wounded Knee defendants.[83]

As European solidarity groups did much to support the Native sovereignty struggle across the Atlantic, one Austro-German ally directly contributed to the movement from within the United States. In May 1975, Richard Erdoes was asked to head the defense committee for AIM medicine man Leonard Crow Dog.[84] For the next two years, the Erdoeses hosted the family in New York City, provided moral support to Crow Dog behind bars, and maintained a logistical base and communications center for the defense work. Yet it was not Richard Erdoes's personal lobbying that eventually swayed Judge Robert Merhige, who had originally sentenced Leonard Crow to prison. The judge summoned the defense team to his court in Virginia, showed them some of the petitions he had received from around the world, and re-sentenced Crow Dog to time already served.[85]

Even as they were working on an overwhelming number of court cases in several locations across the Midwest, WKLD/OC letter writers were communicating across cultures and the Atlantic Ocean with European support groups in the language of solidarity. Europeans supported AIM's legal struggle against the U.S. government because this activity gave them a new way to express their long-standing fascination with American Indians—something that had been nurtured by transatlantic cultural forms of whites and Natives "playing Indian." Solidarity with living Native Americans transformed this older romanticized interest into a political activity—some of which the Europeans also romanticized as an internationalist revolution. East Germans collected signatures and sent petitions and messages of solidarity because this made it possible to express their interest in American Indians and the American West in an officially sanctioned way. Germans on both sides of the iron curtain articulated their solidarity with the radical Indian sovereignty movement not only as a political activity, but also as a way to subtly reassert a common all-German fantasy and pastime: a fascination with the mythical American Indian warriors of the Great Plains.

By the mid-1970s, the transatlantic sovereignty alliance was circulating along a U.S. Heartland–Mitteleuropa axis not only ideas and information, but also material support, and in some cases the bodies of travelers. The transatlantic coverage of the spectacular protest performances of the radical Indian sovereignty movement now combined with an older Central European fascination with American Indians, and it generated continental interest in the current struggle of Native Americans. Circulating copies of the Native press and the calls by visiting Native sovereignty leaders for support prompted Europeans to respond in several ways. While petitions were sent from various European countries, most messages of solidarity arrived from East Germany, where this was one of the few officially sanctioned ways of engaging with the culture and society of the United States. On the other side of the iron curtain, Western Europeans initiated a stream of financial donations, which proved crucial to the morale and the logistical success of WKLD/OC. This European support helped the Wounded Knee Legal Defense/Offense Committee, which represented hundreds of defendants, to achieve an acquittal rate of over 92 percent.[86] The release of AIM activists and their allies in turn confirmed for supporters in Mitteleuropa that their solidarity and donations had made a difference right in the U.S. Heartland—and thus it further strengthened the transatlantic alliance for Native sovereignty.

Breakthrough: Performing Sovereign Indianness on the 1977 Post-Conference Tour

The radical Indian sovereignty movement responded to the U.S. government's legal assault against AIM and their allies not only with vigorous defense in the courts, but also with a sustained transnational campaign. After the June 1974 first International Indian Treaty Conference, the International Indian Treaty Council embarked on a program of transnational diplomacy. The Treaty Council's chief administrator, Jimmie Durham, applied for and, after three years of hard work, achieved nongovernmental organization (henceforth NGO) status in the Economic and Social Council of the United Nations. On the inside, some UN officials in the Special NGO Committee on Human Rights and the

Sub-Committee on Racism, Racial Discrimination, Apartheid and Decolonization had also been moving to accommodate indigenous groups in the United Nations. Prodded by earlier American Indian appeals and the impending arrival of the Treaty Council, they now helped organize the United Nations International NGO Conference on Discrimination against Indigenous Populations in the Americas on September 20–23, 1977, in Geneva, Switzerland. This conference, which I discuss in more detail in Chapter 6, was a breakthrough event in the transatlantic Indian sovereignty alliance because it carried an official recognition of indigenous rights as a transnational issue, it brought a critical mass of Indian activists to Central Europe, it established many social contacts for the alliance, and because the trips that resulted from it established a Switzerland–Germanies–Austria corridor for future tours of Native American activists and their Central European allies.

The aforementioned events and relations of the radical Indian sovereignty movement—the spectacular and prolonged protests and their press coverage, the early European visits and alliance building by Native activists, the transatlantic circulation of information, solidarity and support—all prepared both sides for the breakthrough conference at the UN Palace of the Nations in Geneva, Switzerland, in the fall of 1977. Considering that their relationships had been forged in and baptized by the fire of Wounded Knee and the subsequent court trials, for some Native and European participants the conference and the subsequent tours may have been as much a "reunion" as the first personal encounter with each other.

In June 1973, just weeks after the final stand down at Wounded Knee, Bellecourt informed the press in Geneva, Switzerland, that "[E]ven as the White House breaks its latest agreement, it has opened [a] war against the leaders of the American Indian Movement and the Oglala people in the courts." Nevertheless,

> Wounded Knee provided a very important victory [. . .] For the first time we have shown internationally that Indian people exist as a living society, that we are not only in cowboy-and-Indian movies, in literature, and in museums throughout the world where the bones of our ancestors are put on display.[87]

Bellecourt's statement drives home that he and his fellow Native American activists saw a link between cultural representations of Indians and the sovereignty struggle as a sociopolitical movement. In his formulation,

Indians were breaking through the archival and discursive depictions of the "noble savage" and "vanishing native," and they were reasserting their sovereignty rights through performances of social and political protest. However, dominant cultural representations and political rights are not in binary opposition. As I have argued, subtly or overtly, Indian sovereignty activists themselves manipulated dominant images of Indianness in their performances for political rights.

The 1977 post-conference tour of West Germany by a dozen or so Indian delegates from North and Latin America brought Native activists in personal contact with both Central European solidarity organizations and some of the West German public. In their transnational performances of Indian sovereignty rights, indigenous activists from across the Americas—among them several key members of the American Indian Movement and its International Indian Treaty Council—not only promoted the causes of their respective communities, but together they also presented a public identity for a common indigenous movement. As evidenced by the West German tour's newspaper coverage and the internal documents of the Society for Endangered Peoples (Gesellschaft für bedrohte Völker), the presence and performances of U.S. and Canadian activists in the delegation were vital in defining the cause, and in attracting German audiences and their support. The transnational performances[88] of these Native activists and their German allies also intervened in the transatlantic forms of "playing Indian" by presenting American Indians as living human beings and political actors with considerable agency.

The post-conference tour lasted a little over two weeks and took the Indian delegation from Geneva to Munich, Göttingen, Bonn, Cologne, Bremen, Hamburg, West Berlin, Freiburg, and Tübingen. Their public performances took a variety of forms and addressed various audiences and potential allies. They included press conferences (Bonn, Bremen, Hamburg), the opening of an Indian-themed exhibit (Hamburg), concerts (Hamburg), film screenings and discussions (Göttingen, Bremen), a meeting with Christian clergy (Berlin), and a discussion with some of the federal representatives of the West German Social Democratic Party (SPD).[89] In their performances, the Indian delegation[90] addressed the German-based churches, the press, students, environmental and antinuclear activists, locals, and federal politicians.[91]

For German audiences, the most important element of the Native performances was the drumming and singing by the North American Indian activists. Several newspaper reports of the tour emphasized that Clyde Bellecourt (Ojibwa, AIM, director of a survival school in

Minnesota), Bill Wahpepah (Kickapoo/Sauc-Fox, director of a survival school in California), Francois Paulette (Dene, Northwest Territory of Canada), and Errol Kinistrio drummed and sang "the AIM song," usually as the opening of an event with the delegation.[92] Predictably, some journalists could not resist sensationalizing their reports by describing this activity as "Indians sound[ing] the war whoop," " 'redskins' reporting about their problems in Munich," and "sounding the alarm: Indians."[93] These writers sought to associate the delegates' performance with the long-standing transatlantic form of "playing Indian" in sound: the throbbing of "Indian drums" so familiar from the composed soundtrack of Western films. Other journalists simply used the form to grab the reader's attention with an exotic vignette like "Traditional drumming from North America echoed in the Konsul-Hackfeld-Haus."[94]

Bellecourt and his fellow delegates were fully aware of how their drumming was perceived by many Central Europeans, and they grappled with it. "[The press] call us 'savages.' When we wanted to take to Geneva our holy drums, which represent our culture, they wrote that we conducted a scalp dance. The cliché of the Wild West movies about us [Indians] was still there."[95]

For years before their European tour, the American Indian Movement had been using the drum as a source and conveyor of cultural and spiritual strength in their struggle for Native sovereignty. A year before the siege of Wounded Knee, AIM activists and locals were celebrating that their demonstrations of solidarity and concern had forced an investigation into the death of Raymond Yellow Thunder in the town of Gordon, Nebraska. As part of the celebration, one of the songs performed by Severt Young Bear and his Porcupine Singers moved AIM leaders so much that they adopted it as the official song of the organization.[96] Lakota Sioux medicine man Henry Crow Dog not only confirmed the power of this particular song, but his metaphor also established AIM as an instrument of Native American spirituality: "The Creator took a bit of thunder and made it into a drum. The drum is the thunder and rain. The American Indian Movement is like a drum that speaks all languages and makes people understand. The drum is sacred."[97]

Some of the Native efforts to educate Germans about American Indian drumming and singing proved to be fruitful. At least one journalist used Bellecourt's phrasing when describing the performance—"The Indian leaders said goodbye with a religious song, accompanied by their holy drum."[98] Through the incorporation of this form into the performances of the Indian delegation, the Native activists and their German allies exposed themselves to rhetorical trivialization of their causes, but they nevertheless ended up successfully manipulating this transatlantic form of "playing Indian."

The act of drumming and singing to "frame" their performances,[99] the semantics of the name "American Indian Movement,"[100] and repeated explanations that in Geneva "so many different peoples from many different places of the world were united!" and "despite the differences in languages, traditions, and nations, we spoke with one voice!"[101] made the delegation look and feel like an all-Indian endeavor stamped with the image and concept of AIM. This is all the more striking because of the considerable differences among the Native struggles and their conditions. While the AIM/Treaty Council delegation could tout their progress in setting up their own Native survival schools,[102] and the Canadian Dene representatives could hold up their united Native victory over corporate and government plans for an oil pipeline in the McKenzie River Valley,[103] their Latin American counterparts faced different but related struggles. While Indians in the United States and Canada were only a fraction of the population, in many Latin American countries they were a significant demographic if not an outright majority; the degree of violence against them differed significantly, as did the "nonviolent" means of oppression and exploitation. The shared charge of historical genocide, current intolerable living conditions, and their ongoing oppression logically linked the groups together in a general demand for political recognition and empowerment in all fields of life—and these general shared conditions, grievances, and goals were performed by the Indian delegation.

The most widely covered events of the tour were the collective performances[104] of the Indian delegation.[105] Of these, the best documented event was the one held in the Audimax auditorium at the University of Hamburg on October 8. Named by the Society's planners "Indianer sprechen" [Indians Speak], the event was a cross-performance of lectures, a concert, and a mass rally. According to newspaper accounts and evidenced by photographs taken by the Society's Martin Taureg (himself likely a photo journalist), the event proved to be a success. In spite of glitches with the sound technology—at one point, the performers had to use a loudspeaker[106]—the hall was packed with an audience between 2,000 and 3,000 people, some of whom sat right in front of the stage area.[107] On the back wall of the stage hung a banner with the words "The Indians of America Demand Self-Determination," and the long desk seating the presenters also sported a banner with the full name of the Society for Endangered Peoples. The seating arrangements at the long table reflected the integrated structure of the show, but also the leadership of the transatlantic sovereignty alliance. The AIM and Treaty Council and Dene speakers sat interspersed with Tilman Zülch and Claus Biegert of the Society leadership, and interpreter Gert Hensel—with the Latin American delegates on the other end.[108] Across from the table, the other half of the stage area was taken up by the concert space all the way to be back wall.[109] This way any presenter on the stage floor had a double audience: the thousands of spectators in the hall, and also their fellow delegates sitting at the long table. Their performances therefore were directed at both a general German public and a specialized Native and movement community.

The transatlantic "braiding" of the Hamburg rally for Indian sovereignty manifested itself not only in the seating and order of the performers, but also in the musicians and the kind of music they played. The evening was opened by drumming and singing by U.S.-based AIM/Treaty Council leaders Bill Wahpepah and Greg Zephier; the (presumably German) band Huentelaf played Chilean tunes; the Ougenweide ensemble performed from its Medieval-inspired folk rock repertoire; Errol Kinistino (Ochapowace, Canada)[110] played the guitar with a white (possibly German) female flutist; and former East German Wolf Biermann sang as the highlight of the evening.[111] The order of acts reflects an implicit strategy to back load the night with "the main event"—the Indian delegates from Canada and the Unites States—in itself a reflection of a general German fascination with the Indians of those specific *North* American countries. The succession of a militant Indian ritual, Latin American folk, Teutonic courtly tunes, and all-German protest songs wove the Indian presentations and their German allies together into a transatlantic solidarity happening that spanned the North American Plains, the Native nations of both Americas, the United Nations in Geneva, and linked *both* Germanies across the iron curtain.

The fact that the Society successfully convinced Wolf Biermann to sing for the Indian delegation was significant. Biermann originally moved to East Germany from the Federal Republic to realize his ideals in Communism. In East Germany he had a promising start in theater, but his show about the building of the Berlin Wall was banned and he was gradually forced into internal exile, which was only broken by rare visits from Western artists like Joan Baez. In 1976, while touring in West Germany, Biermann was stripped of his East German citizenship. This act amounted to an official recognition that the East German state could not handle dissent—and it promoted Biermann's reputation as a nonconformist and uncompromising politically committed protest singer. By 1977, Germans on both sides of the iron curtain would have linked Biermann to the leftist working-class and folk protest tradition of North and South America—not only to Woody Guthrie and Pete Seeger, or to the more recently famous Joan Baez, but also to the Canadian Cree singer Buffy Sainte Marie,[112] who had given benefit concerts in the San Francisco Bay Area on behalf of the Native occupiers of the island of Alcatraz.[113] Having Biermann sing, as a newspaper article phrased it, for "the redskins [. . .] songs that deal with the specific problems of the native American population"[114] was an act that linked the various meanings of "red nations" into one transnational performance: a singer who was "red" by conviction but proved to be too radical for the "red" Communist nation of East Germany was now convening with "the reddest of the red" Indians—the activists of the American Indian sovereignty movement.

The Society and their Native allies had carefully cultivated this transatlantic musical protest tradition. Albums recorded by Pete "Wyoming" Bender in 1972 and 1978 featured songs with titles like "Indian War Dance" and "Born to be Indian."[115] A February 1976 diplomatic cable from the U.S. Embassy in West Berlin reported that East Berlin's recently held annual festival of political songs featured "an American Indian singer named 'Wyoming,' who is pictured sitting at the piano singing his own composition, 'Freedom.'" The embassy cable noted that one major East German newspaper described "Wyoming" as "a spokesman for the Indian freedom movement," who was "sentenced to many years in jail last August by American racist justice for his political opinion and action."[116] An undated photograph taken during these years is titled "warrior" and depicts Pete "Wyoming" Bender singing behind the piano, with shoulder-length hair, wearing a beret with a patch that depicts what looks to be a tipi with the U.S. flag upside down—an AIM signal of distress.[117] Wearing a beret similar to that worn by Dennis Banks at Wounded Knee in 1973[118] and also sported by Greg Zephier during the 1977 post-conference tour, this white singer of unclear nationality[119] performed a sovereign Indianness with his on-stage persona. His transatlantic protest performance for Native sovereignty made him appear Indian to German audiences and the U.S. government from across the iron curtain. His performance served as fodder for East German anti-U.S. propaganda, but it also put the U.S. government on alert that American Indians were engaging in diplomacy in the Central European contact zone. It also stretched the transatlantic sovereignty movement to confer a kind of Indian identity on non-Natives who were willing to work for the movement—to engage in "playing Indian" for sovereignty. This performance form was soon continued with a visit to West Germany by Sisseton Sioux singer songwriter Floyd Westerman in the spring of 1978 at the invitation of the Society for Endangered Peoples.[120]

For the Society's organizers and the U.S.-based sovereignty activists, the Hamburg rally was a powerful experience.[121] For American Indian activists who had been working against what they felt was at its best white ignorance and apathy, and at worst the overwhelming assaults of the U.S. government and its corrupt Indian officials, to be speaking to an audience of thousands of sympathetic and interested Germans must have been an immense relief, a vindication of much of their hard work and suffering, and a surge of hope for the future of Native sovereignty.

The West German tour of the Indian delegation was bracketed by two outdoor protest performances that engaged the transatlantic public memory of the first contact between Europeans and the Natives of the Americas. In early September 1977, activists of the American Indian Movement who had arrived in Central Europe for a United Nations conference led a torchlight march of 500 people across Hamburg, West Germany. Carrying a banner calling for an end to the sterilization of Native women, they declared that what had been known as Columbus Day was now going to be a Day of Mourning with American Indians.[122] A month later, on the evening of October 12, 1977, about thirty people gathered in front of the America House on the Hardenbergstraße of West Berlin, Germany. After a few speeches expressing solidarity with American Indians living on reservations, the members of this demonstration approached the steps of the building and publicly burned several Wild West-themed comic books.[123] In their signature move, the AIM/Treaty Council leaders again used a holiday of "American" history to critique the long history of Indian relations and call attention to their current demands. This time, however, the geographical location of their performances made this an intervention in the European as well as U.S. public memory of the first engagement with the peoples of the New World. While the countries that observe Columbus Day are mostly in the Americas (Spain being an exception), these performances aimed to shape the public memory of the age of discovery in Europe.

After the rocky planning of the 1977 tour, the Society for Endangered Peoples (Gesellschaft für bedrohte Völker) expanded the tour it was planning for May 1978. The Society solicited sponsorship from corporations such as Ford and Lufthansa, and pro bono appearances from West German musicians, so that the solidarity concerts could raise money for the trip and the various current projects of the delegates.[124] Heeding the feedback from the previous year's Native delegates and their own volunteers' observations,[125] the organizers now scheduled the delegation for breakout tours to visit a greater number of locales simultaneously, and approached clergy, local mayors, and federal politicians of the Social Democratic Party (Sozialdemokratische Partei Deutschlands, the then governing party of West Germany) for meetings and official patronage.[126]

Another important new feature of the May 1978 tour was its inclusion of more Native women and a stronger focus on their issues. While the only female delegate of the 1977 West German post-conference tour was Winona LaDuke,[127] the 1978 tour included four women: founder of Women of All Red Nations, Phillis Young; recent champion of Native legal and gender equality, Yvonne Wanrow; Marxist historian, feminist and Indian rights activist, Roxanne Dunbar-Ortiz; and Mary Crow Dog's sister, Barbara Moore, who had experienced the trauma of involuntary sterilization that she was now crusading against.[128] Accordingly, the tour's program also included events such as a planned mass rally on women's rights at the Audimax hall of the Technical University of Berlin on May 5.[129] Some of them strong personalities and veteran activists, these women likely forcefully foregrounded Native women's demands and contributions to the sovereignty struggle, and shared their experiences and wisdom about activism with their German audiences and counterparts.

The 1977 post-conference tour established the cultural forms, some of the logistical bases and routes, and found the audiences for the subsequent Native visits in the triangle of Switzerland, West Germany, and Austria. After the 1977 conference, Indian sovereignty activists traveled to Europe frequently enough to be an annual presence there. In addition to the Society's Native tour of that spring, in April and May of 1978 Ulla Bäcksin's Swedish Indian League (Svensk Indianska Förbundet) teamed up with a network of small Central European AIM support groups to bring Eddie Benton Banai and Shirley Blakely of the Federation of Survival Schools on a "European Speech Tour" to West Germany and Austria.[130] In November 1980, AIM-affiliated Native delegates such as Archie Fire Lame Deer participated in the Fourth Russell Tribunal held in Rotterdam, the Netherlands, which focused on the violation of the rights of Indians in the Americas.[131] The following year, the United Nations convened its International NGO Conference on Indigenous Peoples and the Land in Geneva, Switzerland.[132] After 1977 the annual sessions of the United Nations Commission on Human Rights, and after 1982 the UN Working Group on Indigenous Populations all featured delegates of Native North American sovereignty rights organizations.[133] Lakota medicine man Archie Fire Lame Deer spent much of the 1980s touring Europe.[134] Other Native American spiritual leaders and teachers like Vincent LaDuke, a.k.a. Sun Bear, likewise traveled around in Europe, both educating about and marketing Native or Indian-inspired New Age spiritualities.[135]

The Reds and the Greens: American Indian Sovereignty Meets European Environmentalism

> In 1984, when the Americans decided to station their nuclear rockets in Germany, the phone rang at 2 in the morning. I knew that it was either somebody who needed money or somebody who needed planning. I still remember the phone call. It was Carl Amery, who was a writer, an adviser to the Gesellschaft für bedrohte Völker, a writer of Bavarian fiction, of philosophy. Amery said, "Now we need the Indians.[136]
>
> —Claus Biegert

While the U.S. decision to plant Pershing missiles on West German soil in 1984 may have kicked it into higher gear, the alliance between the German environmental and antinuclear movement and the American Indian radical sovereignty struggle had been present in seeds and openings before the mid-1980s. The German interest and hopes for networking are reflected in letters written to Dunbar-Ortiz by the Hamburg Citizens' Initiative for Environment Protection (Bürgerinitiativen Umweltschutz Unterelbe) in the early spring of 1978. This group of the German greens first explained the situation of their own struggle:

> In recent years, the environment protection movement has gained momentum here—especially against nuclear power plants. We had demonstrations of 40,000 people, attempts to take over sites, and campouts on the building sites, and other smaller actions. Now we are in a critical phase. Because of the ever more powerful and more brutal police apparatus and greater number of court cases against environmental activists, many people have been intimidated. The results of demagogic propaganda: "Nuclear stations create jobs," "environmentalists

> are criminals" have led to resignations. There are political divisions in the initiatives about how to continue the resistance. Meanwhile, the destruction of our environment continues.[137]

What the West German greens were most interested in were opportunities to mutually share experiences and the best strategies of resistance and environmental activism. A planned May 6, 1978, meeting between the Indian delegates and some 200 representatives of green groups from Hamburg, Kiel, and Hannover was to focus on attempts to build a different relationship to the environment and fellow humans. Deeming their own actions too weak and experience too little, the environmentalists were interested in Native worldviews and an organization of life not based on exploitation. "We would also like to hear the opinions of Indians about such attempts by white Americans."[138]

The second part of this meeting was to discuss forms of resistance. This included the West German greens' experience with government hearings, demonstrations, publicity, movement work, takeover attempts and actions to obstruct construction and operations, and court proceedings and counter-insurgency programs.[139] In turn, the Germans were eager to hear about the Native struggles:

> We know that you have been active on the behalf of the Sioux Nation and the proceedings after Wounded Knee. We believe that we can learn something from your experiences at least indirectly. We are asking you to share with us if you want to participate in this event, so that we can confirm it.[140]

The West German environmentalists understood themselves as being at an early stage of the development of a social movement that the sovereignty struggle had already gone through. In addition to offering the Native activists opportunities to articulate their own appeals for German support, the greens wanted to learn from their experience of struggling against the U.S. government and corporations' encroachment on the natural resources of Indian communities. Plans for German environmentalist author Carl Amery to give speeches at some of the 1978 tour's events rounded out the participation of this West German group in the Native delegation's visit.[141] Despite differences over approaches to planning between the environmentalists and the Society for Endangered Peoples,[142] the red-green linkup was realized at events like a May 5 Berlin rally, a May 6 Hamburg joint presentation, and a May 7 Berlin session.[143] Thus, the West German greens offered a potential transatlantic alliance to the American Indian sovereignty struggle one year before their own political party was officially launched in 1979.[144]

For the next few years the transatlantic red-green coalition seems to have languished in a gestation stage. The antinuclear cause was slow to gather momentum in West German society, which had accepted the construction of nuclear power plants as a solution to the rising oil prices of the 1970s. However, along with Reagan's hardening anti-Communism, the 1983 decision by the United States, NATO, and their own national government to station new nuclear missiles in West Germany cast a shadow of nuclear apocalypse over the country, alarming larger segments of West German society. Opposition to the arrival of the Pershing missiles linked the West German environmentalists to a new generation of activists critical of the transatlantic military partnership. Now the perceived parallels between the West German situation, uranium mining in the Sioux's sacred Black Hills in South Dakota, and the "Joint Use Area" of the Navajo and Hopi of Big Mountain/Black Mesa in Arizona[145] could establish a transatlantic connection of urgency and activism against corporate encroachment and government domination of "native" natural resources.

Claus Biegert responded to Carl Amery's appeal for Native support by forming a working group, raising money, and organizing a tour of Switzerland and West Germany.

> I put together a group, [. . .] it was called the Journey of Peace. For ten days, many people from Menominee, Anishinaabe, Iroquois, and Lakota, traveled to Germany and honored the mayors of towns and villages to declare their territory nuclear free. Each got an eagle feather. And we met with Petra Kelly, and I drafted a Consensus of Peace and Friendship between both sides I drafted it in a traveling dining car of Munich to Bonn. And I drafted it, and then I wrote it on expensive pergamen [. . .] And this was then signed by Petra Kelly, and of the Greens, and Heimut Stuegel of the Social Democrats, and all the participants of the tour. [. . .] We got nice press coverage. [. . .] And Winona LaDuke was part of this, of the group, and Devasenta, the Grandmother from the Onondaga, who adopted me in her family, and [. . .] Black Hawk who was at Wounded Knee. In Munich it was a huge event. It was huge everywhere.[146]

Biegert's contacts and his knowledge of American Indian cultures helped the activists of the transatlantic alliance to creatively strengthen their coalition. Taking the form of treaty making from the history of European and Euro-American–Native relations,[147] the West German Greens and the radical Indian "reds" now performed a pact that made common cause between the sovereignty rights movement and the Central European peace and environmentalist struggles in this Cold War contact zone.

Claus Biegert's "Journey of Peace" was not the only Native tour of Central Europe in the 1980s. Only in the year 1984, there were two other visits by American Indians in Central European German-speaking countries. In February, five envoys of the Oglala Lakota Sioux tribal council and the Lakota Treaty Council[148] held rallies and press conferences, gave slide show presentations, and met politicians like Petra Kelly, spokeswoman of the West German Green Party that had secured a foothold in the federal parliament the year before, and Social Democrat representative Hans-Jürgen Wischnewski. In August and September of that same year, two Lakota activist-artists, Victor Runnels and Milo Yellow Hair, toured Switzerland, Austria, and West Germany, meeting youth groups, fellow artists, peace and environmentalist groups, and local and federal politicians. The Lakota and the Greens were seeking to convince the West German government to support a resolution in the United Nations General Assembly to refer the Sioux Black Hills land claims to the International Court.

In the reportage resulting from the tour's media blitz,[149] the Society's Renate Domnick and eco-feminist Petra Kelly argued that West Germany's importation of uranium from companies that mined it in the Black Hills made their society complicit in the perpetuation of an injustice recognized by the U.S. Supreme Court.[150] As a politician elected to the national parliament only the year before, in March 1984 Kelly formally asked the federal government of West Germany whether it was ready to lend support to the Lakota case in the United Nations. She received the response that the Black Hills case was an "internal matter" (*innere Angelegenheit*) of the United States—a predictable answer from a staunch transatlantic ally and a UN member state.

Kelly's August 31, 1984, letter to West German foreign minister and vice chancellor Hans-Dietrich Genscher did more than rebut her own government's earlier response to the red-green diplomacy effort.

> In spite of the occupation by the United States, Indian tribes like the Lakota have retained state-like characteristics and

> people's rights. Of all the countries, the Federal Republic should be the last one to doubt this, since under the Potsdam agreements, itself was occupied by the United States. This occupation, which by jurists has been called "trusteeship," did not prevent the Federal Republic from being a state, even though the occupation lasted for a long time. In actuality, the statehood of American Indians has a stronger foundation. The Lakota never capitulated to the U.S. government—unlike Germany did in 1945. Germany had a government installed by the Allied Powers in 1949, whereas the Lakota still have a pre-Columbian form of government in the General Council. Like the Federal Republic was recognized as its own country in 1949, so could the Lakota be recognized as their own state.[151]

In arguing the case of Lakota land claims, Kelly broached the sensitive issue of the very legitimacy of the West German state and its special transatlantic alliance with the United States. Subverting the usual diplomatic argumentation that valorized this transatlantic partnership, Kelly implied that the very dignity of West German self-image—that postwar West Germany was not an occupied colony, but a sovereign state born of a trust relationship—called for the support of the efforts of the Lakota to regain their lands through international arbitration. It was here that this German Green politician directly addressed one of the major issues underlying the ongoing German alliance with American Indians: that of German self-image and identity.

In addition to approaching their own politicians, Kelly, Domnick, Runnels, Yellow Hair, and their allies also promoted sovereignty through what they called "cultural exchange." On their tour of Switzerland, Austria, and West Germany, Runnels and Yellow Hair brought the artistic traditions of their people to the Germans to educate them about the difference between Karl May's literary fantasies, other popular German clichés about Indians, and real creative expression, folkways, and current Native issues and causes.[152] "In order to be taken seriously by West German politicians, the Indians think they must deconstruct the clichés about North American Indians and present a real picture of their history political and cultural situation."[153] Here, the faith of the activists of the American Indian Movement in "sensitizing" Euro-Americans,[154] Richard Erdoes's use of publishing to enlighten audiences about Indian cultures, and the belief of the West German Greens in alternative political consciousness-raising[155] combined to form a sociocultural strategy of the transatlantic Native sovereignty movement.[156]

Conclusion

Native tours in Central Europe continued through the rest of the 1980s and beyond. This chapter traced the rise of the transatlantic alliance for Native sovereignty. It was the siege of Wounded Knee in 1973 that truly catalyzed the transatlantic alliance through its media coverage and Native transnational outreach. During the mid-1970s, leaders of the Native sovereignty movement traveled in Central Europe to establish "support groups" and build a transatlantic alliance. This alliance between the American Indian radical sovereignty movement and groups in especially German-speaking Central Europe proved to be crucial in shoring up the financial strength and boosting the morale of the sovereignty struggle during the court trials of the occupiers of Wounded Knee. Following a 1977 breakthrough United Nations NGO conference on discrimination against American Indians, Native activists and their European allies perfected their North American Plains–Mitteleuropa Axis, along which circulated moral and political support, financial contributions, and human bodies in the transatlantic Indian sovereignty movement. The alliance entered another phase when in the 1980s Central European environmental and antinuclear activists sought the help of Native groups for their struggles.

What happened when people who had been corresponding across the Atlantic finally met in person? How did the American Indian activists and Central European solidarity volunteers navigate their personal relationships and the social dynamics of movement life? Did their egos clash and hinder their solidarity projects, or did they work seamlessly together for their causes? The next chapter will probe the politics of solidarity in the transatlantic alliance for Native sovereignty.

4

The Politics of Solidarity in the Transatlantic Sovereignty Alliance

> Friends: We are young people, living in the German Democratic Republic, loving peace, brotherhood, humanity and our country, its woods, meadows, rivers, villages, towns. We are informed about your problems as Indian people enough to understand your fighting for your identity as a nation, for your own Indian way of life, for the Indian education of your children, against the pollution of your beautiful country, for your landrights and cultural autonomy.
>
> We hope and wish you may be successful. We are feeling in solidarity with you, with the people of Wounded Knee who have given a world-wide signal, with all Indian people defending their existence as Indian people. We like to listen when you speak. We know that thousands of young people here are feeling this way.
>
> We are with you when you go your difficult way.
>
> —Letter with 36 signatures from Rostock, East Germany 1973[1]

An undated photograph by Dick Bancroft titled "Dennis Banks talking with C. Biegert"[2] shows the two men facing each other in a room, some distance from an open door where people are milling about. The West German journalist is sporting a moustache and beard, and is wearing a plaid shirt or jacket. The military tunic-like jacket of the AIM leader bears a patch with the word "Airlift" as well as several movement buttons. Banks's hair is carefully braided and is sporting a feather. Leaning toward each other, Banks and Biegert lock gazes, and share a laugh over mutually knowing looks. Their posture and gestures suggest male camaraderie, a kind of intimacy in solidarity.

Europeans at Wounded Knee

While the interest had been strong and some of the connections had already been made, the event that truly catalyzed the transatlantic alliance for Native sovereignty was the spring 1973 siege of Wounded Knee. The occupiers catered to the press in their performances,[3] and the length of the standoff allowed for the media to build up a presence in and around the village. In turn, the European response to the press coverage was impressive: numerous messages of solidarity arrived at the *Akwesasne Notes* from European countries. A reader from London assured Indian activists of the support of "the English, Scotts, Welsh and Irish Peoples" who have been following their struggle on radio and television. High school students from Denmark expressed their solidarity not only with the goals of Wounded Knee, but with the larger American Indian struggle; a Danish author instructed his publisher to transfer all income from his book to the newspaper's address.[4] The paper also received a letter from Bulgaria signed by twenty-eight supporters, and two missives from young people in East Germany, with fifty-four and thirty-six signatures, respectively, expressing solidarity "with the people of Wounded Knee who have given a world-wide signal, with all Indian people defending their existence as Indian people."[5] A group of Dutch printed an eight-page booklet titled "Wounded Knee Poems by Werner Verstraeten" in English, and sent an autographed copy to the occupiers, which ended up with the Wounded Knee Legal Defense/Offense Committee (WKLD/OC).[6] Whether they were grassroots initiatives or encouraged by Marxist home governments, these messages of solidarity were signs of an interest in the sovereignty struggle from groups living on both sides of the iron curtain.

The only two photographs by Richard Erdoes that show him at Wounded Knee were taken at the Gildersleeve trading post, which was left at the disposal of the occupiers after its managers were moved out. After a series of shots of the store interior that feature three different cigar store Indians, two pictures show the store through the convex mirror hanging from the ceiling in the corner. The clinically bright neon lights and the distorted geometric perspectives of the fish-eye looking glass almost manage to hide the figure of Erdoes himself taking the photographs. Yet it was the photographer whose decisions determined what the images show. Like some forensic software, a close reading of some written accounts can help reconstruct the perspectives closer to the original embodied experience of Europeans at Wounded Knee. Like the fish-eye mirror however, the actual experience was already subjective and has since been mediated through the agendas of the writers, and the ways in which the subjects have made meaning of their own life histories. In this sense, scholars can study only the mediated records of past embodied experiences—never the experiences themselves.

Some of the embodied experience of Europeans at Wounded Knee can be reconstructed from memoirs, opinion pieces, and oral histories. Most of those whose accounts survive were in the international press corps or were amateur journalists.[7] Of these, some tried to maintain a neutral position or even play the role of an independent arbiter. According to Carol Sullivan, "a group of Dutch journalists put an advertisement in the *New York Times*, [titled] 'The Dutch at Wounded Knee,' calling for a sense of proportion and a writing campaign to the [U.S.] Department of Interior asking for a 'lowered voice and reasonable conversation.' "[8] Others were perceived to have crossed the line from observer to participant. As he was escorting a funeral caravan out of the village, Pine Ridge police and the FBI apprehended Danish author and filmmaker Jacob Holdt, stripped him of his press credentials, and kicked him off the reservation.[9]

Two specific tales by Central Europeans at Wounded Knee present critical and conflicting relationships with the radical Indian sovereignty movement. One was "extracted from letters" and published in German in a magazine or anthology, under the title "Wounded Knee: a Defeat?" A photocopy made its way into the papers of Richard Erdoes,[10] which in itself is evidence that such documents circulated in the transatlantic network of sovereignty activists. The author, who was most likely German,[11] claims to have participated in the events at Wounded Knee, and relates his experience to explain his position concerning the sovereignty struggle as a revolutionary movement.

Fictionally named so for the purposes of this writing, Gerhardt starts his narrative by explaining that he had been reluctant to stay with American Indians because of their exploitation by white anthropologists, and because of their depressing history. He nevertheless volunteered to be with them at Wounded Knee, because this was "an armed revolt against the U.S. government," and, like the U.S. left, he too had grown weary of demonstrating and had romanticized armed violence.[12] This reasoning suggests that he was either a member or a careful observer of the 1960s transatlantic counterculture documented by Martin Klimke.[13]

Gerhardt gives two reasons for why he concluded that Wounded Knee was a failure of the radical sovereignty movement. "In our romantic drunkenness we had not considered the physical challenges that you have to overcome when you lie in trenches in snow and mud for months at a time."[14] This reason, however, contradicts his tales of his own exploits. At the funeral ceremony of Frank Clearwater, Gerhardt delivered a speech which—he claims for the first time—placed the siege of Wounded Knee in an international context.[15] Gerhardt also claims to have spent long hours smuggling arms and ammunition into the village while federal agents shot flares to detect him. On one occasion, he led the FBI on a high-speed car chase. He was once apprehended and expelled from the reservation. Another time he was caught, wearing a wig to disguise himself, and he had to talk his way out of a tribal jail cell.[16]

Gerhardt's other reason for dismissing Wounded Knee as a fiasco has to do with the interpersonal conflicts among the occupiers. "I have seen so much quarreling and bickering among the Indians that I would not like to talk about it." Yet for Gerhardt, as for the characters of his account, the real problem seemed to be the hierarchy between the Indians and the non-Indians. "Actually, they considered us white helpers almost like slaves."[17] At one point the Indians even discussed "the question of sending all the whites away," which Gerhardt claims most of them actually wanted to do, but one of their leaders convinced them otherwise.[18] Even after some of the warriors sneaked out of the village and the standoff was arguably over, the remaining defenders kept Gerhardt in the camp "for safety reasons." He felt like a prisoner, but eventually managed to escape and hitchhike to Rapid City.[19]

Regardless of its truth value, Gerhardt's account of his experience at Wounded Knee is indicative of the tensions of an interracial[20] coalition for Indian sovereignty. A problem inherent to such social and political coalitions is the issue of control and representation. Gerhardt's complaints highlight problem areas like the division of labor, leadership, enforcement of security, and the more general and deep-seated question of the ownership of the protest event. For the next two decades and beyond, the transatlantic alliance of the radical Indian sovereignty movement would be grappling with issues of how whites could help the cause the best, when exactly Indians or non-Indians crossed the line in speaking for the movement, and how much and in what ways whites could legitimately perform Indianness for sovereignty.

Claus Biegert[21] tells the story of how he joined the sovereignty movement shortly after the events at Wounded Knee. An amateur journalist and author, Biegert went to the United States with a fellow journalist to report on the sovereignty struggle. They first spent a week at the office of the radical Native paper *Akwesasne Notes* on the Mohawk territory of the New York–Ontario borderlands.

> [W]e both had a book contract. And the people at *Akwesasne Notes* said, "We cannot help you if you are writing a book." "Why?" "Well, writing a book is exploitation. We know you guys now—you stayed here for a week, you helped—we know that you, you're different, you're not anthropologists who, you know, use the information that they get to climb up the academic ladder, but the people who gave the information get nothing, they don't get anything." We knew that we did not have the time to stay at every place for a week, so we said, "We also have this contract with a radio station for a 60-minute feature on the Native American resistance," and they said, "Why didn't you tell us this before? That makes a hell of a difference. No radio channel is going to the hinterland here to listen, nobody talks to us, that's why we need Wounded Knee. So if you cross the Atlantic and are willing to travel from reservation to reservation, of course we will help you.[22]

Recording their broadcast, Biegert and his colleague visited reservations and Native hubs at Onondaga, Buffalo in New York, Chicago in Illinois, the Twin Cities in Minnesota, and North and South Dakota.

> And in South Dakota we went to the office of Ramon Robideaux, the lawyer, in the office was Dennis Banks and [. . .] Bisonnette and someone else . . . and a day later, there was also a John Adams, the head of the [World Council of Churches . . .]. And there we waited—for hours. And then they said, "We appreciate your patience. You're different." So, first lesson: patience.
>
> [. . .]
>
> And then we said we wanted to go to Wounded Knee. "That is our final goal here, to come over." And they said, "Well, we cannot help you. We don't want you to go alone, that is dangerous, and if we come with you, then it is even more dangerous. So our advice is, stay here and talk to us, and go to Wounded Knee some other time. This is not the time."[23]

On his first fact-finding trip to the United States, Biegert met some leading members of the movement who, as he understands in retrospect, tested him and his fellow European journalist by making them wait, listen, and help out.[24] Biegert's first embodied encounter with the radical sovereignty movement was marked by the Wounded Knee experience as a catalyst, but not at the actual site. While Gerhardt's embodied immersion in Wounded Knee led to burnout and disillusionment with sovereignty as a revolutionary project, Biegert's inability to visit the actual site served as a pledge to the transatlantic alliance. Claus Biegert would go on to be one of the major European nodes and facilitators of the transatlantic sovereignty alliance.

The Gender and Sexual Politics of the Radical Indian Sovereignty Movement

Several former activists discussed the gender and sexual politics of the U.S.-based Native sovereignty movement in their memoirs. In her two autobiographies co-authored with Richard Erdoes, Brule/Sicangu Sioux Mary (neé Moore) Crow Dog/Brave Bird articulated a Native approach to feminism that criticized the Sioux male-centered warrior role of the AIM men while still praising them for their bravery in political activism.

> There is a curious contradiction in Sioux society. The men pay great lip service to the status women hold in the tribe. Their rhetoric on the subject is beautiful. They speak of Grandmother Earth and how they honor her. [. . .] The men kept telling us, "See how we are honoring you . . ." honoring us for what? For being good beaders, quillers, tanners, moccasin makers, and child-bearers." Men explain their traditional role as hunters and defenders. "So, go already," I tell them. "Be traditional. Get me a buffalo!"[25]
>
> But to sum up: our men were magnificent and mean at the same time. You had to admire them. They had to fight their own men's lib battles. They were incredibly brave in protecting us, they would literally die for us, and they always stood up for our rights—*against outsiders!*[26]

Brave Bird's alliances with white liberal women were fraught with differences over the goals and means of feminism. At the 1973 siege of Wounded Knee, she recalled that:

> At one time a white volunteer nurse berated us for doing the slave work while the men got all the glory. We were betraying the cause of womankind, was the way she put it. We told her that her kind of women's lib was a white, middle-class thing, and that at this critical stage we had other priorities. Once our men had gotten their rights and their balls back, we might start arguing with them about who should do the dishes. But not before.[27]

Even as she pointed to the weaknesses of a feminist approach to the sovereignty struggle, Brave Bird provided a strong corrective to the male-centered accounts of the movement by AIM leaders like Dennis Banks and Russell Means.[28] In particular, she listed the women activists and described their leadership at crucial junctures of the movement, thus honoring them in writing.[29] According to her, the idea of occupying Wounded Knee was raised by traditionalist Sioux women Ellen Moves Camp and Gladys Bissonette, who in February 1973 encouraged people at Calico Hall to take over the village: "Go ahead and make your stand at Wounded Knee. If you men won't do it, you can stay here and talk for all eternity and we women will do it."[30] She also praised the Women of all the Red Nations, "the first native feminist movement ever,"[31] and insisted that the Hopi and Navajo's "fight for Big Mountain was led by the women" like Madonna Gilbert.[32]

Mary Brave Bird at once laments and celebrates the intense but brief and casual romantic relationships between men and women in the radical sovereignty movement. "Some of the AIM leaders attracted quite a number of 'wives.' We called them 'wives of the month.' " When official, such relationships were sanctioned not by the white man's law, but by the Indian medicine man's pipe ceremony. With death or imprisonment always hanging over the partners' heads,

> [s]hort or long, it was good while it lasted. The girl had somebody to protect and take care of her; the boy had a wincincala to cook his beans or sew him a ribbon shirt. They inspired each other to the point where they would put their

> bodies on the line together. It gave them something precious to remember all their lives.[33]

Such casual relationships may have been expedient for the movement, but not for the Native nations it was serving, or for people who wanted to start a family. At worst, they left the female activists to deal with the fruits of the affair on their own.

> The nicer [men] say: "Warrior woman, let's make a little warrior." Nine months later the woman is nursing her little warrior, but the big warrior is over the hills and far away.[34]

Brave Bird's first child was born of just such a brief movement flame. In her own life as in her memoirs, eschewing mainstream feminism in favor of a kind of Native reproductive activism, Brave Bird asserted that American Indian women were obligated to bear children to revive their nation's population.

> I consider myself a feminist. [. . .] Well, there is a difference between white and Indian feminists—we think that abortion is a right for everybody else, but not for us. [. . .] So there is within us the subconscious urge to reproduce, to make sure that we are not a "vanishing race."[35]
>
> Together with my sisters from many tribes, I am a birth-giver, a rebirth-giver, fighting to ensure a life for unborn generations. I am a Sioux woman![36]

Herself a professed feminist, Northern Cheyenne Roxanne Dunbar-Ortiz described a similar sexual dynamic in the movement, but with destructive consequences.

> Jimmie [Durham]'s [1978 accusatory] letter about me was sent out after I had seen him briefly the month before when I was in New York and spent the night at his apartment, as I had on several occasions. For the first time, he had indicated an interest in me sexually, an interest I did not share, but I responded anyway since I considered him a close friend and comrade. He had a reputation for having many lovers since he and his wife had divorced several years before; however, he was unable to perform with me and seemed to resent me

> for it. Whether this was a factor in his new hostility toward me, I had no way of knowing, but I suspected that it was. This is an old story, not only between male bosses and female employees, but also in social movements, in which as a woman, you're damned if you respond to a comrade's overtures and damned if you don't; which of course goes on all the time but is particularly destructive given the fragile nature of movement organizations.[37]

Dunbar-Ortiz highlighted the dark side of the struggle's skewed gender relations in harsh terms. Under pressure from the U.S. government's legal and clandestine campaign,

> [b]y the time of the national AIM conference, June 6–18, 1975, outside Farmington, New Mexico, the paranoia [among the activists] seemed almost palpable. Even Anna Mae Aquash was being questioned as an FBI plant, a charge that seemed utterly absurd to me, and I feared that all women would be mistrusted, as often happened in male-dominated organizations.[38]

Anna Mae Aquash was found dead the following year—as a later investigation revealed, she had been shot execution style.[39] From her own experience, Dunbar-Ortiz suggests that a double standard persisted in the radical Indian sovereignty movement for women, which kept them vulnerable sexually, questioned their trustworthiness and loyalty to the cause more than the men's, and potentially even put their lives in danger.

Such "movement affairs" may not have been unique to the Indian sovereignty struggle—after all, the sexual revolution of the long 1960s served as the social backdrop to radical Native activism. However, the interracial dimension of the U.S.-based alliance further intensified its sexual politics by bringing together young people of both Native and non-Native backgrounds. Trained by her husband Leonard Crow Dog and other spiritual teachers, Mary Brave Bird started conducting sweat ceremonies in the late 1970s–early 1980s. In her memoirs she recalled that at first the sweats were co-ed, but soon they needed to be gender separate, because some "outsiders who did not know our customs" would cop a feel in the dark and blame it on "the spirit." On one occasion, the white girlfriend of an Indian mistakenly groped another Native man, ruining the whole ceremony.[40] Brave Bird had an honest and scathing opinion of white women who were attracted to Native men and framed their desire as a longing for a spiritual experience:

> There are white women, groupies, who are looking for "a medicine man who will put the power right into me." They are hungering for "a deep sexual experience." They'll sleep with anybody who wears braids or a choker.[41]

Transatlantic Intimacies: Solidarity as Camaraderie, Romance, and Desire

In German author Karl May's 1893 novel *Winnetou I*, the German hero encounters and is immediately attracted to Apache warrior Winnetou and his sister Nsho-tshi, who are described in similar ways:

> [Winnetou's] moccasins were decorated with hedgehog bristles and the seams of his leggings and the hunting with fine, red, decorative embroidery. Like his father, he wore a medicine bag and the calumet on a cord hanging from his neck. Because his head also was uncovered, I could see that his hair was arranged like his father's, except that it was interlaced with the skin of a rattlesnake and showed no feather. It was long and fell heavily and abundantly over his back. Certainly many a woman would have envied this splendid, bluish ornament. His face was almost more noble than his father's and of a subdued, light brown with a tinge of bronze. As I guessed and later discovered, his age was about the same as my own and even that day, when I saw him for the first time, he made a profound impression on me. I felt that he was a good human being and exceptionally gifted. We scrutinized each other at length and then I thought I observed that a momentary, friendly expression came into his eyes, which had a velvety shimmer. It was like a greeting the sun sends to earth through a cloud cover.[42]

> [Nsho-tshi] was clad in a long, shirtlike garment which fitted tightly around the neck and was held together around the waist by the hide of a rattlesnake. [. . .] Her only ornament was her splendid long hair, braided in two pigtails hanging down to

> below her belt, and of a bluish-black color. This hair reminded me of Winnetou's. Her features also resembled his, and her eyes had the same velvety blackness. They were half-hidden by long, heavy lashes like secrets that must not be discovered. There was no trace of the high cheek bones common among Indians. The soft, warm, and full cheeks came together in a chin whose dimples would have suggested playfulness in a European woman. So as not to awaken me, she was speaking softly to the old woman, and when she opened her beautifully shaped mouth in a smile, her teeth glistened like pure ivory. The delicate flare of her nostrils seemed to point to Greek rather than Indian descent. The color of her skin was a light copper-bronze with a touch of silver. The girl must have been around eighteen, and I felt certain that she was Winnetou's sister.[43]

Through a series of adventures that involve grappling with mutual attraction, distrust, and alternating roles of captive and captor, the relationship between German immigrant "Charlie" and Apache warrior Winnetou develop into friendship and beyond—into blood brotherhood.[44] Meanwhile, Nsho-tshi falls in love with Charlie, and at her brother's advice she resolves to go to Saint Louis to "learn the white ladies' ways" to attract him. However, her trip is cut short by the evil and murderous white adventurer Santer, who kills Nsho-tshi and Winnetou's father, the Apache chief, for their gold.[45] At the end of the story, Charlie successfully talks the grieving Winnetou out of his plan of uniting all the Indian tribes and waging war against the whites, thereby latently asserting a Christian pacifist morality.[46]

Katrin Sieg has pointed out how Karl May's characters and original storyline have enabled a series of stage and filmic performances of interracial sexual encounters that include scenarios of homosocial bondage and unfulfilled "miscegenation."[47] An attempt to demonstrate the actual influence of this trope on the ideas, attitudes, and behaviors of the generations of Central Europeans who grew up consuming popular culture products featuring the Winnetou story would require a rigorous and systematic study.[48] Instead, I argue here that this scenario is too similar not to have informed later incarnations of the positioning of a German hero as a subject of romantic and sexual desire both toward and from American Indians. In other words, some of the German and Central European solidarity with the radical Indian sovereignty movement of the late Cold War was motivated by a romantic idea of, and sometimes a sexual desire for, interracial togetherness—which resulted in performances of solidarity and transatlantic intimacy.

This kind of emotional motivation and epistolary self-expression was a characteristic of some of the most mature members of the Central European solidarity groups. In a November 8, 1974 letter to Richard Erdoes, 73-year-old East German professor and popular author of Indian-themed historical fiction Liselotte Welskopf-Henrich fondly recalled the nights she spent on the Pine Ridge Reservation of South Dakota, presumably earlier that year.[49] Hundreds of kilometers away in Northeastern Europe, the spiritual leader of the "Polish Movement of Friends of the American Indians" (Polski Ruch Przyjacioł Indian, PRPI), Stefania Antoniewicz was nicknamed "Indian Grandma" (*Indiańska Babica*) because of her intense and poetic ventriloquizing of American Indian identity and causes. She kept a sample of soil from Wounded Knee under her bed, thus sleeping on what she considered sacred ground. Being in her early eighties and having poor English skills did not keep Antoniewicz from performatively identifying with American Indians to an extent that often seemed sublime to her fellow activists. On at least one occasion, she used the royal pronoun: "When they had taken the Black Hills from *us*. . . ."[50]

From the early 1970s, Antoniewicz corresponded with the racial Native newspaper *Akweasane Notes*, WKLD/OC, and with Native American prisoners like Darryl Wilson, Michael Lee Big Water, and Lance Yellow Hand.[51] Her language expressed an intense longing and identification that went beyond solidarity:

> Reading [Dee Brown's *Bury My Heart at Wounded Knee*], I live in all tragic events: I was hungry, frozen, wounded, beaten, imprisoned. I took part in the desperate heroic battles. I feel deep sadness, but not hopelessness.[52]
>
> I wait for the paper in anxiety and sadness, in a great fear at because of the troubles perhaps AKWESASNE NOTES cannot appear.
>
> For me, there exists no treasure in the world equivalent with NOTES. The news are sorrowful, but not hopeless. They bring strength and unity. My great trouble is where is the editor? and Means Russell? I am constantly unrest of the members of AIM. My spirit and heart will follow you in all events.[53]

> [. . .] And now without news from you. My life surpass in a[n] unceasing despair, unrest and fear, about all Members of AIM, all Liberators of Wounded Knee, prisoners, about all Indian life, and safety. My day begin[s] with a prayer for you, and end with prayer. I wrote in tears.
>
> [. . .]
>
> In Struggle and Solidarity, in Love—
> your with heart and spirit devoted friend Stefania.[54]

Geographical distance and lack of exposure to living Native people are not always an adequate explanation of such hyper-identification on the part of Europeans. Works of Polish juvenile literature like Alfred Szklarski's 1959 novel *Tomek na wojenney ściezce* [*Tomek on the War Path*] narrated the story of how a Polish hero's bravery earned the respect and brotherhood of American Indians, and how he persuaded their warriors to refrain from unnecessary bloodshed[55]—quite like Charlie/Old Shatterhand did in Karl May's *Winnetou*. Antoniewicz and her fellow solidarity activists were culturally rooted in ideas and representations of the ideal relations between American Indians and Europeans.

"Getting Your German, Getting Your Indian": Sexual Politics in the Transatlantic Alliance

Gerhardt's account of his disillusionment with the radical Indian sovereignty movement through his experience at Wounded Knee in 1973[56] not only critiqued the interracial relations of the activists, but also included a rather specific and detailed narrative of his sexual exploits.

> But I do not think that such outside experiences warranted being thrown out of the area. It was a more intimate experience of mine that did it. A leader of Wounded Knee, a Sioux Indian I will name X, became a very good friend of mine. [. . .] We drove on to the Rosebud Reservation, where X suggested that we spend the night at his aunt's place. We got to sleep on a mattress in her kitchen, where [. . .] he said that we should share the mattress, and he explained at length that according to Indian custom it is rude to turn down an invitation. As we lay on the mattress he told me

> in mysterious whisper of the ghosts of his forefathers while the prairie wind howled over the eaves and enveloped us in a peculiar feeling. In his ecstasy he came closer and closer, and he could not fathom why I was unable to see the ghosts in the darkness. His whole body started trembling, and he held me closer. At length the trembling slowly subsided, and he started to kiss me—with long, moist kisses. It was only then that I realized that he was a homosexual, but this was a kind of homosexuality that I had never encountered before. Because of his stubbornness, for him this was not about sexuality, and he would not pull back. He only wanted to live on "a higher plane" which he adorned with ghosts and demons—and he did this in a way that even to this day I wonder if that night he seriously came onto me.[57]

Gerhardt and X spent the following days in the village of Wounded Knee where the Indian leader treated the German like any of the other activists, showing little if any personal preference for him, "so I concluded that the Indian culture strongly suppresses homosexuality." During the funeral of Frank Clearwater, who had been killed by a stray bullet of the federal forces, Gerhardt gave a rousing speech about Wounded Knee being a turning point of world history. Right after his speech,

> My eyes found a girl of the Tipoix Indians, who hitchhiked in red clogs all the way from Minnesota to fight at Wounded Knee. She was beautiful, and we completely fell in love with each other as our gazes met over the casket. We hardly finished smoking the peace pipe and smoothing the dirt over the grave as customary, when Bobby and I started to spend all our time together. We tried to keep our relationship a secret because it was not very popular to see a red girl and a white man going together.[58]

X was bound to find out about the blossoming romance, and when he did, he was mad with jealousy. He gave a speech to the camp condemning the promiscuity that was undignified and disrupting the traditional ways of mourning. He also discussed with the Native leadership the option of banishing the white allies, but eventually decided not to take that step. For Gerhardt, all this had to do with the Native leader's attraction to him—"To cut it short, X was very much in love with me, and I am fully convinced that this was the only reason for why we were permitted to stay in the camp. I was realizing how much X was in love with me."[59]

Gerhardt's sexual adventures were far from over. In order to keep him away from Bobby, X "promoted" him to sleep in the leaders' tent with him and Morningstar, Clearwater's pregnant widow. Here a strange scene unfolded.

> Morningstar lay in the only bed and she chatted with me in the lamplight as I was lying on the ground. She became more and more animated in her talking to me. All of a sudden she asked if she could lie down with me. I was caught off guard, and before I could respond, she already climbed over to me and huddled right into my sleeping bag. I didn't know what to do and just lay there stiffly. In similar situations I often surrendered, but this was something different, and it was unthinkable for me to contemplate sex. It had been only two days since the burial of her husband—the man whose child she was carrying. I was appalled, shocked. [. . .] I do not know what I would have done had X not saved me with his return to the tent from a meeting. When we heard him coming, Morningstar climbed back in her own bed. X put out the light, and lay down beside me like he did in his aunt's house. Ever since that time, he had not dared to give more than the slightest signs of his love for me. Alhough I am not a homosexual, I have to admit that even as he started kissing me that night, he had managed to save me from a very, very painful situation. (As I later found out, such behavior is not unusual for women who had just lost their husbands.)[60]

Gerhardt spent the rest of his time at Wounded Knee under the watchful eye of X, and he was kept in the camp "for security reasons" even after the stand down—until he managed to sneak out, having "had enough of armed rebellion and 'armed love.' "[61]

The sensitive nature of the topic of such sexual acts and the lack of publication information for the account make it well-nigh impossible to corroborate or refute Gerhardt's claims. As such, they need to be treated as a vision of the German protagonist becoming a subject of desire for three different Indians under exceptional circumstances. In his vision, Gerhardt reenacts the role of the German immigrant "Charlie" (Karl) and his performance of Wild West/revolutionary feats—and thereby he also attracts the sexual desire of some of the movement leaders. Meanwhile he develops his own romantic desire for an Indian maiden the like of Nsho-tshi—which remains apparently unfulfilled. Ultimately, Gerhardt claims that in the end it was not necessarily the snow, the cold and the discomfort, or even the flying bullets of the U.S. government, but their own sexual politics that prevented the sovereignty activists from seizing their (rather Marxist-inflected) revolutionary moment in world history—instead, they "fucked it away!"[62]

What Gerhardt's vision construed as homosexual acts are difficult if not impossible to verify.[63] I choose to interpret these as an intensified outlier version of the moment staged or captured by Dick Bancroft's photograph of Dennis Banks and Claus Biegert: a more general homosocial (same-sex) relationship that does not have to have a romantic or sexual component[64]—in other words, same-sex camaraderie. In addition to bisocial (cross-gender) activities and various forms of sexual attraction, such homosociality was a component of the activist camaraderie of the U.S. and the transatlantic wing of the radical Indian sovereignty movement. Other examples of such camaraderie from the movement seem to fit in the current scholarly paradigm that sociality and sexuality form a continuum of acts as opposed to discrete categories[65]—acts realized in performance.

Even as they soon started sending in-kind support to the United States,[66] the young East German Indianists were not content with exchanging officially sanctioned gestures through the media and correspondence. "Chiefi," the leader of a cultural hobbyist club in Triptis took a group to East Berlin to personally meet the AIM delegation of the 1973 World Festival of Students and Youth. Upon their first encounter, the Native activists liked the young and enthusiastic East Germans so much that they invited them to their after-hours campfire. "Of course the security did not want to let us in there" because they were not official delegates to the Festival. At the AIMsters' insistence, they were finally allowed in. "Then we sat and drummed in a staircase until 4 in the morning." The Thüringian youth ended up accompanying the American Indian delegation for the whole week. After the official events of the day, there was dancing and singing every night. After the conference, "Chiefi" and delegate Jim Castilla spent an extra week in Fürstenwalde, where Castilla trained German hobbyists in the traditional sweat lodge ceremony, an important Native religious ritual.[67] Reaching beyond the festival's official slogan of "Anti-Imperialist Solidarity, Peace and Friendship," these performances of transnational Indian diplomacy resulted in more intimate personal and spiritual experiences that strengthened the transatlantic alliance in the making.

While their programming was in high demand, some of the intimacy between Indians and Germans seemed to, at the same time, both enable and interfere with the functioning of the transatlantic sovereignty alliance. By early 1975, the American Indian Movement had opened an office in West Berlin. In February of that year, a German volunteer reported on the challenges of the activists.

> First of all we had to move out of our old [AIM West Berlin] office. It was in a private apartment of a girl who used to work with us, but she has got a heavy problem, she always wants to sleep with Indians, but there are not too many around here. She has got a very strange way to support the Indians. Also she dislikes fat Indians or short-haired Indians. So anyway we moved out of there and finally found a house, we rented it. Five people are living in there, including myself. The rent is very high and we are all working to get together the money to keep the house going. But we have the office in the house and two phone-lines and so we can work now much more efectfully.[68]

By late summer of that year, the same German volunteer herself had become involved head over heels with an American Indian sovereignty activist:

> [. . .] he is from Pine Ridge. People say: now you finally got yourself an Indian. I don't like that saying because I really did not chase him around town, also I did not rope him or threaten him to marry me, this was his idea, but I guess it's true: I finally got myself an Indian.[69]

Similarly to Mary Brave Bird, this German solidarity activist later wrote honestly and with enjoyment about the sexual relations between her and "her Indian."[70]

Some of such personal curiosity and desire for friendship and romance motivated the solidarity correspondence between Europeans and Native organizations. Requests for pen pals had reached such a volume that the editors of the letters section of Native radical newspaper *Akwesasne Notes* decided not to print them anymore as early as 1972.[71] After Wounded Knee 1973, this motivation continued to be a major factor in the transatlantic interactions of German youth and the Wounded Knee Legal Defense/Offense Committee (WKLD/OC). Many letter writers from East Germany asked for addresses of potential pen pals—young Indians.[72] It is not clear if and how the overworked lawyers and their volunteers responded to such requests—they may have simply ignored them, or may have tried to leverage them for more tangible support.

In a long missive, one East German writer tried to articulate her motivation for writing. In March 1975, a young woman from East Berlin wrote to WKLD/OC,

> I am white, and I hate myself for it—it is sure stupid. I love black hair, I love walnut brown hair, and I love strong black eyes.
>
> I am sentimental, and that is not good, I know.
>
> Maybe you will say, "this a crazy white girl who has nothing better to do than to bother us."
>
> Maybe it is not good that I speak of my feelings, but I want to do it, and lift the stone from my breast.
>
> I dream of the great woods, of the Prairie, and of the many big and small tribes. [. . .] I think of all the terrible things the whites have done to you, and still doing them to you today. I could kill them all for it.
>
> It is so hard for me to find the right words, so that I do not [illegible] you, but I reach your hearts. If I were brown and I had black hair and black eyes like you do, maybe it would be easier for me to reach your hearts. [T]he words of the whites have lied to you and still do it today.
>
> Maybe I will say goodbye that I dream of you. I love your people, I wish I was a child of your people.
>
> I love a young Indian, I have seen him in the summer of 1973 in Berlin, but he does not know me. But I love him, him and his people.
>
> He was in prison. Is he free? Is he healthy? His name is [name and address in Canada]. What is he doing? What is he planning to do? Is he all right? Can you answer my questions?[73]

The East German girl's letter was rounded out by five English poems of love and longing. Her prose and verse express a grappling with issues of race and historical justice, a romantic attraction to an "exotic" partner, and a longing to fight by his side—but also a real concern for the well-being of North American Indians that goes beyond her fixation on the young man.

In itself a Teutonic sensibility shared across the iron curtain, this sexual politics of the transatlantic sovereignty alliance was not exclusive to the divided city of Berlin in the mid-1970s. In East Germany, "Kate," who joined the Cheyenne Indianist Interest Group as a nineteen-year-old in 1982, did solidarity work out of conviction. Together with the other members of her club, she corresponded with Indian institutions, did educational outreach, and wrote letters of protest to judges, governors, and other state officials in the United States. However, she dreamed of more—she wanted get to the United States and have a child from an Indian.[74] Reflecting on this dynamic in 1988, Lakota medicine man Archie Fire Lame Deer, who lectured in Europe about Native American spirituality, jokingly claimed that "we are being attacked by German women. [Laughter] My God, they are coming in droves. All our Indian men are not safe right now."[75]

In spite of their fraught nature, such interpersonal relations could still be negotiated in ways that maintained the transatlantic alliance. As they recall, Mary Brave Bird/Crow Dog and Richard Erdoes cleared the air in their own relationship thus:

> She once caught me looking at her and at once confronted me, saying: "I know you are sexually attracted to me." I told her that, being an artist and photographer, I could not help studying people's faces, whether they were men or women, young or old, pretty or ugly. She stared back at me for a moment, shrugged, and said: "Okay, I half believe you." We laughed and I was never suspected harboring designs against her virtue, but the remark was typical of her blunt way of confronting situations.[76]

As in Dick Bancroft's photograph, the homosocial (same-sex non-sexual) relationships could likewise produce powerful experiences, enduring interpersonal alliances, and a broadening of people's worldview. Mary Brave Bird describes her all-female sweat experiences in her memoirs. To white women Mary explained that the darkness of the sweat made them all equal, because skin color was invisible. "There are no leaders here, just women supporting each other."

> I've sweated with women of all colors—with Asian women, with people who have been facing down tanks in Tiananmen Square. I've sweated with South African women from the antiapartheid movement, with women from San Salvador and Guatemala who are Indians like myself. I tell them all: "I can relate to you, because I've been where you are. Whether at Wounded Knee or Soweto, or at Tiananmen Square, it's the same. This sweat is for freedom." And I also sweat for our men to be strong, for the children to be strong against the things that would destroy our people.[77]

In their interpersonal relations, Central European women and men were "reenacting" the homosocial and romantic attraction between Karl May's German hero and Apache characters—the mutual admiration of looks and character, and in particular the Central European fetish for the essentialized bluish-black hue of American Indian hair. Into this mix the flesh-and-blood Native and German sovereignty activists threw a strong dose of sexual desire that was heightened by revolutionary romance and enabled by both a countercultural morality and a sense of living fast and dangerously. At least for a while, this kind of romantic solidarity seemed to strengthen the transatlantic alliance for Indian sovereignty. However, as the female volunteer's account about working at the West Berlin AIM office, as Mary Brave Bird's decision to separate the sexes in sweat ceremonies,[78] and as Claus Biegert's reference to the fickleness of West German student AIM support groups[79] indicate, this dynamic was both volatile and messy. German solidarity leaders, like Biegert, and the Native leadership gradually reasserted their authority and control over transatlantic intimacies and political activism.

"And Think about What Solidarity Means!"[80]: Jealousy and Rivalry in the Transatlantic Alliance

Considering the stakes and intensity of their previous acquaintance, and the Central European interest in the Indian past and struggle, it is no wonder that several of the European support groups jumped at the opportunity to plan programming with the Native participants of the 1977

Geneva conference. Their good intentions notwithstanding, the European work in fundraising and communication did not always match up with the expectations of the American Indian sovereignty organizations, and vice versa. During the fundraising and planning phase, European support groups and American Indian sovereignty organizations ran into differences about principles, control, and representation. Their miscommunication, differences, and discontents reveal much about the dynamic and challenges faced by the transatlantic sovereignty alliance.

In the planning period of the fall 1977 post-conference tours, the transatlantic alliance for American Indian sovereignty experienced friction in communication. A spat between Ulla Bäcksin of the Swedish Indian League and Claus Biegert and Tilman Zülch of the Society for Endangered Peoples brought to the surface issues of representation amongst the European solidarity groups and a struggle to control the access to the Native delegates from the Western hemisphere after the conference. In their subsequent letters to both the Swedish Indian League ("And think about what solidarity means!") and U.S.-based Indian sovereignty organizations, the leaders of the Society reasserted the primacy of their strategy of working with the churches and their prerogative of planning the post-conference tours over the Swedish League and the AIM support groups.[81] On the other side of the Atlantic, Native activists responded to this inter-European rivalry with surprise and frustration: "[P]lease do not present us with your problems, disagreements, jealousies, that are among your own people. We have many other worries and the most important being the survival of our people."[82]

On the part of the Native organizers, the challenges of planning the actual conference and fundraising were compounded by spotty communication. This occasioned a burst of long letters from both sides, outlining the reasons for why each organization was the supreme leader of the sovereignty movement on its own continent, how much they had sacrificed to make the conference and the tours happen, and rebukes about the lack of organized planning and streamlined communication on the other side of the Atlantic.[83] While in their forceful ways both sides tried to improve communication, to the historian their efforts also convey an anxiety about their position in their respective societies as the leaders of the transatlantic solidarity network. Each in his own way, American Indian activists like Robert Antona of the *Akwesasne Notes* and Jimmie Durham of the Treaty Council also reasserted Native control over the work of the European support groups ("We need people to work *with* us, not *for* us").[84]

Conclusion

This chapter provided an analysis of the solidarity between U.S.-based Native activists and Central Europeans in the transatlantic alliance for American Indian sovereignty. It mapped out some of the motivations and impulses that made for the sometimes contradictory forces of attraction, camaraderie, jealousy, and rivalry in the coalition stretching across the Atlantic. Unfolding against the backdrop of the sexual revolution of the long 1960s, the radical Native sovereignty movement itself was fraught with lopsided gender and sexual relations. The older transatlantic cultural imagery and forms of "playing Indian" both enabled and constrained the late Cold War alliance for Native sovereignty. Central Europeans positioned themselves vis-à-vis American Indians as comrades-in-arms, homosocial companions, but also as subjects of romance and desire. In some instances, Central European solidarity groups even competed with each other for access and good relations with American Indian sovereignty organizations. The transatlantic wing was an extension of the sovereignty movement's continuous struggle for control over the political, social, and cultural representation of Indian identity and goals. Two accounts by Europeans at Wounded Knee offered different perspectives on the difficulties of interracial collaboration between Europeans and Native activists. Over time, Native activists asserted control over "working with" and articulated the limits of "speaking for" American Indians in Central Europe, even when that led to friction.

We have seen how the activists of the radical Native sovereignty movement played around with and reinterpreted older stereotypes of Indians. This included the word and the color "red." Yet their reappropriation of older Indian imagery and discourse went deeper—to the level of ideas and ideology. The next chapter will investigate the relations between the radical Indian sovereignty struggle and Marxist movements and régimes.

5

"Red" Nations

Marxist Solidarity and the Radical Indian Sovereignty Movement

> Also, even though we will be going to the world forums, [. . .] the United Nations, the Organization of American States, the Organization of African Unity, the Arab countries, the communist bloc and whatever is necessary for us to get our treaties in court and would give the world forums a chance to hear us, we must realize what we are into. What we are into is revolution, turning that cycle of life always back. It is the sacred hoop that we are talking about.
>
> —Russell Means, International Indian Treaty Council conference, June 14, 1974[1]

Indians Are Not Red: Marxism and the Moderate Sovereignty Movement

The post-World War Two period inaugurated new assaults on Native American communities in U.S. federal Indian policy. The problematic federal Indian Claims Commission, set up in 1946, aimed to adjudicate and give monetary compensation for land taken from a Native nation—in return for them giving up all rights to pursue their claim in the future. Legislation such as the 1953 House Concurrent Resolution 108 and Public Law 280 aimed to transfer Indian reservations from federal into state jurisdiction, in effect ending the long-standing federal management of Indian affairs. These and subsequent acts, which came to be known as the *termination policy*, abolished the federal status of specific Indian tribes, and aimed to break up and sell their remaining communal lands and pay out the proceeds to former tribal members. Concurrent federal programs like those of the 1956 Indian Relocation Act offered assistance in finding jobs and services to Indians who were willing to move to large urban centers. The termination policy aimed to make American Indians completely assimilate into U.S. society by breaking up their cultural and social organization. Termination withdrew federal recognition of even the kind of "impaired" sovereignty[2] that had been achieved through centuries of Native resistance to European and white U.S. colonialism. Termination thus became a baseline, a kind of legally mandated cultural annihilation, which the Indian sovereignty movement mobilized to avert.[3]

It was likely in response to the federal termination policy that one of the earliest postwar encounters took place between Indian activists and a Marxist régime. After years of futile attempts to gain federal recognition as a separate tribe, the Miccosukee band of the Florida Seminoles decided to outflank the U.S. government. In 1959, a delegation of the Miccosukee visited Cuba, where the revolutionary forces of Fidel Castro and Ché Guevara had achieved final victory only months before. The Seminole activists spent three days in Havana as Castro's "personal guests of honor." While there, the Indians officially recognized the revolutionary government and in turn received Cuban recognition as the "duly constituted government of the sovereign Miccosukee Seminole nation."[4] According to Buffalo Tiger, publicity surrounding their trip forced the U.S. government to take them seriously and offer them concessions upon their return home.[5] The Miccosukee's transnational diplomacy—the performative representation of a domestic minority group to a foreign government while bypassing the home government—prodded the U.S. nation-state to address the demands of the Indians in earnest.[6]

At the same time, whether out of genuine conviction or as a politically expedient strategy, the most influential Indian sovereignty activists of the early Cold War professed a stringently patriotic anti-Communism. Daniel Cobb has documented how the National Congress of American Indians and the Association of American Indian Affairs argued that moving toward greater recognition of sovereignty rights was an integral part of the national struggle against Soviet totalitarianism as well as the domestic counterpart of U.S. aid for third-world economic development.[7] They did this not only to play to the media and reassure the U.S. government of their loyalty. The leaders of Indian Country were themselves divided over the strategies of the sovereignty struggle. In January 1961, the Inter-Tribal Council of the Five Civilized Tribes discussed their participation in the upcoming American Indian Chicago Conference. Here principal chief of the Cherokee Nation and Phillips Petroleum CEO W. W. Keeler recalled his business trip to the USSR the previous fall. There some Russians

> took me aside and explained to me how they would like to work with me [on] plans to set up some *Indian Republics* here in the United States. They talked to me about *freeing the Indians* . . . they had the idea Indians are held as prisoners . . . they spoke of the Indian in leg-irons. They said [their information] came from the reports of the *University of Chicago*.[8]

Keeler's report was followed by a statement by Cherokee General Counsel Earl Boyd Pierce, who cautioned that the Chicago Indian conference could become part of a Communist conspiracy to create not only an Indian state but "an overall Government State."[9] For these Native leaders, the Soviets were not so much expressing their solidarity with the sovereignty rights struggle and offering a transatlantic alliance for the movement as threatening a different kind of government control. Whether because of their own anti-Communist convictions, their investment in U.S. capitalism, or their wariness of the power of the U.S. government, these Indian leaders recoiled from an alliance with Soviet Russia.

Shades of Red: Indians and the Communist Bloc

Native attitudes toward Marxist alliances changed in the next decade. By the late 1960s, the Civil Rights Movement and U.S. counterculture had not only developed radical forms of activism, but also built links with transnational and national liberation movements. The next generation of Indian activists—many of them coming out of the University of Chicago and the University of Colorado–Boulder's workshops on American Indian affairs—saw the sovereignty struggle less in the context of Western democracy's conflict with Communism than as part of a global anticolonial movement.[10] This shift in Native positions opened up possibilities not only for alliance building with the Nonaligned Bloc and third-world liberation movements, but also for overtures to Marxist régimes.

With these new horizons, two kinds of attitudes emerged in the radical sovereignty movement towards Marxism and its manifestations.

Some activists regarded Marxist régimes as potential partners in an Indian revolutionary project. In his speech to the First International Indian Treaty Conference in June 1974, American Indian Movement (AIM) leader Russell Means defined the sovereignty struggle itself as "*revolution*, turning that cycle of life always back. It is the sacred hoop that we are talking about." For this Indian revolution to be successful, some activists will have to be willing to spill blood, and sacrifice their lives metaphorically, or even literally, for the cause. This struggle would involve not only confrontations and lobbying within the United States, but also "going to the world forums, [. . .] the United Nations, the Organization of American States, the Organization of African Unity, the Arab countries, *the communist bloc* and whatever is necessary for us to get our treaties in court and would give the world forums a chance to hear us [. . .]."[11] While Native activists and Marxist states may have shared a revolutionary commitment, for Means, the USSR and its socialist satellites were not necessarily ideological kin, but entities which could be enlisted as political allies in transnational Indian diplomacy.

The other kind of Native engagement with Marxism was exemplified by Roxanne Dunbar-Ortiz, a self-professed Marxist revolutionary, feminist-turned-Indian sovereignty activist, and historian. Dunbar-Ortiz first became involved with AIM when she was in law school in 1973, and after working with the Wounded Knee Legal Defense/Offence Committee became one of the early leaders of the International Indian Treaty Council, the transnational arm of the radical sovereignty movement. Committed to a Marxist revolutionary project of national liberation, Dunbar-Ortiz believed that the Indians of the Americas were part and parcel of the downtrodden working class in each country. She insisted that national liberation movements should include indigenous populations, and that revolutionary régimes should recognize Indian sovereignty rights.[12] Importantly, this Native perception of Marxism called for a deep commitment and mutual collaboration between sovereignty activists and revolutionary movements and régimes.

On the other side of the Atlantic, the contemporary interest of European Marxist groups and régimes in the American Indian sovereignty struggle had a long cultural prehistory. By the middle of the Cold War, the Central European fascination with American Indians had become an ideological battleground, as seen in the symbolic dueling between the West German *Winnetou* movies and the Eastern Bloc's *Indianerfilme*. While the former may have recast the special transatlantic relationship between the United States and West Germany, the latter expounded an ostensible "historical accuracy" and the kind of historical materialism that was a hallmark of Marxism as an ideology.[13] The Central European media coverage of the early events of the American Indian radical sovereignty movement also often depicted Native activists as leftist liberation or resistance fighters.[14]

European Marxist governments soon realized the potential of the radical Indian sovereignty movement for anti-U.S. and anti-capitalist propaganda, and moved to exploit it. The German Democratic Republic's recent official campaign titled "1,000,000 Roses for Angela [Davis]!" had provided one model of German solidarity with U.S. radicals that ideologically spanned the iron curtain.[15] When Davis was acquitted of charges of complicity in an armed assault by the Black Panthers in June 1972, Eastern Bloc officials and their enthusiastic grassroots activists proclaimed victory. The experience of this solidarity campaign still echoed in one East German letter sent to WKLD/OC in 1974, which boasted, "We all know what international solidarity can do, if we think of Angela Davis [. . .]."[16] These solidarity campaigns were themselves transnational performances in which Germans on both sides of the iron curtain articulated an alliance with the radical African-American struggle.

Friedrich von Borries and Jens-Uwe Fischer have hyperbolically observed that by the mid-1970s, the East German government had "ideologically annexed the Wild West" when it officially promoted not only the *Indianerfilme*, but also representations of Indians both as historical victims of capitalist expansion on the American continent and as contemporary international working-class resistance fighters against imperialism and colonialism.[17] Among others, such official promotion manifested itself in newspaper coverage. The visit of an AIM delegation accompanying Angela Davis to the 10th World Festival of Youth and Students in East Berlin in 1973 was covered by the East German government papers in detail. The *Neues Deutschland*, the foreign affairs paper *Horizont*, and the official youth daily *Junge Welt* all featured interviews with the AIM activists, and thereby amplified the messages of the radical sovereignty movement.[18]

> *Junge Welt*: How can the young people of [East Germany] help you?
>
> *Monica Charles:* They can morally support us. This is important for the Indians who are in a very difficult struggle. Whoever wants to help the Indians, can send their greetings of solidarity,

> preferably in English, to this address: USA, Wounded Knee Legal Defense/Offense Committee, Rapid City, SD 57761. This is a committee for the defense of Indian rights. Maybe with your support and the support of other countries, we can again fight against our government for the rights we are entitled to.[19]

For their own part, the Indian sovereignty activists reported back to their North American communities about their visits in the Eastern Bloc and the Nonaligned countries. After their breakthrough at the 1977 United Nations Non-Governmental Organizations International Conference on Discrimination against the Indigenous Peoples of the Americas in Geneva, Switzerland, the activists of AIM and its International Indian Treaty Council fanned out across Europe to build alliances. The November 1977 issue of the *Treaty Council News* carried reports about a trip undertaken in the USSR by Allene Goddard, Bill Means, Greg Zephier, and Bill Wahpepah. In Moscow they met with the Soviet Peace Council, government officials, educators, and the press. The group toured the Kremlin, and two of its members visited the Moscow Ballet. A University of Moscow ethnographer presented them with eagle feathers from Siberia, and they appeared on Soviet TV, broadcast to some 180 million viewers. Next the delegation visited the Soviet Republic of Kazakhstan, where they were impressed with the Kremlin's progressive policies for Kazakhs as a minority "of color." Then the group split to cover several countries simultaneously: Goddard visited the Soviet Republic of Mongolia, while Zephier and Wahpepah went to West Germany for a meeting of support groups from all over Europe.

The same issue of the newsletter carried an account titled "These Countries Believe Strongly in Human Rights," written by Russell Means' then fifteen-year-old daughter Sherry about their trip across Bulgaria, Yugoslavia, Hungary, and East Germany in that same year. In Bulgaria, where they were treated as guests of the government, the sovereignty delegation met with members of the country's Central Committee and the World Peace Council. In East Germany, the Indian visitors learned about the history of "the Sorbs," an ethnic minority whose human rights were now protected under socialism. For Sherry Means, "[t]hat goes to show what a lie the Americans are living" with their anti-Communist propaganda. Although the group had to cut short their trip and forego visiting Greece, Czechoslovakia, Romania, and Ireland because her father had to report to court for a bond violation, Sherry Means had seen enough to conclude that "what I have learned in these countries is that they believe strongly in human rights and for our struggle. They aren't the people to feel sorry for. They have no poverty or competition with each other, and nobody wants to get rich because they all have equal opportunities."[20]

Did the sovereignty activists really believe the official Marxist propaganda given them about minority rights in the Eastern Bloc? There are a number of reasons why they may have reported favorably on the policies of these Communist countries. Even though the visitors and some of their hosts sometimes managed to wriggle their way out of supervision (like at the East Berlin youth festival), state control was likely prevalent and tight on their official trips. This probably did not allow them to experience much on their own terms. The travelers may also have decided to report on their experiences strategically. On the pages of the *Treaty Council News*, they likely wanted to boost the sagging morale in Indian Country[21] with depictions of countries where both political leaders and the people lived in harmony and embraced the causes of human rights and sovereignty. If they were read by government officials in Eastern Europe, these reports would have also endeared the Indian sovereignty movement to them. Favorable reporting on Marxist régimes thus worked both ways across the Atlantic.

A Solidarity Too Much?

Solidarity with the radical Indian sovereignty movement in Eastern Bloc countries was shaped not only by the age-old transatlantic and more recent homegrown images and forms of "playing Indian," but also by the responses of the national governments to the engagement of their own populations with American Indians and other parts of U.S. culture. The paradoxical question these Communist governments faced was how to respond to the kind of social movement that was culturally motivated, facilitated by mass communication, and officially sanctioned by the state–but at the same time was potentially subversive against the government.

This dynamic relationship between the government and the solidarity groups played out in variations of the same theme in different Central European Communist régimes. The young activists of the "Polish Movement of Friends of the American Indians" (Polski Ruch Przyjaciół Indian, PRPI) first gathered at a rally of the Polish Scouts Organization,[22] an officially sanctioned group, which was the Polish equivalent of the Pioneer movement in other Communist countries. Not more than a thousand in number, in a country of 40 million people, PRPI members could write and send petitions to the United States in protest against violations of Native sovereignty; but the Polish authorities banned the sending of packages and they also blocked plans for a "Long March" of solidarity,[23] which could have garnered public attention and boosted membership to make the group a real movement. These measures may not have been as much of an overreaction as they first seem: some of the influential works of Polish juvenile literature and the PRPI activists themselves drew parallels between "the" Indian and Polish character and resistance to foreign domination[24]–just the kind of subversive patriotic ideology that was considered an enemy of internationalist Socialism.

In October 1977, Russell Means and his daughter Sherry arrived in Budapest, Hungary, on a leg of their tour of Socialist countries after the Geneva United Nations NGO Conference on Discrimination against Indians in the Americas. Father and daughter toured Budapest, where Sherry noted the many statues from the past; they visited an orphanage where they learned about the disciplinary system and the various facilities; and they "met two famous Hungarian writers."[25] Their other meetings did not make it into the written historical record, but at least one can be reconstructed from the lore of Hungarian hobbyist reenactors of American Indian cultures.

Hungarian hobbyists had been "playing Indian" in the Danube River valley north of Budapest, where gentleman ethnologist Ervin Baktay had started a dude's Western role-playing group back in the 1920s,[26] and in the Bakony mountains, where since the late 1960s political songster and educator Tamás Cseh had developed his group of friends from teenagers playing cowboys and Indians á la Karl May and J. F. Cooper into "tribes" reenacting nineteenth-century Plains Indian life and warfare. For these young people, the Meanses' visit was a once-in-a-lifetime opportunity to communicate with and be validated by live Indians—and not just anyone, but the leaders of the radical sovereignty movement. For the AIM leader, this meeting was a unique opportunity to start building an alliance with a group of hundreds of potential activists behind the iron curtain.

A few members of Tamás Cseh's Bakony group met Russell Means in Budapest on short notice, unclear about the goals of his visit. Hungarian hobbyist lore holds that Cseh himself may have been at the meeting. To the Hungarians, Means looked powerful but worn—a great man whose enemies had tried to break him. The AIM leader was moved by the intimate knowledge of the Hungarian hobbyists of Native cultures, and he gave them a pipe bag.[27] The immediate goals of performing cultural expertise and sovereign Indianness were met in this event of Native transnational diplomacy. Yet the fact that this initial meeting did not lead to any further solidarity relations between Hungarian hobbyists and the radical Indian sovereignty movement may be surprising at first. The cultural and media landscape of the country was similar enough to that of other Eastern Bloc states. The East German *Indianerfilme* had been playing in Hungarian cinemas. While the Hungarian government did not specifically advocate solidarity,[28] its official youth newspaper mentioned North American Indian causes in an editorial response to the 1973 siege of Wounded Knee, in connection with political song writing and activism, and in an interview with U.S. leftist songster and recent East German resident Dean Reed.[29] Among the Hungarian hobbyists there was a strong identification with the Plains Indians of the past. By the mid-1970s, Tamás Cseh had written an "Indian diary" that would later become his 1997 novel *Hadiösvény (1968–69)* [*War Path, 1968–69*], which begins, "Like the other Plains Indians, *we* [the Lakota] too are hunters of the buffalo [. . .]."[30]

The lack of response on the part of Hungarian hobbyists to Means's overtures has several explanations. Hobbyists active during these years have claimed that they felt that contemporary Indian life and issues were simply too depressing and overwhelmingly hopeless[31]—an intellectual position that may well have been the result of the pervasive trope of "the vanishing native." They also stressed that they were aware of how the sovereignty struggle was being used for propaganda by both the Communist governments and the Western powers, and they did not want to become a tool in this ideological war against the United States[32]—a wise contemporary insight, or a retrospective justification of their activities.[33]

The foremost reason that my respondents gave for their lack of solidarity work was that by the early 1970s the two groups of Hungarian hobbyists had already been infiltrated and disciplined by the Communist state.[34] In the early 1960s the Hungarian secret police planted an informer in the Danube Valley group. Known in the state security apparatus as "György Fung," he posed as a cultural anthropologist in training and impressed his fellow hobbyists with his knowledge about North American Indians. "Fung" gathered information about both the Danube group and the Bakony community of reenactors, and he then testified in the 1962–63 trial of five hobbyists on charges of conspiracy to overthrow the Hungarian state.[35]

Melinda Kovai has analyzed the peculiar dynamic of how one defendant, his covert informer cellmate, and the interrogation officers over time collaboratively constructed this case for the court indictment, conviction, sentencing, and eventual pardon. The various incarnations of introspective confessions, cellmate reports, and officer write-ups included claims about the defendant's relations with American Indian organizations dating back to the 1940s, his vision of being given an Indian identity and mission by Native leaders, and the charge that "playing Indian" was the clandestine and continuous reenactment of the 1956 Hungarian uprising against the Communist régime.[36] As Kovai pointed out, the assumption of the authorities was that there must have been something else behind the hobbyist activities[37]—that "playing Indian" was *more than* playing. Based on their previous investigations of the country's Boy Scouts[38] and religious education under the guise of Indian play, the Communist state was all but certain that hobbyism was a foil for similar "clerical" and "reactionary" activities.[39] They wanted to know how much of the Indian hobby involved homegrown reactionaries, and how much of it was incited and used by U.S. and Western agents. Kovai's insight that behind the Indian hobby the Hungarian authorities perceived only the hand of a foreign power and not the agency of actual American Indians or a legitimate subculture of their own citizens[40] attests to the destructive myopia of a totalitarian state. Like their East German counterparts, these Hungarian hobbyists engaged "American" culture in ways that complicated the official ideologically motivated anti-Americanism of the state.

The case occasioned searches of the homes of sixteen people, the interrogation of fifty-six, the arrest of eight, and the conviction of five.[41] The deterrent effect of these efforts should not be underestimated. The informer "György Fung" kept writing reports on Indian hobbyists as well as other youth subcultures for the Hungarian state security until at least 1975. Like their East German counterpart,[42] the Hungarian secret police was shifting its methods from reactive measures to preventative information-gathering and operations as early as during the 1962–63 trial.[43] This likely led to many cases being "resolved" through operative work before they ever reached the trial stage. While the specific individuals informing on any given group may not have been known with certainty, the mere suspicion that there may have been "bricks" or "moles" in the group itself easily discouraged solidarity work and relations with American Indian organizations.[44] At least one former Hungarian hobbyist claimed that he and his peers knew that they were monitored by state security[45]—whether by "Fung" or others.

According to Tamás Cseh, another event drove home the limits of "playing Indian" as an escape from the grey world of the mediocre bureaucracy of the Communist state.

> We slowly pass through 1968, and I am still walking in place. The Czechoslovak revolution is crushed—the Russian tanks roll over the Indian camp in August, we are down there camping [. . .] We had lived with a hope, a desire for freedom, and '68 was one enormous slap in the face for the whole young generation of Eastern Europe: "This is what you get for hoping!" There is no more hope, because the tanks are rolling in, and you are rolling in with them, because the Hungarians [troops] were part of the invasion of Czechoslovakia.[46]

The vision of tanks rolling over the Indian camp became a trope cautioning the Hungarian hobbyists against overreaching—in this case, against reaching out to the current Native sovereignty struggle.

Across the Border into Canada: Agency and State Control in the East German Solidarity Movement

East German and to a lesser extent Eastern Bloc solidarity with AIM was a convergence of a more general grassroots cultural interest in American Indians and a state sanctioned Marxist solidarity with the radical sovereignty movement. *Kulturbund*, the government-controlled cultural association of the German Democratic Republic seized on the figure of the American Indian as a tool of anti-American propaganda.[47] At the same time as it elevated American Indians, the East German state proceeded to "purge" the Wild West fandom in the country. Cowboys, white pioneers, and frontier people were designated as the "henchmen" of U.S. imperialism. Originally opened in 1928, the Karl May Museum of Radebeul was renamed "Indian Museum" in 1956, and references to Indians killing General George Custer or playing in Buffalo Bill's show were removed from the exhibits. Finally, the Museum was moved to Bamberg just one year before the Berlin Wall was completed.[48] As part of the ideologically correct realignment of popular culture, East German and Hungarian authorities also made sure to remove any firearms from Wild West fan communities,[49] and the former also suppressed cowboy fandom. In response, reenactors of white frontiers-people pretended to impersonate Indians in public, and indulged in playing cowboys in private.[50]

Clandestine cowboy life largely came to an end after some clubs were shut down and others reorganized into Indianist fan circles.[51]

While it lasted, the official condoning of solidarity with American Indians by the East German state facilitated some transatlantic contacts. In his October 1974 letter to WKLD/OC, Andreas Erdmann explained, "In summer 1974, during my holidays—I'm 18 years old and (what you would call) a college student—I had a chance to see the 'Indianer Museum' (i.e., a museum concerned with history and life of the Northern American Indians) at Radebeul near Dresden. There I could increase my knowledge about your life, fight, and culture. There I also found your address."[52] By the mid-1970s, the GDR authorities had refashioned the former "reactionary" Karl May Museum into a center that actually fostered anti-imperialist solidarity with American Indians.

With time, however, the official sanctioning of the alliance between Native sovereignty activists and Eastern European[53] solidarity groups reached its limits. As more East Germans raised money, held teach-ins, collected signatures, and sent petitions to the United States on behalf of AIM "political prisoners" like Leonard Peltier,[54] the Marxist state's secret police moved to keep the solidarity movement under control. After all, it was suspicious enough that thousands of hobbyists studied and reenacted Indian lifeways—an aspect of the culture of the United States of America, a mortal enemy for the past three decades.[55] Whether out of real conviction or as a precautionary measure, some East German hobbyist clubs adopted anti-imperialistic mission statements to conform to state ideology.[56] While official and grassroots arguments may have converged in depicting Indians as allies of the international working class and originally following a kind of proto-Communism as asserted by Friedrich Engels,[57] East German solidarity activists were not allowed to visit their comrades in the United States or other Western countries.[58] However, the ultimate fear of those in power was that solidarity activists would move from demanding sovereignty rights for American Indians to asserting freedom of speech and democratic government under their own Marxist state.[59] The metaphors of solidarity threatened to spin out of control and unleash political demands on the East German state itself.

Sometimes the East German state handled cases of "overzealous" solidarity reactively and at the lower levels of its structure. When, in the fall of 1983, Manfred Unnasch of Stralsund began sending the official East German Socialist Unity Party youth newspaper *Neues Deutschland* resolutions of his recently created Indian hobby group regarding Native sovereignty rights in the United Nations, officials became alarmed. Unnasch kept bombarding the letters section editor with his materials and ideas about more effective solidarity. The ensuing correspondence between the newspaper's editors and officials at the central Berlin office of the *Kulturbund* became increasingly hysterical as they failed to reach the officers of the district where Unnasch's group belonged. What followed were five months of anxious correspondence and phone calls trying to find out more about Unnasch and his group. The matter was finally put to rest when local officers gave Unnasch a talking-to, telling him that his Stralsund group should limit themselves to Indianist projects in the theory, folk arts, and cultural realm, and "should not attempt 'to play Indian.' "[60] In this instance, the very phrase "playing Indian" in German was used at one and the same time as a derogatory term referring to the age-old transatlantic form of children playing cowboys and Indians, and as a formula connoting the performance of solidarity with the contemporary Native sovereignty movement.

East Germans activists who insisted on solidarity work and went "too far" in speech and action experienced social pressure, monitoring, investigations, and reeducation by the Marxist state security.[61] As attested by their security files, the East German authorities usually assumed that doing solidarity work with the current Indian sovereignty struggle were in reality a foil for activities against the state. According to Anja Kunze, the East German state security investigated Indian hobbyists if they had contacts with or requested a permit to travel to the West, were suspected or actual members of churches, or were involved in the environmentalist movement.[62]

One early case that surely contributed to such state vigilance was the attempt of two East German teenagers to cross the Czechoslovak border into Austria in the summer of 1976. Caught by the border guards and taken back to East Germany, the two could have been charged with *Übersiedlung nach nichtsozialistischen Staaten*—"emigration to non-Socialist [Western] countries"—a crime that had carried a death sentence a few years before. During weeks of interrogation and cross-examination, the two teenagers stuck to their story: they had wanted to stay in Austria only until one of them reached eighteen years of age and they could earn enough money to travel to Canada, where they wanted to join the independence movement of the American Indians. They recalled that they had grown up reading Indian novels and that a few years before one of them had also collected petition signatures and sent letters to the

United States. The two young men were convicted of a "severe case" of attempted illegal border crossing, and received a prison sentence of at least one year—suspended with a two-year probationary period.[63]

Whether out of conviction or as a pre-calculated defense, the use of solidarity as the reason for an attempt to flee to the West attests to the agency of these East German youth. Their repeated references to their 1974 correspondence with the American Indian Movement about Wounded Knee and Native prisoners[64] leveraged a solidarity sanctioned by the East German government first as an opening to engage a group in the United States, and subsequently as a defense against punishment by the state—in a way claiming, "we only did what you encouraged us to do." They only "overreached" in their thinking that collecting signatures and sending petitions were not enough[65]—and in their subsequent attempt to personally support the sovereignty movement in the heart of North America. These two teenagers acted on the impulse of Andreas Erdmann of Neuruppin, who in October 1974 wrote to WKLD/OC, "Please tell us, if you know about a more efficient help than collecting signatures"; of Angelika Niebuhr of Rostock, who in February 1975 wrote, "I want to help you! I think, it's not enough, to collect signatures. I want to do more. Please, tell me how can I help you?"; and of Andreas Wollmann of East Berlin, who exclaimed, "When I think about how you fight against the many monopolies, then I really feel like fighting with you on the side of the good, for the freedom you want to have."[66] In this case, however, the identification of the solidarity movement led to an action that violated the laws of the totalitarian state.

The Solidarity of Others through the Eye of the State

Considering the case of the two teenagers, it is not surprising that by the 1980s, East German state security regularly monitored and screened the solidarity correspondence of its citizens with U.S. entities. According to Kunze, the fact itself that an individual or group had such communication was enough to arouse the suspicion of the "Stasi" (the citizens' nickname for state security).[67] In an "AIM-Vorgang" operation[68] that spanned five years between 1984 and 1989, the secret police monitored the activities of an Indian hobbyist group at Fürstenwalde and Berkenbrück, which explicitly worked to support the "fight for freedom" (*Freiheitskampf*) and rights of the American Indians.[69] A Stasi informer claimed that at least one club member was an enthusiastic hobbyist who was frustrated that the state authorities suppressed certain forms of support for the Indian sovereignty movement in East Germany.[70] Besides informers' reports, the investigators also used materials discovered during the screening of the international mail in and out of the German Democratic Republic: "73 letters from various senders to 8 different persons and institutions in the U.S.A." According to the report, two of these were sent to American Indian communities by sixteen people who called themselves "Members of Indian Friends Movement of the GDR," and assured the Indians that in "East Germany" there is both knowledge of and support for their struggle.[71]

The letters and petitions in question were sent to President Ronald Reagan, the Arizona relocation commission director, (as claimed by the senders) the BIA area director, the two senators of the state, and the Big Mountain People at Oraibi, Arizona. They protested against the planned "forced relocation" of the Navajo from the "Joint Use Area" of Big Mountain in Arizona. They pointed out that "[w]hile internationally the US defend human rights, the forced relocation constitutes an act of genocide according to the UN Convention on the prevention and punishment of the crime of genocide [. . .]."[72] The English text of the petitions was most likely received from the West or the United States as a template. The petitions and protest letters were signed at the "first central Indian festival" of East Germany, held in August 1986 in Leipzig—probably a national hobbyist convention. The authorities were alerted because the organizers had not requested permission for the petition drive. The state security file also contains a letter between the Fürstenwalde/Berkenbrück hobby group and an address in West Berlin[73]—another serious concern of the state security was the prevention of relations between East and West Germany.

One of the last reports of the file concerns a 1986 visit of the leader of the Fürstenwalde group to the United States Embassy in East Berlin to use its library for gathering information on the life of American Indians.[74] This was neither the first nor the last time the authorities investigated East German solidarity activists for such a visit. Five different state security files mention at least seven such visits by six people, from early 1982 through 1986.[75] Such exposure, albeit brief, to the "propaganda machine" of the U.S. government was a "red flag," a cause for concern for the East German state, which encouraged its citizens to criticize American imperialism and capitalism, but at the same time did not trust their ability to think critically about the United States.

The state's surveillance gradually extended to the various forums of solidarity relations between East Germans and American Indian sovereignty groups. In 1958, the hobbyists of East Germany began holding an annual council of their clubs, which rotated between the various groups and their club houses.[76] After the solidarity actions of the 1970s such as the campaign to free Leonard Peltier, the activists sympathetic to the sovereignty movement coalesced into groups—and state security probably wanted structures that were more transparent. In October 1983, East German hobbyists met in Dresden and established the "Solidarity Readiness Group of the Indianist Groups of the GDR" (Solidaritätsarbeitskreis der Indianistikgruppen der DDR) to coordinate future campaigns. They laid down ground rules and resolved to designate solidarity officers in each club, who were to meet twice every year.[77]

While the solidarity officer of any given club was supposed to be working on solidarity actions, these activities gradually came to be limited by the state. Borries and Fischer described the case of "Kate," who joined the Cheyenne Indianist Interest Group in 1982 at the age of nineteen, and for the next four years threw herself into corresponding with American Indian institutions, petitioning U.S. officials, and organizing action days for solidarity. Gradually, it was no longer enough for her to have the hobby and the annual one week of Indianist camp festival. She no longer wanted to toe the line—she wanted to actually live "their life." Kate dreamed of a trip to the big cities of the United States. "We had been imprisoned and our rights denied. I wanted out. I felt I had more in common with Indians than with Germans." She applied for a permit to travel, and was registered in her hometown as "Case 127. Application for Emigration 1986." The State Security got wind of this and confronted her and her club leader in the club house. They explained to her that she could best support the Indians through solidarity work in East Germany and not elsewhere. If she tried to convince other club members to attempt to emigrate, she would be expelled from the club. Kate was also demoted from her position as solidarity officer.[78]

Another example uncovered by Borries and Fischer illustrates the dynamic of East German agency and government control. Peter K. attempted twice to flee to Canada, and served two years in prison as punishment. After this experience, in 1974 he established the O-hij-jo club to reenact Mohawk culture. To obtain more information about the Six Nations, K contacted Radio Canada International, which gave him the address of the Akwesasne Mohawk. "We [then] received a lot of materials from the Mohawk, and it was clear that we should return it. We asked how we could help—we could not transfer money." Under K's guidance, O-hij-jo worked around the government ban on sending money, and they used the hobby's central solidarity committee meetings to organize a campaign of sending readymade supplies to Indian survival schools: nails and screws, exercise books, crayons, warm blankets and clothing, and beads from Brandenburg. As a sign of gratitude, the Mohawk honored Peter K. with the name *Wahattoke*—"Understanding." He now felt like a "real" Indian.[79] Over a decade, Peter K. and his fellow East German activists tread a fine line between expressing their solidarity in ways both officially sanctioned by their own totalitarian government and materially helpful to their North American Indian allies, and being punished for violating the norms and laws of the suppressive Communist state.

Even when East German activists managed to leverage the official mandate for solidarity and outflank their own government, their work could be frustrated on the other side of the Atlantic. After the fall of the Berlin Wall, Kate accompanied an Indianist support group from Munich to Pine Ridge. Here she learned that U.S. Customs had withheld part of the aid packages they had been sending the Lakota all those years. Kate was outraged that "[t]his is just like in the [East German] Zone," and she eventually got the U.S. government to release 100 woolen blankets.[80]

State surveillance reached through to the central node of the East German solidarity movement. The "Coordinator of the Solidarity Issues of the Indianist Groups of the GDR" himself informed to the Stasi under the name of "Hans." Through him and various other operations, by 1988 the East German state security gathered information that allowed them to get an overview of both the East and the West German solidarity organizations and their national events; their relations across the iron curtain to other European solidarity groups; and their attitudes and some specific links with American Indian organizations such as AIM, the International Indian Treaty Council, the Navajo and Hopi, and the *Akwesasne Notes*. The secret police investigated East German relations with the West German minority rights organization, the Society for Endangered Peoples (Gesellschaft für bedrohte Völker), which had been organizing and hosting the West German tours of the delegations of the above North American Indian groups since 1977. They also kept tabs on a person in Giessen, West Germany, who was another node of solidarity work between AIM, the Treaty Council, and European organizations like the Swiss International Committee for the Indians of the Americas; *Danai*, the Danish International Work Group for Indigenous Affairs; and the Hopi Work Group of Austria.[81] "Hans" reported on at least one meeting where East and West German activists discussed their hopes for collaboration between the GDR's *Kulturbund* and the

West German Society for Endangered Peoples.[82] This kind of solidarity work with and for American Indians was suspicious to the Communist state precisely because it had a potential to reconnect Germans across the iron curtain.

In addition to informing on central solidarity meetings, and East-West German and European solidarity relations, "Hans" also reported on the visits to East Germany of Indian medicine man and spiritual teacher Archie Fire Lame Deer. A member of the same Lakota Sioux family who had befriended the Austro-German émigré photo-journalist and author Richard Erdoes, Archie Fire Lame Deer had joined Leonard Crow Dog in running annual sun dances in Arizona as the Hopi and Navajo's struggle for Big Mountain emerged as a sovereignty cause in the early 1980s.[83] Lame Deer first went to Europe to attend the Bertrand Russell Tribunal on discrimination against American Indians in Rotterdam, Holland, in 1980.[84] He subsequently toured Europe in the 1980s, making at least three visits to East Germany. According to reports by "Hans," Lame Deer visited the country in April and October of 1983, both times at the invitation of the Peace Council of the GDR. In April 1986, he again spent a few days in East Germany, hoping to return with three other Lakota spiritual teachers in early June of that year.[85]

By this time, "Hans" had all but advanced into the position of chief East German coordinator of Indian solidarity projects, in which the national meeting of the hobbyist solidarity officers would confirm him less than a week after Lame Deer's April 1986 visit.[86] The informer reported that Lame Deer brought with him a lady friend who had to wait at the border for a tourist visa to be issued for her. The medicine man visited East Germany specifically to meet the Indian hobbyists of the *Kulturbund* cultural association. The meeting was hosted by the hobbyist club at Triptis, and it involved a four-day happening with forty delegates from ten different East German groups.[87]

In Triptis, Archie Fire Lame Deer did much in the way of maintaining the solidarity relations with the Eastern Bloc. He thanked the East Germans for their solidarity and expressed hope for their continued support. In order to simplify and streamline the communication system for solidarity and financial support, he asked that each country designate just one person to coordinate solidarity relations. Predictably, "Hans" was named as the East German solidarity coordinator. Lame Deer also described schemes to use organs in the Soviet Union to promote the causes of sovereignty. Through the help of the *Komsomolskaya Pravda*, he hoped that 17 million postcards would be sent to the White House demanding a new trial for Leonard Peltier. He also wanted to invite Mikhail Gorbatchev to the sun dance at Big Mountain, Arizona, to help prevent the forced relocation of the Hopi and Navajo from the Joint Use Area.[88]

Like that of the Hungarian hobbyist informer in the early 1960s,[89] the position of "Hans" as both "grassroots" projects facilitator and secret state observer of the German hobbyist scene was morally problematic. The layers of his role were only compounded by the fact that he was the *coordinator* of transnational solidarity work—the East German node of the transatlantic sovereignty alliance. In this sense, he performed an East German national solidarity with American Indian sovereignty—and at the same time performed a loyalty to the East German state that potentially conflicted with his first role. This facilitator of the transatlantic alliance between the "red nations" was at the same time the watchful eye of the "red" state of East Germany.

A Medicine Man in East Germany

On his part, during his visits to East Germany Archie Fire Lame Deer was performing his own kind of "red" solidarity for Indian sovereignty. His talk at the Triptis solidarity rally was carefully calibrated to satisfy the Communist state—or so a sympathetic "Hans" chose to portray it in his report. Discussing his trips to East Germany a few years later in oral history interviews with Richard Erdoes, Lame Deer recalled his encounters of solidarity in East Germany.

> We went to a May Day parade in Leipzig, and as we stood there in the parade, watching all these Russian tanks and missiles, my son says, "My hair keeps blowing in my eyes, I can't see!" Without thinking, I handed him my knife, and he reached over, and he cut the red flag behind us, but we didn't see him, and he tore off the bottom half of the red flag. And all the generals started to look to see what he was doing, and I looked, and there he was, cutting off the bottom half of the American . . . I mean, the Russian red flag . . . I said, Oh-oh, something is going to happen now. All the people on parade, they were looking at us, the soldiers and everybody, and all the people beyond that, they were very quiet. And I helped him cut off the rest of the flag, and I tied it on his head to hold the hair back, as a head band, and I got an applause

> from the people! And later when the parade was over, the general turned to me, and said, "You Indian people are more red than us!" [laughter] This was his immediate reaction. And it felt good, I could feel the people clapping and everything. Of course, this guy was a Russian general, he was not an East German general, he was a Russian general.[90]

As guests of honor of the East German state, the Indian visitors were standing with the generals and party cadres on or near the parade tribune. Yet as Lame Deer's slip of the tongue shows, they still performed a mischievous Indianness that poked fun at the nation-state, whether it was the United States, the German Democratic Republic, or the Soviet Union. In addition to the protest counter-commemorations of the American Indian Movement, Native concepts such as the Ojibwa/Anishinaabe practice of "violating" the white laws by exercising Indian off-reservation hunting and fishing rights,[91] or the contrariness of the Lakota Sioux "heyoka" holy clowns[92] may help scholars understand both the actual behavior and the way they were seen by spiritual leaders like Lame Deer. Most importantly for this context, the Indian boy with a headband had been a stock image of the transatlantic forms of "playing Indian"—immediately recognizable to the East Germans and the Soviet general. Thus, whether intentionally or unwittingly, Lame Deer and his son ended up manipulating the transatlantic stereotype of American Indians, and thereby actually made a statement about solidarity among "red" nations across the Atlantic and the iron curtain.

In his 1986 interview with Richard Erdoes, Lame Deer recalled a meeting with an East German official which resulted in mutual understanding of the shared conditions that made for solidarity between East Germans and American Indians.

> While we were [at the hobbyist encampment], the first day we had a visitor. He was the defense minister of East Germany. He came to the tipi and he knocked on the tipi, and my son and I were sitting inside, we [were] expecting him, we had coffee made and sitting there. And he walked in, and he said good morning, "Guten Morgen." And immediately, my son said "Danke schoen," thank you very much. And the defense minister said "Bitte schoen," you're welcome. And my son answered back "Auf wiedersehen," [*Erdoes laughs*] good bye. And the defense minister sat down, and he looked at me and

> he said in perfect English, "There are many people I would like to say that same thing to, "auf wiedersehen." Right away, the defense minister and I got acquainted.
>
> We discussed world affairs inside that tipi [*Erdoes*: Tell me about that.] About his feelings of the Indian people over here, and themselves, being under the rule of the Russian people. The feeling that they had towards the way they were living today. [*Erdoes*: He was open about that?] Yes, he was very open. [*Erdoes*: He must have trusted you.] [There were] two or three people with us. He trusted me as I would trust him. I trust all people until proven otherwise. [*Erdoes*: And he didn't look upon the Russians as the Great White Father, so to speak?] No, no, I imagine it was because I immediately opened up as an oppressed people of the American people. We are oppressed regardless of what the BIA Indian would say. [. . .] So in the process of all this talking to him of how we were oppressed, he sympathized with us, and he said that the country of East Germany everywhere is open to you, you can come and go as you please, anytime, you and your people can come and go whenever you want to, and you will be treated like you've never been treated in America.
>
> [. . . *Erdoes*: And he indicated that—East Germany was also an oppressed country?] He mentioned the fact that East Germany, "like you, we are in the same boat, we are oppressed just like you." So there is a feeling there, when he left, he said, "Your fight is my fight." And the reason why he said this was, "How long will you come to East Germany?" And I mentioned the fact that "I will come until your fences fall down. Until you two countries are united, and long before that. After that, I will come. I will come, and I will see your fences fall down." And then he turned to me, and he said, "Your fight is my fight. Maybe together, we can make the fences fall down."[93]

The hobbyist tipi—itself a prop for East German Indian play—now served as a space for dialogue in the Central European contact zone. In Lame Deer's understanding, he and the East German official related their shared experience of oppression by a dominant group and its government, and made common cause against the imperialism of the two superpowers. The scene is reminiscent of both the treaty negotiations of the early

(U.S.) national period and the earlier Native contact zone diplomacy of the colonial and revolutionary era.[94] As far as it can be reconstructed, the actual event was a transnational performance of solidarity for sovereignty. Its recall in Lame Deer's oral history interview with Erdoes was itself a collaborative performance that reaffirmed the spiritual leader's original commitment to the people of East Germany.

In his travels, Lame Deer also became mindful of the disadvantages and trappings of collaborating with the Eastern Bloc governments. His description of being tailed by security services echo Russell Means' memories of various U.S. and communist intelligence services bugging his car.[95]

> Of course, you might get in the process of being caught in the trap of one of the governments, by the government asking you to, that they will fund your trip and everything else, and by doing that you are jumping into the pocket of the socialist government. So you have to know exactly what you're doing at all times. We are, many times when we leave, when I leave the East Bloc countries, I'm followed for four days by the KGB, the counterpart of the CIA, they follow me throughout the places where I go to make sure that I don't go to any American embassy, because I see a lot of sensitive information [. . .].[96]

Archie Fire Lame Deer tried to tread a fine line between being co-opted by the East German government for purposes of anti-U.S. political propaganda, and risking being denied access to the people of East Germany, who he wanted to encourage for solidarity and support of the American Indian sovereignty movement. Aware of the dangers, for much of the 1980s he kept traveling, building solidarity relations, and teaching Europeans about Native American spirituality in the Central European contact zone.

The file named after the informer "Hans" was never officially closed—history in the making prevented that. After the Berlin Wall was breached in November 1989, the East German people broke into the buildings of the Ministry of State Security, chanting "No more spying!" Today, the surveillance files of the former East German secret police are kept in a complex of archives—providing citizens with information about their past, and scholars with insights into the relationship between the East German state and the transatlantic solidarity alliance.

Other constraints on the transatlantic solidarity movement were gradually imposed by the Indian sovereignty activists themselves. Retaining control over the movement was a major concern for Native Americans, who for centuries had been dictated to by U.S. government officials and Euro-American reformers in making and implementing policies for their own communities. In September 1975 the sovereignty activists established the Native American Solidarity Committee (NASC) to coordinate "Non-Indians [who] are mobilizing in the support of the American political activists in prison or facing trials [. . .], are taking up the defense of Native American land rights and struggles for political power; and are opening broad discussions on the relationship of the Native American struggle to the class struggle and other oppressed nationality struggles in the U.S."[97] Employing a leftist if not fully Marxist rhetoric, the NASC at the same time attempted to broaden the radical sovereignty coalition and to retain Native control over non-Indian solidarity work.

Nationally, Indian activists educated Euro-Americans about why and how to stop "playing Indian,"[98] and how to make performances and representations of Indians legitimate.[99] Asserting and maintaining Native control over the movement outside the United States proved to be even more challenging. With new solidarity groups and organizations cropping up across and beyond the Germanic countries of Central Europe,[100] it was a daunting task to keep the struggle from turning into a movement of European Indian reformers instead of an alliance for Indian sovereignty rights.

Glenn Penny has investigated how the eventual arrival of Native American voices changed the discourse of Indian authenticity in Germany.[101] In addition to solidarity work, another field of such Native interventions was the European interest in American Indian spirituality. Lakota medicine man Archie Fire Lame Deer[102] spent much of the 1980s touring Europe, and he visited East Germany in 1983 and 1985, educating audiences about Native American approaches to religion and society. In his lectures, workshops, and sweat lodge ceremonies, Lame Deer encouraged and successfully persuaded some East German enthusiasts to look for local spiritual traditions instead of trying to "play Indian."[103] In some instances however, the European propensity to "go Native" elicited more forceful edicts from North American Indians. When European hobbyists wanted to reenact the Sioux sun dance outside Munich in the mid-1980s, AIM-affiliated Native medicine men forced them to call off the event. In his later teachings, Lame Deer used this incident as a narrative argument for not only separate but equal spiritual practices, but also for discontinuing European involvement in the Indian sovereignty movement.[104]

Conclusion

Indian sovereignty activists and their allies attempted to reconfigure the ideological geography of American Indian sovereignty into a fully independent Native America that was to be in alliance with revolutionary Marxism and its own "red" nations around the globe. For their own part, Native activists tried to leverage their developing solidarity relations with Marxist groups and régimes into moral, political, and material support for the sovereignty movement. In turn, Marxist totalitarian governments faced the challenge of how to control a culturally rooted and officially sanctioned solidarity with American Indians among their own citizens. Eastern Bloc states responded with a variety of measures that included co-optation, surveillance, and reactive and preventative suppression and punishment of those who "overreached" in their zeal for solidarity. Even with such measures of state control, efforts by Native activists and Eastern Bloc solidarity groups led to meaningful encounters and some understanding of common causes. Other limits on the transatlantic solidarity alliance were articulated and imposed by American Indian spiritual leaders and sovereignty activists themselves.

While solidarity with groups in Marxist régimes and movements was a major feature of the radical Indian sovereignty struggle, their cause came to its fullest with their participation in the United Nations. How did American Indians come to play a role in the UN? How did they articulate their sovereignty rights in the world body? The next chapter will document the history of American Indian participation in the United Nations.

6

A Trail of New Treaties

Performing American Indian Rights at the United Nations

> We started [marching] from across town, our elders leading the way—Phillip [Deere], carrying the pipe, Leon and Audrey Shenandoah from the Six Nations, David Monongye, a Hopi who had seen more than one hundred winters, and several elders from South and Central America. Right behind them came the drum. We sang the AIM song. As they always did, Indian people flocked to it, filled with pride and spirituality, infused with courage and the feeling of sovereignty, 120 marchers representing the aspirations of a hundred million oppressed but resolute souls. [. . .] UN security people opened the double doors [of Geneva's Palace of the Nations], and we marched up the stairs with the drum, singing all the way to a second-floor conference room where world leaders have met for more than a century.[1]
>
> —Russell Means, *Where White Men Fear to Tread*

The International NGO Conference on Discrimination against Indigenous Populations in the Americas at the Palace of the Nations in Geneva, Switzerland, in September 1977 was both the culmination of a long history of American Indian transnational diplomacy and the beginning of a new phase in the transatlantic alliance for Native American sovereignty. Growing out of a rather informal network of groups, media, and events, the transnational relations of the American Indian rights movement were eventually institutionalized in the indigenous rights régime of the United Nations.

This institutionalization was the result of a series of performed interventions made by Native activists in efforts to build transnational alliances and put pressure on the United States government from the outside for a more progressive Indian policy. In their responses over time, United Nations officials gradually worked with Native activists to accommodate their causes in the world body. I argue that this dynamic relationship resulted in the "channeling" of American Indian sovereignty demands, not into a process of decolonization, but into the UN forums on human rights. Accordingly, the concept of Native North American sovereignty was gradually refashioned from a notion that encompassed *national independence* into that of *indigenous human rights* with political and legal autonomy. The reasons for this transformation lay in historical precedent, the influence at the United Nations of the idea and actual power of the nation-state, and the developing alliances between Native activist organizations and UN officials. The "new" mechanisms for indigenous rights—the UN Commission on Human Rights and the Working Group on Indigenous Populations—did not preclude the effective pressuring of national governments by these transnational activists, but this required careful alliance building, and was limited in its results.

Wounded Knee 1973 and the United Nations

It is clear from the historical record that by the early 1970s, North American Indians had been not only monitoring but also approaching the United Nations through petitions and even personal visits. Back in the 1920s, Deskaheh's personal lobbying for the admission of his Iroquois Six Nations to the League of Nations was greeted with popular support and sympathy in Geneva, but his efforts were rebuffed by the power that Canada and Great Britain wielded in the world body. Nevertheless, on his trip the Haudenosaunee leader exercised his right to travel on his own tribal passport (itself a recurrent performance of Indian sovereignty), used the Native memory of treaty making as an historical argument for sovereign status, and left a memory of goodwill at the seat of the world body.[2] As Daniel Cobb has pointed out, by the 1960s, the discourse of the new generation of U.S.-based Native sovereignty activists was transnational in the sense that they saw their struggle less as a U.S. domestic cause than in the context of decolonization around the world.[3] Between 1970 and 1972, various Native nations like the Chippewa/Ojibwe, the National Indian Brotherhood of Canada, the Iroquois Six Nations, and a coalition of blacks, Hispanics, and Indians again petitioned and traveled to the United Nations with their grievances. These efforts were all, in effect, aimed at placing Native rights outside of U.S. and Canadian jurisdictions and into the field of international affairs.[4] However, it was the 1973 siege of Wounded Knee which finally catalyzed the American Indian rights movement to undertake a concentrated and sustained effort to raise international support for sovereignty, one major forum of which was the United Nations.

"A Place Where We Can't Go any Further"[5]*: The Constraints of Nationalism*

As early as one week into the occupation, the American Indian defenders of Wounded Knee sent a delegation to the United Nations in New York City. By design or following advice, the group sought out the "Secretariat," the office of Secretary-General Kurt Waldheim. At noon on March 2, 1973, they met "chef de cabinet" or Chief of Staff C. V. Narasimhan. The Native delegation was comprised of the American Indian Movement's "roving ambassador" Vernon Bellecourt,[6] Chief Oren Lyons of the Turtle Clan, Onondaga Nation, Chief Waterman, Louis Papineau, Myron McClairy (all residing under the same address as Lyons, which links them to the Six Nations Iroquois Confederacy), and Doreen Menchini of the American Indian Community House, Luckchoe, New York. Narasimhan's handwritten notes, taken during the meeting, and his typewritten report, based on his notes,[7] yield insights into how these American Indian activists performatively claimed Native sovereignty at the United Nations.

In their meeting with Narasimhan, the Native American delegates used several performative forms from American Indian traditions of treaty-making. "Before initiating the discussion, Bellecourt asked me to join the group in a minute of prayer."[8] While Narasimhan's report does not indicate what language the prayer was in, or what it entailed, the move itself may have functioned to establish a connection between those praying together—performatively making them kin, as some Native treaty ceremonies had done.[9]

"Chief Waterman referred to the Two Row Wampum Belt which represented the undertaking that the two forms of government, namely the Indian and U.S., would be parallel and avoid mutual entanglement and involvement." In his handwritten notes, Narasimhan added Waterman's conclusion: the "U.S. should live up to this treaty." The notes also contain a sheet of paper with a drawing (likely by Chief Waterman) of the "Two Row Wampum Belt—Treaty belt between our nations and the white brothers who came to our shore."[10] Here the Iroquois leader visually described an object similar to the wampum belt which Deskaheh took from the Museum of the American Indian back in 1922 to explain Six Nations sovereignty at the League of Nations. It is reasonable to assume that as Chief Waterman was explaining the treaty's principle of "parallel and equal," as visual illustration he was using his drawing of the belt, an object embodying that principle. In this, he was decoding a document taken from the archive to reassert Native sovereignty through a performance of American Indian historical memory. The drawing features the name "Mr. C. V. Narasimhan," possibly as a performative claim made by Chief Waterman on the UN official as an ally.

Even as the American Indian leaders outlined the specifics of their requests, they were placing their grievances in the larger context of U.S. and Canadian Indian affairs, and the colonialism of other settler societies. Vernon Bellecourt first expressed his hope that the siege of Wounded Knee would call "national and *international* attention" to the "popular revolution" happening in Indian communities. He then recounted how the U.S. Bureau of Indian Affairs had created and propped up corrupt puppet tribal governments on Indian reservations, like the one at the center of the Wounded Knee standoff. The previous year's occupation of the BIA headquarters in Washington, DC, was another demonstration against this state of affairs, and both events were proof that there was real broad-based support for this American Indian movement. Bellecourt concluded by explaining that some 371 treaties were signed between the U.S. government and Native nations, which the government had been violating. U.S. capitalists had been exploiting Indian mineral resources, such as Phillips Petroleum in Oklahoma. In turn, Chief Oren Lyons reminded Narasimhan that American Indians were "a sovereign people." Besides the United States, the governments of Canada, Mexico, and a number of Latin American countries had likewise signed treaties with their native populations, and had been "systematically" violating those agreements. More forcefully, "Mr. Bellecourt also drew attention to the genocide that was systematically taking place of Indians in Central and Latin American countries. He wanted to know what the United Nations was doing about it."[11]

Chief Oren Lyons and Louis Papineau used the examples of the Northeast tribes to explain how Native sovereignty had been violated. According to Papineau, the Iroquois Confederacy made a treaty with the United States federal government as early as 1788. The state of New York had been violating such treaties by refusing to return to the tribes some twenty-eight documents, and by keeping the mandated annuities paid to them at 1788 levels. Another example of treaty violation was the denial of free transit across the U.S.–Canadian border to the Six Nations who lived there. The interference of the U.S. government with Native religion, culture, and language, Lyons concluded, could not be tolerated anymore.[12]

According to Lyons, the Native movement had exhausted all recourses available within the nation-state. "The Indian people had no one to turn to except the United Nations, which was based on humanitarian principles. The Indian people were the victims of their own humanity to their white brothers. They appealed to the UN for justice and freedom and a friendly hearing. He claimed that those in the room represented millions of their Indian brothers." Vernon Bellecourt explained that they "wanted the leaders of the movement to be able to address the Security Council and to ask for UN Observers to be sent to places like Wounded Knee, where Indian lives were in jeopardy. He also wanted to be allowed to address the General Assembly, to report that their minerals had been stolen and that they should be allowed to protect their rights against U.S. Government and the tribal chiefs who were the Government's puppets."[13]

Even as they were noticeably different in the forcefulness of their approaches—Bellecourt's militancy contrasting with Lyons' respectful entreaties—the Wounded Knee delegation linked their cause to the larger issue of treaties between American Indian populations and national governments in the colonial settler societies of the Americas. In this, they were attempting to put the indigenous rights of the Western hemisphere, a humanitarian issue transcending the nation-state, on the agenda of the United Nations. Narasimhan's note that Chief Lyons "claimed that those in the room represented millions of their Indian brothers,"[14] attests to a powerful performance of the delegates' bodies standing in for Native communities across the countries of the Western hemisphere. This was a performative representation of Indian sovereignty at an event of transnational diplomacy.

Narasimhan responded to the Native presentation by claiming that he was allowed merely to relay the communication to the Secretary-General, and that the Secretariat itself "had no authority to bring these matters to the attention of either the Security Council or the General Assembly. That could be done by a Member Government. I also drew attention to Article 2 paragraph 7 of the Charter." The chef de cabinet was using a document from the archive of the United Nations to justify his own performance as representing the United Nations.

Narasimhan's response to the American Indian leaders was concerned with why procedure did not allow for the consideration by the United Nations. Article 2 paragraph 7 of the United Nations Charter of 1945 prohibits the international body from "intervening in matters which are essentially within the domestic jurisdiction of any state or [. . .] requir[ing] the Members to submit such matters to settlement under the present Charter."[15] Based on this answer, as an institution comprised of member (nation) states, the United Nations did not have a way to accommodate transnational issues raised by groups that did not go through a nation-state's UN representation. According to Narasimhan, neither his own standing as "only a Civil Servant in the Secretariat," nor the purview of the cabinet of the Secretary-General allowed for anything to be done about the request. The chef de cabinet did not share anything about the powers of Waldheim to pursue the issue in other ways, for example by bringing it to the attention of the Security Council based on Article 99 of the UN Charter.[16]

> Replying to this point, Chief Lyons said that the Indians were a sovereign people, although their territory was surrounded by the United States. They wanted to know what the procedure was if they to apply for membership of the United Nations in their capacity as a sovereign people. I told them that the procedure for such applications was for them to be dealt with by the Security Council in the first instance and by the General Assembly on its recommendation. At their request, I provided them with copies of the Charter of the United Nations.[17]

In light of the information Narasimhan had just given the group about UN procedure, Lyons's suggestion was logical. If only a member state can bring such an issue to the United Nations, then American Indians should pursue membership as a nation-state. Obtaining member-state status was also in keeping with the developing goals of the American Indian rights movement. However, Narasimhan's explanation that such a membership request could be handled only by the Security Council did nothing to demystify the workings of the UN—it did not clarify *how* a membership application *could* reach the Security Council. Instead, he gave copies of the UN Charter, an archival document, to the delegates, to use as a script for their performances of Native diplomacy.

While Narasimhan claimed that his primary responsibility in the matter was to inform the Secretary-General about the meeting, it is remarkable that likely even before he did that, and only hours after the event, he "informed Ambassador Tapley Bennett, Deputy Permanent Representative on the Security Council at the United States Mission, of the substance of my conversation with the representatives of the American Indian community at 6.45 p.m. on 2 March. He was grateful for the information I gave him."[18] Here, the chief of staff to the Secretary-General of the United Nations seemed to put aside his allegiance to the international body in favor of transmitting his report along national lines. In its documents and embodied repertoire, the United Nations broke down along the ideology of nationalism, which prioritized the nation-state as the organ of power and engine of this body.

"Nixon Fell Apart at the Knee!": Crossing the Line at UN Plaza

The standoff at Wounded Knee dragged on. Even when the defenders were not facing another deadline with the threat of a full-scale invasion by the FBI and U.S. marshals, they were strafed with deadly gunfire, which claimed several casualties on both sides. These life-and-death confrontations were punctuated by continued negotiations between various levels of the U.S. government and the defenders. Several agreements were brokered but then fell through, and the parties blamed each other. Even as those in the village were drawing on their cultural and spiritual resources to hold out, they were also using their social, ethnic, and activist networks to keep their struggle in the public mind and increase pressure on the federal government to accede to their demands.

In early May of 1973, AIM and the Oglala made another push to enlist the United Nations as an ally in their cause. Native, white, and black sympathizers held benefits and rallies to support the struggle at Wounded Knee in several cities of the United States, the most remarkable of which was a demonstration at the United Nations in New York City on May 4, 1973. It was at this event that the performers of American Indian sovereignty rights not only pushed the boundaries, but literally transcended the U.S. nation-state.[19]

The Native demonstration took place in the place now called UN Plaza, in front of the United Nations Headquarters in New York City.

Running parallel and adjacent to the UN complex is First Avenue, here divided in the middle, and carrying dense traffic in both directions. The pedestrian walkway between the fence of the UN compound and the street is but a few feet wide. The narrowness of this walkway would have made it difficult to hold a demonstration without monopolizing the space for foot traffic.[20] As Richard Erdoes's photographs attest, the demonstrators were further corralled by wooden road barriers painted "Police line—do not cross."

Even as they were hemmed in by barriers and police officers between the traffic of New York City and the fence of the United Nations compound, the protesters used their space creatively to perform political statements about the cause of Wounded Knee. In addition to marching between the barriers in both directions parallel to the UN fence, the activists also hung some of their signs on the barriers, and leaned or sat on them. Richard Erdoes used his skills of photo-journalism to amplify and dramatize this performance. One of his pictures shows a middle-aged protester wearing a cowboy hat, leaning on the barrier with his hands holding in place a sign draped over the bar, with the words "Nixon fell apart at the Knee!!!" Another photo features a long-haired demonstrator wrapped in the U.S. flag, leaning against a barrier with his back to the camera. In both images, an American Indian is standing between the two lines of barriers, which bear the words "Line" and "Police," suggesting that these human beings are literally being corralled, and by transference reminding the viewers that American Indians have been confined to the narrow spaces of the reservations. At the same time, the human figure wrapped in the flag likely expresses patriotism and identification with the nation-state that had marginalized this group, thus creating a tension. As the flag-draped body of the Indian protester critiques the body of the nation-state, so does the phrase "Nixon fell apart at the Knee" conjure up the body of the president of the United States falling over as his legs give way. As visually suggested by Erdoes, these demonstrators were pushing against the "line"—the limits of the nation-state—and they were reconfiguring the body of the United States by asserting that Nixon as national leader and Indian policymaker failed to stand on Wounded Knee.[21]

Switching sides in space but not in mind, Erdoes took another tension-ridden photograph—this one of a police officer leaning on the barrier with one hand, the other in his pocket, looking in the direction of the street, while just behind the barrier ("Police Line") stand a row of Indian protesters, in effect forming their own cordon, facing the United Nations buildings.[22] Juxtaposing the police officer standing in for the law of the nation-state, looking inward as he is bodily supporting the United States, and the Native demonstrators looking to the United Nations for assistance in forcing the nation-state to open their confines. Erdoes masterfully captured the essence of this Native American protest performance.

Erdoes was mindful to show the parts of the UN demonstration beyond the marching. Many of his photos in the series are taken from a higher point on the UN side, where leaders such as Oren Lyons, Mad Bear Anderson, Eddie Benton Banai (all in Six Nations regalia), and Clyde Bellecourt (in Native-inspired folksy clothing) congregated and directed the event. Four images show Bellecourt, Anderson, and others standing in a circle and looking inward, suggesting a drum circle.[23] Drumming and singing over the noise of the traffic passing by would have strengthened the spirit of the demonstrators and also drawn the attention of any UN workers in the buildings adjacent to the protest. This is another early example of the revival of drumming, a Native cultural form, for performances in the ethno-political repertoire of the American Indian rights movement of the late Cold War.

The champions of Wounded Knee would not be contained. A photo providing a wider pan around the figure wrapped in the Stars and Stripes also reveals that at least one protestor had already crossed to the UN side of the barrier. Three other shots show several more people standing on the UN side of the wooden police corral. In the sequential context of Erdoes's original contact print, these images show the demonstrators gradually loosening their corrals and spilling over the police line to the side of the United Nations buildings.[24]

Performing Petitions of Sovereignty

The second half of Erdoes's photographs of the event, corroborated by United Nations reports, helps to flesh out how the American Indian performance eventually transcended the U.S. nation-state and reached into the United Nations as an international forum and territory. The pictures on the second contact print sheet show Ojibwe AIM leader Eddie Benton Banai, wearing a fringed buckskin shirt and flanked by an Indian and an African-American activist, ascending some steps, then standing by as his black companion gives an interview.[25] A close comparison of the image with pictures taken by the author during a walkthrough of the site confirms that the rails of the steps in the original photo are those of the steps of the visitor entrance of the United Nations.[26] This means that at least three Wounded Knee demonstrators managed to enter the premises of the United Nations, having crossed from U.S. legal jurisdiction to international territory.

A member of this Native delegation had called ahead to speak with Chef de Cabinet C. V. Narasimhan, but—because it concerned the placing of American Indian issues "on an international plane"—the call was put through to the UN Office of Legal Affairs.[27] Subsequently, "this morning [of May 4, 1973 . . .] a delegation of five American Indian Chiefs who were among a number of Indians demonstrating outside the Headquarters Building [. . .] were admitted to the building by the Chief of Security and Safety Section, Mr. Trimble, for the purpose of presenting the communication."[28] The UN officials' moves of directing the phone call and delegation to the Office of Legal Affairs seem to contradict their earlier statements to the press corps that the Secretary-General and his Secretariat would not seek legal advice on the Indian appeals.[29] At the same time, the fact that Trimble allowed the Indian delegation to enter the UN Headquarters premises was a victory for the Wounded Knee demonstrators. A decision by an official of the international organization overrode the rules of U.S. traffic and law enforcement, and allowed Native activists to transcend the limits of the American nation-state.

Named by the documents in the delegation were Onondaga Oren Lyons and Sioux Meredith M. Quinn, accompanied by New York lawyer Omar Ghobashy. In the United Nations compound, the Native activists had an audience with UN Legal Counsel Constantin Stavropoulos. "[R]eturning from discussions in Washington where they believed they had obtained come measure of sympathetic understanding," Lyons and Quinn first explained that based on their historic treaty relationship, the United States is a guardian of sovereign Native nations. Then they asked the legal counsel if there was any way for the American Indian communities to raise their issues with the United States at the forum of the United Nations. Predictably, Stavropoulos responded that Article 2 paragraph 7 of the Charter prevented the UN from addressing a topic "essentially within the domestic jurisdiction of any State."[30]

However, the UN legal counsel went further by reminding the Indians that they had "the right of individual petition to the Commission on Human Rights, a procedure which the members of the delegation informed him they were already pursuing."[31] From the institution's point of view, this was a favorable outcome, and the report's closing paragraph reflects an attitude toward the Native petitioners that can in turn be read as either benevolent or rather complacent and paternalistic.

> The entire interview was a very harmonious one, lasting for over an hour, the delegation appearing to understand the difficulties in the way of presenting their case on a full international plane. They appeared to be pleased that a senior official of the United Nations had agreed to see them, and they mentioned that they might wish at some later date to meet again with Mr. Stavropoulos to discuss their problems and give their views.[32]

That same day the American Indian delegation also had a meeting with "Mr. Lawson and Mr. Moller of the Division [of Human Rights]" in the office of Trimble, the head of UN security. Here they were to present a petition to UN officials. "They did not bring a written communication with them, but dictated it after the procedures for handling such communications had been made clear to them.[33] Faced with the UN's archival rule requiring them to submit their appeal in writing, the Native delegates performed their petition of sovereignty by dictating it on the spot. Their performance is imprinted in the document titled "Petition by the Six Nation Iraquois [*sic*] Confederation Agency on behalf of the Indians of the Oglala Nation," which was later attached to the United Nations file on Wounded Knee.[34]

In the petition, addressed to both the Secretary-General and the chairman of the UN Commission on Human Rights, the Six Nations offered their services in resolving the dispute at Wounded Knee, and requested that, as a "humanitarian measure," the UN intervene to provide free access for the media, food, medicine, and spiritual and legal counsel to those in the village. Among the further demands of the defenders were the withdrawal of the U.S. military from Wounded Knee, and "the removal of censorship" of the Indian side of the siege.[35]

"The Chiefs requested that their communication should be drawn to the attention of the Secretary-General, as an urgent matter, as soon as possible. We will deal with the communication under the procedures set out in the relevant resolutions."[36] After two months of lobbying by American Indians and prodding by its press corps, the United Nations seemed to be trying to accommodate Native sovereignty rights, even if anxiously following procedure. Having officers from the UN Human Rights Division meet the Indian demonstrators was in line with Narasimhan's March 9, 1973 note that he would direct any further such inquiries to that office,[37] and attests to ongoing UN efforts to channel the issue of American Indian sovereignty into the field of human rights.

This is important in that it reveals not only a choice in embodied procedure, but also a rhetorical move: instead of being raised in the Security Council, in the General Assembly, or in the Decolonization Committee, any of which would have had far-reaching implications, American Indian sovereignty was being framed at the United Nations as human rights.

From "Independence" to Indigenous Rights: Institutionalizing the Radical Native Sovereignty Movement

Following repeated petitions and delegations to the UN in the early 1970s, the June 1974 First International Indian Treaty Council conference adopted a program of transnational diplomacy for sovereignty rights, including a sustained engagement with the United Nations.[38] In that same month, Jimmie Durham of the International Indian Treaty Council (IITC) initiated the process of gaining status in the UN Economic and Social Council.[39] After three years of correspondence, meetings, and submission of paperwork, in May 1977 the world body finally granted the IITC Category II nongovernmental organization observer and consultative status[40] under the Economic and Social Council (ECOSOC), the counterpart of the UN General Assembly in the social and economic realm. This NGO status opened the door for the Treaty Council and its peer organizations[41] to attend and participate in the annual sessions of the United Nations' Commission on Human Rights, and its subsequent Working Group on Indigenous Populations (established in 1981, first convened in 1982).

In her article on the UN Working Group on Indigenous Populations, Andrea Muhlebach pointed out that "[l]ike all [transnational activists], indigenous delegates have had to negotiate over time and agree upon the purposeful frames, effective symbols, and discursive strategies that have now come to characterize the transnational indigenous movement and its discourses."[42] Gaining access to the United Nations indeed carried a price for the radical sovereignty activists. This price was the transformation of some of the movement into a nongovernmental organization with a structure that was recognizable and transparent for the United Nations offices that would grant it access to the world body. At least on paper, the International Indian Treaty Council had to have a governing board, bylaws, statements of finances, and regular reports about its activities. With three years of hard work, Jimmie Durham and his fellow volunteers produced this structure and met the attendant UN requirements.[43]

A more subtle but very serious price of UN access for the movement was scaling back their discursive concepts of sovereignty. We have seen how, in these years, movement leaders and their lawyers grappled with and refined their concepts of Native sovereignty.[44] In his correspondence to gain status with the United Nations, Jimmie Durham had now to resolve the contradiction between aiming for Indian independence and becoming a nongovernmental organization. Only four months after the lawyers of the Treaty Council discussed independence as their ideal status for native nations, Durham submitted to the UN NGO Committee the sovereignty movement's June 1974 *Declaration of Continuing Independence*. On June 13, 1975, UN NGO Council Affairs Officer Lola Costa sent a handwritten note to "Mr. Marcella" of the UN legal section.

> This is a delicate matter where I would need your advice. Please have a quick look at the "Declaration" attached herewith and let me know if you feel that this org.'s goals are in conflict with Article 2.7 of the [UN] Charter.[45] This is a strong declaration yet Mr. Durham's 16 March letter is clearly [. . .] explicit—making a strong argument for admittance as an NGO. Though they would fit more under the title of "sovereign nature nations." [. . .] Is it possible to reply at this late date and not sound as though we're purposely putting them off?[46]

Costa was seeing the *Declaration*'s goal of attaining a sovereign nation status as a possible violation of the UN Charter's clause on nonintervention into the "domestic" matters of its member states. Marcella likely concurred, for on June 19, 1975, Lola Costa wrote to a lawyer of the Treaty Council,

> Particular attention should be drawn to page 4 of the Declaration [. . .] where it is stated that "The International 2nd Treaty Council established by the conference is directed to make the application to the United Nations for recognition and membership of the Sovereign Native Nations." It would seem doubtful, to me, that the Committee on Non-Governmental Organizations will consider native nations as non-governmental organizations. Furthermore, I wish to draw your attention to the fact that membership in the United Nations is limited

> to independent sovereign states. I suggest that this aspect of the declaration be clarified before the application is received by the Committee.[47]

Costa was grappling with the correct UN category for native nations as well as to see how the goals of the Treaty Council conference were guiding the nature of the organization she was negotiating a UN status for. At the core of Costa's misgivings was the principle stressed by Andrea Muehlebach—that "manifestations of self-determination [. . .] always imply a people's right to determine its political status freely, including the right to secede."[48] Costa and other UN officials were trying to make sure that this potential of the radical sovereignty movement would be suppressed or at least effectively contained in the UN forums and mechanisms that they would have access to.

Jimmie Durham responded to the issue by finessing the Treaty Council's mission. On June 27, 1975, he wrote to a "Mr. Rizzo" that

> The [Declaration] was merely a declaration and was not drafted by lawyers in precise legal language. The declaration does not fit within the definitions of the constitution, by-law, or annual report, nor is it considered as any of the above by the Treaty Council.
>
> The Treaty Council has not made application for membership as Nations nor does it have plans to do so. The only decision it has made is to persue [*sic*] its goals, i.e., to create an interest in, to gather and disseminate information concerning, and to develop and implement mechanisms for governments to honor treaties made with Native American tribes and Nations, and to advance their struggle for human rights, freedom, dignity, independence, to combat colonialism, and to foster and nurture Native American culture and pride therein. As part of its effort to achieve these goals the Treaty Council has decided to apply for non-governmental status with the Office of Public Information, recognizing that the exchange of information in educational, social, and human rights fields, and in combatting racial intolerance and colonialism will help both the Treaty Council and the United Nations. This is the only form of recognition the [T]reaty Council is seeking—that of an NGO.[49]

In these responses, Durham was trying to reconcile the bold plans of the *Declaration of Continuing Independence* with the realpolitik-driven application strategy that the Treaty Council was pursuing with the United Nations. His goal was attaining UN status through the mechanism most readily and easily available for the Treaty Council—a process that was still taking three years of work. Durham's maneuver in effect strategically abdicated the radial Indian sovereignty movement's reach for independence in order to acquire it access to the United Nations. Thus, in the UN mechanism, the radical sovereignty struggle was transformed from a movement with a national liberation potential into a nongovernmental organization dedicated to indigenous human rights.

Performing American Indian Sovereignty at the 1977 UN NGO Conference

By the spring of 1977, UN officials in certain key positions had decided to help open a way for the representation of indigenous populations in the world body. Since 1972, Ecuadorian UN ambassador José R. Martínez Cobo had been working on a "Study of the Problem of Discrimination against Indigenous Populations" commissioned by the United Nations' Sub-Commission on the Prevention of Discrimination and Protection of Minorities. According to Roxanne Dunbar-Ortiz, Cobo had been convinced to propose the Study by the UN human rights secretariat's Augusto Willemsen-Diaz, who was motivated by his growing concern for the Maya communities in his native Guatemala. Through Cobo's ongoing study and directly, Willemsen-Diaz placed indigenous issues as a category on the UN human rights agenda.[50]

Dunbar-Ortiz claims that by the mid-1970s, Cobo's study was languishing without annual reports due to a lack of interest and political will among the members of the Sub-Commission, who were all closely associated with their own national governments.[51] This suggests that their closeness to the ideology of the nation-state made them reluctant to support a study the results of which would have challenged national governments over their treatment of Indians and other native communities.

While Williemsen-Diaz and Martínez Cobo were working on the inside, American Indian activists worked on the outside to open doors. Dunbar-Ortiz credits the Treaty Council's Jimmie Durham with building relations while living in Geneva, and gradually convincing international organizations such as the World Council of Churches (where his wife Ann had worked), the World Peace Council, the Women's International League for Peace and Freedom, and the International Commission of Jurists to sponsor a conference on Indian issues at the United Nations.[52] On September 20–23, 1977, the radical sovereignty movement held its breakthrough Non-Governmental Organizations International Conference on Discrimination against the Indigenous Peoples of the Americas in Geneva, Switzerland.

The conference was attended by representatives affiliated with thirty-eight different "international organisations," including the above sponsors, human rights organizations such as Amnesty International and the International Federation for Human Rights, youth movements such as the World Alliance of YMCAs and the World Federation of Democratic Youth, professional bodies such as the International Organisation of Journalists and the Union of Arab Jurists, women-focused associations like the International Federation of University Women and the International Council of Women, faith-based groups such as the Lutheran World Federation and the Muslim World League, international organizations such as the Afro-Asian Peoples Solidarity Organisation and the International Movement for Fraternal Union among Races and Peoples, and indigenous rights groups such as the Scandinavian-based International Work Group for Indigenous Affairs and the Canadian-based National Indian Brotherhood. Indigenous delegates participated from Argentina, Bolivia, Canada, Chile, Costa Rica, Guatemala, Ecuador, Mexico, Panama, Paraguay, Peru, Surinam, Venezuela, and the United States. In addition to the above countries, national governments sent representatives from Australia, Columbia, Cuba, Czechoslovakia, Denmark, France, the German Democratic Republic, Hungary, Iraq, Italy, Israel, Jamaica, Mauritania, Morocco, the People's Republic of Mongolia, the Netherlands, Norway, the Syrian Arab Republic, and the Arab Republic of Yemen. The Palestine Liberation Organisation was listed as a separate non-state entity.[53]

Native North American participants included the leadership of the Six Nations Iroquois Confederacy (Leon Shenandoah, Oren Lyons, and others) and the "United States" delegates (including AIM and Treaty Council leaders and core members Russell Means, Phillip Deere, Larry Red Shirt, Pat Bollanger, Clyde Bellecourt, Allene Goddard, and Roxanne Dunbar Ortiz, and the Institute for the Development of Indian Law's Robert T. Coulter). On the European side the participants included the volunteers and leadership of the Swiss International Committee for the

Indians of the Americas (Incomindios); the Swedish American Indian League; the West German Society for Endangered Peoples (Gesellschaft für bedrohte Völker); the Netherlands Action group for North American Indians, and—although he was not on the official list of participants—journalist Claus Biegert.[54] Many additional Native participants were listed as "observers"[55]—a category which provided them with access, if not with full conference privileges.

The conference was organized by the Special NGO Committee on Human Rights of the United Nations Sub-Committee on Racism, Racial Discrimination, Apartheid and Decolonization. Several of the above NGO representatives had also been officers at the Sub-Committee and now took a leading role in the conference—for example, Edith Ballantyne, the general secretary of the Women's International League for Peace and Freedom, and the president of the conference of NGOs in Consultative Status with ECOSOC, became the conference chair. The other UN offices attending the conference were the Human Rights Division, the UN High Commissioner for Refugees, the UN Institute for Training and Research, the International Labour Office, and UNESCO.[56]

Constructed for the League of Nations in the 1930s in Ariana Park overlooking Lake Leman, the Palace of the Nations is a monumental and imposing complex of buildings connected by gates, halls, and corridors.[57] Its individual buildings include the ECOSOC Council Chamber, the Assembly Hall, the Library, and the conference facilities building, which houses both smaller and larger conference rooms, as well as the Bar Serpent lounge. The entrance way to the Palace is a complex of successive outdoor and inner courtyards, anterooms, and gateways, which, along with the carefully landscaped park grounds, positively evoke an eighteenth-century palace with its "power gardens."[58]

The Native delegates opened the conference with a march on the Palace of the Nations. Considering that there were over 100 Indian participants, this required some planning. Means's memoir reveals that it was AIM leader Clyde Bellecourt who suggested the performance: "We're going to march on that building, all as one, singing our sacred songs. We're going up there proud of who we are."[59] Contemporary photographs and the author's personal walkthrough[60] suggest that the march took the Avenue Giuseppe-Motta to the Square of Nations (Place des Nations), crossed the square, and entered the Palace through the Gate of the Nations, which is the official entrance, adorned by two rows of the flags of the member states. The double doors Means referred to were likely at the end of the inner courtyard where the Gate led to the entrance to the ECOSOC Council Chamber building.

> We started [marching] from across town, our elders leading the way—Phillip [Deere], carrying the pipe, Leon and Audrey Shenandoah from the Six Nations, David Monongye, a Hopi who had seen more than one hundred winters, and several elders from South and Central America. Right behind them came the drum. We sang the AIM song. As they always did, Indian people flocked to it, filled with pride and spirituality, infused with courage and the feeling of sovereignty, 120 marchers representing the aspirations of a hundred million oppressed but resolute souls. [. . .] UN security people opened the double doors [of Geneva's Palace of the Nations], and we marched up the stairs with the drum, singing all the way to a second-floor conference room where world leaders have met for more than a century.[61]

These outdoor spaces were designed to inspire and successively increase awe for the power of the United Nations. Means's description of marching through these successive stages reinterprets the effect and tells of an increasing sense of momentousness, dignity, and power that the marchers brought to, as much as received from, the buildings and their history. The sight of the many Native delegates wearing regalia signaling their tribal belonging, carrying sacred objects such as pipes and fans, and hearing their singing and drumming echo off the walls[62] must have greatly increased their own sense of recognition and victory. At other times, the European photographers and journalists milling around the marchers with microphones and portable recording equipment would have appeared as gawkers and white media people trying to cheapen the occasion. Here however, together with the UN officials watching the march and occasionally mingling with the delegates, they likely confirmed the importance of the event. Journalists included Claus Biegert and Tilman Zülch of the Society for Endangered Peoples, and UN officials included conference chairwoman Edith Ballantyne.[63] In addition to the drum, the fragile physique and dignified presence of Hopi elder David Monongye provided a center for the gathering. This march was repeated at the opening of the 1981 International NGO Conference on Indigenous Peoples and the Land, but this time the marchers took up the whole width of the avenue.[64]

In her article on American Indian transnationalism, Shari Hundorf uses David Wilkins's definition to drive home the fact that Native American communities "are *nations* in the most fundamental sense of the word. That is, they are separate peoples inhabiting specific territories that they wield some governmental control or jurisdiction over."[65] The 1977 march and subsequent conferences of the Indians of the Americas in Geneva were a performed diplomatic assertion of their status as nations different from but equal to the nation-states that created and sustained the United Nations. Even if only through assuming the form of "non-governmental organizations," the "red nations" of the Americas now were present at a major forum of the nation-states of the world, and they could not be ignored.

In a break of the conference, Greg Zephier, Ted, Bill, and Russell Means, Phyllis Young, and other young activists held a picturesque photo op at the globe sculpture, *The Celestial Sphere*, in a reflecting pool on the palace grounds.[66] Here the group posed for several shots, including one with their right fists in the air, and another one in which one young woman struck the same Red Power pose, while another put her hand behind the poser's head, her index and middle finger extended to form a victory sign or two feathers in her hair[67]—the AIM Indian profile on patches, flags, and letterheads. With the globe in the background, this visual arrangement physically performed a global victory for the American Indian sovereignty movement.

Both the conceptual design of the gathering and the large number of attendees—which was in the hundreds—necessitated that the delegates hold breakout sessions where they worked in a variety of committees in several conference rooms.[68] The vast majority of the photographs of the sessions of the 1977 conference, the 1981 conference, and the meetings of the UN Commission on Human Rights and its Working Group on Indigenous Populations—the latter two annually held through the end of the Cold War—show rather similar settings: committee members sitting at their desks designated by name plates or tags, speaking into microphones, occasionally standing and using some visual aids to illustrate their oral interventions.[69]

The UN indigenous conferences' visual record also reveals how sovereignty activists were doing crucial work outside the halls of power. Claus Biegert's discerning camera recorded views of the corridor outside the conference rooms where most Native delegates, NGO, UN, and national government representatives took their breaks, and where they could mingle and have conversations off the record. Three of his shots show Native Hawaiian activist Hanuani Kai-Trask lobbying a white man in a suit and tie, and a white woman wearing glasses, sitting in the corridor by the window, and one captured Roxanne Dunbar-Ortiz in a similar setting in 1983.[70] These were the same spaces where 1992 Nobel Peace Prize winner Guatemalan Quiché Indian Rigoberta Menchú lobbied and built alliances. One of the most powerful embodied experiences of such UN spaces was described by Roxanne Dunbar-Ortiz, who at the 1981 Human Rights Commission session met relatives of the disappeared of several South American countries.

> The Serpentine Lounge next to the conference room where the Commission met was full of these wounded and traumatized people. I saw them and for the first time I fully realized that the UN human rights organizations were a matter of life and death, and not simply talk and bureaucracy.[71]

For Dunbar-Ortiz, the survivors of the South American disappearances were embodied witnesses to the importance to her work at the UN Commission on Human Rights. The power of the embodied presence and voice of these witnesses and the indigenous representatives at the United Nations are not to be underestimated—they engaged in lobbying and other forms of pressure on national governments throughout the rest of the Cold War.

An Archive for the Repertoire of Native Sovereignty: The Indigenous Peoples' Documentation Center at the United Nations

According to anthropologist Andrea Muhlebach, "[a]n overview of these [hundreds of indigenous interventions made before the UN Working Group on Indigenous Populations] reveals a remarkable consistency in the cultural political arguments made by indigenous delegates since their emergence on the global scene."[72] This was as much a result of the years of discussions and strategizing among delegates and between them and UN officials, as it is a product of the work of a group of European volunteers, who over time built up a logistical base for the annual visits of Native representatives at the United Nations.

Before and during the gathering, the Indian participants of the 1977 conference—among them the Treaty Council's team[73]—identified the need for office space and secretarial services for Native delegations in Geneva. Relying on the interest generated by the conference as well as previous indigenous causes like that of the Yanomami in Brazil,[74] the following year the Swiss pulled together a volunteer base from university and other circles. The group, soon to be called The Indigenous Peoples' Documentation Center (henceforth doCip), was for the next decade or so a foster child of the United Nations. The doCip was given an office in the Palais Wilson, but they received no funding for their activities, their facilities had no heating, and they had to work hard to convince UN officials to even give them a photocopying machine.[75]

While some of the doCip volunteers may have been influenced by older transatlantic romanticized notions about American Indians,[76] they were committed to serving them, which required building and maintaining trust with indigenous organizations like the International Indian Treaty Council and the World Council of Indigenous Peoples. The doCip tried to steer clear of the politics of indigenous representation at the United Nations. For the first decade of their existence, they eschewed funding from member state governments, which was a difference and a point of friction between the above two organizations. The doCip leaders knew that state funding often came with strings attached, and that such money was used to censor indigenous speech—like when the Assembly of First Nations presented on Canadian Indian rights in an international forum, and the Canadian government punished them by cutting their funding. Nor did doCip expand into publicity, for fear of "folklorizing" and commercializing the causes of their Native clients.[77]

As a "paper secretariat," doCip did not produce any tangible product. Instead they provided services in drafting, translating, copying and storing documents. Their policy has been to listen to the requests coming from indigenous delegations and complying with those they could reasonably satisfy. The doCip provided the paperwork, but they did not advise indigenous delegates about the actual sessions—that was to be the learning experience of the representatives themselves.[78]

The doCip has been at the same time a logistical base and archival depository for the indigenous delegations at the UN. Their files contained manuals on the UN's human rights mechanisms, obtaining consultative UN NGO status, and the current drafts of the major indigenous UN projects, such as the "Declaration of Principles for the Defense of the Indigenous Nations and Peoples of the Western Hemisphere," which was drafted during the 1977 conference, and subsequently served as the basis of the *Declaration of Principles for the Rights of Indigenous Peoples*[79] drafted between 1985 and 1993 by the Working Group on Indigenous Populations, and adopted by the UN General Assembly in 2007.[80] Until most of the doCip office files were destroyed by fire in 1988, they also contained the drafts of José R. Martínez Cobo's "Study of the Problem of Discrimination against Indigenous Populations," which had been deposited there by its instigator and drafter, the UN human rights secretariat's Augusto Willemsen-Diaz.[81]

To use Diana Taylor's Performance Studies framework,[82] the doCip has been serving as an archive for the performances of Native rights by indigenous delegates at the United Nations. The manuals, drafts, and previous statements which current delegates have been able to access at the doCip have in turn informed the performance strategies of their own written submissions and oral interventions in the Commission on Human Rights, the Working Group on Indigenous Populations, and the post-Cold War UN indigenous rights forums. Some of these performances by indigenous delegates have been recorded and deposited in the doCip archives—and have in turn served as scripts to choreograph new embodied interventions for indigenous rights. Thus, the doCip's archive and the indigenous delegates' performance repertoire combined to make political claims for the rights of Native Peoples at the world forum of the United Nations.

One embodied link between these archival documents and the performances for Native sovereignty rights was the person of Augusto Willemsen-Diaz, whose concern for the Maya in his native Guatemala originally prompted him to advocate for an indigenous rights mechanism. In addition to being the chief instigator, drafter, and promoter of Martínez Cobo's "Study of the Problem of Discrimination against Indigenous Populations," Willemsen-Diaz is also credited for training a number of Native delegate-activists in how to use the UN mechanisms to their advantage.[83] Roxanne Dunbar-Ortiz recalls that Willemsen-Diaz had orchestrated the Study

> until Native Americans arrived in 1977 to assume responsibility for their own liberation. During the following decade before he retired, Augusto transferred his vast knowledge of UN/NGO workings to us, and some of us, including me, trained others, and that is how our numbers multiplied and we became an unlikely force within the UN's immense bureaucracy and influential among its many member states.[84]

Thus, Augusto Willemsen-Diaz was an important node not only in the transatlantic sovereignty alliance, but to use Joseph Roach's Performance

Studies framework, he was an early link in the "genealogy of performances"[85] by Native delegates at the United Nations. A decade before the doCip and the Treaty Council started giving workshops on the topic,[86] Willemsen-Diaz was transmitting the embodied practices of transnational diplomacy—lobbying, alliance building, and drafting and performing interventions for indigenous rights—through personal mentoring on and off "stage."

Strange Bedfellows[87]: Ideology and "Red" Alliances in the United Nations

In contrast to the Carter White House's engagement with the United Nations, the Reagan Administration refashioned the role of the UN in U.S. foreign policy. This presented challenges for the radical sovereignty movement's activities in the world body. According to Roxanne Dunbar-Ortiz, ending with the 1981 Human Rights Commission session, NGOs were allowed to make 15-minute oral interventions and could also submit written statements for each of the dozen or so agenda items, with assistance in drafting and translation by UN services. The Reagan White House withheld some U.S. dues from the UN, while it earmarked others for non-human rights UN initiatives, which led to the elimination of these NGO privileges due to "budgetary considerations."[88] The loss of these opportunities directly affected Native sovereignty activists' ability to performatively claim rights for their indigenous constituencies.

Dunbar-Ortiz condemns the Reagan Administration for "forging human rights into a hammer rather than leaving the Commission" on Human Rights.[89] Scholars have argued for and against the "turnaround thesis"—that the White House did not really engage with human rights in its foreign policy until late in Reagan's tenure—and some asserted that the administration actually used human rights in a strategic manner.[90] Blaming the U.S. government solely for the increasing politicization of human rights in the Commission in this period would overlook the motivations of various other state and non-state actors in using the issues to further their own goals. However, as it will be discussed below, it is clear from Dunbar-Ortiz's memoir that the Reagan Administration utilized the topic of indigenous rights in and outside of the United Nations in its efforts to destabilize the Sandinista régime of Nicaragua.

For the sovereignty movement, much of the work in the United Nations involved lobbying and alliance building for keeping issues on the agenda and passing resolutions and recommendations. According to Roxanne Dunbar-Ortiz, the Socialist Second World's propensity to support Third-World initiatives in the UN prompted Indian activists to build alliances with Third-World countries, as well as their more radical national liberation organizations such as the African National Congress, the Pan-African Congress, the Southwest Africa Peoples Organization, and the Palestine Liberation Organization. In addition to winning Third-World states—whose 77-member bloc wielded serious voting power in the UN—there were a few other countries the support of which held the key to accomplishing any major task in the world body.[91]

> In those days [the 1980s], getting Sweden, Yugoslavia and the nonaligned countries together was a dream combination for winning in the UN (except for the Security Council) because the socialist bloc would never oppose anything supported by the nonaligned countries, and the European states would support Sweden and Yugoslavia, both of which were considered neutral. But the Reagan administration opposed nearly everything, including the existence of the U.N.[92]

The 1981 creation of the UN Working Group on Indigenous Populations (WGIP) was the work of just such diplomacy and alliance building. Theo van Boven, the head of the UN Human Rights Division—who had also opened the 1977 NGO conference—had privately informed Dunbar-Ortiz that "if anything were to be developed for indigenous people within the UN system, it would have to emerge from this meeting"—the August 1981 session of the Sub-Commission on the Prevention of Discrimination and Protection of Minorities. With permission from the Treaty Council, Dunbar-Ortiz and Wally Feather first drafted a petition by the NGOs for the creation of a working group with no term limits and a broad mandate, open to indigenous groups outside of the United Nations. With NGO signatures, the petition was then circulated among the Sub-Commission member states, who were also lobbied through back doors by van Boven. After a few hiccups, the Sub-Commission passed the resolution to create the Working Group—in the absence of the United States representative. According to Dunbar-Ortiz, this was a historic commitment "to creating international law machinery for dealing with Native Americans and other indigenous communities."[93]

As a result of preexisting ties and relationships as well the continued efforts to out-maneuver the United States, the UN human rights body witnessed the emergence of a peculiar alliance between radical sovereignty activists and Marxist régimes and organizations. The unspoken agreement seems to have been that while the Native American representatives defended the revolutionary régimes against U.S. and other Western criticism, the Marxist and nonaligned representatives would support American Indian initiatives and criticize the indigenous rights record of the U.S. government. This was especially true in the case of AIM member Leonard Peltier, who had been serving consecutive life sentences in the United States since 1977 for the shooting of two FBI agents. From 1978 onwards, the IITC raised Peltier's and other political detainee cases in the Commission's annual meetings, while representatives from Cuba, the USSR, Syria, or Afghanistan blasted the United States for its poor record of human rights for blacks, Latinos, and Indians.[94]

On at least some occasions, such alliances yielded some successes. At the Commission's 1981 session, the Treaty Council tried to refute U.S. charges about a "shipment of Communist arms to El Salvador leftists," who included indigenous groups. At the same time, the IITC called for more pressure on Chile because of the indigenous land rights abuses of its rightist government. Next, the Treaty Council and the Syrian Arab Republic both expressed concern about the treatment of Leonard Peltier, who they considered a political prisoner of the United States. Syria threatened that it was willing to pursue the issue through to the UN General Assembly. Whether as a result of their intervention or a coincidence, Peltier's solitary confinement was rescinded a few days after the session.[95]

The commitment of Indian activists to this alliance with Marxist régimes for indigenous rights could be seen as either admirably persistent or foolhardy. As late as in 1989, Tony Gonzales of the International Indian Treaty Council not only pursued the case of Peltier, but also defended Cuba's human rights record on the floor of the UN Commission on Human Rights. In return, the representative of Cuba spoke out on behalf of American Indians and urged a UN investigation of human rights in the United States.[96] This dynamic was part of the swashbuckling "resolution wars" of the United States and Cuba, neither of which usually managed to pass a motion to have the other one investigated.[97] To the chagrin of the United States and its allies, Indian sovereignty activists and Marxist representatives built and maintained a transcontinental "red" human rights alliance in the late Cold War.

After years of repeated lobbying and petitioning, the arrival of American Indian delegates in the United Nations revitalized the world body's languishing attempts to accommodate these transnational groups in the Americas. José R. Martínez Cobo's "Study of the Problem of Discrimination against Indigenous Populations" was finally published in 1982, a whole decade after it was commissioned. First created during the 1977 NGO conference, the "Declaration of Principles for the Defense of the Indigenous Nations and Peoples of the Western Hemisphere" went through several incarnations and subsequently served as the basis of the *Declaration of Principles for the Rights of Indigenous Peoples*[98] drafted between 1985 and 1993 by the Working Group on Indigenous Populations, and adopted by the UN General Assembly in 2007.[99] Created in 1981 and convened for the first time the following year, the UN Working Group on Indigenous Populations (WGIP) opened the door wider to indigenous rights organizations both vying for UN NGO status and not affiliated with the word body.[100] The broad mandate of the WGIP and the increasing number of participating indigenous groups gradually developed this forum into the Special Rapporteur on the rights of indigenous peoples (2001–),[101] the Permanent Forum on Indigenous Issues (2002–),[102] and the Expert Mechanism on the Rights of Indigenous Peoples (2007–).[103] Together, these mechanisms now function as an indigenous rights régime in the United Nations, studying, reporting, and advising about indigenous issues around the world, and using their supranational status to pressure national governments to improve their treatment of Native peoples and respect their rights to self-determination—the right to define their own political status, including through forms of full integration or autonomy in another nation-state.[104] The development of these forums with their many indigenous, UN, governmental and other NGO participants redefined the terms and the scope of the discussions from "Indian" to "indigenous," from "nations" and "people" through "populations" to "peoples." These mechanisms, however, could not have been created without the hard work, bravery, and persistent embodied transnational diplomacy of the American Indian radical sovereignty movement of the late Cold War.

Conclusion

This chapter provided an account of how the radical Indian sovereignty movement gained entry and participated in the United Nations in the Late Cold War. The spring 1973 siege of Wounded Knee catalyzed the UN outreach of the champions of sovereignty rights. In their appeals, petitions, and demonstrations, Native activists temporarily transcended the U.S. nation-state as they sought to place their demands in the world body. However, in the early 1970s the United Nations could not accommodate transnational issues such as Indian sovereignty because it functioned in a framework of nation-states. In order to be able to gain UN NGO status, in their subsequent transnational diplomacy the radical Indian sovereignty movement scaled back their demands for a decolonization process and recast them as a crusade for indigenous human rights.

The 1977 International NGO Conference on the Indians of the Americas in Geneva, Switzerland, was a breakthrough for the sovereignty movement and it inaugurated an indigenous presence at the United Nations that continues to this day. The needs of the conference and the subsequent indigenous delegations to the world body resulted in the creation of the Indigenous Peoples' Research and Documentation Center, which came to serve as an archive for Native repertoires. The late 1970s saw the development of a peculiar coalition at the United Nations between the radical Indian sovereignty movement, various Nonaligned countries, national liberation struggles, and Marxist states and movements.

Mapping the transnational relations of the radical Indian sovereignty movement must include the most powerful player: the United States government. Just how easy was it for Indian activists to "leave the American sector"? How did the U.S. government react to their international organizing? The next chapter will be a survey of the U.S. government's responses to the transnational movement for Native sovereignty.

"Pehriska-Ruhpa of the Dog Band of the Hidatsa tribe of Native Americans." Illustration by Karl Bodmer for Maximilian zu Wied's *Travels in the Interior of North America in the Years 1832 to 1834.*

The cover of Karl May's 1893 edition of *Winnetou I-III*.

Dennis Banks (right) talking with Claus Biegert, preparing for an AIM conference in 1982, Minneapolis. Courtesy of Dick Bancroft and Claus Biegert. Photo archive of the Gesellschaft für Bedrohte Völker, Göttingen, Germany.

Demonstration in solidarity with those inside Wounded Knee, held in UN Plaza of New York City, May 4, 1973. Photos by Richard Erdoes. The Richard Erdoes Papers. Courtesy of the Yale Collection of Western Americana, Beinecke Rare Book & Manuscript Library.

American Indian Movement delegation posing in front of the United Nations' *The Celestial Sphere* statue at the 1977 United Nations International NGO Conference on Discrimination against Indigenous Populations in the Americas, September 20–23, 1977, in Geneva, Switzerland. Courtesy of Claus Biegert and Gesellscahft für Bedrohte Völker. Photo archive of the Gesellschaft für Bedrohte Völker, Göttingen, Germany.

7

States of Control

U.S. Government Responses to the Transnational Sovereignty Movement

> If Indians are killed, we can surely expect sharp and widespread foreign condemnation of this U.S. government action. It would come at a particularly unpropitious time, giving Arab governments an excuse to fog up the terrorist issue.
>
> —United States Information Agency cable, spring 1973[1]

Containing a Contagion: The U.S. Government and the First International Indian Treaty Council Conference

The U.S. federal government's responses to the First International Indian Treaty Council held in June 1974 may be in part anecdotal, but they are nevertheless indicative of a general attitude that ranged from dislike to blacklisting, surveillance, and persecution. According to AIM leader Russell Means, on the first day of the conference, a federal Health Service expert announced that he confirmed a case of hepatitis in the gathering. The publicity of the infection forced a number of high profile delegates, including United Nations observers, to cancel their participation. On site, the immune booster shots soon ran out, and the health inspector threatened quarantine. When confronted with a request for a culture from the original patient, the doctor admitted that he had misdiagnosed the case.[2] This incident may have been simply the work of an incompetent doctor—or it was a planned maneuver to derail the gathering with the threat of disease spreading at the event. The federal government may have used the specter of literal contamination to contain the spread of ideas and best practices in the transnational movement for Native sovereignty. The United Nations observers' cancellation was probably a severe blow to the conference organizers' goal of putting their event and organization on an international plane.

Another instance of governmental interference in the matters of the conference involved the U.S. court system. As has been established by both scholars and veterans of the sovereignty movement, after Wounded Knee 1973 the federal government embarked on a policy of prosecution against any and all AIM members regardless of the foreseeable outcome, in order to tie up the movement in court, and to deplete their funds.[3] At the trial of the leaders of Wounded Knee in 1975, Louis Moves Camp testified for the prosecution. He alleged that, through Communist agents disguised as news crews, the AIM occupiers of Wounded Knee had received support from countries such as Italy, Germany, the USSR, Czechoslovakia, and China. Moves Camp also claimed that at the First International Indian Treaty Council gathering, Communist agents in attendance offered Russell Means money, ammunition, and weapons.[4] Although his testimony was soon discredited and stricken from the record for undue FBI involvement,[5] Moves Camp's charges are revealing about how the federal government attempted to make Indian activists and conference organizers appear "alien" to the body of the nation-state even as its officials insisted that all Indians properly belonged under United States jurisdiction—and as such they should be tried in U.S., not international, courts.

"Operation Bicentennial": Transnational Indian Diplomacy, Historical Memory, and National Security in 1976

Scholars and veteran activists have discussed the domestic campaign of the United States government against the American Indian Movement through police action and litigation.[6] While I cannot provide a complete account of U.S. government responses to the radical sovereignty movement's transnational diplomacy, a few specific measures are worth discussing here, because they involved the commemoration of the U.S. Bicentennial.

The U.S. Bicentennial celebrations were supposed to be a respite for a country weary of social and political strife and economic difficulties.

The Vietnam War, by many regarded as a mistaken commitment to a controversial conflict in a faraway country, had ended in U.S. withdrawal and the dramatic fall of Saigon, but not before it tore American society apart. The assassinations of political leaders like John F. Kennedy and Robert Kennedy and Civil Rights Movement icons Martin Luther King, Jr. and Malcolm X had sown disillusionment among liberals, youth, and African Americans, some of whom were turning to militant radicalism in organizations like the Weathermen and the Black Panther Party. Revelations about and the subsequent investigation of President Richard Nixon's role in the break-in at the Watergate building became a sinkhole that not only precipitated Nixon's resignation, but led to a national crisis of faith in the character of holders of high office.

By early 1976, the relations between the radical Indian sovereignty movement and the U.S. government had also reached a low point. Since the deadly standoff and firefights of Wounded Knee 1973, the confrontations, however sporadic, had even increased in intensity. On June 26, 1975, after an FBI car drove onto the Jumping Bull Ranch of the Pine Ridge Reservation of South Dakota, a firefight ensued. When the dust settled, one Indian and two FBI agents were dead. In the following months, U.S. federal authorities arrested Dino Butler and Bob Robideau, and conducted a manhunt for AIM leader Dennis Banks on charges from Wounded Knee and previous activities. After having been on the run for over seven months, in February 1976 Leonard Peltier was extradited from Canada to the U.S. government.[7] That same month, the dead body of AIM activist Anna Mae Aquash was found on the Pine Ridge Reservation—a delayed autopsy revealed that she had been shot at point blank range. By early 1976, the U.S. federal government was prosecuting AIM in the courts, and hunting its leaders as armed and dangerous. Both the federal authorities and the Indian activists were on edge.

As the FBI surveillance of AIM continued, the language of the agency's reports evolved, not only criminalizing the organization, but reaching a pitch near hysteria. In late May of 1976 the Director of the FBI sent a memo to, among other agencies, the Deputy Attorney General's Analysis and Evaluation Unit, the Attorney General's sections of General Crimes and Internal Security, the U.S. Marshals Service, the U.S Secret Service, and the Department of the Interior. The specificity of the text contrasts with the way it obscures its sources: "A source, with whom insufficient contact has been made to determine reliability but who is in a position to furnish reliable information, advised as follows on May 21, 1976" that

> "Dog soldiers," who are pro-American Indian Movement (AIM) members, who will kill for the advancement of AIM objectives, have been training since the Wounded Knee, South Dakota, incident in 1973. These dog soldiers, approximately 2000 in number, have been training in "the Northwest Territory" (not further described) and also an unknown number have been training in the desert of Arizona. These dog soldiers are allegedly undergoing guerilla warfare training experiences (not further determined).
>
> The dog soldiers are to arrive at the Yankton Sioux Reservation, South Dakota (Wagner, South Dakota) in order to attend the traditional Sioux sun dance and International Treaty Conference. The sun dance and the conference are to occur on the Yankton Reservation in early June of 1976 and this sun dance and conference are to serve as cover for the influx of dog soldiers. (The second biennial International Indian Treaty Conference is scheduled for May 28–June 6, 1976, Yankton Reservation.)[8]

The text implies that the militants had been trained by a named AIM expert in the use of explosives, and it claims that they would be armed with M-16 rifles, carbines, and dynamite. According to this and a second informer, the guns and explosives would be stored and transported by "Russell Means' 'hit men' ": Sam Moves Camp, Greg Zephier, Wilburt Provost, and Wallace "June" Little. One of the specified safe houses for gun running included the residence of Charles Abourezk, son of South Dakota Senator James Abourezk.[9]

After this exposition, the document unfolds a scenario that is both apocalyptic and reminiscent of the history of U.S. Indian relations. After receiving their specific assignments, the "dog soldiers" would wreak havoc across the state of South Dakota. They would blow up the Lake Andes Court House and the Fort Randall Dam; hit the Sioux Falls State Penitentiary to kill an inmate; attack farmers, shoot up equipment, and blow up BIA buildings in the Wagner area; invade Mount Rushmore and the State Capitol in Pierre; attempt to assassinate the governor of South Dakota; and put out snipers to shoot tourists along the South Dakota interstate highway.[10]

If read as a script for a performance, the document projects a scenario of domestic terrorism. At the same time, this scenario is also reminiscent of accounts of Indian frontier raids and Native campaigns against white settlers in the (white) history of North American Indian relations. Under the pretense of the traditional cultural and spiritual event of the Sioux sun dance and the hemispheric Indian treaty conference, the crazed "dog soldiers" of the radical Indian sovereignty movement were said to be preparing to turn the U.S. Bicentennial celebrations into chaos, sabotage, and bloodbath. Here, the FBI's memo brought together the traditional Native cultures and their current transnational diplomatic initiatives and depicted them as bodies not only alien but murderous to the U.S. nation-state—"red" bodies that would in effect reenact an Indian uprising familiar from "white" Euro-American U.S. historical memory. By implication, the document does not allow for further verification; it easily suggests that the only way to respond to this information is by a preventative performance—"hit them before they strike." The parallels between the kind of terror this 1976 telegram evokes with its claims about the Sioux sun dance on the one hand, and the murderous response at Wounded Knee in 1890 of the 7th Cavalry to the Indian ghost dance movement on the other, cannot be lost on a critical reader.[11]

The radical Indian sovereignty movement acquired the FBI memo and responded with a barrage of press releases. Both in a separate teletype and in a statement through the Wounded Knee Legal Defense/Offense Committee (WKLDOC), Charles Abourezk, Renee LeDeaux, and Sam Moves Camp quoted the memo, and denied any knowledge of a society of dog soldiers and the charges of gun running. They explained that their own rules would not allow for this, since "Sam Moves Camp is an Oglala Sioux medicine man and cannot carry any kind of weapons, only the sacred pipe."[12] In their own press release, the Native American Solidarity Committee explained that summer was "a time when [Native Americans] are traditionally on the move travelling the pow-wow circuit and to ceremonies scheduled around the country," and clarified that

> In fact, Indian people came to Yankton from many points to participate in the traditional sundance, an annual religious ceremony. The subsequent treaty conference brought together more than 600 Native peoples from North and South America and aboriginal Australia, Puerto Rico and Zanu to build a strategy for the struggle for sovereign rights and self-determination.
>
> Likewise, Rapid City will be a meeting place for Indian people on June 25 travelling by caravan to a centennial ceremony at Little Big Horn, Montana, the site of Custer's Last Stand against the Sioux.[13]

Thus, these activists were protesting against the U.S. government's criminalization of all three cultural forms in the ethno-political repertoire of the radical Indian sovereignty movement: Native cultural rituals like the sun dance; transnational conferences about Indian sovereignty; and the Indian counter-commemoration of an anniversary of the U.S. nation-state (replacing the birth of the United States with the Indian victory at Little Big Horn a century later).

The radical Indian organizations responded to the federal allegations with allegations of their own. Both the WKLDOC and the NASC charged that the FBI memo was a measure in "Operation Bicentennial," a part of larger ongoing clandestine federal campaigns like COINTELPRO, Operation Chaos, and Operation Garden Plot against domestic and foreign radical groups.[14] Whether arranged by Indian activists or as an independent initiative, the June 24–30, 1976 issue of the *Washington Newsworks* carried a lengthy article titled "Operation Bicent: The Latest Step in the Military's Plans to Take Over the Police," placing the FBI's recent measures in the larger context of the U.S. military's contingency plans for a gradual introduction of martial law in case of domestic disturbances at political conventions and the Bicentennial celebrations. The report cited as examples the summer 1975 federal raid on Pine Ridge, as well as the recent admission by Russell Means's security chief, Douglass Durham, that he had informed on the AIM leadership to the FBI.[15]

These federal programs had been launched to gather intelligence on the domestic dissent movements of the 1960s, their possible foreign infiltration, and to plan for restoring order in the case of mass domestic disturbances such as the urban riots of 1967. The programs were allegedly discontinued in the early 1970s; however, the high secrecy surrounding active programs as well as the records of discontinued ones had prevented verification.[16] Indian activists have, since the 1970s, charged that they were subjected to continued harassment by the FBI, CIA, BIA, and other U.S. federal agencies. The fact that such programs ever were in place indicates the lengths to which certain branches of the U.S. federal government went in order to counter the efforts of domestic dissenters to mobilize and build transnational relations—with measures reminiscent of the suppression of the link-up between early black civil rights activists and the global anticolonial movement in the early Cold War.[17]

The most rational but nevertheless damning assessment of the effects of the FBI memo came from the Wounded Knee Legal Defense/Offense Committee, the domestic public relations and legal arm of the radical Indian sovereignty movement established during Wounded Knee

1973. "[W]e feel this memo and others of this nature serve as a method of provoking already tense law enforcement people who have been told to expect anything this summer, to a point where fear and violence could be their only possible reaction." Whatever its originating motives, the immediate result of the document would be terror among law enforcement—and a narrowing of their options for preventive and responsive measures. Native Americans traveling in groups would be regarded as potential terrorists, and interacting with them would be correspondingly harsh, with little room for benefit of the doubt in case of a misunderstanding.

Even as the Indian organizations fired back in their press statements, the federal government moved to codify the radical Indian sovereignty movement as an enemy of the state. On June 18, 1976, the U.S. Senate's Committee on the Judiciary held a hearing in its "Subcommittee to Investigate the Administration of the Internal Security Act and Other Internal Security Laws." Their performance resulted in a 168-page document titled "Threats to the Peaceful Observance of the Bicentennial."[18]

After ordering the protestors in the room to remove their signs and cease chanting,[19] Chairman and South Carolina Senator Strom Thurmond opened the hearing. Thurmond established that the Subcommittee was taking testimonies about groups planning potential "acts of terrorism" threatening the Bicentennial celebrations.

> One need not be paranoid to observe the obvious—there are those who see our Bicentennial Celebration and perhaps our two political nominating conventions as historic opportunities to test the strength of our fiber. [. . .]
>
> It is the hope of the subcommittee, in taking today's testimony, that bringing the facts to the attention of the Congress and the public about the various organizations involved in the upcoming Bicentennial *counterdemonstrations* will contribute to the keeping of the peace, not only on July 4, but throughout the Bicentennial period.[20]

This was recognition that the symbolic significance of the U.S. Bicentennial and presidential nomination gatherings made them a stage for performances for ethno-political rights—including performances of violence. The U.S. government had learned from the radical civil rights guerilla theater and the recent counter-commemorative performances of the radical Indian sovereignty movement, and was now determined to prevent breaches of security.

The hearing consisted of evidence and testimonies given by President of the Leadership Foundation Martha Roundtree; University of Pennsylvania political science professor and President of the Foreign Policy Research Institute Dr. William Kintner; Philadelphia Police Department Inspector George Fenel; and Washington, DC, Metropolitan Police Department Deputy Chief Robert L. Rabe. More than their specific testimonies, the documents submitted, including newspaper articles, press releases, letters, and fliers, enabled the Subcommittee to link various organizations in the radical Indian sovereignty movement to a larger coalition of U.S. and foreign radical groups, some of which had advocated or had engaged in violent action.

Through leaders and activists like Clyde and Vernon Bellecourt and Jimmie Durham, the American Indian Movement, the International Indian Treaty Council, and the recently established Native American Solidarity Committee (NASC) were shown to be cooperating with the so-called "July 4 Coalition." A larger solidarity alliance of a variety of leftist and radical organizations including the Palestinian Liberation Organization and the Puerto Rican Solidarity Committee, the July 4 Coalition had been organizing counterdemonstrations for the period of the official U.S. governmental commemorations of the Bicentennial. One of the Coalition's member organizations was the Prairie Fire Organizing Committee, which could have been linked to the Weatherman/Weather Underground, a group who had engaged in violence and bombings of government buildings to protest the U.S. intervention in Vietnam. The Subcommittee specifically used these ties to include AIM, IITC, and NASC in its list of organizations that were potentially planning terrorist acts over the Bicentennial season.[21] Even though the hearing was ostensibly convened to prevent the disruption of the commemorations by informing the general public,[22] the performance and its resulting document in effect classified the radical Indian sovereignty movement as a terrorist threat to the internal security of the U.S. nation-state.

The U.S. government responded to the strengthening transnational ties of the radical sovereignty movement with radical measures not only within but also without the nation-state proper. As early as in December 1973 and January 1974, the U.S. State Department alerted its Western European posts that "February 27 anniversary date of takeover at Wounded Knee could be occasion for bomb attacks against U.S. embassies. Posts urged take extra precautions that date." Signed by Secretary of State Henry Kissinger, the cables were titled "Bomb Threat to Embassies from American Indian (Movement) Extremists," and bore the identifying conceptual tags "paramilitary forces," "embassies," "plots," "American Indian," "American Indian Movement," "AIM," "(Banks, Dennis James)."[23] Such communication within the U.S. government's diplomacy arm is evidence that some officials in the nation-state interpreted the transnational reach of AIM and its allies as an external threat to the very institution of the United States government.

Keeping Them "America's Indians": U.S. Cultural Diplomacy and Indian Sovereignty

The above discussed diplomatic cable notwithstanding, the U.S. State Department did not seem to have a coherent strategy for managing the image of changing U.S. Indian relations overseas.[24] Scholars like Richard T. Arndt, Frances Stonor Saunders, David Caute, and Walter L. Hixson have mapped out the various strategies, stages and forms that U.S. cultural diplomacy took during the Cold War. These ranged from the hard-core rollback propaganda of early Radio Free Europe and the Voice of America[25] through the covert CIA funding of the Congress for Cultural Freedom,[26] the teaching of English as a foreign language around the world, the Fulbright grants and the American embassy library system,[27] to traveling art exhibitions, displays at world expositions, and cultural exchange tours by plays, classical, jazz, ballet and modern dance performances.[28] While several of these forms of cultural diplomacy carried content about American Indians, only rarely did they overtly address the contemporary sovereignty rights struggle.

One notable exception to the State Department's silence on current Native rights was its response to the transatlantic coverage of the siege of Wounded Knee in the spring of 1973. As we have already seen, during the siege the State Department cabled several of its embassies with instructions on how to respond to demonstrations and questions regarding the oppression of American Indians. As the United States Information Agency cautioned, "If Indians are killed, we can surely expect sharp and widespread foreign condemnation of this U.S. government action. It would come at a particularly unpropitious time, giving Arab governments an excuse to fog up the terrorist issue."[29] This was an internal recognition that the outcome of Wounded Knee 1973 would reflect on American foreign policy and would be used as propaganda. Quietly, the State Department also sent to Wounded Knee a journalist from the Voice of America (VOA), one of the U.S. government's media organs overseas.[30] It is not clear if the VOA did broadcast programming about the siege.

The State Department went further in its crisis management by devoting to Indian affairs one whole 1973 issue (vol. 6, no. 2) of *Dialogue*, "the quarterly journal of analysis and opinion" of the agency, published for the elites of both East Germany and the Soviet Union.[31] As much as it can be reconstructed from a later undated USIS booklet for New Zealand, the original issue contained articles including "The New Activism" by Vine Deloria, Jr., "The First Americans" by Albert Roland, Richard Bradford's "Annual Indian Lore Lecture," Carl N. Degler's "Assimilation vs. Separatism," "Excerpts from Messages on Indian Affairs" by President Richard Nixon, "Taking the System and Making It Work" by "Nyoka," and an unattributed text titled "Festival of the Whale." A variety of pieces on American Indian art rounded out this issue of *Dialogue*.[32]

According to the introduction by editor Nathan Glick, "[a]lthough the Indian has often been a troubling, and sometimes a sympathetic, presence in American thought and writing, the dominant popular stereotype have vacillated between [the] two extremes" of Rousseau's "natural man" and Hollywood's "cruel and savage warrior." According to his overview,

> [t]he articles [in] the middle section suggest that the reality was more complex and less exotic. Albert Roland describes a widely separated galaxy of social organizations ranging from nomadic hunters to sedentary farmers and fishermen. Carl N. Degler traces the pendulum swing in U.S. government policy from paternalistic separatism to pressures for assimilation into the surrounding "Anglo" society. President Nixon's Message on Indian Affairs recognizes the present clear preference of most Indians for the preservation of their tribal identities although full participation in the larger society remains open to those who choose it.[33]

It is not a stretch to "reverse engineer" some of the initial response by the State Department to the siege of Wounded Knee based on a few of these articles. For example, both Vine Deloria, Jr., and Martin Seneca, the focus of "Nyoka's" biographical interview "Taking the System and Making It Work," likely worked and lived in Washington, DC, at the time of the siege. Deloria was the director of the Institute for the Development of Indian Law, while Seneca served as White House Fellow and legislative advisor to the Nixon Administration.[34] When the USIA was casting about for Native voices for its publication during the siege, its editors did not go far from the White House.

Correspondingly, the most important articles reflect a rhetorical position closest to the State Department's. The above two articles—two of the four authors designated as Indian in the issue—present the view of the Native establishment. Even as he described the major Native grievances and the issues of concern in a measured way, Deloria's sentences like "[a] series of recent dramatic confrontations reflect both [the Indian's] improved status and his sharpened awareness of grievances that have yet to be redressed" and "[u]nfortunately, the federal government moved too slowly and offered too little to satisfy the growing militancy of urban Indians" played an apologist for the U.S. government. After all, he attributed the recent militancy of Native activism to the improved conditions that were the result of the government's Indian policy.[35] More specifically, Deloria explicitly defended the current government:

> It should also be noted that when the Nixon administration took office in 1969, it appointed an Indian, Louis R. Bruce, as head of the Bureau of Indian Affairs, and he in turn hired a number of articulate and reformist young Indians who helped somewhat to revitalize that traditionally conservative agency.[36]

Deloria likewise depicted the 1972 Trail of Broken Treaties as encouraged by Nixon's recent and pending Indian legislation. Again, "[u]nfortunately, the unhappy events that occurred when the caravan reached Washington diverted the public's attention away from the substance of these demands to arguments over tactics. [. . .] Angered by the destructive behavior of AIM militants, the government gave only perfunctory responses to the Twenty Points, and this casual treatment of their demands created a great many new Indian supporters for the militant cause."[37] Deloria also claimed that the government and the tribal governments even strengthened their alliance in response to the rise of militancy among the younger activists.[38] According to him, the siege of Wounded Knee 1973 was occasioned by the clashing egos of Oglala tribal chairman Richard Wilson and AIM leader Russell Means.[39] In the face of this inter-Indian conflict,

> [t]he federal government proved to be incredibly patient with the AIM militants. [. . .] To prevent bloodshed, it conducted

> prolonged negotiations with the embattled Indian protesters, thereby winning the gratitude and confidence of the great majority of Indians whose strongest concern was to prevent any loss of life.
>
> As I write, the siege of Wounded Knee continues. [. . .][40]

In his conclusion titled "Mutual Responsibilities," Deloria called on the federal government to keep moving in the right direction by reviewing its past Indian policy and upholding treaty rights; and he expressed hope that on their end, Native communities will be able to create and maintain "stable and progressive" tribal governments.[41] In effect, his message was the same as that of Martin Luther King, Jr.'s to Radio Prague back in the 1960s: "we have made considerable progress, but there is a long way ahead."[42] For Deloria, the solution to the current crisis lay with the new Native activists "occupying a middle ground" between AIM and the tribal governments. According to Deloria, these people believed in tribal governments as a tool of governance, but they also espoused most of the goals of the militant movement without its violence—yet they were often rejected by both groups. In his eyes, they were the ones who through higher education had mastered the skills crucial for helping Native communities—and they were willing to do the hard work that it required.[43]

One of those "articulate and reformist young Indians" hired by the Nixon administration was Martin Seneca, featured in Nyoka's "Taking the System and Making It Work." This piece effectively showcased Seneca's success in education and his subsequent appointment as White House Fellow as a triumph of the will of the individual.

> [B]oth my mother and father instilled in me the belief that I could do anything that I wanted to do. They would say, "Don't ever back away from anything. You can do it."[44]

Accordingly, Seneca likewise praised the Nixon Administration, for whom he had been working.

> Mr. Seneca put some of his knowledge to use in helping to draft the Indian legislation which the Nixon Administration proposed to Congress this year. The main point of that legislation is movement toward autonomy and self-determination for Indians—letting them, rather than the federal government, decide what is best for Indians.

> For the first time someone is asking what we want and then trying to get it for us. I've had a lot of faith in the Nixon administration because, for the first time, it began giving Indian lands back—a sacred lake to one tribe, and a mountain to another, for example—rather than trying to buy us off.[45]

In the article, Seneca positioned himself as one of the new activists described by Deloria earlier.

> Mr. Seneca thinks of himself as a "radical, but a realistic, pragmatic radical rather than a rhetorical one." "Pragmatic radicals," who take the system and work within it to bring about change are the only truly effective ones, to him, and he maintains that all minority groups "will have to realize that point before they get anything done."
>
> What it is all about is taking the system that exists and making it work. The key is to learn how to read the laws, to work with them, to have them changed if necessary, to know Congressmen, government officials, the people who can help you get needed change.[46]

Beyond his tenure in Washington, Seneca was planning to serve as legal counsel to the Cherokee Nation, and "eventually I suppose I'll go into politics. [. . .] Who knows? I may even be the first Indian president of this country."[47]

In the journal's only two articles that directly and at length addressed the contemporary Native rights struggle, one of the most important Indian leaders and an up-and-coming Native government worker praised the Nixon Administration's prudent treatment of Native protests and their progress in legislating Indian rights. Their faith in the new cadre of educated young Indians who can bridge the militant and the conservative activism also overtly advocated for Native collaboration, and not confrontation, with the U.S. government. Glick and his fellow USIA editors probably thought that the transatlantic media coverage had already adequately publicized the grievances, demands and confrontational tactics of both AIM and the traditionalist groups of Native America. *Dialogue* needed to serve as a corrective for overseas public opinion by strengthening Native voices supporting the Nixon Administration. Interestingly, the USIA communicated this message by placing it among a number of articles on the long history of Indian policy and Native American art.

This latter strategy in effect both downplayed the urgency of the ongoing sovereignty rights struggle and diffused the reader's interest among a number of other fields.

In his book *The First Resort of Kings*, Richard T. Arndt discusses the role of the U.S. embassy library system and exhibitions in American cultural diplomacy during the Cold War.[48] An examination of USIA documents and diplomatic cables reveals that in the early- to mid-1970s the State Department had a number of Indian-themed projects in its programming. An "American Indian handicrafts exhibit" was open in two locations in Poland from April through early June 1974, when it moved on to Belgrade, Yugoslavia.[49] An exhibit of the Amon Carter Museum on the American West was shown in March 1974 in three locations in Romania.[50] Between September 1974 and November 1975, the Smithsonian Institution's "George Catlin's American Indian Paintings" toured Iran, Egypt, Sri Lanka, Israel, Hungary, Yugoslavia, and Bulgaria.[51] An "American Frontier Days" exhibit was on display in Tokyo, Japan, in October 1975.[52] In January 1976, the U.S. Embassy in Rome, Italy, was working to book space for an "American Indian exhibit."[53] Several posts expressed an interest on the part of locals for including elements of American Indian cultures—artifacts or performances—in the planned Bicentennial programming.[54]

The early- to mid-1970s State Department programming mostly re-presented the dominant images of American Indians in U.S. art and popular culture. These included artwork by Frederick Remington, Charles Russell, George Catlin, Thomas Moran, and Albert Bierstadt; historical artifacts as well as crafts objects; the embassies' additional cultural programming included the screening of the feature films *How the West Was Won*, *Shane*, *True Grit*, *Stage Coach*, *The Big Sky*, *Red River*, and *Will Penny*, and the documentaries *American Indian Art of the Pacific Northwest*, *Catlin and the Indians*, and *Old Chiefs*; live concerts of country and western music; and numerous lectures and reports in the national media. In this, the State Department responded to the ongoing Indian sovereignty struggle "by default" by offering to its overseas target audiences the age-old Euro-American and transatlantic forms of "playing Indian." While such programming certainly provided pleasure and entertainment, it also most likely further reinforced the attitudes held by those audiences toward both the U.S. government and Native Americans.

Several of the Indian-themed exhibitions were official events under the aegis of the local embassy of the United States. Only one of the opening addresses by U.S. government officials made any reference to the current sovereignty rights struggle. On October 5, 1976, Vice President of the United States Nelson Rockefeller opened the "2000 Years of North American Indian Art" exhibit at London's Hayward Gallery.

> My interest in what [is] commonly and wrongly described as primitive art goes back a good many years, but I never cease to be thrilled by it . . . I never cease to make new discoveries. And, I must admit, I never cease to be astonished by its beauty and creativity. This exhibit lives up to its billing as the most definitive collection of North American Indian art ever shown. [. . .]
>
> I confess to a mild case of jealousy—that this collection is being shown here first, instead of on the North American continent, where the craftsmen and artists of yesterday and today lived and worked. But facts are facts: it was the British and the continental Europeans who were the first to appreciate distinctiveness and beauty in the ethnic art of the American Indian. In fact, many of the finest works on display here come from collections in Britain and on the continent. It is only in recent years that the settler Americans discovered what the first Americans had been doing all those centuries.[55]

Here, Rockefeller rhetorically performed a variation of the European discoverer of American Indians—this time, an admirer of Native American art. However, he went further by expanding this role to all European colonizers of the New World, thus reinforcing a shared transatlantic identity as the discoverer and connoisseur-collector of American Indian culture. In her polemic exposition *Primitive Art in Civilized Places*, Sally Price has cited the same Nelson Rockefeller as an example of the Western cultural and ideological construction of "primitive art."[56] In his opening address, Rockefeller rehearsed a Euro-American position of control over representing and "playing Indian."

> I am convinced this exhibition will be a great success—and the reason is not simply because it is awesome in size and ambition, beautiful and mystic in content. Rather, it is because the Indians of North America are a people of absorbing interest throughout the world.
>
> They have been subjected to myth and misunderstanding as perhaps no other people. Wrongly, they have, at various

> times, been romanticized and ridiculed; tragically, they have been persecuted and isolated, patronized and overprotected.
>
> The reality is that America's Indian community of today—almost one million and growing—is as complex as is the rest of our society, as diverse in their own views of what is right or wrong for them as are our other ethnic groups. No single person, no single organization, can speak for them—but if there is a single point on which all agree, it is that they want to share in America's prosperity; they want to retain their distinctive cultural life and pass it on to their next generation.[57]

Recognizing the widespread interest in American Indians among people outside of the United States, Rockefeller asserted that this fascination also led to abiding misunderstandings of the nature and aspirations of Native American communities. The vice president claimed that the lowest common denominator among Indians was that they all wanted to succeed as members of the body of the U.S. nation-state. To use Sally Price's analytical categories, Rockefeller "anonymized" the American Indian activists of the past and the present[58]—he anonymized them into a glorious mass of diverse tribes, too diverse even for effective political representation. Thus, Vice President Rockefeller's speech on Native American art in London in effect delegitimized the claims and demands of the transatlantic sovereignty rights movement.

> For two hundred years, our government made wide swings to find the proper course. It moved from an early policy of assimilation into white society to one of protective paternalism in the form of isolation on tribal reservations.
>
> Ironically, an Indian chief of one hundred years ago, Chief Joseph of the Nez Perce tribe, expressed then in magnificent words the yearning of the Indian—perhaps of every person trapped between two worlds. "Let me be a free man," wrote Chief Joseph, "free to travel, free to stop, free to work, free to trade where I choose, free to choose my own teachers, free to follow the religion of my fathers, free to think and talk and act for myself—and I will obey every law or submit to every penalty."
>
> In a very real sense, this is our approach today. Our present policy provides freedom of choice for America's

> Indians; they now have the legislative authority to decide what is best for them and the right to administer their own development programs.
>
> It represents the highest values of American society. We cannot, should not, force assimilation; we cannot, should not, encourage separation. Freedom of choice is the essence of our national life, and we have extended it, finally, to the first Americans.[59]

In another assertion of U.S. progress, here Rockefeller masterfully enlisted and ventriloquized Chief Joseph as a predictor and proponent of current Indian policy. For the vice president, the Nez Perce leader served as a historical proxy or witness to the goodness of the U.S. government's current position in Indian affairs—the "best of all possible worlds."

> One of our famed authors, Zane Grey, wrote a generation ago of the Indian, "that melancholy figure," as he described him, "[was] diminishing, fading, vanishing." I'm glad to say this is no longer the case; America's Indians are not only visible on the American map today—but they are assuming their rightful place in the politics and economics and culture of our land. Their contributions are mounting steadily as their talents are nurtured by their own self-development.
>
> It is not an easy road, this attempt to sustain different cultures in a society that often demands conformity as the passport for success. But we think we are on the right path, finally, after several centuries of experiment and failure.[60]

In wrapping up his discussion on current Indian affairs, Rockefeller used the trope of "the vanishing native" to contrast it with the current state of Indian affairs—and to celebrate American democracy and social diversity.

Similarly to its strategy with jazz music and civil rights in the 1950s and '60s,[61] in its cultural diplomacy programs the State Department attempted to showcase American Indian art as proof of the enduring value of Native Americans in U.S. culture. In the case of Rockefeller's speech, this entailed the elevation of folk crafts and what was called "primitive art" into the realm of high culture.

> But this exhibit raises the level of our recognition to where it belongs—in exhibitions such as this. These are treasures, to

> be seen and appreciated, indeed, to be pondered as we trace the diversity of our culture for our roots.[62]

The very act of exhibiting American Indian artifacts as art was now presented as U.S. governmental recognition and linked to the current legislative "progress" in Indian policy. In turn, recent federal legislation on Native self-determination was held up as proof of the supremacy of U.S. democracy and diversity.

The State Department responded to the transatlantic sovereignty alliance in at least one other way: by monitoring the activities of U.S. travelers, and foreign media coverage of the Indian rights struggle. The U.S. Embassy in Moscow reported on the Soviet press coverage of the court cases ensuing after Wounded Knee, especially focusing on Dennis Banks and Russell Means.[63] In a December 14, 1973 cable to the U.S. embassy in the Hague, the State Department refuted that a speaking tour at European universities planned by the Survival of American Indians Association was cancelled due to interference from the U.S. government.[64] In August of 1975, Washington cabled its embassy in Lisbon, Portugal that among the U.S. delegation to the "meeting of European Democrat Students" were representatives of the National Indian Youth Council, a radical sovereignty organization.[65] In October 1975, the U.S. embassy in Berlin relayed to Washington, the USIA, and a large number of Western, Central, and Southern European embassies a report of the recently held world congress of women, with a "U.S. delegation [that] contained several representatives of the American Indian Movement," who, along with the "majority of naïve participants, [. . .] were most probably "thoroughly snowed" by what they saw and experienced."[66] A February 1976 diplomatic cable from the U.S. Embassy in West Berlin reported that East Berlin's recently held annual festival of political songs featured "an American Indian singer named 'Wyoming,' who is pictured sitting at the piano singing his own composition, 'Freedom.' " The embassy cable notes that one major East German newspaper described "Wyoming" as "a spokesman for the Indian freedom movement," who was "sentenced to many years in jail last August by American racist justice for his political opinion and action."[67] Even if it did not interfere with their free travel, the State Department certainly served as the eyes and ears of the U.S. government in monitoring the members of the transatlantic alliance for Indian sovereignty.

While it is not possible to show if it had any involvement by Native sovereignty activists, the U.S. Bicentennial celebrations in at least one country were disrupted in a manner reminiscent of AIM's counter-commemorations. At the July 4, 1976, festival's official ceremony in Copenhagen, Denmark,

> As Queen [Margrethe] began her brief greetings to the US, [. . .] group of youths around fringes of gathering began to chant in American Indian style. [. . .] Demonstrators then moved closer carrying placards, Vietnamese flags, etc. One got close enough to throw sack of animal blood onto stage narrowly missing queen but splashing prince. Program continued as ambassador read president's message. Police slowly began to pull demonstrators from center area and remainder of event went on as planned. [. . .]
>
> Group continued to try to disrupt proceedings by arriving on horseback in Western dress, putting on Ku Klux Klan demonstration and trying to haul down flags.[68]

While of the roughly 200 demonstrators some 56 were arrested, the U.S. embassy rather focused on how in the national media and government most voices condemned the demonstrations, and took this as a sign of the enduring goodwill of the Danish towards the United States. In the hopes of one embassy official, these disruptive events "perhaps will lead the Danes to realize that even if they permit dissident groups to demonstrate, they should do so in manner which does not interfere with others."[69]

Jimmy Carter's Human Rights Foreign Policy and American Indian Sovereignty at the United Nations

It was no mere coincidence that Indian activists asserted Native American sovereignty as human rights at the United Nations simultaneously with U.S. President Jimmy Carter's decision to make human rights an important element of U.S. foreign policy.[70] President Carter's human rights-based foreign policy initiative offered a potential departure from the previous binary framework of geopolitics. In his June 1977 commencement address at Notre Dame University, Carter said,

> Being confident of our own future, we are now free of that inordinate fear of communism which once led us to embrace any dictator who joined us in that fear. [. . .] Our policy

> during [the post-World War Two] period was guided by two principles: a belief that Soviet expansion was almost inevitable but that it must be contained, and the corresponding belief in the importance of an almost exclusive alliance among non-Communist nations on both sides of the Atlantic. That system could not last forever unchanged. Historical trends have weakened its foundation. The unifying threat of conflict with the Soviet Union has become less intensive, even though the competition has become more extensive. [. . .]
>
> We will cooperate more closely with the newly influential countries in Latin America, Africa, and Asia. We need their friendship and cooperation in a common effort as the structure of world power changes. [. . .] We have a special need for cooperation and consultation with other nations in this hemisphere—to the north and to the south. We do not need another slogan. Although these are our close friends and neighbors, our links with them are the same links of equality that we forge for the rest of the world. We will be dealing with them as part of a new, worldwide mosaic of global, regional, and bilateral relations. [. . .]
>
> And we are confident of the good sense of the American people, and so we let them share in the process of making foreign policy decisions.[71]

In this articulation of his foreign policy doctrine, President Carter moved away from seeing the world as three blocs, and formulated a concept that potentially cut across ideological and political lines. As he announced U.S. overtures to the Soviet Union to scale back the arms race, he placed human rights in his foreign policy plank, and reasserted the U.S. intention to strengthen ties with countries in both the decolonizing world and the Western hemisphere. At the same time, Carter seemed to want to empower his own citizens to participate in U.S. foreign policy. Seizing an opportunity in such changing international relations, the Indian sovereignty movement now embarked on a transnational campaign to shine a light on the violations and denial of rights to Native communities by the very government which touted its commitment to human rights everywhere in the world.

The fact that in May 1977 the member states of the UN Sub-Commission on the Prevention of Discrimination and Protection of Minorities voted to admit the International Indian Treaty Council to

NGO status in the UN Commission on Human Rights[72] could be explained by a variety of reasons. Governments who were allied with the United States may have wanted to support Carter's foreign policy with hopes that his government would return the favor, while Communist states may have admitted the Treaty Council as a prospective partner in anti-U.S. propaganda and alliance building. Perhaps more than the first two groups, Nonaligned and "Third World" government representatives may have also genuinely believed in the power of a human rights doctrine in international relations. AIM's relations with national liberation movements such as the Palestine Liberation Organisation, the Puerto Rican Socialist Party, and the Northern Irish independence struggle would have also appealed to this latter group.

As pointed out earlier, the U.S. government monitored the Treaty Council's admission process to the UN. A January 1975 cable from the State Department to all East Asian and Pacific diplomatic posts and select Eastern European embassies predicted that after recognizing the Viet Cong as a national liberation movement or provisional government, the UN may extend similar status to the American Indian Movement.[73] In November 1976, the United States mission at the UN alerted Washington that the world body was preparing to hold a conference "on subject of discrimination against American Indians," and recommended that they send a representative from the Bureau of Indian Affairs.[74]

The rhetorical value of Carter's human rights doctrine was used by Native activists already at the 1977 Geneva conference. At the plenary session, Onondaga leader of the Six Nations Iroquois Confederacy Oren Lyons said,

> The president of the USA has brought forth into the forum of the international world the issue of human rights. It affords us the opportunity at this time to present our positions on the issue of human rights. It is strange indeed that we have to travel this far to the east, to the European continent, to turn and face the president of the US and ask him about our human rights.[75]

The Iroquois leader who had traveled on his own passport was now using his new geographical vantage point to critique the foreign policy of a superpower the history of which was predicated on Westward colonial expansion. The major threat and counterbalance to the influence of the United States now were not the Indian nations of the American West, but the Eastern Bloc—the Communist countries of Eastern Europe and Asia. The activists of the Indian radical sovereignty movement were now meeting representatives of the other "red" peoples and nation-states of the world in the contact zone of Central Europe. In their performed interventions for Native rights, Indian activists would continue to leverage their geographical reach, international status, and their subsequent alliances for enhanced recognition and enforcement of their rights.

Even as they may have recognized their own policy's weaknesses, the Carter Administration initially cooperated with the organizers of the 1977 conference. Otherwise a harsh critic of the various U.S. administrations and their foreign policy, Dunbar-Ortiz praises Carter appointee, U.S. Ambassador to the United Nations Andrew Young, for being a partner for the event even though he did not agree with the strategy of taking Indian rights to the UN.[76] Himself a leading member of the U.S. Civil Rights Movement, Young was tasked with representing the Carter human rights doctrine at the UN. Faced with a conference likely critical of the U.S. government's past and current treatment of Native Americans, he almost certainly recalled past African American efforts to use the world body to shed light on ongoing U.S. racism and pressure the American government into legislating racial equality.

Inasmuch as the final report of the 1977 conference can be read as a record of some of the delegates' performances of their claims of Native sovereignty, the gathering confronted the U.S. government about its treatment of American Indians. For example, the "Representatives of the Lakota Nation" recommended to the NGOs to take to the UN Committee on Decolonization the issues of the "status of American Indians under international law, violations of United Nations covenants and agreements, treaty recognition by the United Nations, land reform, autonomy and increased land base." They also recommended that NGOs censure the U.S. government and force it to ratify the 1948 Genocide Convention, that individual nation-states recognize the 1868 Fort Laramie Treaty as international law, and that the UN call an international convention on Indian rights in 1978.[77] The Lakota representatives (who were closely associated with AIM and its Treaty Council) were calling for the permanent placing of their relations on an international plane, with actions that carried the implicit potential of full decolonization.

Through its UN missions, the United States government parried the Lakota's charges both in the conference documents and in the press. On September 23, 1977, *The Washington Post* carried a distilled report of American Indian grievances.[78] Two days later the paper reported that

William van den Heuvel, U.S. ambassador to the UN's European office in Geneva, objected that official U.S. representative Gloria Gaston-Shapiro was prevented from reading her government's statement at the NGO conference's closing session. The statement would have refuted the "anti-American accusations" that had been made at the gathering. The conference's organizers in turn denied that Gaston-Shapiro's request was rejected.[79] Beyond the facts, this spat is indicative of the importance that each side attached to the embodied performances of sovereignty at the conference.

The official final report of the conference did contain the U.S. government's statement. In the discourse of liberal public diplomacy, the text expressed an openness and eagerness to constructively engage with the issues discussed at the conference.

> We are pleased that the original people of our country have gathered here in Geneva to discuss these matters of vital importance to human rights. We are warmed by the initiative you have shown in carrying your concerns to this forum. This kind of dialogue can only happen in open societies, societies that are not afraid to learn from past mistakes.
>
> As you know, President Carter insists that the United States will discuss human rights violations wherever they occur. It would be useless, and moreover, a disservice to gloss over the injustices suffered by native peoples in the United States, as well as by other ethnic groups. Ambassador Andrew Young has positively supported the United States' participation here out of his conviction that vigorous efforts must be made to eliminate grievances at home as well as abroad. While rejecting hyperbole, the United States remains concerned about and is sensitive to any serious charges of human rights abuses committed against United States citizens. In accordance with President Carter's statements on our human rights policies, the United States will investigate any serious charges presented and take corrective actions which prove necessary. [. . .]
>
> The new Administration intends to learn from the past. Therefore, it is committed to hearing the truth from the voices of the native peoples themselves.[80]

Next, the government's statement pointed to a number of domestic studies and legal and legislative initiatives dealing with Indian issues such as the U.S. Congress's American Indian Policy Review Commission, the Indian Self-Determination and Education Assistance Act (both of 1975), and an impending investigation of Indian affairs by the U.S. Commission on Civil Rights. In its statement the U.S. government also recognized the importance of "prison systems and processes"—for the Department of Justice, the criminal justice system and U.S. society at large. The U.S. government also promised to pay heed to the ongoing investigation of the forced sterilization of Native women.

> However, the United States categorically rejects the charges of genocide which is defined in Article II of the Convention on the Prevention of the Crime of Genocide as "acts committed with the intent to destroy" a group.[81]

Neither the self-image of the U.S. nation-state, nor its international implications allowed for anything but a vehement denial of the charge that the U.S. government had committed genocide against American Indians. The government was asserting that it was handling Indian issues within the framework of the nation-state, and it was not open to any attempts to leverage them as transnational issues or matters of international law.

The radical sovereignty movement's demands about dissenters being incarcerated did not achieve material results, but it may have informed U.S. UN ambassador Andrew Young's remark to a French reporter less than a year later. Discussing the discrimination against Jewish dissidents in the Soviet Union, a U.S. foreign policy issue, Young quipped, "We still have hundreds of people that I would categorize as political prisoners in our prisons." He explained that he meant primarily civil rights and anti-war activists who were arrested for being dissenters, and that the due process of U.S. law soon set them free.[82] In the eyes of the Indian sovereignty movement, he could have also meant the defendants of the Wounded Knee trials, and other prisoners such as Leonard Peltier. These self-critical remarks by a civil rights leader-turned U.S. government official earned Ambassador Young a failed impeachment resolution in the U.S. House of Representatives.[83]

"Triangulation" in the Middle East: The Iranian Hostage Mail Exchange Service

The high period of U.S. cooperation with the radical Indian sovereignty movement in the United Nations may have been the little-known tenure of the International Indian Treaty Council as sponsor and facilitator of mail delivery for the hostages at the Tehran U.S. embassy in 1980. While an in-depth chronicle of this initiative awaits more research, it can be reasonably pieced together from United Nations and U.S. government documents, as well as the memoirs of Native sovereignty activists.

The ties between the American Indian Movement and various national liberation organizations dated back to the early 1970s, and were baptized in the fire of Wounded Knee 1973, the ensuing violence on Pine Ridge, and the U.S. government's legal and covert campaigns against the movement. Correspondence and occasional meetings between AIM activists and the Palestine Liberation Organization, the Puerto Rican Socialist Party, or the Northern Irish independence movement all appear in the historical record. Key activists of the radical Indian sovereignty movement like Jimmie Durham and Roxanne Dunbar-Ortiz promoted a strategy of cooperation with the national liberation struggles of the Nonaligned and the Third World.[84] These transnational relations were both the result of and further facilitators of the distinction of the Indian sovereignty movement as an entity distinct from the U.S. nation-state—a transnational actor. They also provided Native sovereignty activists with access to groups and governments who were opponents or outright enemies of the United States.

The unlikely involvement of the radical Indian sovereignty movement in the Iranian hostage crisis developed out of such ties. According to a White House memorandum, in early 1980 at a California college a Native American AIM activist befriended an Iranian student close to the Ayatollah Khomeini, and gave him a pipe as a gift to the religious leader. Subsequently, at the request of Khomeini for a personal pipe ceremony,[85] another AIM activist visited Tehran, met the U.S. hostages and their captors, and collected mail from the hostages. Upon his return to the U.S., his AIM colleague was contacted both by departing Iranian diplomats and the Ayatollah to discuss the status of the hostages at a pipe ceremony. It was at this point that one of the Native activists told about these overtures to Ed Torres, special assistant to President Carter.

> [AIM activist's name redacted] related to me that he is disposed to make contact with the Iranians, but does not want to become embroiled in any action that would be used as propaganda against the U.S. (In spite of his animosity and adversary position towards the U.S. Government.) He does, however, want to be helpful and placed himself at our disposal.[86]

In a rare effort of cooperation for the sake of the hostages or perhaps as a strategic move from sovereignty towards U.S. patriotism, the AIM activist set aside his distrust of the U.S. government and relayed them vital information about the potential for both humanitarian aid and backdoor diplomacy.

After the Carter Administration's appeals to the United Nations and the failure of Secretary-General Kurt Waldheim's personal visit to even gain audience with the Ayatollah,[87] it became crucial that the parties find a mediating entity that was acceptable to the hostage takers, the Iranian religious leadership, the United Nations, and the United States government. According to Russell Means, John Thomas had been touring the Middle East as an AIM "ambassador" early that year.[88] The most complete description of the Hostage Mail Exchange Service during the crisis claims that it originated in discussions between Thomas of the International Indian Treaty Council and the Iranian Student Council at the U.S. Embassy in Tehran on January 8–9, 1980. The same document claims that a mail transfer by a hostage to Thomas was made on January 11.[89] Thomas was probably also the person referred to in a January 14 UN telegram as "an American Indian met with one of the hostages yesterday and was given more mail from captives for their relatives."[90] The first hostage mail delivery in the United States took place on January 17–25. The document anticipated full mail runs afterwards about twice each month—except for a brief pause for the Indian couriers to celebrate the 7th anniversary of Wounded Knee 1973.[91]

A photograph of the UPI/Bettman Archive in Russell Means's memoir, *Where White Men Fear to Tread*, shows Adams and Thomas in an airport terminal, pushing carts with large canvas bags designated in printed white letters as "Hostage Mail Exchange Service." Adams wears a suit jacket over his dark sweater and clerical collar; Thomas sports shoulder-length dark hair, sunglasses, a choker, and a necklace similar to Clyde Bellecourt's—obvious signs of his Indianness, which in the outdoors were covered with his coat and scarf, items that suggest winter or early spring.[92] Traveling together across oceans and the borders of nation-states moving closer to war, this priest and Indian activist were performing a kind of transnational sovereignty for humanitarian aid and backdoor diplomacy. Together, the blaring white letters "Hostage Mail Exchange Service" and any references to the Treaty Council's United Nations status likely smoothed their transit through national checkpoints.

The terms under which the Hostage Mail Exchange Service operated reveal the importance of the radical Indian sovereignty movement as a third-party intermediary. The Service was "sponsored by" the Treaty Council, whose vice president, John Thomas, served as courier. The program was "facilitated by" the Board of Church & Society of the United Methodist Church, which collected donations, provided its facilities in New York City and its liaison, the reverend John P. Adams. The initiative was "sanctioned by" the Muslim students who held the hostages, who also read any letters arriving and being sent. Finally,

> The commitment which Mr. Thomas made to the students holding the Embassy was that the letters would be hand carried to the families to whom they were addressed by the hostages and that the mail would not be put into the United States mail service or delivered to an agency of the United States government. Consequently, American Indians, and clergy of the United Methodist Church and other denominations, in 26 states are making mail deliveries.[93]

The conditions of this operation made for American Indian sovereignty activists collaborating with clergy to deliver mail to and from the hostages in Tehran. A U.S.-based transnational organization with NGO status in the United Nations, the International Indian Treaty Council was now temporarily supplanting the functions of the U.S. government in diplomacy and mail delivery. In effect, this transnational social movement proved its supremacy to the nation-state in facilitating humanitarian communication in an international crisis.

It is unclear if and to what extent President Carter knew about the Hostage Mail Exchange Service before late spring 1980. Reverend John Adams's February 1, 1980 letter to UN Chef de Cabinet Rafeeuddin Ahmed begins, "[s]everal times in recent days and nights I have spoken with Ambassador [Glenn] Olds,"[94] the U.S. envoy to the Economic and Social Council, the UN office that had granted NGO status to the Treaty Council two years before. Yet Carter may have learned of this opening for backdoor diplomacy only from his Chief of Staff Hamilton Jordan, after he received a memo from White House special assistant Ed Torres on May 22, 1980. Since some of the diplomatic correspondence from these years remains classified, this question remains to be answered by future research.

Whether or not the Hostage Mail Exchange Service flew under the U.S. government's radar, by late spring of 1980 U.S. officials had realized that their involvement was not advisable. Special assistant Ed Torres's

May 22, 1980 memorandum to Carter's Chief of Staff Hamilton Jordan received the handwritten response "I believe it would be best for us to let [AIM activist's name redacted] to do whatever he wants to do so he is not accused of being "an agent."[95] In a lucid moment of sound judgment, Jordan realized that the way to enable such transnational diplomacy is to keep the nation-state out of the initiative. The key to any hope for such an unlikely collaboration was precisely to use the reputation of the radical sovereignty movement as independent from and often at odds with the U.S. government—as American Indian, and not U.S. American. Thus the convergence of AIM's ties with national liberation movements and Nonaligned and Third World régimes, the Treaty Council's recognition by the United Nations, and the lucid judgment of Native activists as well as UN and U.S. officials facilitated a rare triangulation[96] for delivering this special kind of humanitarian aid.

The Iranian Hostage Crisis spelled the end of President Carter's unique attempt to base U.S. foreign policy on universal human rights. However, the Indian sovereignty movement had lost their greatest ally in the U.S. UN administration even before the crisis began. On July 26, 1979, Ambassador Andrew Young personally lobbied a PLO representative to delay a UN recommendation to create a Palestinian state. This action was a direct affront to the Israelis, who had been against U.S. contacts with the Palestinian liberation movement. To preserve the U.S. peace effort in the Middle East, Young resigned from his post in August 1979. [97] Engaging in the kind of transnational ties with liberation movements that enabled the sovereignty movement to supplant the U.S. government in the hostage crisis got Ambassador Andrew Young fired—a definite sign of the limits of the foreign policy of the American nation-state. With the changes in U.S. foreign policy after the election of Ronald Reagan, the radical sovereignty movement would face even greater challenges in its transatlantic diplomacy.

Driving a Wedge in Solidarity: Race against Revolution[98] in Nicaragua

The ultimate test of the mutual commitment to the alliance between the sovereignty struggle and Marxist revolutionary movements came with their involvement in Nicaragua in the 1980s. After the Sandinista National Liberation Front successfully overthrew the military dictatorship of Anastasio Somoza Debayle in 1979, the former rebels embarked on a project of Marxist revolutionary nation-building. The Indian communities of Nicaragua's Atlantic coast, who had largely stayed away from the power struggle, now came under pressure to submit to Sandinista policies made without their assent. The Reagan Administration and its anti-Communist allies opposed the Sandinista régime, and they openly and covertly worked to overthrow it through much of the 1980s. Thus the rights of the indigenous Sumu, Rama, and Miskito Indians of Nicaragua became a rallying point for the radical Indian sovereignty movement at the same time as the issue was being deployed by the U.S. government in its anti-Communist foreign policy.

North American Indian activists felt compelled to choose between an anti-Communist pro-indigenous stance, and a pro-Marxist position that subordinated Native rights to the revolutionary project. By 1980, AIM leader Russell Means had dismissed Marxism as a political partner for being just another European ideology that reproduced the colonialist status quo for indigenous people even as it aimed to reorder society.[99] On the other hand, Roxanne Dunbar-Ortiz maintained that it was possible to reconcile indigenous rights with the Marxist nation-building project through power sharing that respected human rights and even autonomy.[100] Along with others, both activists engaged with the issue of Nicaragua: in the early to mid-1980s, Means visited the region three times,[101] while Dunbar-Ortiz spent much of the decade in Nicaragua as an activist, observer, and a shuttle diplomat trying to resolve conflicts.[102]

As the Miskitos took opposing sides on the ground, and as the U.S. government continued its campaigns against the Sandinistas, so fractured the Indian sovereignty movement on the issue. Early on, the American Indian Movement and the International Indian Treaty Council, dominated by Russell and his brother Bill Means, supported the Sandinista government and praised its "Literacy Crusade," which they saw as aiming at instilling national unity, raising revolutionary consciousness, and giving agency back to the indigenous and other Nicaraguans.[103] However, as the tensions mounted between the Sandinistas and the coastal Indians, and counterrevolutionary forces started to mobilize in the Nicaragua-Honduras border region, these U.S. Native organizations increasingly feared a U.S. intervention.[104] In late 1981 or early 1982, AIM and the IITC were invited by the Nicaraguan government to undertake their first fact-finding mission to Nicaragua. They found that

> the former National Guardsmen of Somoza were operating out of Honduras trying to get the Miskitos to rise up against the new government of Nicaragua. They were attacking Indian villages dressed up as Sandinistas, and were kidnapping people and burning villages, trying to create a climate of fear and terror in the area, forcing the Indians to leave Nicaragua and join the counter-revolutionaries in Honduras. It is widely suspected that the CIA is behind much of the trouble.[105]

AIM and the IITC noted that under the leadership of Steadman Fagoth, some Miskitos had been convinced to cross into Honduras and train to fight against the Sandinistas[106] in what came to be called the Contra forces. Other Miskitos stayed either neutral or loyal to the Sandinista régime, and these were the Indians who AIM and the IITC met and chose to believe on this and subsequent visits. In repeated press statements, the IITC's Bill Means and Dunbar-Ortiz expressed outrage over what they saw as U.S.-orchestrated terror and guerilla raids, and affirmed their faith in the Sandinista government's ability to satisfactorily include the Nicaraguan indigenous in the process of revolutionary nation building.[107]

AIM leader Russell Means, on the other hand, attempted to leverage his organization's support of the Sandinista government for the recognition of U.S. Indian sovereignty rights. In March 1982, he pressed Nicaraguan Commandante Jaime Wheelock to endorse the 1868 Fort Laramie Treaty as an international agreement in return for the IITC's continuing support of the Sandinista régime.[108] After Wheelock asked for time to consider the deal, Means gave an interview to the North American sovereignty flagship newspaper, *Akwesasne Notes*, in which he denounced Nicaragua's record of indigenous rights: "I feel they are Marxists; and I feel that Marxists are the most racist people on earth."[109] Publicly, Dunbar-Ortiz attempted to patch up the rift by pointing out that Means spoke only for himself, not on behalf of the IITC, and reiterating the organization's official position.[110] Privately, she thought Means was out for celebrity status.[111] After his own fact-finding trip to the region, Means publicly pledged to recruit North American Indians for an armed struggle against the Sandinistas, which positively outraged AIM, the U.S. left, and some of the general public.[112]

Even as the IITC continued to associate and conference with the pro-Sandinista indigenous of Nicaragua,[113] the anti-Sandinista Miskito sought out U.S. Indian organizations to build anti-Marxist and pro-indigenous alliances. Indian rebel commander Brooklyn Rivera was favorably received by the conservative National Congress of the American Indians,[114] while Miskito exile Armstrong Wiggins found a home at the Washington, DC-based Indian Law Resource Center (ILRC), a former ally of the IITC.[115] The IITC publicized that "their" Miskito disputed the right of these pro-Sandinista Indians to represent the indigenous of Nicaragua.[116] In one of his later responses, Wiggins of the ILRC castigated Bill Means of the IITC for his organization's public statements on Nicaragua.[117] Soon, however, even the IITC fractured when Bill Means decided to expel fellow activist and representative to the UN Glenn Morris from the organization over his activities regarding Nicaragua. In an internal letter, Morris accused Means of selling out indigenous rights for the sake of political expediency—a continued alliance with the Marxist Sandinistas.[118] Western European indigenous rights advocacy organizations like the British Survival International and Cultural Survival likewise took an anti-Sandinista position.[119] The East German government, like much of the Eastern Bloc, sided with the Sandinista régime, and promoted an active solidarity among its citizens.[120]

The falling out over Nicaragua thus spilled over from the Indian sovereignty movement into the U.S. public sphere and to the world stage. Dated November 30, 1985, veteran sovereignty activist Hank Adams circulated a long letter addressed to President Ronald Reagan and copied to half of the U.S. government, Indian organizations and the media, in which he publicly condemned the pro-Sandinista group within AIM.[121] At the sessions of the United Nations Commission on Human Rights, the Nicaraguan representative and the IITC were now pitted against the U.S. government and the ILRC in a struggle over the meaning of the Nicaraguan revolution for indigenous human rights.[122] In a twist that gives yet another meaning to the word "red," some prominent Indian leaders like Hank Adams now questioned the very Indianness of Roxanne Dunbar-Ortiz, who was still committed to a Native-Marxist alliance.[123] Thus, now it was not only brother against brother and sister—Miskito against Miskito, Hank Adams and Russell Means against Bill Means and Roxanne Dunbar-Ortiz. The use of Nicaraguan Indians in U.S. foreign policy now pitted Native sovereignty organizations against one another: AIM against itself, the International Indian Treaty Council against the Indian Law Resource Center and the National Congress of the American Indians. Finally, it was "red nation" against "red nation": the IITC against the Miskito Contras, and AIM and the ILRC against the Nicaraguan Marxist government. The solidarity alliance between Indian sovereignty activists and Marxist movements fractured along the lines of "race against revolution."[124] Even as the Reagan Administration's Iran-Contra arms sales unraveled in a 1986 public scandal,[125] inter- and intra-Indian power struggles and renunciations continued for much of the rest of the 1980s.

The era of such heady but tenuous alliances came to an end in 1990, when Communism in Eastern Europe crumbled and fell, and its former régimes transitioned to other models of government. That same year, the Sandinistas were unseated by an opposition coalition in the Nicaraguan elections. These national and global changes would occasion a realignment in the international alliances of the U.S. nation-state and the transnational relations of the radical Indian sovereignty movement.

Conclusion

Through a number of examples, this chapter reviewed the various responses of the U.S. government to the transnational relations of the radical Indian sovereignty movement in the late Cold War. During and after Wounded Knee 1973 and the First International Indian Treaty Council conference, the U.S. government attempted to disrupt the transnational communication and relations of the Native rights struggle by classifying and persecuting them as a contagion or ideology alien to the body of the nation-state even as they insisted that the government had full and sole jurisdiction over the crimes committed by Native activists. In the years leading up to the Bicentennial, this approach escalated when the U.S. government classified the American Indian Movement and their allies as domestic terrorist organizations that posed a serious threat to the celebrations of the birth of the U.S. nation-state.

The arm of the U.S. government that most directly responded to the transnational relations of the radical Indian sovereignty movement was the State Department. While this institution initially may not have had a strategy for managing the image of U.S. Indian relations overseas, the United States Information Agency responded to the spring 1973 crisis at Wounded Knee by publishing a whole journal issue in which select Native activists defended the Nixon Administration's Indian policy. The State Department's subsequent cultural diplomacy programs—traveling exhibitions, concerts, lectures and film screenings—often presented foreign audiences with older transatlantic images of Indianness, thus reinforcing age-old stereotypes. Other cultural programs elevated Indian crafts and artifacts into the realm of art, and, along with recent legislation on Indian self-determination, used this move as proof of a new recognition of Native American contributions to U.S. diversity, and granting them their rightful place in American democracy. All the while, the State Department and its network of U.S. diplomatic posts regularly monitored and reported on the travels of Native activists and the foreign media coverage of the Indian sovereignty movement.

President Carter's human rights-centered foreign policy doctrine afforded Native activists with opportunities to frame the Indian sovereignty struggle as human rights just as they were gaining NGO status at the United Nations. The Carter Administration cooperated with the UN and the Native organizers of the 1977 Geneva UN NGO conference on discrimination against the Indians of the Americas, and it subsequently parried the criticism of the U.S. government articulated by the gathering. The high point of cooperation between the U.S. government and the radical Indian sovereignty movement came when as an NGO in the United Nations, the International Indian Treaty Council operated the U.S. embassy's only mail service during the Iranian Hostage Crisis. Here, because of its relations with various national liberation struggles and Nonaligned countries, the radical Indian sovereignty movement in effect supplanted the functions of the U.S. national government in humanitarian diplomacy.

After the election of Ronald Reagan to the presidency, the U.S. government's new foreign policy put the Indian sovereignty movement in a bind. The Reagan Administration's hard-line anti-Marxism used Nicaragua's Miskito Indian population in its attempts to overthrow the country's Sandinista government. By training the Miskito as Contras and through its international information campaigns about alleged Sandinista atrocities against indigenous Nicaraguans, the U.S. government drove a wedge in the transnational alliance for Indian sovereignty. U.S.-based Native sovereignty activists and their foreign allies split into a Marxist and pro-Sandinista camp on the one hand, and into an anti-Sandinista side that aligned with the U.S. government's professed concern for the indigenous of Nicaragua. Even as the Reagan Administration was forced to scale back its campaigns after the Iran Contra scandal, the issue caused a painful and enduring rift in the transnational sovereignty alliance.

Conclusion

The Transatlantic Sovereignty Alliance and its Legacy

This book presented an analytical history of the transatlantic relations between the American Indian radical sovereignty movement, Central European solidarity groups, and the United Nations in the late Cold War era. Its scholarly thesis was that such an alliance actually existed because, since the nineteenth century, transatlantically circulating representations and cultural forms of "playing Indian" had been consumed and reproduced by generations of Central Europeans in and beyond the primarily German-speaking populations of Switzerland, Germany and Austria. These cultural imaginaries had created interest and good will toward American Indians in Central European societies, and their specific manifestations in novels, stage plays, popular adventure films and the Indian reenactment hobby had created a pool of potential solidarity activists.

My investigation confirmed that such an alliance indeed came into being in the mid-1970s and endured through at least the end of the Cold War. Even though there had been interest, vision and overtures before, it was the siege of Wounded Knee in 1973 that truly catalyzed the transatlantic alliance through its media coverage and Native transnational outreach. From the mid-1970s, the leaders of the Native sovereignty movement traveled in Central Europe to establish "support groups" and build a transatlantic alliance. This alliance between the American Indian radical sovereignty movement and groups in especially German-speaking Central Europe proved to be crucial in shoring up the financial strength and boosting the morale of the sovereignty struggle during its supreme test—the court trials of the occupiers of Wounded Knee. Following the 1977 breakthrough United Nations NGO conference on discrimination against American Indians, Native activists and their European allies perfected their North American Plains–Mitteleuropa Axis, along which circulated moral and political support, financial contributions, and human bodies in the transatlantic Indian sovereignty movement. The alliance entered another phase when, in the 1980s, Central European "green" environmental and antinuclear activists sought the help of Native groups in their struggles.

This book's probing of how the preceding cultural forms of white Americans and Europeans "playing Indian" informed the transatlantic alliance uncovered a complex dynamic. The older transatlantic imaginaries of American Indians both enabled and constrained the transatlantic alliance for sovereignty. For their own part, Native activists grappled with the colonialist tropes of "the vanishing native," the "bloodthirsty warrior," and Indian "primitive art"—but they also manipulated some of these older images in their media and diplomatic performances for sovereignty. On the other side of the Atlantic, U.S. and Central European novels, stage plays, films, and reenactment hobby about Indian history and cultures had not been fully accepted as truth by Central Europeans; nevertheless, they had generated sympathy and good will toward Native Americans, especially because they often positioned Europeans in alliance with Indians. These fictional ideals were more than likely an added (if not always admitted) impetus for Central Europeans to actively support the radical Indian sovereignty movement. More ambiguous aspects of these imaginaries were their homosociality and interracial romances, which in the transatlantic alliance made for camaraderie, but also for personal and movement relationships based on romantic and sexual attraction. Tensions and arguments between Native activists and their European allies over who represented American Indian rights and how, and over the control of performances of Native cultural and spiritual rituals, also frustrated the transatlantic movement for sovereignty. Such politics of sexuality and representation delineated the limits of the transatlantic alliance.

My other assumption was that the cause of Indian sovereignty rights became important on a transatlantic plane as a result of a convergence of factors. These forces included the rise of the radical Indian sovereignty movement in and beyond the United States; the recent transatlantic counterculture and anti-Vietnam war protest networks; the importance of culture as a Cold War battleground for hearts and minds between U.S. democracy and Soviet Communism; and the peculiar geopolitical location of Central Europe as a Cold War "frontline" or zone straddling the iron curtain—more specifically the Germanic countries of (neutral) Switzerland and Austria, and (the divided) West and East Germany. In my historical analysis of the transatlantic sovereignty alliance, I argued that for these reasons Central Europe in the Late Cold War constituted (in Mary Louise Pratt's words) a "contact zone," where American Indian sovereignty activists and their European allies challenged the status quo of Indian rights and status in their performances of transnational diplomacy.

Radical American Indian activists, in particular, employed (in Daniel Cobb's words) an "inside-outside strategy," in which they represented themselves as being outside the U.S. nation-state, and articulated their ideal political status as autonomy, and often as full independence through decolonization under UN supervision. While Native performances of this imaginary independence strategically used the trappings of nationalism as defined by Benedict Anderson, at least one group of Indian activists persistently sought to actually realize this vision of a Native America as a group of independent countries. They were one of the few groups who worked with United Nations officials to gain status for Indian rights organizations in the world body. In the long run, in return for taking their transnational issues to the forum of the United Nations, these Native activists had to shift their position from demanding full decolonization to leveraging the evolving doctrine of human rights in UN forums for improvements in Indian policy within the framework of their own respective national governments. Ultimately, these alliances did not achieve Native American independence from the United States. Over time however, Native activists and their UN partners managed to build a mechanism that aims to protect indigenous rights around the globe, and which in 2012 sent UN Special Rapporteur Dr. James Anaya to investigate the conditions and issues of Indian communities in the United States.[1]

Successive doctrines of Cold War U.S. foreign policy presented opportunities but also posed challenges for the transatlantic alliance for American Indian sovereignty. By the end of the U.S. involvement in Vietnam, both the radical Indian sovereignty activists and their opponents placed Native America outside of the U.S. nation-state, and likened it to Vietnam as a battleground between the powerful forces of colonialism, Communism, and indigenous national liberation struggles. In this and other formulations, Indian activists critiqued current U.S. foreign policy, and articulated their own alternatives to it. President Jimmy Carter's human rights-centered foreign policy initiative afforded Native activists and their Central European allies political leverage and attention in the international community. Carter's U.S. ambassador to the United Nations, Andrew Young, collaborated with the organizers of the breakthrough 1977 UN International NGO Conference on Discrimination against Indians in the Americas. The high point of collaboration between the radical Indian sovereignty movement and the U.S. government came with the operation of the Iran Hostage Mail Exchange Service by the International Indian Treaty Council in 1980. However, the implementation of President Ronald Reagan's hard-line anti-Communist foreign policy doctrine posed a difficult challenge to the radical Indian sovereignty movement. The U.S. government's clandestine funding and training of the Contra rebels in Nicaragua and its public relations campaigns to destabilize the Marxist Sandinista régime in that country used the issue of the welfare and rights of the Nicaraguan Miskito, Sumu, and Rama Indians to sway public opinion. Eventually, even as various Native North American activists made fact-finding tours in Central America, the radical Indian sovereignty movement split over the issue of Nicaraguan indigenous rights into a pro-Contra and a pro-Sandinista faction. Here, the Native North American sovereignty movement broke down into camps of Indian rights activists versus Marxist nation builders; anti-Communists versus Indians as citizens of a "red" Marxist state—along the binary of race against revolution.

The United States and various European governments on both sides of the iron curtain responded to the rise and activism of the transatlantic Indian sovereignty alliance in a variety of ways. Veteran activists and scholars have largely mapped out the U.S. government's role in the siege of Wounded Knee in 1973, their domestic legal assault against the American Indian Movement, the FBI's clandestine campaign of planting informants and casting suspicion on leading members of the movement, and the BIA's and FBI's peculiar sluggishness and bungled investigations of the ensuing waves of violence on the Pine Ridge Reservation of South Dakota. As the radical Indian sovereignty movement was expanding its transnational outreach, the U.S. government responded with renewed alarm and disruptive activities. FBI reports used the transnational ties of the Native sovereignty struggle as further evidence of "foreign" influences and their warnings eventually resulted in the Congressional classification of AIM as a potential terrorist organization posing a threat to the official observations of the Bicentennial in 1976. The FBI's domestic hysteria about alleged plans of American Indian "dog soldiers" committing acts of terrorism in South Dakota spilled over into State Department cables about an AIM plot to bomb several U.S. embassies around the world. The State Department not only monitored and reported on the foreign coverage of the radical Indian sovereignty movement and on the travels of its Native activists, but that they also attempted to "manage" the global image of U.S. Indian policy through overseas cultural exchange programs, including USIS publications, traveling exhibitions, concerts, and film screenings. In the early- to mid-1970s, these programs presented Nixon's and Ford's recent legislation on Native self-determination as proof of the progress that the U.S. government had been making in its Indian policy.

On the other side of the iron curtain, Marxist totalitarian governments faced the challenge of how to control a culturally rooted and officially sanctioned solidarity with American Indians by their own citizens. Here, while some hobbyist groups desisted from solidarity work for fear of being persecuted or manipulated, other groups and individuals used solidarity as a pretext to engage with various aspects of U.S. culture and society in a climate of official Marxist anti-Americanism. Eastern Bloc governments responded with a variety of measures that included co-optation, surveillance, and reactive and preventative suppression and punishment of those who "overreached" in their zeal for solidarity with American Indians.

The legacy of the transatlantic alliance for American Indian sovereignty is carried on in several ways. German journalist Claus Biegert likes to point out that the alliance continues to be active.[2] During my visit to their office, the staff of the International Indian Treaty Council were engaged in a struggle with U.S. government officials to be a tax exempt organization based on its domestic and international activities.[3] While I was busy looking through their decades-old office files, staff at the German Society for Endangered Peoples were looking to facilitate Leonard Peltier's release by nominating him for international prizes and awards.[4] Both organizations also regularly attend and participate in the annual indigenous forums of the United Nations. Roxanne Dunbar-Ortiz follows hemispheric affairs and UN work, and in her publications she explains the current importance of past American Indian activism in the world body.[5]

Indeed, Native participation in the United Nations is still a powerful force. One day in May 2012, I was at my computer workstation in the archives when I received an email alert from the International Indian Treaty Council. The message contained an Internet link which pulled up a live video feed of Sinte Gleska University on the Sioux Rosebud Reservation of South Dakota. For the next several hours, I sat and watched a number of Indian leaders give testimony to United National Special Rapporteur Dr. James Anaya about the living conditions and discrimination that their Native communities have had to endure. A few days later, as he was wrapping up his official UN fact-finding tour in Native America, Anaya boldly asserted that the Black Hills should be returned to the Sioux so that the process of healing and reconciliation could begin.[6] Anaya's statement occasioned speculation that the UN would initiate some "intervention" process in the United States on behalf of American Indians.[7] Such expectations were likely one of the factors that have motivated President Barack Obama's increased engagement with Indian affairs.[8]

Tracing just how the transatlantic sovereignty alliance contributed to U.S. legislation on Indian self-determination rights requires extensive and systematic research beyond this study. Yet the influence of the North American Plains–Mitteleuropa axis on U.S. lawmaking is not to be dismissed. In federal policy, termination was overturned and self-determination advanced on the agenda. In the period between Wounded Knee 1973 and the end of the Cold War in 1990, the U.S. nation-state passed the Indian Self-Determination and Education Assistance Act of 1975; the American Indian Religious Freedom Act of 1978; the Indian Child Welfare Act of 1978; the Indian Gaming Regulatory Act of 1988; the Aleut Restitution Act of 1988; the Native American Graves Protection and Repatriation Act of 1990; the Indian Arts and Crafts Act of 1990; and the Native American Languages Act of 1990. Yet the Indian Claims Limitations Act of 1982 and some of the Indian land claims settlements extinguished Native title to land on what is now U.S. soil. On balance, directly or indirectly, the mainstream as well as the radical Indian sovereignty movement successfully pressured the U.S. government for progressive legislation on Native rights.

Another legacy of the transatlantic Indian sovereignty movement lies in its practical implications for the work of transnational nongovernmental organizations. The transatlantic coalition presents an example of how a social or political movement can attempt to "outflank" a particular country's national government and build alliances outside of the nation-state. These transnational relations can then be used to pressure the particular national government to seriously address the demands of the movement. This strategy has to do with the nation-state's rhetoric and self-image, and its diplomatic relations. Like the transnational sovereignty alliance, a social or political movement can mobilize resources from outside its strictly defined geography, and use these resources to bolster its position vis-à-vis its national government or other opponents. The recognition and pressure from such transnational resources can also help the movement build its institutional infrastructure both in its home society and beyond the reach of its national government. While a group's struggle against a multinational corporation may take different forms, it may still contain some elements of this dynamic. International Relations scholars and practitioners of transnational advocacy would be able to show if and to what extent the transatlantic sovereignty alliance is a model that can be replicated for other causes—how old and new struggles for justice can use strategies of "leaving the American Sector."

Notes

Introduction

1. In 1975, American Indian Movement leaders Dennis Banks and Vernon Bellecourt visited author Liselotte Welskopf-Henrich in East Berlin. Lakota medicine man Archie Fire Lame Deer spent much of the 1980s touring Europe, and he visited East Germany in 1983 and 1985, educating audiences about Native American approaches to religion and society. For more, see Glenn Penny, "Red Power: Liselotte Welskopf-Henrich and Indian Activist Networks in East and West Germany," *Central European History* 41 (2008), 447–476. "Ceremony & Sundance, Europe, Do's & Don'ts; Beer & Alcohol, etc., Europe?" Undated audio recording, 1/2. The Richard Erdoes Papers.

2. Such events included the American Indian occupation of San Francisco Bay's Alcatraz Island between 1969 and 1971; the October 1972 Trail of Broken Treaties to Washington, DC; the subsequent takeover of the headquarters of the Bureau of Indian Affairs; the February 1973 riots at Custer, South Dakota; and the subsequent takeover and standoff at Wounded Knee, South Dakota, in the spring of 1973.

3. Activists in militant sovereignty organizations like the American Indian Movement included Natives from Canada, the United States, and Mexico.

4. Paul Chaat Smith and Robert Allen Warrior, *Like a Hurricane: The Indian Movement from Alcatraz to Wounded Knee* (New York: The New Press, 1996), 269. For another version of this argument, see Troy R. Johnson, *Red Power: The Native American Civil Rights Movement* (New York: Infobase Publishing, 2007), 81.

5. Solidarity groups also existed in France, Italy, the United Kingdom, Ireland, Poland, and likely in Czechoslovakia.

6. Some of this scholarship includes Johnson, and Smith and Warrior.

7. Scholars who have made the same point include Kevin Bruyneel, *The Third Space of Sovereignty: The Postcolonial Politics of U.S.–Indigenous Relations* (Minneapolis, London: University of Minnesota Press, 2007), 126.

8. For more on the patriotic and anti-Communist rhetoric of Indian activism, and Native alliance building with the Kennedy and Johnson administrations,

see Daniel Cobb, *Native Activism in Cold War America: The Struggle for Sovereignty* (Lawrence: University Press of Kansas, 2008).

9. Within North America, arguably the most important group of such non-Native allies were the lawyers who defended many AIM members in the court cases resulting from the siege of Wounded Knee in 1973, and who also strategized with Native activists about the transnational approaches that are the subject of this book. Outside of North America, such allies included leading members of Central and South American indigenous struggles; leaders of national liberation struggles including in Northern Ireland and Palestine; United Nations officials; and European solidarity groups.

10. Smith and Warrior, 132.

11. Ibid., 24, 28–29.

12. Arnold Krupat, *The Voice in the Margin: Native American Literature and the Canon* (Berkeley: University of California Press, 1989), 206, fn 4; Bruce Elliott Johansen, Barbara Alice Mann, eds., *Encyclopedia of the Haudenosaunee* (*Iroquois Confederacy*), (Westport, CT; London: Greenwood Press, 2000), 16; Bruce E. Johansen, *Akwesasne Notes*. American Indian Heritage Month: Commemoration vs. Exploitation. ABC-CLIO History and the Headlines. Online: http://www.historyandtheheadlines.abc-clio.com/ContentPages/ContentPage.aspx?entryId=1171842&currentSection=1161468&productid=5. Accessed October 5, 2011. Front page, *Akwesasne Notes*, July–Aug 1972; Jan–Feb 1972, 2–3. Underground Newspaper Collection.

13. See Russell Means with Marvin J. Wolf, *Where White Men Fear to Tread: The Autobiography of Russell Means* (New York: St. Martin's Press, 1995), 275; Smith and Warrior, 215; and Dennis Banks and Richard Erdoes, *Ojibwa Warrior: Dennis Banks and the Rise of the American Indian Movement* (Norman: University of Oklahoma Press, 2004), 179.

14. See Charles Wilkinson, *Blood Struggle: The Rise of Modern Indian Nations* (New York: Norton, 2005), 133; Thomas W. Cowger, *The National Congress of the American Indians: The Founding Years* (Lincoln and London: The University of Nebraska Press, 1999), 6, 9, 11–12, 15; Johnson, 38, 40; Smith and Warrior, 26, 33, 54, 79, 88.

15. For some recent scholarship on the sovereignty movement, see Smith and Warrior; Wilkinson; Johnson; and Cobb, *Native Activism in Cold War America*.

16. Among these were a number of West German AIM support groups, regarded by the more established solidarity organizations as too temporary and fickle for real movement work. Solidarity organizations beyond Central Europe included the Swedish Indian League, the "Polish Movement of Friends of the American Indians," the Irish Committee for the Defense of Wounded Knee, and the "KIVA group, Friends of the North American Indians in the Netherlands." Respectively, July 5, 1977 letter from Claus Biegert, Munich to Ulla Bäcksin, Sweden, Records of the Gesellschaft für bedrohte Völker (Society for Endangered

Peoples); Ewa Nowicka, "The 'Polish Movement Friends of the American Indians.'" Christian F. Feest, ed., *Indians and Europe: An Interdisciplinary Collection of Essays* (Aachen: Edition Herodot Rader-Verlag, 1987), 599–608; "For favor of publication," in January 11 and February 6, 1974 letters from the Irish Committee for the Defense of Wounded Knee; June 3, 1974 letter from J. Heijink of "KIVA group, Friends of the North American Indians in the Netherlands"; article in March 11, 1974 letter from Pierrette Désy of "Comité francais de soutien á AIM" Paris, France; article "For a Policy of Solidarity towards the Indians of Wounded Knee" by Pierrette Désy, published in *La Guelue ouverte* in Paris, France. Records of the Wounded Knee Legal Defense/ Offense Committee.

17. While non-U.S. Americanists may have been engaging in Transnational American Studies in the forms of comparative, immigration and reception studies for much longer, in the United States Transnational American Studies emerged as a paradigm in the (inter)discipline of American Studies in the mid-1990s, when scholars such as Jane Desmond and Virginia Dominguez started to spearhead this theoretical framework. By the dawn of the new millennium this approach had gained ground: in her 1998 presidential address at the American Studies Association, Janice Radway explored the possibility of the ASA refashioning its name after The International Forum for U.S. Studies, a research organization co-founded and co-run by Desmond and Dominguez. See Jane C. Desmond and Virginia R. Dominguez, "Resituating American Studies in a Critical Internationalism," *American Quarterly* 48, no. 3 (1996): 475–490; Janice Radway, "What's in a Name? Presidential Address to the American Studies Association, 20 November 1998," *American Quarterly* 51, no. 1 (1999): 19. Also see the website of the International Forum for U.S. Studies, now at the University of Illinois at Urbana-Champaign: http://www.ips.uiuc.edu/ifuss/. Accessed February 7, 2015.

In the new millennium, the ascent of Transnational American Studies culminated in its official recognition as a full-blown paradigm: the proclamation of the so-called "Transnational Turn in American Studies" in Shelley Fisher Fishkin's 2004 presidential address to the American Studies Association. In Fisher Fishkin's formulation, Transnational American Studies interrogates the power, potential, and limits of the United States as a nation and a system of cultures—transnational scholarship "see[s] the inside and outside, domestic and foreign, national and international, as interpenetrating." In that it considers "the ways in which ideas, people, culture, and capital have circulated and continue to circulate physically, and virtually, throughout the world, both in ways we might expect, and unpredictably," Transnational American Studies acknowledges and critically examines aspects of the United States in a supra-national context: in a regional or global setting, or as part of "web of contact zones." Shelley Fisher Fishkin, "Crossroads of Cultures: The Transnational Turn in American Studies. Presidential Address to the American Studies Association, November 12, 2004," In *American Quarterly* 57, no. 1 (March 2005): 21–22.

18. For more, see Shari M. Huhndorf, "Picture Revolution: Transnationalism, American Studies, and the Politics of Contemporary Native Culture," *American Quarterly* 61, No. 2 (June 2009): 359–381.

19. As recently as 2010, the British authorities refused to recognize the tribal passports of the Iroquois lacrosse team, in effect denying them entry to an international championship in Manchester, England. Thomas Kaplan, "Iroquois Defeated by Passport dispute." *The New York Times* July 17, 2010, page D1. Online: http://www.nytimes.com/2010/07/17/sports/17lacrosse.html. Accessed May 29, 2015. For earlier Mohawk activism for transnational passage rights, see *You Are on Indian Land* (dir. Mort Ransen, National Film Board of Canada, 1969).

20. Helen H. Jackson, *A Century of Dishonor: A Sketch of the U. S. Government's Dealings with Some of the Indian Tribes* (New York: Harper and Brothers, 1881), 68, 70.

21. In a more general sense, the history of American Indian transnationalism is a case study of alternative modernities—inasmuch as Native Americans have maintained forms of governance and human communities alternative to the modern nation-state.

22. The 1830 U.S. Supreme Court ruling in *Cherokee Nation v. Georgia* said, "it may well be doubted whether those tribes which reside within the acknowledged boundaries of the United States can, with strict accuracy, be denominated foreign nations. They may, more correctly be denominated domestic dependent nations." *Cherokee Nation v. Georgia*, 30 U.S. 1 (1831). Legal Information Institute, Cornell University Law School. Online: https://www.law.cornell.edu/supremecourt/text/30/1. Accessed May 29, 2015.

23. Paul C. Rosier, *Serving Their Country: American Indian Politics and Patriotism in the Twentieth Century*. (Cambridge, MA: Harvard University Press, 2009), 9, 10–11.

24. Ibid., 225.

25. Bruyneel, xvii.

26. Smith and Warrior, 269; for another version of this argument, see Johnson, 81.

27. Cobb, *Native Activism in Cold War America*.

28. See ibid. and Daniel Cobb, "Talking the Language of the Larger World: Politics in Cold War (Native) America." In Daniel Cobb and Loretta Fowler, eds., *Beyond Red Power: American Indian Politics and Activism since 1900* (Santa Fe, NM: School for Advanced Research, 2007), 161–177.

29. For more on emerging scholarship of American Indians as transnational actors, see Jace Weaver, *The Red Atlantic: American Indigenes and the Making of the Modern World, 1000–1927* (Chapel Hill: University of North Carolina Press, 2014); Shari M. Huhndorf, *Mapping the Americas: The Transnational Politics of Contemporary Native Culture* (Ithaca, NY: Cornell University Press, 2009); and Lucie Kyrova, "Native American International Activism and Political

Thought during the Cold War, 1950–1989." Unpublished doctoral dissertation. Department of History, College of William and Mary, May 2016.

30. See Ronald Niezen, *The Origins of Indigenism: Human Rights and the Politics of Identity.* (Berkeley, CA; London: University of California Press, 2003).

31. See Weaver, *The Red Atlantic.*

32. H. Glenn Penny, *Kindred by Choice: Germans and American Indians since 1800* (Chapel Hill: The University of North Carolina Press, 2013), 197.

33. See Penny M. Von Eschen, *Race Against Empire: Black Americans and Anticolonialism, 1937–1957* (Ithaca, NY; London: Cornell University Press, 1997).

34. See Martin Klimke, *The Other Alliance: Student Protest in West Germany & the United States in the Global Sixties* (Princeton NJ; Oxford: Princeton University Press, 2010). I will confine myself to using the term "transatlantic" instead of "global," since probing the latter requires a greater scholarly apparatus and scope than the one at my disposal.

35. See Von Eschen, *Race Against Empire*; and Mary L. Dudziak, *Cold War Civil Rights: Race and the Image of American Democracy* (Princeton, NJ; Oxford: Princeton University Press, 2000).

36. See among others, Von Eschen, *Race Against Empire*; Dudziak, *Cold War Civil Rights*; Penny M. Von Eschen, *Satchmo Blows Up the World: Jazz Ambassadors Play the Cold War* (Cambridge, MA: Harvard University Press, 2004); Megan Threlkeld, "The Pan-American Conference of Women, 1922: Successful Suffragists Turn to International Relations," *Diplomatic History* 31, no. 5 (November 2007): 801–828; Megan Threlkeld, *Pan American Women: U.S. Internationalists and Revolutionary Mexico* (Philadelphia: University of Pennsylvania Press, 2014); Molly Wood, "'Commanding Beauty' and 'Gentle Charm': American Women and Gender in the Early Twentieth-Century Foreign Service," *Diplomatic History* 31, no. 3 (June 2007): 505–530; and Allison Blakely, Linda Heywood, Charles Stith, and Joshua C. Yesnowitz, eds., *African Americans in U.S. Foreign Policy From the Era of Frederick Douglass to the Age of Obama* (Champaign, IL: University of Illinois Press, 2015).

37. Such scholarship includes Richard White, *The Middle Ground: Indians, Empires, and Republics in the Great Lakes region, 1650–1815* (Cambridge, New York: Cambridge University Press, 1991); Leonard J. Sadosky, *Revolutionary Negotiations: Indians, Empires, and Diplomats in the Founding of America* (Charlottesville: University of Virginia Press, 2009); Timothy J. Shannon, *Iroquois Diplomacy on the Early American Frontier* (New York: Viking, 2008); Tom Arne Midtrød, *The Memory of All Ancient Customs: Native American Diplomacy in the Colonial Hudson Valley* (Ithaca, NY: Cornell University Press, 2012); John T. Juricek, *Colonial Georgia and the Creeks: Anglo-Indian Diplomacy on the Southern Frontier, 1733–1763* (Gainesville: University Press of Florida, 2010); Charles A. Weeks, *Paths to a Middle Ground: The Diplomacy of Natchez, Boukfouka, Nogales, and San Fernando de las Barrancas, 1791–1795* (Tuscaloosa:

University of Alabama Press, 2005); Gilles Havard, *The Great Peace of Montreal of 1701: French-Native Diplomacy in the Seventeenth Century* (Montreal; Ithaca, NY: McGill-Queen's University Press, 2001); and Vine Deloria and Raymond J DeMallie, eds., *Documents of American Indian Diplomacy: Treaties, Agreements, and Conventions, 1775–1979* (Norman: University of Oklahoma Press, 1999).

38. See Wilkinson, 133; Cowger, 6, 9, 11–12, 15; Johnson, 38, 40; Smith and Warrior, 26, 33, 54, 79, 88.

39. For the concept of the *contact zone*, I am indebted to the scholarship of Mary Louise Pratt, *Imperial Eyes: Travel Writing and Transculturation* (London, New York: Routledge, 1992)

40. Ibid., 6.

41. While as Anderson defined it, the nation is "an imagined political community—and imagined as both inherently limited and sovereign," the fact that it is imagined does not make it any less socially real—people continue to kill and die for it. Benedict Anderson, *Imagined Communities: Reflections on the Origins and Spread of Nationalism* (originally 1983, revised edition London and New York: Verso, 1991), 5.

42. United States Supreme Court ruling in *Cherokee Nation v. Georgia*, 1830.

43. Anderson, 5.

44. Rebekah J. Kowal, "Staging the Greensboro Sit-Ins," *The Drama Review* vol. 48, no. 4 (Winter 2004): 137.

45. Ibid., 138.

46. Ibid., 150.

47. Smith and Warrior, ix.

48. Diana Taylor, *The Archive and the Repertoire* (Durham, NC: Duke University Press, 2003), 19, 20.

49. Ibid., 21.

50. See Joseph Roach, *Cities of the Dead: Circum-Atlantic Performance.* (New York: Columbia University Press, 1996); Katrin Sieg, *Ethnic Drag: Performing Race, Nation, Sexuality in West Germany* (Ann Arbor: University of Michigan Press, 2002); and Diana Taylor, "Performance and/as History," *The Drama Review* 50, no. 1 (Spring 2006): 67–86.

51. Philip J. Deloria, *Playing Indian.* (New Haven, CT; London: Yale University Press, 1998)

52. While the "representations of Indigenous Peoples (in literary texts and visual and popular culture)" is one of the major branches of Indigenous Studies, it is often open to criticism when "studies of American Indians must situate Indian peoples (or simply their invented image) in the gaze of Europeans." D. Anthony Tyeeme Clark and Norman R. Yetman, ""To Feel the Drumming Earth Come Upward": Indigenizing the American Studies Discipline, Field Movement," joint issue of *Indigenous Studies Today: An International Journal* and *American Studies* (incorporating *American Studies International*) (Fall 2005): 12; and Carter

Meland, Joseph Bauerkemper, LeAnne Howe and Heidi Stark, "The Bases Are Loaded: American Indians and American Studies," in ibid., 402.

53. Ibid., 8.

54. The idea that these categories are socially and culturally constructed, and enacted and challenged through performance, makes them no less socially real. This performance framework also establishes the concept of "authenticity" as a performed category—not something inherently fixed. Therefore, I will treat authenticity as a discursive term, a trope at once enabling and constraining the performances of the transatlantic sovereignty alliance. For more on authenticity as a discursive term, see Glenn Penny, "Elusive Authenticity: The Quest for the American Indian in German Public Culture." In *Comparative Studies in Society and History*, vol. 48., no. 4 (October 2006), 798–819.

55. I do not apply notions of performativity inclusively such as Erving Goffman did when he theorized "the presentation of the self in everyday life"; nor as Judith Butler did in her paradigm of performative constructions of gender and sexuality. See Erving Goffman, *The Presentation of Self in Everyday Life* (Garden City, NY: Doubleday, 1959); Judith Butler, *Gender Trouble: Feminism and the Subversion of Identity* (New York: Routledge, 1990); and Judith Butler, *Bodies that Matter: On the Discursive Limits of "Sex"* (New York: Routledge, 1993). For a wide-ranging discussion of the notion in Performance Studies, see "Performativity" in Richard Schechner, *Performance Studies: An Introduction* (New York, London: Routledge, 2002), 110–141.

Chapter 1

1. Box 135, Folder 631. "Archie Fire, Tape 3; Wolakota." Audio recording, 1/2. March 2, 1986. The Richard Erdoes Papers. Transcription by the author.

2. One place of departure for a more comprehensive overview is Colin G. Calloway, "Historical Encounters across Five Centuries," in Colin G. Calloway, Gerd Gemünden and Suzanne Zantop, eds., *Germans and Indians: Fantasies, Encounters, Projections* (Lincoln and London: University of Nebraska Press, 2002), 47–82.

3. See Stephen S. Witte and Marsha V. Gallagher, eds., *The North American Journals of Prince Maximilian of Wied I-II.* (Norman: University of Oklahoma Press, 2008). Also see Calloway, 65.

4. See William H. Goetzmann et al., *Karl Bodmer's America* (Lincoln: Joslyn Art Museum and University of Nebraska Press, 1984).

5. See George Catlin, *The Manners, Customs and Condition of the North American Indians* (London: the author, 1841).

6. For more on Catlin's European tour with these groups, see Christopher Mulvey, "Among the Sag-a-noshes: Ojibwa and Iowa Indians with George Catlin in Europe, 1843–1848," in Christian F. Feest, ed., *Indians and Europe:*

an Interdisciplinary Collection of Essays (Aachen: Edition Herodot, Rader Verlag, 1987), 253–275.

7. See George Catlin, *Catlin's Notes of Eight Years' Travels and Residence in Europe with his North American Indian Collection: with Anecdotes and Incidents of the Travels and Adventures of Three Different Parties of American Indians Whom He Introduced to the Courts of England, France, and Belgium* (New York: Burgess, Stinger & Co., 1848). For more on Catlin's gallery and performances, see W. H. Truettner, *The Natural Man Observed: A Study of Catlin's Indian Gallery* (Washington, DC: Smithsonian Institution, 1979); Brian W. Dippie, *Catlin and His Contemporaries: The Politics of Patronage* (Lincoln: University of Nebraska Press, 1990); and Joan Carpenter Troccoli, *First Artist of the West: George Catlin Paintings and Watercolors* (Tulsa, OK: Gilcrease Museum, 1993).

8. Catlin as cited in Mulvey, 256–258.

9. An early indication of the sexual politics of such transatlantic encounters is an episode in Maungwudaus's account where some British military officers request that the Indians allow themselves to be kissed by the officers' wives, who likely were prostitutes in reality. The Ojibwe obliged, but then commented that these women were not good for anything else, certainly not to be wives. Here, the joke first seemed to be on the Indians, then on the women—and possibly on the officers, who proved their bad taste in women, and were very rude as hosts. Maungwudaus as cited in Mulvey, 269. For more, see Maungwudaus, *An Account of the Chippewa Indians, Who Have Been Travelling Among The Whites, in the United States, England, Ireland, Scotland, France, and Belgium* (Rochester, NY: privately published, 1848).

10. Mulvey, 272–273. For more on Catlin's tours of Europe, see Peter Bolz, "Indian Images for the King: George Catlin in Europe." In Pamela Kort, Max Hollein, eds, *I Like America: Fictions of the Wild* West (München, New York: Prestel, 2006), 68–85.

11. L. G. Moses, *Wild West Shows and the Images of American Indians, 1883–1933* (Albuquerque: University of New Mexico Press, 1996).

12. Ibid., 271.

13. Sieg, *Ethnic Drag*, 125–126. For more on these shows and their Indian performers, see Rudolf Conrad, "Mutual Fascination: Indians in Dresden and Leipzig." In Christian F. Feest, ed., *Indians and Europe: An Interdisciplinary Collection of Essays* (Aachen: Edition Herodot Rader-Verlag, 1987), 455–473; Peter Bolz, "Life Among the "Hunkpapas": A Case Study of German Indian Lore." In Feest, 480–484; and Eric Ames, "Seeing the Imaginary: On the Popular Reception of Wild West Shows in Germany, 1885–1910." In Kort and Hollein, 212–229.

14. Irmgard Egger, "*The Leatherstocking Tales* as Adapted for German Juvenile Readers." In George A. Test, ed., *James Fenimore Cooper: His Country and His Art*, Papers from the 1984 Conference at State University of New York College—Oneonta and Cooperstown.), 41–45. Also an excerpt online: http://external.oneonta.edu/cooper/articles/suny/1984suny-egger2.html. Accessed May 29, 2015.

15. Beadle and Adams Archives online finding aid. University of Delaware Library Special Collections Department. Online: http://www.lib.udel.edu/ud/spec/findaids/beadle.htm. Accessed May 29, 2015.

16. Earlier Indian captivity narratives may have been published in Great Britain as well, since they could capitalize on both the exoticism of their theme as well as the Anglophone readership on the isles.

17. The figure of Winnetou first appeared in Karl May's writing in 1875, and subsequently became a more refined and idealized character. Sieg, 88. In the early 1890s, May's stories were republished in three major volumes: Winnetou I–III. "Karl May—Life And Works. The Years 1875–1912." Online: http://www.karl-may-stiftung.de/engl/biograph2.html. Accessed May 29, 2015. For more on Karl May's creation of Winnetou, see Karl Markus Kreis, "German Wild West: Karl May's Invention of the Definitive Indian." In Kort and Hollein, 249–273.

18. Sieg, *Ethnic Drag*, 81.

19. I base this conclusion of mine on the scholarship of Jacki Rand on the mid to late-nineteenth century life of the Kiowa, Comanche and other native nations in the region of the Southern Plains. Jacki Thompson, *Kiowa Humanity and the Invasion of the State* (Lincoln: University of Nebraska Press, 2008).

20. Conversations with Germans about Karl May's Winnetou novels. In July 2007, a tour guide at the Karl May Museum in Radebeul claimed that by the time May visited the United States for the first time, he had already written several of his Winnetou books; and his journey took him only as far as a Tuscarora reservation in New York State. Author's personal visit to the Karl May Museum in Radebeul, Germany, July 2007.

21. Personal visit and tour of the Karl May Museum in Radebeul, Germany, July 2007. For more on the museum, see http://www.karl-may-museum.de/web/start.php. Later in the 1960s, the West German Winnetou movies spawned a Central European mini-industry of home-made material culture, at the center of which stood the replicas of the heroes' rifles. Personal visits to the *Po stopě Karla Maye*/*Tracing Karl May* exhibition in the Náprstek Museum of Asian, African and American Cultures, Prague, January and February, 2013.

22. Klekih-petra, friend of the Apache and teacher of Christianity to Winnetou, came to the Wild West to atone for his sins of inciting terrorism with his demagogy in his native Germany. Sam Hawkens, trapper, scout for the railroad surveyors, and tutor and friend to Karl, also turns out to be German. Karl May, *Winnetou*. Translated by Michael Shaw. (New York: The Seabury Press, 1977), 82–86.

23. Ibid., 88.

24. These include the narrator's reference to the historical context and the moral position of Germanness: "It was the eve of the Civil War. [. . .] As a German, I could not see eye to eye with the Southerners regarding the slave question, and might arouse suspicion. And I did not feel inclined to involve myself in complications whose resolution I could not foresee." Ibid., 411.

25. Such a literary positioning of a European hero in alliance with American Indians may not have been unique to Germany. In the 1980s, a

Polish solidarity group derived their initial interest in American Indians from *Tomek na wojenney ściezce* [*Tomek on the War Path*], a novel of Polish juvenile literature published in 1959 by Alfred Szklarski. Here young Tomek's alliance with American Indians is motivated not only by his upright character and sense of justice, but also his observations that the Polish and American Indians share a history of oppression by other nations. Ewa Nowicka, "The 'Polish Movement Friends of the American Indians.'" In Feest, 606–607.

26. May, 331, 364.

27. May, 71, 92.

28. May, 271.

29. May, 202, 288, 328–329.

30. The author's research on the internet in 2007 revealed at least a dozen such locations in the German-speaking countries of Central Europe. In July 2007, the author also personally visited for field research two such locations: Elspe, and Bad Segeberg.

31. Sieg *Ethnic Drag*, 76. Sieg's analysis of the theater festivals as well as German cultural hobbyism leads her to argue that Germans, who after the Second World War had to banish the issue of race from their public discussions, used Karl May's Western fantasies to exonerate themselves from the collective feeling of guilt over the Holocaust. In Sieg's reading, the German immigrant-turned frontiersman Old Shatterhand's brotherhood with the Apache chief Winnetou is a *Wiedergutmachung*—the use of a distant American historical era and its native characters as a proxy or *surrogate* to finally right the wrongs committed against Jews by Germans in the Second World War. I disagree with Sieg's analysis because it attempts to subsume in its framework the multiple and diverse ways in which several postwar generations of Germans produced and consumed fantasies about American Indians in a variety of media.

32. Another of these forms of playing Indian at the theme parks is a store where the visitors can have their photos taken in the surplus Wild West costumes of the stage plays. Author's visit to the Karl May stage festival in Elspe, Germany, July 2007.

33. It is important to point out that while the strongest sources of such fan cultures were the German-speaking countries (Germany, Austria and Switzerland), other Central European countries such as Poland, Czechoslovakia, and Hungary also had Western or Indian clubs or societies. See my discussion of the early Hungarian and Czechoslovak hobbyism later. As Katrin Sieg observes, the annual Indian hobbyist meetings in Germany came to have participants "from almost every other Europoean country." Sieg, *Ethnic Drag*, 123.

34. These include Bolz; Yolanda Broyles Gonzales, "Cheyennes in the Black Forest: A Social Drama." In Roger Rollin, ed., *The Americanization of the Global Village: Essays in Comparative Popular Culture.* (Bowling Green, KY: Bowling Green State University Popular Press, 1989), 70–86; Birgit Turski, *Die Indianistikgruppen in der DDR: Entwicklung, Probleme, Aussichten* (Idstein: Baum, 1994); *If Only I Were an Indian.* (dir. John Paskievich, Winnipeg: National

Film Board of Canada, 1995); *Das Pow-wow* (dir. Marta Carlson, 2001); Marta Carlson, "Germans Playing Indians." In Colin G. Calloway, Gerd Gemünden, and Suzanne Zantop, eds., *Germans and Indians: Fantasies, Encounters, Projections* (Lincoln and London: University of Nebraska Press, 2002), 213–216; Katrin Sieg, "Indian Impersonation as Historical Surrogation." In ibid., 217–242; Katrin Sieg, "Winnetou's Grandchildren: Indian Identification, Ethnic Expertise, White Embodiment." In Sieg, *Ethnic Drag*, 115–150; Friedrich von Borries and Jens-Uwe Fischer, *Sozialistische Cowboys: Der Wilde Westen Ostdeutschlands* (Frankfurt am Main: Suhrkamp Verlag, 2008); and Petra Tjitske Kalshoven, *Crafting the Indian: Knowledge, Desire and Play in Indianist Reenactment* (Beghahn Books, 2012).

35. Sieg, *Ethnic Drag*, 82, 122; Von Borries and Fischer, 17.

36. Bolz, 484. Other clubs established in the 1910s included the *Cowboy Club* of Munich, and the *Wild West* and *Cowboy Club Buffalo* of Freiburg, Germany. Von Borries and Fischer, 17.

37. Respectively, ibid., 14, and Bolz, 480.

38. Raul Baktay made at least one trip to Montana, where he studied the traditions and history of the Blackfeet. The photos of Baktay's "cowboy" meetings used props and were posed to look much like scenes from the early Western films. Baktay's own Indian name is possibly a reference to Sitting Bull, the famous Hunkpapa Lakota Sioux chief of the late nineteenth century. Author's visit to the Baktay Ervin Museum of Cowboy and Indian/Western Games, Kisoroszi, Hungary. Tour and conversation with tour guide, himself a veteran reenactor. July 2, 2011.

39. Paskievich. For more on Thompson Seton's ideology and forms of playing Indian, see "Natural Indians and Identities of Modernity." In Deloria, 95–127.

40. Author's visit to the Baktay Ervin Museum of Cowboy and Indian/Western Games, Kisoroszi, Hungary. Tour and conversation with tour guide, himself a veteran reenactor. July 2, 2011.

41. Von Borries and Fischer, 14, 29.

42. László Bérczes and Tamás Cseh, *Cseh Tamás: Bérczes László beszélgetőkönyve* [*Conversations with Tamás Cseh by László Bérczes*] (Budapest: Palatinus, 2007), 71–72.

43. Deloria, 128–135.

44. Ibid., 135.

45. Katrin Sieg observed that this suppression of notions of race opened the door for hiring Germans to perform Indians on stage and claimed that this also transferred to German Indianist hobbyism. Sieg, *Ethnic Drag*, 2, 4, 22, 123.

46. Over the years, both the Karl May Museum in Radebeul and the Karl May Festival at Bad Segeberg hosted some Native American visitors and performers. Ibid., 82, 109, 110. Author's visit to the Karl May Museum in Radebeul, and the Karl May Festival at Bad Segeberg and Elspe, Germany, July 2007.

47. Cseh recalls cutting up an unused leather sofa set owned by the parents of a friend to make buckskin clothing as seen in a French Wild West

comic book—and then later meeting with two other hobbyists, whose accurate replicas of Plains Indian objects and clothing taught him humility about his own expertise. Bérczes and Cseh, 72–73; Author's visit to the Baktay Ervin Museum of Cowboy and Indian/Western Games, Kisoroszi, Hungary. Tour and conversation with tour guide, himself a veteran reenactor. July 2, 2011.

48. Sieg, *Ethnic Drag*, 123.

49. *Frankfurter Nachrichten* June 23, 1983 as quoted in Peter Bolz, 477.

50. Ibid., 486.

51. Author's interview with long-time member and leader of the Bakony group, June 2011. Source kept anonymous due to research ethics regulations.

52. Sieg, *Ethnic Drag*, 124; also see Bolz, 478.

53. The words "accuracy" and "authenticity" are used not as analytical terms, but are descriptive of the notions important to the German Indian hobbyist movement.

54. Sieg, *Ethnic Drag*, 118; Michael Schubert quoted in Bolz, 477; Von Borries and Fischer, 42, 56.

55. Sieg, *Ethnic Drag*, 122.

56. Bolz, 485–486; Sieg, *Ethnic Drag*, 123.

57. Von Borries and Fischer, 54; Sieg, *Ethnic Drag*, 123.

58. Ibid., 118.

59. Von Borries and Fischer, 48.

60. Sieg, *Ethnic Drag*, 130–131

61. Sieg, *Ethnic Drag*, 122.

62. Von Borries and Fischer, 18–19, 31–32.

63. Von Borries and Fischer, 32–33; Author's interview with long-time member and leader of the Bakony group, June 2011. Source kept anonymous due to research ethics regulations.

64. Von Borries and Fischer, 31–32, 54.

65. Von Borries and Fischer, 35.

66. Sieg, *Ethnic Drag*, 82; Von Borries and Fischer, 18–19.

67. Gonzales, 78; Glenn Penny, "Elusive Authenticity," 800.

68. *Die Söhne der Großen Bärin* [*The Sons of the Great Mother Bear*] cycle of books were as follows: *Über den Missouri* [*Over the Missouri*] 1951; *Der junge Häuptling* [*The Young Chief*] 1951; *Heimkehr zu den Dakota* [*Return to the Dakota*] 1951, 1963; *Die Höhle in den schwarzen Bergen* [*The Cave in the Black Hills*] 1963; *Der Weg in die Verbannung* [*The Path in Exile*] 1962; *Harka* 1962.

69. Penny, "Elusive Authenticity," 800.

70. The author remembers that as he was growing up in Hungary in the 1980s, he read in Hungarian translation at least two of Welskopf-Henrich's books titled *The Sons of the Great Bear* and *The Return of Tokei-ihto*, as well as seeing at least one of the film adaptations in the cinema. Personal recollection.

71. Sieg, *Ethnic Drag*, 144.

72. Glenn Penny, "Elusive Authenticity," 800.

73. Katrin Sieg, *Ethnic Drag*, 24.

74. These films included the 1962 *Der Schatz im Silbersee* [*The Treasure of Silver Lake*], the 1963 *Winnetou 1.*[*Apache Gold*]; the 1964 *Old Shatterhand*; the 1964 *Winnetou 2.*[*Last of the Renegades*]; the 1964 *Unter Geiern* [*Frontier Hellcat*]; the 1965 *Der Ölprinz* [*Rampage at Apache Wells*]; the 1965 *Winnetou 3.* [*Winnetou: The Desperado Trail*]; the 1965 *Old Surehand 1.* [*Flaming Frontier*]: the 1966 *Winnetou und das Halbblut Apanatschi* [*Half-Breed*]; the 1966 *Winnetou und sein Freund Old Firehand* [*Thunder at the Border*]; and the 1968 *Winnetou und Shatterhand im Tal der Toten* [*Winnetou and Shatterhand in the Valley of Death*].

75. Sieg, *Ethnic Drag*, 103–104; Von Borries and Fischer, 46.

76. These films included the 1966 *Die Söhne der Großen Bärin* [*The Sons of the Great Mother Bear*]; the 1967 *Chingachgook, die große Schlange* [*Chingachgook, the Great Serpent*]; the 1968 *Spur des Falken* [*The Trail of the Falcons*]; the 1969 *Weiße Wölfe* [*White Wolves*]; the 1969 *Tödlicher Irrtum* [*The Fatal Mistake*]; the 1971 *Osceola*; the 1972 *Tecumseh*; the 1973 *Apachen* [*The Apache*]; the 1974 *Ulzana*; the 1975 *Blutsbrüder* [*Blood Brothers*]; the 1977 *Severino*; and the 1983 *Der Scout* [*The Scout*]. As a child in Hungary in the 1980s, the author remembers seeing *Osceola*, *Apachen*, and *Blutsbrüder* in the cinema.

77. Von Borries and J. Fischer, 49. For more on the East German *Indianerfilme*, see Gerd Gemünden, "Between Karl May and Karl Marx: the DEFA Indianerfilme." In Calloway, Gemünden and Zantop, 243–256; and Anna Bánhegyi, "Where Marx Meets Osceola: Ideology and Mythology in the Eastern Bloc Western." Unpublished PhD dissertation. History Department, Southern Methodist University, 2012.

78. Sieg, *Ethnic Drag,* 105.

79. Von Borries and Fischer, 49, 50–51.

80. As Gemünden shows, the *Indianerfilme* were just as guilty of stereotyping American Indians as the classic Western. Gemünden, "Between Karl May and Karl Marx," 245–246.

81. Ibid., 244–245.

82. Ibid., 245.

83. Ibid., 245. In the movie, this phrase took the idea of pan-Indianism, which had been expressed by the name of Red Power organizations like Indians of All Tribes (who by the release of the film had been demonstrating on Alcatraz Island for years), and reappropriated it to depict Indians as "red" members of international solidarity against capitalist imperialism.

84. For a more nuanced scholarly analysis of the Eastern Westerns and their context, please see Anna Bánhegyi, "Where Marx Meets Osceola: Ideology and Mythology in the Eastern Bloc Western." Unpublished PhD dissertation. History Department, Southern Methodist University, 2012.

85. Peter Bolz traces this image back to what he calls the "massive appearance of Sioux Indians in Germany between 1890 and 1914" in ethnic shows, zoos, and Wild West shows. Peter Bolz, 483.

86. While a definitive claim requires more research, it is likely that during the transatlantic reworkings of the image of the Indian warrior in the late

twentieth century, this painting was the source of much glorification and vilification of the so-called dog soldiers or dog society of the Cheyenne and other tribes. The assertions of radical sovereignty activists that AIM was a warrior society that any Native community could call for help, as well as the 1976 "dog soldiers" memo of the FBI seem to have resonated with this image. In the early 1980s, the annual gatherings of West German Indianist hobbyists over the Pentecost weekend also featured "men's societies like the Dog Soldiers, who exercise[d] a kind of police power." Bolz, 487; Von Borries and Fischer, 141. In the early 1990s, the author heard a Hungarian Indianist hobbyist explain that in a battle, the members of the dog society would pin their train into the ground to signal that they will fight until they win or die—and that they would do this in order to cover the withdrawal of their fellow warriors. Personal recollection.

87. Gemünden, "Between Karl May and Karl Marx," 245–246.

88. In Sieg's words, some German hobbyists saw themselves as a community of the "persecuted yet defiant." I generalized and complemented her model to apply across a variety of forms of playing Indian. The "overwhelming forces" was an interchangeable component of the meaning of whites playing Indian. They could stand for a communist bureaucracy, the oppressive state, consumer society, U.S. imperialism, big corporations, or modern society in general. See Sieg, *Ethnic Drag,* 144.

Chapter 2

1. The model for this title was Paul Gilroy's seminal *"There Ain't No Black in the Union Jack": The Cultural Politics of Race and Nation* (Chicago: University of Chicago Press, 1991).

2. "Meeting Between Traditional Sioux Chiefs and White House Delegation" Carol Sullivan, "After the Occupation . . . South Dakota Impressions May, 1973" 4–5. Self-standing manuscript. Carol Sullivan Papers.

3. Photo contact print sheet 58, folder 332, The Richard Erdoes Papers.

4. One of the major strategies of the defense in the Wounded Knee trials of the mid-1970s was the presentation of Indian treaties as binding international law. "The Sioux Treaty of 1868": Memorandum prepared by Larry Leventhal, March 18, 1974." Evidentiary hearing regarding motion to dismiss for governmental misconduct. *U.S. vs. Russell Means and Dennis Banks* (St. Paul, MN). Also "Press/publicity motion to dismiss for lack of jurisdiction under the Sioux Nation–U.S. Treaty of 1868"; "1868 Treaty (copies)"; "Red Cloud's interpretation of the 1868 treaty"; "Treaty law"; "Sioux treaty of 1868: Position paper by Larry B. Leventhal, undated and 1974. 2 folders"; "Other treaty materials." All in Treaty defense hearing and appeal. Also "Appellants' closing brief: treaty issue, October 10, 1975." U.S. Court of Appeals for the Eighth Circuit. Also "*U.S. vs. Russell Means and Dennis Banks*: Defense exhibit P-8, certified copy of 1868 treaty." Also "*U.S. vs. consolidated cases*: Treaty hearing transcripts, December 21

and 23, 1974 and January 2, 1975. 2 volumes." Wounded Knee Legal Defense/Offense Committee Records.

5. See Von Eschen, *Race Against Empire.*

6. For more see chapter 3 "Dilemmas," in Cobb, *Native Activism in Cold War America*, 58–79.

7. The Haudenosaunee or Six Nations Confederacy is a prime historical example of a transnational Native people living in the interstices of two North American nation-states. The Akwesasne Territory of the Mohawk straddles the border between the state of New York and the Canadian provinces of Ontario and Quebec. The struggle of the Mohawk for transit rights came to a head in late 1968, when Native activists blockaded the International Bridge, which connects the two countries, to force a lifting of the restrictions on passage. According to its own account, the flagship radical Native newspaper, *Akwesasne Notes*, originated in efforts to document the Haudenaosaunee's reassertion of their territorial rights—which was itself a performance of transnational protest. By the early 1970s *Akwesasne Notes* had developed into one of the Native papers with the largest circulation—averaging 10,000 copies per issue, and on occasion claiming as high as 38,000. Selling for 50 cents and running on volunteer labor and financial contributions, the hard-copy paper was published by the Indian Studies Program of Wesleyan University in Middletown, CT, and its actual editorial offices were located in Hogensburg, NY, as well as at Route 3, Cornwall Island, Ontario—on both sides of the international border of the St. Regis Reservation. Arnold Krupat, *The Voice in the Margin: Native American Literature and the Canon (*Berkeley: University of California Press, 1989), 206, fn 4; Johansen and Mann, 16; Johansen, "Akwesasne Notes." Front page, *Akwesasne Notes*, July–August 1972. January–February 1972, 2–3. Underground Newspaper Collection.

8. "Indians Don't Need Draft" by Hank Adams, and "Puyallup Indian Suit Asks Men Of Tribe To Be Exempted from Draft," *Akwesasne Notes*, March 1971, 7. "Indian Draft Resistance Growing," in April 1971, 42. "From the Tomahawk Statement," "From the Statement of Sid Mills," "An Indian GI's Testimony on Racism," and "Caught in the Draft," in April 1971, 42–43. "Indian Refuses Draft because of His Religion," in March–May 1972, 13. "Hidatsa Remembers Indian Teaching and Refuses to Kill in Vietnam," in May–August 1972, 16. *Americans Before Columbus*, December 1969–January 1970, 8. "Lieutenant William Calley, Meet Kit Carson" by John Nichols in *Akwesasne Notes* July–August 1971, 40–41. "How Cruel the Whites' Eyes Look: Tom Hayden on the War in Indochina," in March–May 1972, 32. "The Frontier Moves West: The U.S. Has Got Itself Some New Indians" by Thom Marlowe, *Akwesasne Notes*, March–May 1972, 32."The Fruits of Racism." Uncredited photo in April–June 1972, 34. Underground Newspaper Collection.

9. "Latin America" in *Akwesasne Notes* issues of summer 1971; "Brazil" in June 1972; "In the Colonies" in June 1970, 41; "Third World View" in June 1972, 11 and in July–Aug 1972, 26; "Australia" in June 1970; Sept 1970;

Sept 1971, 29; "The Pacific Peoples" in July–Aug 1972, 29 and June 1972, 27; news on Lapplanders in June 1972, 11, April–June 1972 30, May–Aug 1972, 34. "Third World View," in July–Aug 1972, 26. "Wise Words on 'The Movement' by from Chicano Leader, Corky Gonzales," in June 1972, 11. "Irish Republican Army Inspired by Indian Fishing Struggle in U.S." in December 1971, 11. "World Ambassador," by Da Na Waq (White Beaver), in June 1970, 48. "Roland—trip of a lifetime," in September 1971, 34, in May–Aug 1972, 27, and in March–May 1972, 40. "Use of Iroquois 'passport' questioned by British MP," "Chief's Iroquois passport said good for travel abroad," and "Indian chief with 'own' passport: it was up to the man on the barrier," in September 1970, 40. "Chief's Iroquois passport said good for travel abroad" by Rudy Platiel, in September 1970, 40. "Indians Seek Foreign Aid" (United Press International), in December 1971, 6. "Appeal to UN" in April 1971, 7. "Indian Voices from Sweden" by Robert C. Cowen, in April–June 1972, 30; "Samer är också indianer: Our People in Stockholm" in May–Aug 1972, 34. "Lapps Meet with Our People" in May–Aug 1972, 34. Underground Newspaper Collection.

10. "Harassment of Traditional Mohawks!" "Editor of *Akwesasne Notes* Arrested!" "Two Longhouse Families Threatened with Eviction!" "Traditional Peoples Land Seized!" " 'Indian Way' School in Danger!" all in *Akwesasne Notes*, July–Aug 1972, front page/1–2. Underground Newspaper Collection. Also, see Johansen, "Akwesasne Notes."

11. These works include Johnson; Wilkinson; William Sayer, *Ghost Dancing the Law: The Wounded Knee Trials* (Cambridge, MA: Harvard University Press, 1997), and Smith and Warrior.

12. Johnson, 63; Banks and Erdoes, 177; Smith and Warrior, 212.

13. For various such charges, made on and off the record, see Means and Wolf, 276, 328; Banks and Erdoes, 176, 220; Smith and Warrior, 192, 207; and William S. White, "The Red Storm-Trooper Phenomenon" (originally Associated Press, March 7, 1973), in *Akwesasne Notes*, April 1973, 16. Underground Newspaper Collection.

14. See, respectively, Thom Marlowe, Pacific News Service/Liberation News Service, "The Frontier Moves West: The U.S. Has Got Itself Some New Indians," in *Akwesasne Notes*, March–May 1972, 32; John Nichols, "Lieutenant William Calley, Meet Kit Carson" (originally *The New Mexican*, June–July 1971) in July–Aug 1971, 40–41; "The Fruits of Racism" in April–June 1972, 34. Underground Newspaper Collection.

15. *Akwesasne Notes*, April 1973, 43, Underground Newspaper Collection.

16. Means and Wolf, 279; Smith and Warrior, 206

17. Smith and Warrior, 207.

18. Woody Kipp, *Viet Cong at Wounded Knee: The Trail of a Blackfeet Activist* (Lincoln: University of Nebraska Press, 2004), 126.

19. Banks and Erdoes, 163.

20. Ibid., 176.

21. Means and Wolf, 231; Banks and Erdoes, 137.

22. Means and Wolf, 275; Smith and Warrior, 215; Banks and Erdoes, 179.

23. Banks and Erdoes, 182.

24. Banks and Erdoes, 184.

25. Smith and Warrior, 219.

26. Banks and Erdoes, 184.

27. Banks and Erdoes, 182–183; Smith and Warrior, 218.

28. "Meeting Between Traditional Sioux Chiefs and White House Delegation" Carol Sullivan, "After the Occupation . . . South Dakota Impressions May, 1973," 4–5. Self-standing manuscript. Carol Sullivan Papers.

29. Smith and Warrior, 219.

30. Carol Sullivan, "The Indians and the Media" in "Perspectives on the Occupation of Wounded Knee," 5–9. Self-standing manuscript. Carol Sullivan Papers. The U.S. Embassy in Moscow reported on the Soviet press coverage of the court cases ensuing after Wounded Knee, especially focusing on Dennis Banks and Russell Means. December 18, 1975, April 16, 1976, and May 7, 1976 cables from Moscow to Secretary of State, Washington, DC, State Department Records online database. Iona Andronov, "Další Americká tragédie." [The Next American Tragedy] in *Nová doba*, the Czechoslovak issue of the Russian *Новое время* [*New Times*], March 12, 1973, 12. Communication with Lucie Kýrová, The College of William and Mary, August 25, 2014.

31. "Clearwater's Body Taken to Crow Dog Camp" in *Wounded Knee Seed*, May 4, 1973. The Richard Erdoes Papers.

32. "Nierderlage in Wounded Knee?" [Defeat at Wounded Knee?]. Undated and uncredited article in German. The Richard Erdoes Papers.

33. Means and Wolf, 295; Banks and Erdoes, 202.

34. *Akwesasne Notes*, Aug–Oct 1973, 44–46. Underground Newspaper Collection.

35. Such attempts included petitions charging the U.S. government with genocide, pleas to the UN to send observers or peacekeepers to the land and fishing rights struggles, and Native activists traveling to Western Europe to attend alternative conferences parallel to the UN assemblies. See "They Charge Genocide" in *Akwesasne Notes*, Sept 1970, 46; "Appeal to UN" in April 1971, 7; "Indian Voices from Sweden" in April–June 1972, 30; "Samer är också indianer: Our People in Stockholm" in May–Aug 1972, 34; "It is the People Who Belong to the Earth" in May–Aug 1972, 34; "National Brotherhood Looks to U.N., Europe for Minority Attention" in June 1972 34. Underground Newspaper Collection.

36. Waldheim, an Austrian diplomat, served as Secretary-General of the United Nations between 1972 and 1981, then as president of Austria between 1986 and 1992. As a Central European, Waldheim would have been familiar with the various transatlantic and home grown representations and forms of "playing Indian." How exactly these may have influenced his attitudes toward American Indian issues during his tenure at the UN and in Austria is a matter

of further research. "We Want a Voice" in *Akwesasne Notes*, April 1973, 29. Underground Newspaper Collection.

37. Carol Talbert, "Wounded Knee: 1973" April 1973, 18. Self-standing manuscript. Carol Sullivan Papers; Smith and Warrior, 228.

38. Smith and Warrior, 227–228.

39. Photo contact print 58, folder 332, contact print 63, folder 339. The Richard Erdoes Papers.

40. "Wounded Knee." U.S. Mission to the United Nations telegrams to Secretary of State, May 4 and 5, 1973. State Department Records.

41. "Offer to Mediate in Wounded Knee Dispute." American Embassy Mexico City telegram to Secretary of State, March 27, 1973. State Department Records.

42. Ibid. State Department Records.

43. Smith and Warrior, 236.

44. Photocopies of Wounded Knee press credentials. Location 146.H.13.2F, Box 93. Records of the Wounded Knee Legal Defense/Offense Committee. As part of its cultural diplomacy programs, the State Department's United States Information Service published a number of articles on American Indian issues in the vol. 6 no. 2 1973 issue of its English language overseas publication *Dialogue*. Some of these articles, including pieces by Vine Deloria, Jr., and President Richard Nixon, were then reprinted in other USIS publications. "The American Indians" undated booklet, United States Information Service, New Zealand. State Department Papers. A more general description of *Dialogue* can be found in Hans N. Tuch, *Communicating with the World: U.S. Public Diplomacy Overseas* (New York: St. Martin's Press, 1990), 60–61.

45. "Telegram from Ms. Alicia Castillo S. to the President." Referred from the State Department to the Department of the Interior, May 23, 1973. State Department Records.

46. "Wounded Knee." U.S. Mission to the United Nations telegram to Secretary of State, May 5, 1973. State Department Records.

47. Ibid. Emphasis added.

48. Ibid.

49. Quoted in Cobb, *Native Activism in Cold War America*, 125.

50. Ibid., 126.

51. "Wounded Knee." U.S. Mission to the United Nations telegrams to Secretary of State, May 4 and 5, 1973, State Department Records.

52. Smith and Warrior, 205.

53. See Wilkinson.

54. Pratt, 6.

55. Smith and Warrior, 205.

56. "Treaty signing by William T. Sherman and the Sioux at Fort Laramie, Wyoming. Photographed by Alexander Gardner, 1868." American Indian Select List number 30, identifier 531079. Pictures of Native Americans in the United States. National Archives. Online: http://www.archives.gov/research/native-amer-

icans/pictures/select-list-030.html. Accessed February 13, 2015. Photograph by Jim Mone/Associated Press of assistant U.S. Attorney General Ken Frizzell sitting in a tepee, negotiating with AIM leaders Dennis Banks, Russell Means, Lakota traditionalist medicine man Leonard Crow Dog, and others. Featured in Means and Wolf, among photographs after page 206.

57. "'The Sioux Treaty of 1868': Memorandum prepared by Larry Leventhal, March 18, 1974." Evidentiary hearing regarding motion to dismiss for governmental misconduct. *U.S. vs. Russell Means and Dennis Banks* (St. Paul, MN). Also "Press/publicity motion to dismiss for lack of jurisdiction under the Sioux Nation—U.S. Treaty of 1868"; "1868 Treaty (copies)"; "Red Cloud's interpretation of the 1868 treaty"; "Treaty law"; "Sioux treaty of 1868: Position paper by Larry B. Leventhal, undated and 1974. 2 folders"; "Other treaty materials." All in Treaty defense hearing and appeal. Also "Appellants' closing brief: treaty issue, October 10, 1975." U.S. Court of Appeals for the Eighth Circuit. Also "*U.S. vs. Russell Means and Dennis Banks*: Defense exhibit P-8, certified copy of 1868 treaty." Also "*U.S. vs. consolidated cases*: Treaty hearing transcripts, December 21 and 23, 1974 and January 2, 1975. 2 volumes." Wounded Knee Legal Defense/Offense Committee Records.

58. Sayer, 228; "Wounded Knee Legal Defense/Offense Committee: An Inventory of Its Records at the Minnesota Historical Society." Online finding aid: http://www.mnhs.org/library/findaids/00229.xml. Accessed May 29, 2015.

59. I will discuss these developments in subsequent chapters. "Study on Treaties, Agreements and Other Constructive Arrangements Between States and Indigenous Populations. Final report by Mr. Miguel Alfonso Martinez, Special Rapporteur. July 1997, reported to the UN for the 'Working Group on Indigenous Peoples.'" The University of Minnesota Human Rights Library. Online: http://www1.umn.edu/humanrts/demo/TreatiesStatesIndigenousPopulations_Martinez.pdf. Accessed May 29, 2015.

60. Treaty of Managua 1860. In Folder "R&D: (CA) Nicaragua, Miskito Nation. Interview W/B. Wahpepah." Records of the International Indian Treaty Council.

61. Roxanne Dunbar-Ortiz, *Blood on the Border: A Memoir of the Contra War* (Cambridge, MA: South End Press, 2005), 129, 135–136; Means with Wolf, 459–460.

62. I will discuss these developments in subsequent chapters.

63. For more on the divergence of ideologies and means between these two generations of Indian leadership, see Daniel Cobb, *Native Activism in Cold War America*.

64. For more on Indian stereotypes in media coverage, see Smith and Warrior, 100, 207, 210; and "After the Occupation . . . South Dakota Impressions," 5–9. Manuscript by Carol Sullivan. Carol Sullivan Wounded Knee Papers.

65. Smith and Warrior, 269.

66. Means with Wolf, 324.

67. See, respectively, Roxanne Dunbar-Ortiz, *Indians of the Americas: Human Rights and Self-Determination.* (London: Zed Books Ltd, 1984), 33; and Means with Wolf, 324.

68. Means with Wolf, 325; "Declaration of Continuing Independence by the First International Indian Treaty Council at Standing Rock Indian Country June 1974." Roger A. Finzel American Indian Movement Papers. Online: http://www.iitc.org/about-iitc/the-declaration-of-continuing-independence-june-1974/ Accessed May 29, 2015.

69. Means with Wolf, 325.

70. "International work" was the shorthand designation among Native American activists for what I analytically call American Indian transnational diplomacy. For one example, see "Trying to See Clearly," by Jimmie Durham. *Treaty Council News* August 1978, 2–3; "Russell Means Faces Prison Term," *Treaty Council News* August 1978, 4. Records of the International Indian Treaty Council.

71. "Declaration of Continuing Independence," cover. Roger A. Finzel American Indian Movement Papers.

72. Ibid. Roger A. Finzel American Indian Movement Papers.

73. "Preamble." Emphasis added. Ibid. Roger A. Finzel American Indian Movement Papers.

74. Ibid., 1–2. Roger A. Finzel American Indian Movement Papers.

75. Ibid., 3. Roger A. Finzel American Indian Movement Papers.

76. "Glossary," 1. Emphasis added. Ibid. Roger A. Finzel American Indian Movement Papers.

77. Ibid., 3. Roger A. Finzel American Indian Movement Papers.

78. Ibid., 3–4. Roger A. Finzel American Indian Movement Papers.

79. Ibid., 2. Roger A. Finzel American Indian Movement Papers.

80. Ibid., 2–3. Roger A. Finzel American Indian Movement Papers.

81. Ibid., 3–5. Roger A. Finzel American Indian Movement Papers.

82. "Map for Indian Nationhood 1973." In "S-0271-0001-04. American Indians—Wounded Knee, South Dakota (2)." Electronic file version of hard copy documents. United Nations Archives and Records Management Section.

83. "Declaration of Continuing Independence," Map. Roger A. Finzel American Indian Movement Papers.

84. See Leonard Crow Dog's suggestion that the IITC use the 1868 Fort Laramie Treaty "as the arrowhead and combine with other tribes that have other important treaties so that a "heavy" package can be presented to the U.S. government. "International Indian Treaty Council Meeting—June 13, 1974." Roger A. Finzel American Indian Movement Papers.

85. For more on his model, see Anderson, 4, 45, 67, 81, 87, 99, 135, 157, 184–185

86. As any other nonprofit organization that runs on volunteer labor and grant-based financing, the International Indian Treaty Council lost some of its institutional records over the four decades of its existence. In the early 1980s its

New York City office was closed, while in the early 2000s the basement of its San Francisco office was flooded, and the water and mold destroyed some files. Other records were simply discarded to make space for new documentation. Author's visit to the International Indian Treaty Council's San Francisco office and communication with Dr. Alberto Saldamando, May 2010.

87. While few internal records are available from this early period, Suzanne Dunbar-Ortiz's *Indians of the Americas* cites some IITC files in her scholarship.

88. Dunbar-Ortiz, *Indians of the Americas*, 33–34.

89. In her *Indians of the Americas*, Roxanne Dunbar-Ortiz cites this document as "From the Archives of the International Indian Treaty Council, New York. File dated February, 1975: Report from Meeting of International Lawyers." Since I did not find this document in the Treaty Council's San Francisco Office, I have to assume this file fell casualty to the above mentioned office downsizing or water damage.

90. Dunbar-Ortiz, *Indians of the Americas*, 34. Emphasis added.

91. Dunbar-Ortiz, *Indians of the Americas*, 34. Emphasis added. Dunbar-Ortiz's note on page 68: "George Duke, Professor in International Law, Boalt Hall, University of California, Berkeley, held this view."

92. Ibid., 34.

93. Ibid., 34.

94. While the conference was held in June, the reference to the July 1976 federal raid of Pine Ridge suggests this version of the "Red Paper" was finished in the latter month or even later.

95. "Red Paper, The Second International Indian Treaty Conference, Yankton Lakota (Sioux) Country, South Dakota, June 13–20, 1976." 3, 6, 7–8. Records of the International Indian Treaty Council. Those on trial at this point were mostly indicted for their activities at Wounded Knee in Spring 1973. Anna Mae Aquash, a prominent member of AIM, was found dead on the Pine Ridge Reservation in February 1976. After an autopsy which gave exposure as cause of death, it took several requests from AIM, relatives, and the FBI before a second autopsy was conducted, which found that she had been shot to death at point blank range. Suspects for her murder were still being tried in the early 2000s.

96. Ibid., 4.

97. Ibid., 4.

98. Ibid., 8.

99. Ibid., 10.

100. For more on the difference between the two generations of sovereignty activists (represented by the National Congress of the American Indian on the one hand and Indians of All Nations, the National Indian Youth Council, and the American Indian Movement on the other, see Cobb, *Native Activism in Cold War America*.

101. "International Treaty Council Meeting—June 14, 1974," 4. Roger A. Finzel American Indian Movement Papers.

102. Specifically, they quote the United Nations General Assembly's Resolution 1514 (XV) of December 14, 1960 including "Declaration on the Granting of Independence to Colonial Countries and Peoples," and its Resolution 1654 (XVI), of November 27, 1961 [sic, 1962] establishing the special committee to oversee the implementation of the Declaration. "Red Paper," 11–12. Records of the International Indian Treaty Council.

103. "Red Paper," 17–18. Records of the International Indian Treaty Council.

Chapter 3

1. "Wounded Knee" Bilingual (English–French) booklet, 2. "Foreign publications, 1973–1974." Records of the Wounded Knee Legal Defense/Offense Committee.

2. Penny Von Eschen, *Race Against Empire*.

3. Martin Klimke, *The Other Alliance*. I will confine myself to using the term "transatlantic" instead of "global," since the latter requires a greater scholarly apparatus and scope than the one at my disposal.

4. According to Klimke, "In the first decade after the Second World War, American 'cultural diplomacy' aimed at a democratization of German political culture, in other words an 'Americanization from above.' The years that followed, from 1955 to 1965, in contrast, can be viewed as a starting point for a 'grassroots Americanization,' whereby official political goals were complemented and even replaced by an immense cultural influence on West German society and the political landscape." Martin Klimke, *The Other Alliance*, 6.

5. For more, see "Many Roads" in Cobb, *Native Activism in Cold War America*, 147–170

6. These included Lakota medicine man John Fire Lame Deer's autobiography, *Lame Deer: Seeker of Visions* (1971); with Mary Brave Bird, *Lakota Woman* (1990) and its sequel *Ohitka Woman* (1993); with Archie Fire Lame Deer, *The Gift of Power: The Life and Teachings of a Lakota Medicine Man* (1992); with Leonard Crow Dog, *Crow Dog: Four Generations of Sioux Medicine Men* (1995); and with Dennis Banks, *Ojibwa Warrior: Dennis Banks and the Rise of the American Indian Movement* (2004). Biographical note, *Guide to The Richard Erdoes Papers*. Online: http://hdl.handle.net/10079/fa/beinecke.erdoes. Accessed May 29, 2015.

7. These included Erdoes's first book about an American Indian tribe, *Pueblo Indians*, for the Young Readers' Indian Library series (1967); his *American Indian Myths and Legends* (1984) and *American Indian Trickster Tales* (1998), both co-edited with Alfonso Ortiz. Ibid.

8. "Portraits of Henry Crow Dog, Rosebud Sioux, done at 251 W89 NYC 1969." Photo contact print. The Richard Erdoes Papers.

9. "John Fire Lame Deer on tour with me, fall 1970; Jackie riding at Crow Dog's place; Rachel Strange Owl's baby in cradleboard." Photo contact print. The Richard Erdoes Papers.

10. For more on scholarship on Native modernities and engagement with twentieth-century U.S. life, see Philip Deloria, *Indians in Unexpected Places* (Lawrence, KS: University Press of Kansas, 2004)

11. "Lame Deer at Mount Rushmore Black Hills, S. Dakota, Late summer 1971 with Lee Brightman." "Take over of BIA Bldg Nov. 1972." Photo contact prints. The Richard Erdoes Papers; "Brave Bird with Erdoes," 201.

12. Biographical note, *Guide to The Richard Erdoes Papers*. Online: Accessed November 17, 2011; "Crow Dog and Erdoes," 112, 197, 226; "Brave Bird with Erdoes," 205.

13. Ibid., 86–"88; Crow Dog and Erdoes," 232, 238–239.

14. Implicitly, Erdoes's story also serves to prove he had suffered and sacrificed for his Native friends, and the causes of cultural revival and sovereignty. This proof of his devotion also shores up his own performance-based movement identity. "Archie Lame Deer." Recording. Includes Archie Fire, Erdoes, and "Andy" talking about teaching and traveling in Europe. Oct. 1, 1988, Side ½. The Richard Erdoes Papers.

15. "Crow Dog and Erdoes," 35; "Brave Bird with Erdoes," 19.

16. "With Werner and Hannelore at Wounded Knee August 1977." "Kirchmeiers, Rolf + Ruth Ohlhausen, Erdoeses (Erich), Crow Dog's Leonard, Francine, Little Ina 1970." Photo contact prints. The Richard Erdoes Papers.

17. Letters to Richard Erdoes from Liselotte Welskopf-Henrich, 8/11/1974; 1/4/1975. The Richard Erdoes Papers. I discuss the role of Liselotte Welskopf-Henrich in shaping East German perceptions and representations of American Indians in chapter 1 and her connections with the radical sovereignty movement in subsequent chapters.

18. Aribert Schroeder, " 'They Lived Together with Their Dogs and Horses:' 'Indian Copy' in West German Newspapers 1968–1982." In Feest, 527.

19. These included not only the 1969–1971 occupation of Alcatraz, but also the takeovers in 1970–1971 of Forts Lawton and Lewis, Washington, the former military installations in Richmond, California, Belmont in Chicago, and the abandoned National Coast Guard station near Milwaukee, Wisconsin. Other major events covered were the 1972 Trail of Broken Treaties to Washington, DC, and the subsequent takeover of the Bureau of Indian Affairs (BIA) building there; the siege of Wounded Knee, South Dakota, in spring 1973; the subsequent trials of Dennis Banks and Russell Means; the 1975–1976 Senate subcommittee hearings regarding the 1890 Wounded Knee massacre; the early 1975 takeover of a monastery near Gresham, Wisconsin, by Menominee activists; the June 1975 shootout between AIM and the FBI at Oglala; and the Longest Walk of 1978. Schroeder 528–530.

20. Schroeder, 530–531.

21. Schroeder, 531–532, 533.

22. As Martin Klimke has shown, West German students and activists had already adopted a transatlantic critique of the United States involvement in Vietnam as they worked in coalition with the American antiwar movement. See Klimke.

23. Schroeder, 533–534.

24. Penny, "Elusive Authenticity," 798–818.

25. Schroeder, 534, 535–536, 538.

26. *Allgemeine Zeitung* Oct 8, 1977, cited in Schroeder, 541. For my discussion of Bodmer's artwork as some of the early transatlantic representations of American Indians, see chapter 1.

27. Dénes Kiss, "A legutolsó mohikánok," [The Last of the Last of the Mohicans] *Ifjúsági Magazin* [*Youth Magazine*] June 1973, 29.

28. Schroeder, 537. Emphasis added.

29. Smith and Warrior, 102.

30. Bernd C. Peyer, "Who is Afraid of AIM?" In Feest, 551.

31. Smith and Warrior, 61.

32. Smith and Warrior, 99.

33. Crow Dog and Erdoes, *Lakota Woman*, 5, 125; Brave Bird with Erdoes, *Ohitika Woman*, 186.

34. Schroeder, 538.

35. Schroeder, 542.

36. "A group of your German readers" in letters section of *Akwesasne Notes*, Sept 1970, 45. Underground Newspaper Collection.

37. "German View" by Waltraud Wagner, *Akwesasne Notes*, Sept 1970, 2. Underground Newspaper Collection.

38. Other evidence of Native American G.I. activism in Germany include their plans to join AIM, to establish a Native American club on a base, and plans of American Indian service personnel stationed in the West Berlin area to finance and host the delegates of the 1977 UN NGO conference on discrimination against Indians in the Americas. Letter to Richard Erdoes from Regina Mayer, February 13, 1975. The Richard Erdoes Papers. "The Indians are Coming." *BZ* [most likely *Berliner Zeitung*], September 29,1977, 5. Records of the Gesellschaft für bedrohte Völker.

39. This is not to say that all letters came from people in Europe. There were letters from countries as far away as Australia.

40. "Paola Ludovici, Rome, Italy" in letters section of *Akwesasne Notes*, Aug–Oct 1973, 46. Ruth M. Benjamin in letters section of April–June 1972, 45. Underground Newspaper Collection.

41. Ruth M. Benjamin in letters section of *Akwesasne Notes*, April–June 1972, 45. Underground Newspaper Collection.

42. At the end of 1971, Pete "Wyoming" Bender sent the *Notes* a letter from "Western Germany" calling for Indian musicians to join his project of putting together an Indian musical with lyrics from the poetry section of *Notes*, as a fundraiser for the paper. Four years later Bender was volunteering at the

American Indian Movement's West Berlin office. In a letter titled "German View" in the September 1970 issue of the paper, Waltraud Wagner of Horneburg, Germany, claimed that "several groups from Germany have sent supporting letters to the Mohawks, groups like workshops on Third-World problems and the World University Service." One year later, Wagner was listed in the *Akwesasne Notes* as one of the people who distributed the paper overseas. Presumably in the same period, Wagner received from members of the Swiss group Incomindios (Committee for the Indians of the Americas) a newsletter about traditional Indian land and life. By the early 1970s, Wagner was one of the leading members of the Arbeitskreis für Nordamerikanische Indianer (Working Circle for North American Indians), building relations between the solidarity organizations across the German-speaking countries of Central Europe. Letters section of *Akwesasne Notes*, Dec 1971, 47; Sept 1970, 2; Sept 1971, 47. Underground Newspaper Collection. February 13, 1975 letter from Regina Mayer to Richard Erdoes. The Richard Erdoes Papers. Arbeitskreis für Nordamerikanische Indianer flier to order bulletin and papers; Committee for Traditional Indian Land and Life Newsletter issue 2, May 1969, sent to Waltraud Wagner in Germany. Organizational Records at the office of Incomindios Switzerland.

43. Letters section of *Akwesasne Notes* April 1971, 47; April–June 1972, 46; April–June 1972, 45; July–Aug 1972, 47; Jan–Feb. 1972, 47; April–June 1972 47. Underground Newspaper Collection.

44. "German View." Letters section of *Akwesasne Notes*, Sept 1970, 2; July–Aug 1972, 47. Underground Newspaper Collection.

45. *Akwesasne Notes*, May–Aug 1972, 46; July–Aug 1972, 46; Sept 1971, 46; Jan–Feb 1972, 44; March 1971, 47; Jan–Feb. 1972, 44. Underground Newspaper Collection.

46. Phrasing from Philip Deloria's *Playing Indian* and *Indians in Unexpected Places*.

47. Letters section of *Akwesasne Notes*, Sept 1970, 45; Sept 1971, 46; April–June 1972, 45; July–Aug 1972, 47; July–Aug 1972, 47; April 1971, 47; June 1972, 44. Underground Newspaper Collection.

48. Richard Erdoes's photo contact print features eight shots of Russell Means sitting on a tree trunk and talking to the press, giving either an interview or, just as likely based on the subsequent photos of the warrior ritual, an orientation about the ritual about to take place. "Wounded Knee 1973 Leonard Crow Dog Painting Warriors' Faces for War." The Richard Erdoes Papers.

49. In addition to the European letters to the *Akwesasne Notes* cited earlier, a group of Dutch printed an eight-page booklet titled "Wounded Knee Poems by Werner Verstraeten" in English, and sent an autographed copy to the occupiers, which was later archived by the Wounded Knee Legal Defense/Offense Committee (WKLD/OC). "Wounded Knee Gedichten" anthology of poems. Records of the Wounded Knee Legal Defense/Offense Committee.

50. "Wounded Knee" Bilingual (English–French) booklet, 2. "Foreign publications, 1973–1974." Records of the Wounded Knee Legal Defense/Offense Committee.

51. Ibid., 3. Records of the Wounded Knee Legal Defense/Offense Committee.

52. The committee name in the original was "Schweizerisches Wounded Knee Verteidigungskomitee" [Swiss Wounded Knee Defense Committee]. Translated from German by the author. Ibid., 3. Records of the Wounded Knee Legal Defense/Offense Committee.

53. Author's interview with Claus Biegert, Munich, Germany, July 2011.

54. Peyer, 551.

55. Von Borries and Fischer, 44, 47.

56. Letters to Richard Erdoes from Liselotte Welskopf-Henrich, 8/11/1974; 1/4/1975. The Richard Erdoes Papers.

57. For more on Liselotte Welskopf-Henrich, see Glenn Penny, "Red Power: Liselotte Welskopf-Henrich and Indian Activist Networks in East and West Germany," *Central European History* 41 (2008), 447–476; and H. Glenn Penny, *Kindred by Choice: Germans and American Indians since 1800* (Chapel Hill: The University of North Carolina Press, 2013), 188–198.

58. Peyer, 551.

59. Letter to Richard Erdoes from Regina Mayer, February 13, 1975. The Richard Erdoes Papers.

60. Ibid., The Richard Erdoes Papers.

61. Ibid., The Richard Erdoes Papers.

62. Letters section of *Akwesasne Notes*, Dec 1971, 47. Underground Newspaper Collection.

63. "Vernon-Dennis-Pete." "Die fruehen Jahre—The early years" online photo gallery. Pete Wyoming Bender's public website at http://www.pete-wyoming-bender.de/. Accessed November 29, 2011. (Moribund)

64. Chemnitz, Germany, was called "Karl-Marx-Stadt" [Karl Marx City] under East German Communist rule.

65. Undated (presumably spring 1974) letter from WKLD/OC to Axel Schulze-Thulin of the Deutsch-Indianischer Kreis—German American Indian Group, Stuttgart, Germany. Records of the Wounded Knee Legal Defense/Offense Committee.

66. December 11, 1973 and February 23, 1974 letters from WKLD/OC to Irish Committee for the Defense of Wounded Knee. April 10, 1974 letter from WKLD/OC to Ingrid Jakob of Coburg, Germany. May 1, 1974 letter from Ann Durham of WKLD/OC to Bry Bruno, Cosne sur Loire, France. Records of the Wounded Knee Legal Defense/Offense Committee.

67. April 29, 1974 letter from Ellen Heinemann of Geneva, Switzerland, to WKLD/OC. January 25, 1974 letter from Gesellschaft für bedrohte Völker to WKLD/OC. Letter from WKLD/OC to Axel Schulze-Thulin of Deutsch-Indianischer Kreis—German American Indian Group. Records of the Wounded Knee Legal Defense/Offense Committee.

68. Their correspondence shows that in the period of 1973–1975, WKLD/OC received the amounts of £12 from Ireland; an unknown sum; $50, $55, and

$10 from West Germany; $75, $100, and another $100 from the Netherlands; $20 from Switzerland; and $72 from France. On January 25, 1974, the West German "Society for Endangered Peoples" (Gesellschaft für bedrohte Völker) offered WKLD/OC $743 in German currency. WKLD/OC advised them to reinvest it into outreach. Records of the Wounded Knee Legal Defense/Offense Committee.

69. February 12, 1974 letter from WKLD/OC to Irish Committee for the Defense of Wounded Knee. May 1, 1974 letter from Ann Durham of WKLD/OC to Pierrette Désy of Paris, France. Undated letter from WKLD/OC to Axel Schulze-Thulin of Deutsch-Indianischer Kreis—German American Indian Group. Records of the Wounded Knee Legal Defense/Offense Committee.

70. April 1, 1974 letter from Kiva Group, Friends of the North American Indians, of Netherlands. February 6, 1974 letter from the Irish Committee for the Defense of Wounded Knee. Records of the Wounded Knee Legal Defense/Offense Committee.

71. Letters in Records of the Wounded Knee Legal Defense/Offense Committee.

72. "For favor of publication," in January 11 and February 6, 1974, letters from the Irish Committee for the Defense of Wounded Knee; June 3, 1974 letter from J. Heijink of "KIVA group, Friends of the North American Indians in the Netherlands;" article in March 11, 1974 letter from Pierrette Désy of "Comité francais de soutien á AIM" Paris, France; article "For a Policy of Solidarity towards the Indians of Wounded Knee" by Pierrette Désy, published in *La Guelue ouverte* in Paris, France. Records of the Wounded Knee Legal Defense/Offense Committee.

73. "Letters of Solidarity," Box 24, Location 151.K.3.9B. "Letters," Box 93. "Correspondence: Foreign fund-raising, solidarity, and information requests." Box 95. Undated petition in English. "Petitions: Foreign and domestic," Box 100. "Petitions: Foreign and domestic." Location 146.H.13.4F. Records of the Wounded Knee Legal Defense/Offense Committee.

74. December 5, 1973 letter from Seán O Cionnaith of International Affairs Bureau of the Irish Republican Movement, Dublin, Ireland. Records of the Wounded Knee Legal Defense/Offense Committee.

75. October 1974 letter from Andreas Erdmann of East Germany. February 21, 1975 letter from Andreas Wollmann, East Berlin. Undated letter from H. Marius Spanier of Hannover, West Germany. Records of the Wounded Knee Legal Defense Offense Committee.

76. June 3 and July 30, 1974 letters from Kiva Society of Friends of the North American Indians in the Netherlands. Records of the Wounded Knee Legal Defense/Offense Committee.

77. Quoted in von Borries and Fischer, 66. Translation by Toth. In "Letters of Solidarity," Box 95, Location 151.K.3.9B, and in "Petitions: Foreign and domestic," Box 100, Location 146.H.13.4F. Records of the Wounded Knee Legal Defense/Offense Committee.

78. May 20, 1974 letter from How-kola-Klub Völkerkundliche Kulturgruppe Zur Pflege des Brauchtums der Prärieindianer. Records of the Wounded Knee Legal Defense/Offense Committee.

79. April 5, 1974 letter from Ingrid Jakob, Coburg, West Germany. September 27, 1974 letter from Marion Busch from East Germany. Records of the Wounded Knee Legal Defense/Offense Committee.

80. Undated letter to Ingrid Jakob of Coburg, West Germany. April 10, 1974 letter to unnamed addressee. February 12, 1974 letter from WKLD/OC to Irish Committee for the Defense of Wounded Knee. Records of the Wounded Knee Legal Defense/Offense Committee.

81. June 5, 1974 letter to Miss Marlis Horn of Hamburg, West Germany. Undated letter to Axel Schulze-Thulin of German American Indian Group. Records of the Wounded Knee Legal Defense/Offense Committee.

82. "Petitions: foreign and domestic." Records of the Wounded Knee Legal Defense/Offense Committee.

83. September 27, 1974 letter from Marion Bush from East Germany. October 18, 1974 letter from C. Sänger, East Berlin. October 13, 1974, letter from Herbert Leisdahner of "Committee American Indian Movement, Betriebschule des VEB Robur." Records of the Wounded Knee Legal Defense/Offense Committee.

84. "Brave Bird with Erdoes," 86–88,

85. "Crow Dog and Erdoes," 238–239. While there were solidarity groups in other European and non-European countries, West Germany was of special importance for the officials of the U.S. government due to that nation being an experiment in post-war re-education in democracy and it being a major frontline ally against Soviet Communism.

86. Sayer, 228; "Wounded Knee Legal Defense/Offense Committee: An Inventory of Its Records at the Minnesota Historical Society." Online finding aid: http://www2.mnhs.org/library/findaids/00229.xml. Accessed May 29, 2015.

87. "Wounded Knee" Bilingual (English–French) booklet, 1. "Foreign publications, 1973–1974." Records of the Wounded Knee Legal Defense/Offense Committee.

88. The considerable variety of transatlantic performances of the radical Indian sovereignty movement make it highly difficult to fit them into existing categories formulated in historical scholarship and Performance Studies. They ranged from diplomatic meetings and activist strategy sessions through street marches to press conferences, presentations, concerts and rallies. In their forms, goals and content, they straddle the continuum between commemorations, social protest events, and cultural programming. My theoretical approach places these performances along the scale constituted by the scholarship of Richard Schechner (social protest as performance), Rebekah J. Kowal (protest as "staged events"), and Diana Taylor (history as a political resource, the archive informing the performance repertoire to make for political claims). See, respectively, Kowal, 137, 138, 150; Taylor, "Performance and/as History," (*The Drama Review*, Spring

2006, vol. 50, no. 1), 70; Taylor, *The Archive and the Repertoire* (Durham, NC: Duke UP, 2003), 19, 20, 21, 28.

89. July 8, 1977 letter from Society for Endangered Peoples to the Institute for the Development of Indian Law, the International Indian Treaty Council, *Indigena*, and *Akwesasne Notes*. September 1, 1977 letter from the Society for Endangered Peoples to the International Indian Treaty Council. Records of the Gesellschaft für bedrohte Völker (Society for Endangered Peoples). "Friedlicher Feldzug der Indianer" [Peaceful Campaign of the Indians]. *Vorwärts*, October 13, 1977. Wolfgang Lehmann, "Wir sind kein zoologischer Garten," *Der Tagesspiel*, October 13, 1977. Informationsdienst, October 15, 1977 with a notice about an information session October 13 in Berlin. Photo with caption about visit, Die Kirche, October 16, 1977. Records of the Gesellschaft für bedrohte Völker (Society for Endangered Peoples).

90. The delegation included Clyde Bellecourt (Ojibwa, AIM, U.S.), Bill Wahpepah (Kickapoo/Sauc-Fox, AIM/International Indian Treaty Council, U.S.), Greg Zephier (AIM, U.S.), Phillip Deere (Muscogee/Creek, AIM/International Indian Treaty Council, U.S.), Winona LaDuke Westegard (Ojibwa, U.S.), George Erasmus (Dene, Indian Brotherhood of the Northwest Territories, Canada), Francois Paulette (Dene, National Indian Brotherhood, Canada), Constantino Lima (Aymara, Bolivia), Julio Tumeri (Aymara, MINK'A, Bolivia), Juan Condorie Uruchi (Quechua, Bolivia), Simeon Jimenez (Quiche-Maya, Venezuela), Manuel Tzoc Megia (Maya, Guatemala), and José Mendoza Costa (Panama).

91. The West German tour afforded the Native delegates with access to and opportunities for building alliances with a variety of European groups, some of which wielded considerable influence. On their October 3 visit in the West German capital, the Indian activists met with federal representatives of the country's Social Democratic Party (SPD). On October 9, the Native leaders met with Bishop Martin Kruse of the Evangelical Church of West Berlin. It can be assumed that the Native delegation gave the bishop the same demands as to the politicians: the withdrawal of the missionaries from Indian communities in Latin America or their unconditional and material support of the Native struggles there. In addition to their immediate political significance, their performances of Indian sovereignty rights at these meetings also presented the Native leaders as political agents. These were not the exotic spectacle of Wild West comics and movies, the bloodthirsty red men, or the noble savage of the vanishing race. Nor were they the stereotypical Indian chiefs awed by the splendor of Eastern U.S. or European cities, cluelessly giving away their people's land in treaty negotiations. They were indigenous activists lobbying the chairman of the German Federal Parliament's committee for economic cooperation about the government's position on an undertaking of the Intergovernmental Committee for European Migration. See ibid.

92. Dieter Fabritius, "Indianer stimmten "Kriegsgeschrei" [Indians Sound the War Whoop]. *TZ* Oct. 3, 1977; Heidrun Graupner, "Elf Indianer führen Klage" [Eleven Indians Air Grievances] *SZ* [Süddeutsche Zeitung?] Oct. 3,

1977; "Bellecourt: Das Klischee der Wildwest-Filme ist immer da" [Bellecourt: the Western Film Cliché is Always There] *Spandauer Volksblatt*, Oct. 12, 1977; "Traditionelle Trommelklänge aus Nordamerika" [Traditional Drumming from North America] *Bremer Nachrichten*, undated clipping. Records of the Gesellschaft für bedrohte Völker.

93. Dieter Fabritius, "Indianer stimmten "Kriegsgeschrei" [Indians Sound the War Whoop]. *TZ* Oct. 3, 1977. Records of the Gesellschaft für bedrohte Völker (Society for Endangered Peoples).

94. "Traditionelle Trommelklänge aus Nordamerika" [Traditional Drumming from North America] *Bremer Nachrichten*, undated clipping. Records of the Gesellschaft für bedrohte Völker (Society for Endangered Peoples).

95. "Bellecourt: Das Klischee der Wildwest-Filme ist immer da" [Bellecourt: the Western Film Cliché is Always There] *Spandauer Volksblatt*, Oct. 12, 1977. "Der Rote Mann verlangt sein Recht" [The Red Man Demands His Right] *Deutsche Volkszeitung*, Oct. 13, 1977. Records of the Gesellschaft für bedrohte Völker. Translation by Toth.

96. Banks and Erdoes, 118.

97. Ibid., 312.

98. "Bellecourt: Das Klischee der Wildwest-Filme ist immer da" [Bellecourt: the Western Film Cliché is Always There] *Spandauer Volksblatt*, Oct. 12, 1977. Records of the Gesellschaft für bedrohte Völker.

99. Describing the structure of "public performance," Richard Schechner claims that "a performance is whatever takes place between a marked beginning and a marked end. This marking, or framing, varies from culture to culture, epoch to epoch, and genre to genre. In the performing arts in mainstream Western genres, lowering the houselights and bringing the stage lights up, raising or opening curtains, and other procedures mark the start of a performance or portion of a performance. The closing or dropping of a curtain, the dimming of stage lights, the applause of spectators, and the actors taking bows mark the end of mainstream performances. [. . .] For every genre, in every culture, there are usually very clear markers signaling the start and finish of a public performance." Richard Schechner, *Performance Studies: An Introduction* (London, New York: Routledge, 2002), 205.

100. German journalists and the solidarity activists who developed their press materials struggled with accurately translating the English name: "amerikanischen I[n]dian Movement," "Indian Movement," "amerikan. Indianer-Bewegung," "amerikanischen Indianerbewegung (AIM)," or simply within or without quotation marks, the "American Indian Movement." Despite their discussions of the living conditions and struggles of Native populations in individual countries of the Americas, the semantic ambiguity of the English word "movement" and its German counterpart "Bewegung" helped make the perception of the indigenous delegation and their shared goals and demands as "pan-Indian," as both the Society's volunteers and the journalists called it. Originating with AIM's founders, this designation was imprinted in the documents generated by

their transnational performances of sovereign Indianness in the Central European contact zone. Heidrun Graupner, "Elf Indianer führen Klage" [Eleven Indians Air Grievances] *SZ* [Süddeutsche Zeitung?] Oct. 3, 1977; Flier for Clyde Bellecourt's talk at the Volkshochschule Wyhler Wald (Wyhler Forest Community College) on Oct. 12, 1977; "Bellecourt: Das Klischee der Wildwest-Filme ist immer da" [Bellecourt: the Western Film Cliché is Always There] *Spandauer Volksblatt*, Oct. 12, 1977; Wolfgang Lehmann, "Wir sind kein zoologischer Garten" *Der Tagesspiel*, Oct. 13, 1977; poster and information sheet "Indianer sprechen in Tübingen" [Indians Speak in Tübingen] for Friday, Oct. 14, 1977; "Sturm" überzeugte die Zuhorer" ["Storm" convinces the listeners] undated article on Bellecourt's Oct. 12, 1977, apprarance at at the Volkshochschule Wyhler Wald (Wyhler Forest Community College). Box "Amerikanische Indianer 72–77." Records of the Gesellschaft für bedrohte Völker.

101. "Vereinigte Indianer" [United Indians] *Berliner Sonntagsblatt*, Oct. 23, 1977. Records of the Gesellschaft für bedrohte Völker.

102. "Bellecourt: Das Klischee der Wildwest-Filme ist immer da" [Bellecourt: the Western Film Cliché is Always There] *Spandauer Volksblatt*, Oct. 12, 1977; "Informationsdienst," Oct. 15, 1977 with a notice about an information session Oct. 13 in Berlin; "Sturm" überzeugte die Zuhorer" ["Storm" convinces the listeners] undated article on Bellecourt's Oct. 12, 1977, apprarance at at the Volkshochschule Wyhler Wald (Wyhler Forest Community College); "Vereinigte Indianer" [United Indians] *Berliner Sonntagsblatt*, Oct. 23, 1977. Records of the Gesellschaft für bedrohte Völker.

103. "Sie machten uns viele Versprechen" [They made us many promises] *Kommunistische Volkszeitung*, Oct. 17, 1977. Records of the Gesellschaft für bedrohte Völker.

104. Here I am using *performance* as an analytical term. The German phrase used for these was *Veranstaltung*, which could be translated as *presentation*, *performance*, *rally*, or *event*.

105. These usually took place in a mid-size local venue—like an unnamed location in Munich on September 30 or October 1, the Audimax auditorium at the University of Hamburg on October 8, a lecture hall of the Technical University of West Berlin on October 10, or the Neue Mensa student cafeteria in Tübingen on October 14, 1977. These locations were designed for crowds and spectacles, and the delegation's presentations drew estimated audiences of 1,500 in Munich, between 2,000 and 3,000 in Hamburg, and 800 in West Berlin. Dieter Stäcker "Schon vor tausend Jahren den Kommunismus gelebt" [Lived in Communism for Millenia] FR Oct. 10, 1977; "Bellecourt: Das Klischee der Wildwest-Filme ist immer da" [Bellecourt: the Western Film Cliché is Always There] *Spandauer Volksblatt*, Oct. 12, 1977; Dieter Fabritius, "Indianer stimmten "Kriegsgeschrei" [Indians Sound the War Whoop] *TZ* Oct. 3, 1977. Records of the Gesellschaft für bedrohte Völker.

106. "Indian Delegates in Hamburg. An Overflowing [Auditorium] Makes an Encore Necessary. Indians and Churches Against Multinational Concerns,"

and Oct. 12, 1977; "Sie machten uns viele Versprechen" [They made us many promises] *Kommunistische Volkszeitung*, Oct. 17, 1977. Records of the Gesellschaft für bedrohte Völker.

107. "0131/33. Ind. Del. '77 Hamburg Großveranstaltung." Folders "Pan Amerika Deleg 1977.," "Panindianische Rundreise 1977." Photo archive of the Gesellschaft für bedrohte Völker.

108. "0131/33. Ind. Del. '77 Hamburg Großveranstaltung"; "0131/4" Greg Zephier, Tilman Zülch, Gert Hensel (escort and interpreter) at Hamburg Indian delegation. Folders "Pan Amerika Deleg 1977" and "Panindianische Rundreise 1977." Photo archive of the Gesellschaft für bedrohte Völker.

109. Inscription on the banners reconstructed from photos by Toth. Folders "Pan Amerika Deleg 1977" and "Panindianische Rundreise 1977." Photo archive of the Gesellschaft für bedrohte Völker.

110. In the Society's photos, he is named as "Errol Cree," but in at least one newspaper photo he is credited as "Errol Kinistrio." It is almost certain that he is Erroll Kinistino (Ochapowace, Canada). Heidrun Graupner, "Elf Indianer führen Klage" [Eleven Indians Air Grievances] *SZ* [Süddeutsche Zeitung?] Oct. 3, 1977. Records of the Gesellschaft für bedrohte Völker (Society for Endangered Peoples). "0131/54 Errol Cree Kanada," "0131/56 Errol Cree Kanada," "0131/57 Errol Cree Kanada." Photo archive of the Gesellschaft für bedrohte Völker.

111. April 18, 1977 Letter from Klaus Humann to Wolf Biermann as invitation to sing at the event. Records of the Gesellschaft für bedrohte Völker (Society for Endangered Peoples). "0131/52 Wolf Biermann Hamburg." Photo archive of the Gesellschaft für bedrohte Völker.

112. "Wir wollen nicht mehr Opfer sein: Buffy Ste. Marie spricht" [We Don't Want to be Victims Anymore: Buffy Ste. Marie Speaks]. Translation by Anneliese Rudwaleit from *Akwesasne Notes*, early winter 1976, 29. Records of the Gesellschaft für bedrohte Völker. A 1974 article in the Hungarian Communist Party's youth magazine listed both "The Trail of Tears" by "the Indian half breed Peter La Farge," and "Now That the Buffalo's Gone" by Buffy Sainte Marie. "Politizáljatok, gitárok!" [Guitars Playing Politics], *Ifjúsági Magazin* [Youth Magazine], December 1974, 37. Fővárosi Szabó Ervin Library.

113. Smith and Warrior, 26.

114. "Biermann bei Rothäuten" [Biermann with the Redskins]. Preview of the event. *Hamburger Abendblatt* September 29, 1977. Box "Amerikanische Indianer 72–77." Records of the Gesellschaft für bedrohte Völker.

115. "Discography LP's." Pete Wyoming Bender homepage.

116. February 11, 1976, cable from the U.S. Embassy in Berlin to the Secretary of State, Washington, DC, State Department Records. Online database.

117. "pete–revo," "pete–warrior" Photographs on Pete Wyoming Bender homepage.

118. One of the photographs recording this is "Russell Means and Dennis Banks" Unidentified Artist, 1973 NPG.2005.32 in the online database of the Smithsonian National Portrait Gallery: http://npgportraits.si.edu/eMuseumNPG/

code/emuseum.asp?rawsearch=ObjectID/,/is/,/100121/,/false/,/false&newprofile=CAP&newstyle=single. Accessed May 30, 2015.

119. According to his English biography on his website, Bender was born in France but spent much of his childhood in the United States before moving with his father "back to Germany." The lyrics of his hit "Born to be Indian" were "written by his brother Zeph Zephier, Sr., (a Yankton Sioux). Pete was adopted by the family and tribe. Pete was also member of the American Indian Movement and speaker for the German office for some time." This kind of positioning of a white person "adopted" by Native North Americans and being a member of the radical sovereignty movement is itself a transatlantic form of "playing Indian." Biography. Pete Wyoming Bender homepage.

120. Another musical response to the radical Indian sovereignty movement was the West German Krautrock/progressive rock band Gila's 1973 record titled "Bury My Heart at Wounded Knee" with song titles like "Sundance Chant," "Young Coyote," "The Buffalo Are Coming," and "Black Kettle's Ballad." "Gila" entry on German rock e.V. website. Online: http://www.germanrock.de/lexikon_show_band.php?ID=610. Accessed May 30, 2015.

121. Martin Taureg's photographs show Bellecourt during his presentation, widely gesturing with one hand and holding a pipe in the other. Subsequent pictures show the AIM/Treaty Council delegation sitting and standing on stage—Bellecourt, Bill Wahpepah, and Greg Zephier raising their fists in the air as a Red Power victory sign, with dignity, pride, and relief on their faces, Wahpepah visibly moved and close to tears. "0131a/31," "0131a/32," "0131a/33," "0131a/34": Clyde Bellecourt USA/Chippewa/AIM 1977. Photo: Martin Taureg. "Von liks nach rechts: Bill Wahpapah, Greg Zephir und Clyde Bellecoürt von der "American Indian Movement." Photo: Martin Taureg; "0131/3 von links: Tilman Zülch (GfbV) Francois Paulette (Indian Brotherhood) Clyde Bellecourt (American Indian Movement—AIM) 1977 Panindian Rundreise auf Einlandung der GfbV." Photo: B. Stammer. Photo archives of the Gesellschaft für bedrohte Völker.

122. It is possible that the date was closer to October 12, Columbus Day, since the AIM leaders were still in the Berlin area. "Improvised torchlight procession for the day of the so-called "discovery of America" by Columbus. This was declared the "Day of Mourning" by the Indian organizations. Hamburg, September 1977. Photo: Martin Taureg. Translation from German by Toth. Photo archive of the Gesellschaft für bedrohte Völker.

123. "Pro Indianer" [For/on behalf of Indians]. *Der Abend* of West Berlin, Oct. 13, 1977. Records of the Gesellschaft für bedrohte Völker.

124. April 6, 1978 letter from Society to the Ford plant in Köln, Germany. Spring 1978 letters between society and Lufthansa about discounts on plane tickets for the Indian delegation. March 15, 1978 letter from Society to Team Musikon. Records of the Gesellschaft für bedrohte Völker.

125. Undated "Gespräche mit Indianern und Eindrücke während der Delegation" + "Vorschlage für die nächste Delegation. [Conversations with

Indians and Impressions from the Delegation]." "Vorschläge für die nächste Delegation [Suggestions for the Next Delegation]." Records of the Gesellschaft für bedrohte Völker.

126. A December 21, (presumably 1977) letter from the Society to Debbie DeLancey of the Indian Brotherhood of the Northwest Territories explained that the organizers divided up the visitors among the Society's regional groups. Undated "Endgültiger Terminplan für die Indianerdelegation '78 [Final Schedule of the Indian Delegation in 1978]." April 8, 1978 letter from Society to its members regarding the schedule of Indian delegation. April 5, 1978 letter from the Society to an Evangelical pastor in Berlin. March 10, 1978 letter to the Society from Siesbaden Ministerpräsident. March 12, 1978 letter from the Society to the mayor of Romer-Hamburg. February 24, 1978 letter from the Society to "MdB Manfred Coppik, Bundestag [Member of the German Federal Parliament]," Bonn. Records of the Gesellschaft für bedrohte Völker.

127. Some of the other delegate groups included women such as Allene Goddard and Sherry Means. "Indian Delegation Visits Soviet Union." *Treaty Council News*, Nov. 1977, 3; "These Countries Believe Strongly in Human Rights" by Sherry Means. *Treaty Council News*, Nov. 1977, 4. Original title in quotation marks. Records of the International Indian Treaty Council.

128. Women of Red Nations was a mid-1970s offshoot of the American Indian Movement, focusing on indigenous women's issues such as forced sterilization, pollution and women's health, as well as treaty rights and the elimination of demeaning Indian stereotypes in U.S. culture. Yvonne Wanrow had been convicted of murder for the shooting of a man in the defense of her children; her sentence was commuted in 1979. Barbara Moore was sterilized without her consent and against her will by personnel in the Indian Health Service in 1975. Meg Devlin O'Sullivan, "We Worry About Survival: American Indian Women, Sovereignty, and the Right to Bear and Raise Children in the 1970s," 63. Unpublished PhD dissertation. Department of History, the University of North Carolina at Chapel Hill, 2007. Online: http://dc.lib.unc.edu/cdm/singleitem/collection/etd/id/2128/rec/19. Accessed May 29, 2015. Jael Silliman et al., eds. *Undivided Rights: Women of Color Organize for Reproductive Justice*. (Cambridge, MA: South End Press, 2004), 112. "0132/62-65. Performance Göttingen Delegation '78. Photo Baugert," and various other photographs. Photo archive of the Gesellschaft für bedrohte Völker. On Barbara Moore, see Crow Dog and Erdoes, 4, and Brave Bird with Erdoes, 193.

129. Undated "Endgültiger Terminplan fur die Indianerdelegation '78 [Final Schedule of the Indian Delegation in 1978]." April 8, 1978 letter from Society to its members regarding the schedule of Indian delegation. Records of the Gesellschaft für bedrohte Völker.

130. The Federation of Survival Schools was established in 1975 to advocate and administer Native controlled education that taught both traditional Indian cultures and activism. December 17, 1977 letter from AIM Support Group Hamburg to the Society for Endangered Peoples. March 29, 1978 letter

from AIM Support Group Hamburg to the Society. Records of the Gesellschaft für bedrohte Völker.

131. "Archie Fire, Tape 3; Wolakota," March 2, 1986, 1/2. "Ceremony & Sundance, Europe, Do's & Don'ts; Beer & Alcohol, etc., Europe?" Undated, 1/2. "Archie Fire; Sundance at Crow Dogs; Europe and Life Support Groups," 1988. Audio recordings by Richard Erdoes of Archie Fire Lame Deer. The Richard Erdoes Papers. Flier for fundraising for 1980 Rotterdam Russell Tribunal. Report of the Fourth Russell Tribunal, November 1980, Rotterdam. Report of the Fourth Russell Tribunal on the Rights of the Indians of the Americas. Opening Session. Rotterdam 1980. Report of the Fourth Russell Tribunal on the Rights of the Indians of the Americas. Conclusions. Rotterdam 1980. March 12 1981 letter from the Society to friends to reflect on Russell Tribunal. Brochure "The Rights of the Indians of the Americas Fourth Russell Tribunal" report "A WIP Publication, Amsterdam Summer 1981." Tribunal program in sepia booklet. Records of the Gesellschaft für bedrohte Völker.

132. Rules of Procedures for 1981 NGO Conference on Indigenous Peoples and the Land + sessions schedule, and "Katrin's" handwritten notes on the sessions. International NGO Conference on Indigenous Peoples and the Land, Palais des Nations, Geneva, Switzerland, 15–18, September 1981. Records of the Gesellschaft für bedrohte Völker.

133. Minutes of the United Nations Commission on Human Rights, 1977–1990. United Nations Library, Palace of the Nations, Geneva, Switzerland. Records of the UN Working Group on Indigenous Populations, 1982–1990. United Nations UNOG Registry, Records and Archives Sub-Unit.

134. Archie Fire Lame Deer was the son of John Fire Lame Deer, with whom Richard Erdoes had co-authored the book *Lame Deer, Seeker of Visions* (New York: Simon & Schuster, 1972). Lame Deer visited East Germany in 1983 and 1985.

135. Ward Churchill, "Spiritual Hucksterism: The Rise of the Plastic Medicine Men." In *Z Magazine*, December 1990. Subsequently collected in Ward Churchill's *From a Native Son: Selected Essays in Indigenism, 1985–1995*. (Boston: South End Press, 1996). Online: http://www.culturalsurvival.org/publications/cultural-survival-quarterly/united-states/spiritual-hucksterismthe-rise-plastic-medicin. Accessed May 30, 2015. "The Party Crasher," by Peter Ritter. Minneapolis City Pages. October 11, 2000. Online: http://www.citypages.com/2000-10-11/news/the-party-crasher/. Accessed May 30, 2015

136. Author's interviews with Claus Biegert, Munich, Germany, July and December 2011.

137. Pre-April 6, 1978 draft letters to Roxanne Dunbar-Ortiz, James Kootshongie, George Erasmus and Oren Lyons from the Bürgerinitiativen Umweltschutz Unterelbe. Translation by Toth. Records of the Gesellschaft für bedrohte Völker.

138. Ibid.

139. Ibid.

140. Ibid.

141. March 12, 1978 letter from the Society to Carl Amery. April 8, 1978 letter from Society to its members regarding the schedule of Indian delegation. Records of the Gesellschaft für bedrohte Völker.

142. The greens drafted their letter to Dunbar-Ortiz, and sent it to the Society for approval, which never came. In a later letter, they criticized the Society's centralized hierarchy for controlling the planning and communication with the members of the Indian delegation. April 6, 1978 letter to the Society from Bürgerinitiativen Umweltschutz Unterelbe. Records of the Gesellschaft für bedrohte Völker.

143. Undated "Endgültiger Terminplan fur die Indianerdelegation '78 [Final Schedule of the Indian Delegation in 1978]." Records of the Gesellschaft für bedrohte Völker (Society for Endangered Peoples).

144. The German green movement officially announced the formation of their political wing, the Alternative Political Union, the Greens (Sonstige Politische Vereinigung, Die Grünen) in March 1979 in Frankfurt. David P. Conradt, "Green Party of Germany." *Encyclopædia Britannica Online.* Online: http://www.britannica.com/EBchecked/topic/931089/Green-Party-of-Germany. Accessed May 30, 2015.

145. Reserved for the Sioux under the 1868 Fort Laramie Treaty, the Black Hills were nevertheless overrun by gold prospectors a few years later and for all intents and purposes confiscated by the U.S. government. By the 1970s, various mining companies were prospecting for uranium in the Northern Black Hills. Big Mountain or Black Mesa is an area rich in coal and stretching into territories of both the Navajo and the Hopi nations. In the 1960s, the Peabody Company signed highly favorable contracts with both tribes, allowing for it to both extract coal from the area and use the ground water in transporting the coal through a pipeline. The company's use of ground water polluted the environment, violated spiritual edicts, and drained the water resources of the two Native nations, many of which claimed that the contracts were fraudulent.

146. Author's interviews with Claus Biegert, Munich, Germany, July and December 2011.

147. For more on the use of treaty making as sacred ceremonies in American Indian history, see "Treaties as Sacred Texts" in Robert A. Williams, Jr., *Linking Arms Together: American Indian Treaty Visions of Law and Peace, 1600–1800* (New York: Oxford University Press, 1997), 40–61.

148. The visitors were Joe American Horse, Mike Her Many Horses, Fred Brewer, Milo Yellow Hair, and Birgil Kills Straight. February 1984 "Einladung zur Pressekonferenz der Oglala Lakota" [Invitation to the Press Conference of the Oglala Lakota]. February 22, 1984 "Einladung zur Pressekonferenz der Oglala Lakota" from Arbeitsgruppe Indianer Heute (Working Group on Indians Today) of Vienna, Austria. Records of the Gesellschaft für bedrohte Völker.

149. "Die Black Hills sind heilig—sie sind nicht zu verkaufen." [The Black Hills are Holy—They are Not for Sale]. Undated (before September 17, 1984), uncredited article. "Sioux in Hamburg." *OXMOX*, September 1984, 21–22, by

Renate Domnick. Photo and caption in *Kölner Stadt-Anzeiger* no. 52, March 1, 19(84). February 1984 press wire of (*adp*). Menschenrechte—Lakota Indianer Suchen Unterstützung in Europa" [Human Rights—akota Indians Seeking Support in Europe]. "Güne Streiten für die Indianer" [The Greens Argue for the Indians] *Süddeutsche Zeitung* no. 51, March 1, 1984, 56. "Grüne unterstützen Lakota" [The Greens Are Supporting the Lakota] *Frankfurter Rundschau*, March 1, 1984. Photo and caption in *O. Ö. N.* (Noted as Austria) February 23, 1984. Photo in *Tiroler Tageszeitung*, no. 45, February 23, 1984. "Sioux-Oglala werben um Hilfe bei europäischen Regierungen" [Oglala Sioux Visit for Help from European governments] *AZ*, February 23, 1984. "Black Hills sind nicht zu verkaufen." [Black Hills are Not for Sale] *Wiener Zeitung*, February 23, 1984. "Rote Brüder suchten einen Freund" [The Red Brothers Were Looking for a Friend] *Kurier* (noted as Austrian), February 22, 1984. "Sioux beim 'weißen Bruder' " [The Sioux at the "White Brothers"] *AZ*, February 22, 1984. "Die Black Hills sind nicht zu verkaufen" [The Black Hills are Not for Sale] *De Schnüss* magazine, no. 10, October 1984. "Als Indianer überleben!" [To Survive as Indians!] *Hamburger Rundschau*, September 13, 1984. "Mit Indianischer Kunst zur praktischen Solidarität" [With Indian Art to Practical Solidarity] by H. J. Heinrich, *Taz*, Sept. 24, 1984. "Gold in den Black Hills" [Gold in the Black Hills] *Deutches Allgemeines Sonntagsblatt*, March 25, 1984. Records of the Gesellschaft für bedrohte Völker.

150. In 1979–80, the U.S. Supreme Court ruled that the confiscation of the Black Hills by the federal government was a violation of the treaty; however, it refused to take a position on rectifying the situation. Subsequently, the federal government offered the Sioux over $100 million to settle their claims once and for all. Their tribal government rejected this money for fear they would lose their land claim forever. Later Mario Gonzales (also active in the International Indian Treaty Council and the Leonard Peltier Defense Committee) filed a claim for $11 billion and the land.

151. August 31, 1984 letter from Petra K. Kelly to Federal Foreign Minister Hans-Dietrich Genscher. Records of the Gesellschaft für bedrohte Völker.

152. "Als Indianer überleben!" [To Survive as Indians!] *Hamburger Rundschau*, September 13, 1984. "Mit Indianischer Kunst zur praktischen Solidarität" [With Indian Art to Practical Solidarity] by H. J. Heinrich, *Taz*, Sept. 24, 1984. Records of the Gesellschaft für bedrohte Völker.

153. "Mit Indianischer Kunst zur praktischen Solidarität" [With Indian Art to Practical Solidarity] by H. J. Heinrich, *Taz*, Sept. 24, 1984. Records of the Gesellschaft für bedrohte Völker.

154. Leonard Crow Dog quoted in Mechelle Powers "Custer Courthouse Riot of 1973," 400. Online: http://moh.tie.net/content/docs/CusterCourthouseRiotof1973.pdf. Accessed April 26, 2010; Means with Wolf, 241–242.

155. Theorists of the Green Party like Petra Kelly conceptualized it as primarily a social movement, with a its so-called "standing leg" grassroots social movement using the parliamentary party as a "kicking leg" or propaganda

arm, much like in soccer. Accordingly, Kelly and her fellow activists wanted to change public thinking and opinion before entering into any political alliances. Tad Shull, *Redefining Red and Green: Ideology and Strategy in European Political* Ecology (Albany: State University of New York Press, 1999), 58–59.

156. It is beyond the scope of this book to gauge the extent to which such cultural exchange and sensitization actually transformed the West German discourse on American Indians. Glenn Penny's "Elusive Authenticity" as well as his book *Kindred Choice* provide some of this much-needed perspective.

Chapter 4

1. *Akwesasne Notes,* Aug–Oct 1973, 44. Underground Newspaper Collection.

2. "Dennis Banks im Gespräch mit C. Biegert. © Dick Bankroft." Folder "Panindianische Rundreise (1978)." Photo archive of the Gesellschaft für bedrohte Völker (Society for Endangered Peoples).

3. Richard Erdoes's photo contact print features 8 shots of Russell Means sitting on a tree trunk and talking to the press—giving either an interview or, just as likely based on the subsequent photos of the warrior ritual, an orientation about the ritual about to take place. "Wounded Knee 1973 Leonard Crow Dog Painting Warriors' Faces for War." The Richard Erdoes Papers.

4. *Akwesasne Notes,* Aug–Oct 1973, 44–46. Underground Newspaper Collection.

5. Ibid.

6. "Wounded Knee Gedichten" anthology of poems. Records of the Wounded Knee Legal Defense/Offense Committee.

7. The press credentials distributed by the occupiers feature names and media from Spain, Canada, Switzerland, Brazil, Mexico, and—remarkably—the Voice of America. It seems that at least one organ of the U.S. State Department sent representatives, thereby implicitly recognizing the role of Indian sovereignty rights in U.S. foreign relations. Photocopies of Wounded Knee press credentials. Records of the Wounded Knee Legal Defense/Offense Committee.

8. Carol Sullivan, "The Indians and the Media" in "Perspectives on the Occupation of Wounded Knee" 5–9. Self-standing manuscript. Carol Sullivan Papers.

9. "Clearwater's Body Taken to Crow Dog Camp" in *Wounded Knee Seed,* May 4, 1973. The Richard Erdoes Papers.

10. "Nierderlage in Wounded Knee?" [Defeat at Wounded Knee?]. Undated and uncredited article in German. English translation by Toth. The Richard Erdoes Papers.

11. While it is possible that the article was originally written by a white American and then translated from English into German, the expert opinion of Vera Grabitzky, PhD in Second Language Acquisition (University of Iowa) holds

that based on the language of the writing, the author was a native speaker of German. Personal communication, December 2, 2011. Recently, Martin Kasler from Denmark pointed out that "Gerhardt" was in fact Danish author Jacob Holdt, and the piece was translated from his Danish book *Amerikanske Billeder* [*American Pictures*] by a native German friend of his. Both the original and the German translation were published in the late 1970s in several European countries, and it was translated into English in the following decade. The book's success and critical depiction of class and racial divisions in the United States predictably resulted in plans to use it as Communist anti-American propaganda, and allegations about the author's and the translator's relationship with the Eastern Bloc's state security and intelligence services. It is up to the reader to decide if my analysis of "Wounded Knee: A Defeat?" still stands in the light of such revelations about its author and translator. "To Dr. György Tóth concerning 'Gerhardt.'" Public communication from Martin Kasler, August 25, 2015. *Reaktionære Refleksioner. Martin Kaslers blog*. Online: https://reaktionaererefleksioner.wordpress.com/2015/08/25/to-dr-gyorgy-toth-concerning-gerhardt/. "Defeat at Wounded Knee?" In Jacob Holdt, *American Pictures*. English translation. Copenhagen: American Pictures Foundation, 1985. 49–51. Online: http://www.american-pictures.com/english/book/American%20Pictures-small-size.pdf. Accessed August 27, 2015.

12. "Nierderlage in Wounded Knee?" [Defeat at Wounded Knee?].

13. See Klimke.

14. "Nierderlage in Wounded Knee?" [Defeat at Wounded Knee?].

15. Ibid., 43. In the light of the transnational discourse of groups like the National Indian Youth Council and papers like the *Akwesasne Notes*, Gerhardt was giving himself too much credit.

16. Ibid., 43.

17. Ibid., 43.

18. Ibid., 44.

19. Ibid., 45.

20. Here I use "race" as a social category made real through representations and performances, not as a biological category.

21. Author's interview with Claus Biegert, Munich, Germany, July 2011.

22. Ibid.

23. Ibid.

24. Ibid.

25. Crow Dog and Erdoes, 65–67.

26. Ibid., 69.

27. Ibid., 131.

28. See Banks and Erdoes; Means with Wolf.

29. Among those listed by Mary Crow Dog/Brave Bird are Madonna Gilbert on Alcatraz in 1970; Micmac Annie Mae Aquash at Plymouth in 1970; Sioux Lizzie Fast Horse and Minnie Two Shoes at Mount Rushmore in 1971; Oklahoma Cherokee Martha Grass in Washington, DC, in 1972; Oglala Lakota

Ellen Moves Camp and Gladys Bissonette at Calico Hall in February 1973; Lorelei de Cora at Wounded Knee in 1973; Dennis Banks's wife Kamook giving birth in jail in 1975; Mary's sister Barbara Moore, an activist against forced sterilization (including on the 1978 West German tour).

30. Crow Dog and Erdoes, 124.

31. Ibid., 249.

32. After the U.S. government opened the Big Mountain Reservation of Arizona to commercial mining in 1974, the area's Navajo and Hopi nations increasingly mobilized for resistance to the involuntary relocation of their Native residents, the violation of their cultural and spiritual sites, and the environmental degradation of the area. In addition to civil disobedience, lobbying and litigation, the Navajo and Hopi took advantage of the developing transatlantic Indian sovereignty alliance. Brave Bird with Erdoes, 131, 229.

33. Crow Dog and Erdoes, 78.

34. Brave Bird with Erdoes, 183.

35. Ibid., 58–59.

36. Ibid., 58–59.

37. Dunbar-Ortiz, *Blood on the Border*, 44–45.

38. Ibid., 30.

39. Two Indians were convicted of the murder of Aquash in the early 2000s. What the case shows is the murderous potential of the violence against Native women, whether they were part of the sovereignty movement or not. Scholars like Jacki Rand are doing invaluable and urgent work on the violence against Native women so prevalent in and around American Indian communities.

40. Brave Bird with Erdoes, 97, 100.

41. Ibid., 240.

42. May, 71.

43. Ibid., 202.

44. Blood brotherhood here is but one version of the popular trope of the white hero being "adopted" into a North American Indian tribe, which authenticates his authority. Ibid., 271, 275.

45. Ibid., 288, 328–329.

46. Ibid., 330–331, 334.

47. Sieg, *Ethnic Drag*, 90, 109.

48. For an examination of the ideas of a century of German fascination with American Indians, see H. Glenn Penny, *Kindred by Choice: Germans and American Indians since 1800* (Chapel Hill: The University of North Carolina Press, 2013).

49. November 8, 1974 letter to Richard Erdoes from Liselotte Welskopf-Henrich. The Richard Erdoes Papers.

50. Ewa Nowicka, "The 'Polish Movement of Friends of the American Indians.'" In Feest, 604–605.

51. Memorial website for "Stefania Antoniewicz—Indiańska Babcia." In Polish. Online: http://www.indianie.eco.pl/bylo/babcia.html. Accessed May 30, 2015.

52. In letters section of *Akwesasne Notes*, April–June 1972, 47. Underground Newspaper Collection.

53. In letters section of *Akwesasne Notes*, July–Aug 1972, 46. Underground Newspaper Collection.

54. November 16, 1974 letter from Stefania Antoniewicz, Warsaw, Poland to WKLD/OC. Records of the Wounded Knee Legal Defense/Offense Committee.

55. Nowicka, 606–608. Similarly to Welskopf-Heinrich, Szklarski (with his wife) wrote in the mid- to late-1970s a cycle of books about the historical battles of the Sioux for the Black Hills. Szklarski is said to have regarded the struggles of American Indian nations as similar to the Polish wars of independence. Witold Gałązka, "Na tropach Alfreda Szklarskiego." [On the Trail of Alfred Szklarski], Jan 20, 2012. Gazeta Wyborcza Katowice. Online: http://katowice.gazeta.pl/katowice/1,126076,11004736,Na_tropach_Alfreda_Szklarskiego__Odkurzyc__Tomki_.html. Accessed May 30, 2015. Piotr Kapuściński, "Alfred Szklarski." Great Poles. DumnizPolski.pl. March 25, 2006. Online: http://dumnizpolski.pl/index.php?option=com_content&task=view&id=72&Itemid=37. Accessed May 30, 2015.

56. Gerhardt is a fictional name used for the purposes of this analysis. "Nierderlage in Wounded Knee?" [Defeat at Wounded Knee?]. Photocopy of undated and uncredited article in an untitled German magazine, 42–45. English translation by Toth. The Richard Erdoes Papers.

57. Ibid., 43.

58. Ibid., 43–44.

59. Ibid., 44.

60. Ibid., 44–45.

61. Ibid., 45.

62. Ibid., 45. Interestingly, this ultimate criticism of the radical Indian sovereignty movement did not make it into the English translation of Jacob Holdt's book *American Pictures*.

63. Mary Crow Dog/Brave Bird briefly discusses one role for gay people in Sioux society: called *winkte*, the gay among the Sioux are sometimes asked to give a newborn baby a secret name that would transfer their longevity to the child. Later Brave Bird claims that the Sioux are fearful of incest, but non-relatives are rather open and straight forward about sexual relations—perhaps implying that homosexuality was not particularly proscribed or condemned. She also mentions that she knew at least one *winkte* who participated in the sun dance, a ritual revived by her husband Leonard Crow Dog as a spiritual resource for AIM in particular and Indians in general. Crow Dog and Erdoes, 158, 171.

64. For some of the scholarly thinking about homosociality and sexuality, see "Conceptualising Homosociality," in Mel Storr, *Latex and Lingerie: Shopping for Pleasure at Ann Summers Parties* (New York: Berg Publishers, 2003), 39–54.

65. See ibid.

66. Von Borries and Fischer, 78–79, 153, 155–156.

67. Quoted in Von Borries and Fischer, 55. The authors of the book changed the German names to protect the privacy of their respondents.

68. Letter to Richard Erdoes from German solidarity volunteer, February 13, 1975. The Richard Erdoes Papers. Anonymized to protect personal identity.

69. Letter to Richard Erdoes from German solidarity volunteer, August 6, 1975. The Richard Erdoes Papers. Anonymized to protect personal identity.

70. Letter to Richard Erdoes from German solidarity volunteer, August 6, 1975. The Richard Erdoes Papers. Anonymized to protect personal identity.

71. In letters section of *Akwesasne Notes*, Jan–Feb. 1972, 44. Underground Newspaper Collection. Center for Southwest Research, Zimmerman Library, The University of New Mexico, Albuquerque, NM.

72. January 18, 1975 letter from Gabriele Herrmann, East Germany; February 21, 1975 letter from Andreas Wollmann, East Berlin; Undated, no year, letter from Marina Walinsky of Tschernitz, East Germany. Box 95. Location 146.H.13.4F. Records of the Wounded Knee Legal Defense/Offense Committee.

73. March 1975 letter from a young woman from East Berlin. Translation by Toth. Box 95. Location 146.H.13.4F. Records of the Wounded Knee Legal Defense/Offense Committee.

74. Von Borries and Fischer, 68–69. Name changed by original authors.

75. "Archie Lame Deer." Recording made by Richard Erdoes. Oct. 1, 1988, Side 1 of 2. The Richard Erdoes Papers.

76. Brave Bird with Erdoes, xii.

77. Ibid., 98.

78. Ibid., 97, 100.

79. July 5, 1977 letter from Claus Biegert, Munich to Ulla Bäcksin, Sweden. Records of the Gesellschaft für bedrohte Völker.

80. July 5, 1977 letter from Claus Biegert, Munich to Ulla Bäcksin, Sweden. Records of the Gesellschaft für bedrohte Völker.

81. April 12, 1977 postcard from Ulla Bäcksin to Tilman Zülch, Survival International, Hamburg. "Auszüge aus einem Brief von Ursula Wolf vom 23. 6., über die Standing Rock Conference [Extracts from a letter by Ursula Wolf of 23. 6., about the Standing Rock Conference], 6–7. July 5, 1977 letter from Claus Biegert, Munich to Ulla Bäcksin, Sweden. July 6, 1977 letter from Society to Institute for the Development of Indian Law, Inc., DC., IITC, Indigena, and *Akwesasne Notes*. July 30, 1977 letter from Ulla Bäcksin to Insitute for the Development of Indian Law, Inc., International Indian Treaty Council, Indigena, the *Akwesasne Notes*, and Society offices in Hamburg and Munich. Records of the Gesellschaft für bedrohte Völker.

82. August 2, 1977 letter from Robert Antona of *Akwesasne Notes* staff to Margaret Selaskowski in Hamburg. Records of the Gesellschaft für bedrohte Völker.

83. August 18, 1977 letter from the International Indian Treaty Council to the Society for Endangered Peoples. September 1, 1977 letter from Tilman Zülch

of the Society for Endangered Peoples to Jimmie Durham of the International Indian Treaty Council. Records of the Gesellschaft für bedrohte Völker.

84. August 18, 1977 letter from the International Indian Treaty Council to the Society for Endangered Peoples, 3. Records of the Gesellschaft für bedrohte Völker.

Chapter 5

1. "14 June 1974 Speech to the International Indian Treaty Council Meeting" by Russell Means, 1–2. Roger A. Finzel American Indian Movement Papers.

2. The term "impaired sovereignty" was first used in the *Johnson v. McIntosh* decision of the so-called Marshall trilogy of U.S. Supreme Court rulings on Indian rights. This judicial opinion claimed that tribal sovereignty, while impaired by European colonization, still needs to be taken into consideration.

3. For more on the sovereignty movement's struggle to roll back the postwar federal termination policy, see Wilkinson.

4. "Seminoles Win Cuban Recognition," by Bob Reno, *The Miami Herald*, July (no day), 1959. Miccosukee Seminole Nation Department of Public Information. Online: http://www.miccosukeeseminolenation.com/cuban_recognition_1959.htm. Accessed May 30, 2015. Also see Dina Gilio-Whitaker, "When Mad Bear Met Fidel: How Castro's Cuba Advanced Native Sovereignty." *Indian Country Today Media Network*, July 14, 2015. Online: http://indiancountrytodaymedianetwork.com/2015/07/14/when-mad-bear-met-fidel-how-castros-cuba-advanced-native-sovereignty-161064. Accessed August 27, 2015.

5. "International Affairs: Treaty with Cuba" Miccosukee Seminole Nation Department of Public Information. Online: http://www.miccosukeeseminolenation.com/cuba.htm. Accessed May 30, 2015. Excerpts from Peter Matthiessen's *Indian Country* (New York: Viking Press, 1984). Miccosukee Seminole Nation Department of Public Information. Online: http://www.miccosukeeseminolenation.com/indian_country.htm. Accessed May 30, 2015.

6. One embodied link between the Miccosukee Seminole initiative and the later radical Indian sovereignty movement was Wallace "Mad Bear" Anderson, who was a leading member of the delegation to Cuba, and subsequently was a key leader in Haudenosaunee protests for sovereignty rights on both sides of the U.S.–Canadian border, and also appeared at the May 1973 pro-Wounded Knee demonstrations at the United Nations in New York City. Ibid.; "Clyde Bellecourt Mad Bear Anderson at demonstration early spring 1973, before U.N., New York, in support of Wounded Knee." Photo contact prints. The Richard Erdoes Papers; "Anderson, Wallace Mad Bear." American Indian Heritage Month: Commemoration vs. Exploitation. History and the Headlines. ABC-CLIO Schools. Online: http://www.historyandtheheadlines.abc-clio.com/

ContentPages/ContentPage.aspx?entryId=1171847&currentSection=1161468. Accessed May 30, 2015.

7. Cobb, *Native Activism in Cold War America*, 14, 18–21.

8. Quoted in ibid., 38. Emphasis in the original.

9. Quoted in ibid., 38.

10. For more see Chapter 3 "Dilemmas," in ibid., 58–79.

11. "14 June 1974 Speech to the International Indian Treaty Council Meeting" by Russell Means, 1–2. Emphasis added. Roger A. Finzel American Indian Movement Papers.

12. Dunbar-Ortiz, *Blood on the Border*, 17, 20, 51, 261.

13. Von Borries and Fischer, 46–51. All subsequent quotes translated by the author into English. For more on the infusion of Marxism in the East German *Indianerfilme*, see Anna Banhegyi's doctoral dissertation "Where Marx Meets Osceola: Ideology and Mythology in the Eastern Bloc Western." Unpublished Phd dissertation. Department of History, Southern Methodist University, 2012.

14. Peyer, 551.

15. For the West German solidarity campaigns for the release of Angela Davis, see Klimke, 134–142. Klimke is currently researching the East German solidarity campaigns. Personal communication, January 6, 2012. For posters of the East German government's solidarity campaign for the release of Angela Davis, see the website "The Civil Rights Struggle, African-American GIs, and Germany." Online: http://www.aacvr-germany.org/AACVR.ORG/index.php?option=com_content&view=article&id=114&Itemid=70. Accessed May 30, 2015.

16. Oct. 28, 1974, letter from Andreas Erdmann of East Germany. Records of the Wounded Knee Legal Defense/Offense Committee.

17. Von Borries and Fischer, 41–43.

18. Ibid., 63–66.

19. "Interview mit der AIM-Indianerin Monica Charles." *Junge Welt*, August 17, 1973. Quoted in ibid., 65–66.

20. "Indian Delegation Visits Soviet Union." *Treaty Council News*, Nov. 1977, 3; "'These Countries Believe Strongly in Human Rights.'" By Sherry Means. *Treaty Council News*, Nov. 1977, 4. Original title in quotation marks. Records of the International Indian Treaty Council.

21. By the late 1970s, the U.S. government's relentless legal campaign against AIM, and tribal chairman Dick Wilson's reign of terror on the Pine Ridge Reservation of South Dakota were taking their toll on the radical Indian sovereignty movement. Some of their leading activists, like Pedro Bissonette and Anna Mae Aquash, had been killed; others, like Dennis Banks, Russell Means, Leonard Crow Dog, and Leonard Peltier, were either being prosecuted in court or had already been sentenced to prison terms up to life.

22. Nowicka, 606.

23. Ibid., 599, 602.

24. Ibid., 606–607.

25. As in other countries, the meeting with the Hungarian authors was likely sanctioned or arranged by the Hungarian Cultural Ministry, the country's PEN Club chapter, or the Council for Peace. *Treaty Council News*, Nov. 1977, 4. Underground Newspaper Collection.

26. Author's visit to Baktay Ervin Memorial House and Museum of Western Games/Cowboys and Indians, July 2, 2011.

27. Author's interview with anonymous Hungarian hobbyist of the Bakony group, Budapest, Hungary, July 2011. Special thanks to Adrienn Kácsor for assistance with research in Hungary.

28. Ibid.

29. The hobbyist also confirmed that the Hungarian media covered the Indian sovereignty struggle. Ibid. Dénes Kiss, "A legutolsó mohikánok" [The Last of the Last of the Mohicans], June 1973, 29; "Politizáljatok, gitárok!" [Guitars Playing Politics], Dec. 1974, 37; "What's New?" Interview with Dean Reed, Nov. 1975, 20; *Ifjúsági Magazin* [Youth Magazine]. Fővárosi Szabó Ervin Library.

30. Tamás Cseh, *Hadiösvény (1968–69)* [War Path] (Konkrét Könyvek, Budapest 2008), 1. Emphasis added. Translation from Hungarian by Toth.

31. Author's interview with anonymous Hungarian hobbyist of the Bakony group, Budapest, Hungary, July 2011.

32. Ibid.

33. Ibid. One pitfall of oral history interviews is that the respondent will sometimes give information on cause and effect and motivations in ways that justify past events from the perspective of the present—rationalizing their own past actions. This kind of retroactive justification is part of the individual's process of meaning making, and should be distinguished from actual past motivations.

34. One respondent mentioned a case of young Hungarian hobbyists arrested for the use of firearms they found accidentally. He recalled being interrogated about the hobby and being told that their use of weapons was suspicious. He also recalled that his group of hobbyists were monitored by the state. Another respondent mentioned that the recent Hungarian play and film *The Apache* [*Apacsok*] (play by Géza Bereményi and Krisztina Kovács, 2009; film by dir. Ferenc Török, 2010) uses the case of surveillance as a cultural backdrop. Publicity of the play explicitly linked the performance to the "Fung" case by featuring text from Kovai's (then forthcoming) study. The author's interview with anonymous Hungarian hobbyist of the Danube valley group, Kisoroszi, Hungary, July 2011. The author's interview with anonymous Hungarian hobbyist of the Bakony group, Budapest, Hungary, July 2011. Promotional description and interviews for the play. Online: http://engine.szinhaz.hu/index.php?id=404&cid=35901. Accessed December 23, 2010.

35. Melinda Kovai, "Az "Indiánok" fedőnevű ügy" [Operation "Indians"] In *AnBlokk* magazine special issue on Surveillance, vol. 3, 2009 (Budapest and Pécs, Hungary), 40. Translation from Hungarian by Toth.

36. Ibid., 43, 45, 47.

37. As depicted in the Hungarian comedy *Witness* (dir. Péter Bacsó, 1969) and analyzed in scholarly literature, the show trials [*koncepciós perek*] of the Hungarian Communist state from the late 1940s through the early 1960s were public performances in which the roles of defendant, witnesses, defense, prosecutor, and judge were carefully scripted and choreographed.

38. The Boy Scout movement was banned in Hungary by the Communist régime in 1948, and was replaced by the Pioneer and Young Communist movements.

39. The Communist state's Marxist ideology designated the clergy, the bourgeoisie, and the nobility as "reactionary" to the revolution. Until 1989, the official line claimed that the 1956 uprising against the régime was the work of such forces. Personal recollection of the author.

40. Kovai, 47.

41. Kovai, 40–52.

42. Von Borries and Fischer, 126, 131–134, 136. For more on the methods and operational approaches of the East German state security, see Anja Kunze, "Die Indianistikszene der DDR" [The Indianistic Scene of the German Democratic Republic]. Unpublished Master's Thesis in European Ethnography and Geography. Humbold University of Berlin, October 2006), 70–71.

43. Kovai, 41.

44. In the early- to mid-1980s, the author's parents, not connected to Hungarian Indian hobbyists, held weekly gatherings in their family home, where a large group of friends and acquaintances listened as a "guest of honor" (an intellectual, scientist, scholar, or artist) briefly described his or her ideas and current projects. In retrospective conversations in the 1990s, the author's father claimed they had suspicions that there was an informer in the group, and he claimed that on one occasion the state security had cars waiting, ready to arrest the group—which he prevented by switching up the speaker at the last minute. Regardless of the factual value of these statements, they attest to the degree to which the *perception* of state surveillance among people influenced their behavior in advance of any positive proof of monitoring. Author's personal recollections.

45. The author's interview with anonymous Hungarian hobbyist of the Danube valley group, Kisoroszi, Hungary, July 2011.

46. Bérczes and Cseh, 82.

47. Sieg, *Ethnic Drag*, 122.

48. Von Borries and Fischer, 18–19, 31–32.

49. Ibid., 32–33; Interview with long-time member and leader of the Bakony group, June 2011. Source kept anonymous due to research ethics regulations.

50. Von Borries and Fischer, 31–32, 54.

51. Ibid., 35.

52. October 28, 1974 letter to WKLD/OC from Andreas Erdmann of Neuruppin. Original in English. In "Letters of Solidarity." Records of the Wounded Knee Legal Defense/Offense Committee.

53. I am using the term "Eastern European" not as a geographical designation, but to refer to the Communist countries of Central Europe—such as Poland, Czechoslovakia, Hungary, and East Germany.

54. In 1977, Leonard Peltier was sentenced to consecutive life terms in prison relating to the killing of two FBI agents on the Jumping Bull Ranch in June 1975. The radical Indian sovereignty movement embarked on a still ongoing international campaign to win the release of Peltier. Von Borries and Fischer, 67; the Treaty Council's Jimmie Durham also attended a peace conference in Warsaw, Poland, May 1977, which issued resolutions calling for international campaigns supporting "political prisoners" Skyhorse, Mohawk, and Peltier. "Treaty Council at World Peace Conference," *Council News*, June 1977, 2. Records of the International Indian Treaty Council.

55. Von Borries and Fischer, 33.

56. Sieg, *Ethnic Drag,* 142.

57. Von Borries and Fischer, 41, 43, 60, 86–87.

58. Ibid., 68–69, 78–79.

59. Ibid., 135–136. For such a perspective among Czechoslovak Indian hobbyists, see the documentary *If Only I Were an Indian* (dir. John Paskievich, Winnipeg: National Film Board of Canada, 1995).

60. DY 27 6507. Kulturbund. Landes und Bezirksorganisationen, Kreisorganisationen und Ortsgruppen. Bezirke. Allgemeines. Bd.: 2 Tätigkeit der Fachgruppe Indianistik im Kulturbund Stralsrund, 1983–1984. Federal Archive, Reich and GDR Department, Archive of the Parties and Mass Organizations of the GDR, Berlin, Germany.

61. Ibid., 136. Such measures of state control were not exclusive to East Germany. Hungarian state security also monitored Indianist hobby groups. See Kovai.

62. Kunze, 65–66. Library of the Federal Commissioner for the files of the State Security Service of the former German Democratic Republic.

63. Summary of file "Dresden/XII 1589/76." Federal Commissioner for the files of the State Security Service of the former German Democratic Republic.

64. Ibid., 000067, 000080. Federal Commissioner for the files of the State Security Service of the former German Democratic Republic.

65. Ibid., 000080.

66. While the privacy policies of the Federal Commissioner for the files of the former East German State Security Service in Berlin do not allow for the identification of the two defendants, in the records of the Wounded Knee Legal Defense/Offense Committee at the Minnesota Historical Society in St. Paul I have uncovered solidarity letters that reflect how some East Germans were contemplating taking action beyond the usual state-sanctioned solidarity work. This is but one example of how multi-sited historical research can recover transnational links and thereby contribute to our knowledge about the dynamic relations between state and non-state actors across the Atlantic. October 28, 1974 letter to WKLD/OC from Andreas Erdmann of Neuruppin. February 22, 1975

letter to WKLD/OC from Angelika Niebuhr, Rostock. February 21, 1975 letter to WKLD/OC from Andreas Wollmann, East Berlin. Handwritten in German, handwritten English translation, presumably by a WKLD/OC volunteer. Records of the Wounded Knee Legal Defense/Offense Committee.

67. Kunze, 65–66.

68. In an ironic coincidence, during the Cold War the East German Ministry of State Security used the acronym AIM for "archivierter IM [Inoffizieller Mitarbeiter]-Vorgang"—an "archived operation with an unofficial collaborator (informer)"—the same acronym that designated the American Indian Movement. *Abkürzungsverzeichnis* [List of Acronyms] Federal Commissioner for the files of the State Security Service of the former German Democratic Republic, Berlin, 2009. Online: http://www.bstu.bund.de/DE/Wissen/Publikationen/Publikationen/E_abkuerzungsverzeichnis.pdf?__blob=publicationFile. Accessed May 30, 2015.

69. Original group name in English. Summary of file "IM-Vorgang [Unofficial collaborator/informer operation] V1591/84, Frankfurt." Federal Commissioner for the files of the State Security Service of the former German Democratic Republic.

70. Ibid., 000046.

71. The term "East Germany" was a sore point for the German Democratic Republic's government, since they positioned the country as the one true anti-fascist and democratic heir to the entity of Germany. Ibid., 000061.

72. Ibid., 000065–71.

73. Ibid., 000073–75.

74. Ibid., 000083.

75. "MfS-Abt. XI Nr. 953" twice; "MfS-HA II Nr. 23092; MfS-HA XIX Nr. 1367; MfS-HA II Nr. 23224; MfS AOPK 2709/85 I. Federal Commissioner for the files of the State Security Service of the former German Democratic Republic.

76. Von Borries and Fischer, 54; Sieg, *Ethnic Drag*, 123.

77. Name modified for privacy by the authors. Von Borries and Fischer, 68.

78. "MfS BV Dresden, OPK 833/88." Federal Commissioner for the files of the State Security Service of the former German Democratic Republic. Also in von Borries and Fischer, 68–69. Name changed for reasons of privacy by the authors.

79. Quoted and summarized in ibid., 78–79.

80. Ibid., 153.

81. File "XIV 1418/85, Karl-Marx Stadt, 'Hans.' 000069. Federal Commissioner for the files of the State Security Service of the former German Democratic Republic.

82. Ibid., 000292.

83. Brave Bird with Erdoes, 126.

84. "Archie Fire, Tape 3; Wolakota." Audio recording, 1/2. March 2, 1986. The Richard Erdoes Papers.

85. File "XIV 1418/85, Karl-Marx Stadt, 'Hans.'" 000025, 000173. Federal Commissioner for the files of the State Security Service of the former German Democratic Republic.

86. Ibid., 000173.

87. Ibid., 000173.

88. Ibid., 000173.

89. In rather Foucauldian fashion, the Hungarian term "megfigyelés" both denotes *observation, monitoring,* and *surveillance.* For an analytical essay on the relationship between the personae of "the Indian" (hobbyist), the ethnographic participant observer, and the state informer in the person of László Borsányi, see Kata Horváth, "A Borsányi név: A politikai és a tudományos megfigyelés határai" [The Name Borsányi: The Borders of Political and Scientific Observation] In *AnBlokk* magazine special issue on "Surveillance," vol. 3 (2009) 30–38.

90. "Archie Fire, Tape 3; Wolakota." Audio recording, 1/2. March 2, 1986. The Richard Erdoes Papers.

91. For an analysis of "violating" as a form of Ojibwe resistence and identity maintenance, see Larry Nesper, *The Walleye War: The Struggle for Ojibwe Spearfishing and Treaty Rights* (Lincoln: University of Nebraska Press, 2002), 49–56.

92. Crow Dog and Erdoes, 131. In characteristic humor and identification, Richard Erdoes himself used the figure of the "heyoka" in his incomplete autobiography to describe his activities in Europe before emigrating to the United States. Autobiography in incomplete manuscript. The Richard Erdoes Papers.

93. "Archie Fire, Tape 3; Wolakota." Audio recording, 1/2. March 2, 1986. The Richard Erdoes Papers.

94. Such scholarship includes Richard White, *The Middle Ground: Indians, Empires, and Republics in the Great Lakes region, 1650–1815* (Cambridge, New York: Cambridge University Press, 1991); Leonard J. Sadosky, Revolutionary Negotiations: Indians, Empires, and Diplomats in the Founding of America (Charlottesville: University of Virginia Press, 2009); Timothy J. Shannon, *Iroquois Diplomacy on the Early American Frontier* (New York: Viking, 2008); Tom Arne Midtrød, *The Memory of All Ancient Customs: Native American Diplomacy in the Colonial Hudson Valley* (Ithaca, NY: Cornell University Press, 2012); John T. Juricek, *Colonial Georgia and the Creeks: Anglo-Indian Diplomacy on the Southern Frontier, 1733–1763* (Gainesville: University Press of Florida, 2010); Charles A. Weeks, *Paths to a Middle Ground: The Diplomacy of Natchez, Boukfouka, Nogales, and San Fernando de las Barrancas, 1791–1795* (Tuscaloosa: University of Alabama Press, 2005); Gilles Havard, *The Great Peace of Montreal of 1701: French-Native Diplomacy in the Seventeenth Century* (Montreal; Ithaca, NY: McGill-Queen's University Press, 2001); and *Documents of American Indian Diplomacy: Treaties, Agreements, and Conventions, 1775–1979* (Norman: University of Oklahoma Press, 1999).

95. Means with Wolf, 368, 369.

96. "Ceremony & Sundance, Europe, Do's & Don'ts; Beer & Alcohol, etc., Europe?" Undated audio recording, 1/2. The Richard Erdoes Papers.

97. "Defends Indian Rights: NASC Advances Struggle," by Rusty Conroy. *Guardian*, April 7, 1976. In "Threats to the Peaceful Observance of the Bicentennial," 91–93; "Discussion Paper—NASC [Native American Solidarity Committee] as a Non-Indian Solidarity Organization." Underground Newspaper Collection.

98. Here I use Philip J. Deloria's analytical term "playing Indian" for the performance of Indianness by white Americans to fashion a variety of collective identities for themselves. See Deloria, 5, 7–8.

99. One example is the early AIM demonstrations against the depiction of Indians in the 1970 Hollywood film *A Man Called Horse*. James S. Olson, ed., *Historical Dictionary of the 1970s* (Westport, CT; London: Greenwood Press, 1999), 32. Another instance is the permission by the Zuni Indians to the Koshare Dancers of the Boy Scouts of America to reenact specific Native rituals.

100. For more on the fluidity characteristic of Germanic solidarity groups, see Bernd C. Peyer, "Who is Afraid of AIM?" In Feest, 552–553.

101. See Penny, "Elusive Authenticity," 798–818.

102. Archie Fire Lame Deer was the son of John Fire Lame Deer, with whom Richard Erdoes had co-authored the book *Lame Deer, Seeker of Visions* (New York: Simon & Schuster, 1972).

103. Von Borries and Fischer, 82–84, 97.

104. "Ceremony & Sundance, Europe, Do's & Don'ts; Beer & Alcohol, etc., Europe?" Undated audio recording by Richard Erdoes of Archive Fire Lame Deer. The Richard Erdoes Papers. Peyer likewise refers to the same or possibly another similar instance at the 1983 "1st European Medicine Wheel Gathering and Spiritual Camp" in the Black Forest. Peyer in Feest, 560.

Chapter 6

1. Means with Wolf, 371.

2. See Deskaheh, *The Redman's Appeal for Justice*. (Aug. 6, 1923). Howard R. Berman Collection, The State University of New York at Buffalo Law Library. Online: http://law.lib.buffalo.edu/collections/berman/pdfs/Redmanappeal.pdf. Accessed May 30, 2015. Also in Laurence M. Hauptman, *The Iroquois Struggle for Survival: World War II to Red Power*. (Syracuse, NY: Syracuse University Press, 1986), 206. Also in Ronald Niezen, *The Origins of Indigenism: Human Rights and the Politics of Identity*. (Berkeley, CA; London: University of California Press, 2003), 31–32.

3. For more see chapter 3 "Dilemmas," in Cobb, *Native Activism in Cold War America*, 58–79.

4. Diplomatic "airgram" from The United States post at the United Nations (USUN) to the U.S. Department of State (State), August 19, 1970. State Department Records. "They Charge Genocide," no author. *Akwesasne Notes*, September 1970, 46. "Appeal to UN," no author. Seattle, AP. In *Akswesasne*

Notes, April 1971, 7. "Indian Voices from Sweden:" In *Akwesasne Notes*, April–June 1972, 30. "United Nations Committee Rules Puerto Rico is Entitled to be Free." *Akwesasne Notes*, June 1972, 11. Underground Newspaper Collection.

5. Leonard Crow Dog about Wounded Knee, quoted in Smith and Warrior, 202.

6. Means with Wolf, 295; Banks and Erdoes, 202.

7. "Note for the Record" March 2 1973, by C. V. Narasimhan. In "S-0271-0001-04. American Indians—Wounded Knee, South Dakota (2)." Electronic file version of hard copy documents. United Nations Archives and Records Management Section.

8. Ibid.

9. For more on the use of treaty making as sacred ceremonies in American Indian history, see "Treaties as Sacred Texts" in Robert A. Williams, Jr., *Linking Arms Together: American Indian Treaty Visions of Law and Peace, 1600–1800* (New York: Oxford University Press, 1997), 40–61.

10. "Note for the Record" March 2, 1973, by C. V. Narasimhan. In "S-0271-0001-04. American Indians—Wounded Knee, South Dakota (2)." Electronic file version of hard copy documents. United Nations Archives and Records Management Section.

11. Ibid. Emphasis added.

12. Ibid.

13. Ibid.

14. Ibid.

15. Charter of the United Nations. Chapter I: Purposes and Principles. Electronic version on the website of the United Nations. Online: http://www.un.org/en/documents/charter/chapter1.shtml. Accessed May 30, 2015

16. Ibid., chapter XV: The Secretariat.

17. "Note for the Record" March 2, 1973., by C. V. Narasimhan. In "S-0271-0001-04. American Indians—Wounded Knee, South Dakota (2)." Electronic file version of hard copy documents. United Nations Archives and Records Management Section.

18. Ibid.

19. For more on the agreements and legal status of the United Nations compound and its surroundings, see "99 (I) Arrangements required as a result of the establishment of the Permanent Headquarters of the United Nations in the United States of America"; "169 (II) Agreement between the United Nations and the United States of America regarding the Headquarters of the United Nations." Hundred and second plenary meeting, October 31, 1947, 96, 97–98, 102; "100 (II) Headquarters of the United Nations." Sixty-fifth plenary meeting, Dec. 14, 1946, 94–95, 195–197. Document attachment to electronic message from UN Reference Team, Dag Hammarskjöld Library, United Nations Headquarters, New York, November 26, 2010; and "Convention on the Privileges and Immunities of the United Nations," adopted by the General Assembly on February 13, 1946. Online: http://www.unog.ch/80256EDD006B8954/(httpAssets)/C8297

DB1DE8566F2C1256F2600348A73/$file/Convention%20P%20&%20I%20(1946)%20-%20E.pdf. Accessed May 30, 2015.

20. Author's visit and photographs of the United Nations Headquarters, New York City in January 2010.

21. Photo contact print sheet 58, folder 332, The Richard Erdoes Papers.

22. Ibid.

23. Ibid. Sign transcribed with assistance from Colleen Kelley.

24. Ibid.

25. Photo contact print sheet 63, folder 339. The Richard Erdoes Papers.

26. Author's photographs of the United Nations Headquarters, New York City in January 2010.

27. "Meeting between the Legal Counsel and an American Indian delegation." United Nations Interoffice Memorandum from Senior Legal Officer J. F. Scott to head of Secretariat Georg Hennig, May 4, 1973. In "S-0271-0001-04. American Indians—Wounded Knee, South Dakota (2)." Electronic file version of hard copy documents. United Nations Archives and Records Management Section.

28. Ibid. and "Communication concerning human rights received from delegation of American Indians." United Nations Interoffice Memorandum from Director of the Division of Human Rights Marc Schreiber to Under-Secretary-General for Political and General Assembly Affairs Bradford Morse, May 4, 1973. In "S-0271-0001-04. American Indians—Wounded Knee, South Dakota (2)." Electronic file version of hard copy documents. United Nations Archives and Records Management Section.

29. "OPI Daily Press Briefing." March 8, 1973. In ibid.

30. "Meeting between the Legal Counsel and an American Indian delegation." In ibid.

31. Ibid.

32. Ibid.

33. "Communication concerning human rights received from delegation of American Indians." In ibid.

34. "Petition by the Six Nation Iraquois [*sic*] Confederation Agency on behalf of the Indians of the Oglala Nation." May 4, 1973. In ibid.

35. Ibid.

36. "Communication concerning human rights received from delegation of American Indians." In ibid.

37. "Note for the Record," by C. V. Narasimhan. March 9, 1973. In ibid.

38. "Declaration of Continuing Independence." Roger A. Finzel American Indian Movement Papers. Also online at http://www.iitc.org/about-iitc/the-declaration-of-continuing-independence-june-1974/. Accessed May 30, 2015.

39. IITC application for NGO consultative status in the Economic and Social Council of the United Nations (ECOSOC). June 21, 1974. In Consultative Arrangements and Relations with the International Indian Treaty Council-OR 340 (958), Pt. 1. S-0446-0264-0003, UN. Registry Section, Archive Series-Box

S-0446-0264, Registry Archive Group—Organizational (OR). United Nations Archives.

40. Letter from Virginia Saurwein of UN Committee on Non-Governmental Organizations to Jimmie Durham of IITC, May 18, 1977. In ibid.

41. The other early indigenous world organization was named the World Council of Indigenous Peoples (WCIP), and was created in 1974–75 by the National Indian Brotherhood (Canada), the National Congress of American Indians (U.S.), and the Nordic Sami Council ("Lappland" of Scandinavian countries). The National Indian Brotherhood had been given ECOSOC status as a "place holder" in 1974 with the understanding that a truly international organization would take over as soon as it was recognized by the UN—and WCIP was and took the spot in 1978. In subsequent years, an increasing number of indigenous rights organizations were granted ECOSOC status and joined the table at the Commission on Human Rights and the Working Group on Indigenous Populations. These included the Indian Law Resource Centre (from 1980), the Four Directions Council (from 1983), the Indian Council of South America (from 1982), the Indigenous World Association (from 1984), the National Aboriginal and Islander Legal Services Secretariat (from 1986), and the Grand Council of the Crees (from 1986), and the International Work Group for Indigenous Affairs (from 1990). Other NGOs in ECOSOC status that usually collaborated with the indigenous representatives were the International Anti-Slavery Society (from 1949), Afro-Asian Peoples' Solidarity Organization (from 1970), and Survival International (after 1980). Relevant years of the Yearbook of the United Nations. Online: http://unyearbook.un.org/index.html. Accessed May 30, 2015. Also relevant years of the bound volumes of the reports of the United Nations Economic and Social Council at the Library of the United Nations at Geneva.

42. Andrea Muehlebach, "'Making Space' at the United Nations: Indigenous Cultural Politics at the U.N. Working Group on Indigenous Populations." *Cultural Anthropology* 16, no. 3, (2001): 442.

43. Correspondence in Consultative Arrangements and Relations with the International Indian Treaty Council-OR 340 (958), Pt. 1. S-0446-0264-0003, UN. Registry Section, Archive Series-Box S-0446-0264, Registry Archive Group—Organizational (OR). United Nations Archives.

44. For more on this, see chapter 2, and Roxanne Dunbar-Ortiz, *Indians of the Americas*, 33–34.

45. Article 2 paragraph 7 of the United Nations Charter of 1945 prohibits the international body from "intervening in matters which are essentially within the domestic jurisdiction of any state or [. . .] requir[ing] the Members to submit such matters to settlement under the present Charter." Charter of the United Nations. Chapter I: Purposes and Principles. Electronic version on the website of the United Nations. Online: http://www.un.org/en/documents/charter/chapter1.shtml. Accessed May 30, 2015.

46. June 13, 1975 handwritten letter from Lola Costa to Marcella. Consultative Arrangements and Relations with the International Indian Treaty

Council-OR 340 (958), Pt. 1. S-0446-0264-0003, UN. Registry Section, Archive Series-Box S-0446-0264, Registry Archive Group—Organizational (OR). United Nations Archives.

47. June 19, 1975 letter from Lola Costa to Jeremiah Gutman, Counselor at Law. In ibid.

48. Muehlebach, 439.

49. June 27, 1975 letter from Jimmie Durham of the International Indian Treaty Council to "Mr. Rizzo," presumably a lawyer or UN official. In his July 17, 1975 letter to Costa, Durham was reiterating the same points in a more condensed form. July 17, 1975 letter from Jimmie Durham to Lola Costa. Consultative Arrangements and Relations with the International Indian Treaty Council-OR 340 (958), Pt. 1. S-0446-0264-0003, UN. Registry Section, Archive Series-Box S-0446-0264, Registry Archive Group—Organizational (OR). United Nations Archives.

50. Dunbar-Ortiz, *Blood on the Border*, 38. Also see Roxanne Dunbar-Ortiz, "What Brought Evo Morales to Power? The Role of the International Indigenous Movement and What the Left is Missing." *Counterpunch*, February 10, 2006, i–ii, vii–viii. Online: http://www.counterpunch.org/2006/02/10/what-brought-evo-morales-to-power/. Accessed May 30, 2015.

51. Dunbar-Ortiz, "What Brought Evo Morales to Power?" i–ii.

52. Dunbar-Ortiz, "What Brought Evo Morales to Power?," viii.

53. List of participants in "Report of International NGO Conference on Discrimination Against Indigenous Populations in the Americas—1977," 43–49. Records of the Indigenous Peoples' Information and Documentation Center.

54. Author's interview, Munich, Germany, December 19, 2011.

55. The funding of the trip allowed for the official Native delegates to bring with them a significant number of people in observer status. This made it possible for most members of the Shenandoah family and the Means family to be present at the conference and come along for the trip. It also indicates that in two of the most transnationally active Native nations—the Six Nations Iroquois and the Lakota Sioux—sovereignty activism involved several members of the same families. This is very much in keeping with the obligations of the social unit of the *tyiospaye*, the extended family in Lakota society as described by Mary Crow Dog/Brave Bird. In these two Native communities, cultural and political activism ran in the same families, in this case the Lame Deers and Crow Dogs. At the conference, the next generation of activists was represented not only by the younger members of the Shenandoah and Means clans, but also by seventeen-year-old Winona LaDuke, whose father would soon become known in the esoteric European Indianist scene as Sun Bear, and who later herself would become active in the Native resource and environmental protection movement. Crow Dog and Erdoes, 13, 174. List of participants in "Report of International NGO Conference on Discrimination Against Indigenous Populations in the Americas—1977," 47. Records of the Indigenous Peoples' Information and

Documentation Center. *Die Donnervogelfrau* [Thunderbird Woman] (Claus Biegert and Bertram Verhaag, dirs., 1995).

56. List of participants in "Report of International NGO Conference on Discrimination Against Indigenous Populations in the Americas—1977," 43–49. Records of the Indigenous Peoples' Information and Documentation Center.

57. For more on the history of the United Nations buildings and grounds in Geneva, see George Scott, *The Rise and Fall of the League of Nations* (London: Hutchinson & Co LTD, 1973), 67. Author's visit to an exhibition on the history of the Palace of the Nations. League of Nations Museum, Geneva, Switzerland, June 2010.

58. Here I am referring to the ways and the resulting structures of how architecture and landscaping was used to project the political and economic power of the owner or commissioner of specific mansions or palaces—a European tradition going back to at least the eighteenth century.

59. Means with Wolf, 371.

60. Personal photographs of the United Nations Palace of the Nations and ground. July 2010. Photographs of the 1977 UN NGO conference opening march. Many images taken and copyrighted by Claus Biegert. Photo archive of the Gesellschaft für bedrohte Völker.

61. Means with Wolf, 371.

62. Personal photographs of the United Nations Palace of the Nations and grounds. July 2010. Photographs of the 1977 UN NGO conference opening march. Many images taken and copyrighted by Claus Biegert. Photo archive of the Gesellschaft für bedrohte Völker. Film footage in the documentary *Indian Summer in Geneva*, (Pierrette Birraux and Volkmar Ziegler, dirs., Kisos Films and doCip, 1986).

63. Photographs of the 1977 UN NGO conference opening march. Many images taken and copyright by Claus Biegert. Photo archive of the Gesellschaft für bedrohte Völker.

64. Photograph accompanying the article "Geneva Conference," *Treaty Council News* vol. 3, no. 5, 1981. Records of the International Indian Treaty Council.

65. David Wilkins quoted in Shari M. Huhndorf, "Picture Revolution: Transnationalism, American Studies, and the Politics of Contemporary Native Culture," *American Quarterly* vol. 61, no. 2, June 2009, 363.

66. "*The Celestial Sphere* (United States, 1939). Gift of the Woodrow Wilson Foundation. The spherical frame is adorned with constellations and stars. The 85 constellations are gilded and the 840 stars are silvered. The sphere is equipped with a motor to revolve slowly around an axis turned to the Pole Star. Unfortunately, this motor no longer works." The Palais des Nations. The United Nations in the Heart of Europe official web site. Online: http://www.unog.ch/80256EE600581D0E/(httpPages)/1CF0E20D6BC97A1680256EF700594A1C?OpenDocument. Accessed May 30, 2015.

67. "021//23." Photo archive of the Gesellschaft für bedrohte Völker.

68. The committees of the 1977 conference were the Economic Commission, the Legal Commission, and the Social and Cultural Commission. Commission reports in the "Report of International NGO Conference on Discrimination Against Indigenous Populations in the Americas—1977," 43–49. Records of the Indigenous Peoples' Information and Documentation Center.

69. Photographs in folders "Pan Amerika Deleg 1977," "Panindianische Rundreise 1977," "0.2.3. Genf 84-85," "0.2.4. Genf 87-91." Photo archive of the Gesellschaft für bedrohte Völker.

70. 023/37-39. Photo archive of the Gesellschaft für bedrohte Völker.

71. Dunbar-Ortiz, *Blood on the Border*, 66.

72. Muehlebach, 421.

73. They included Roxanne Dunbar-Ortiz, Jimmie Durham, Paul Smith, Fern Eastman, Chockie Cottier, Bill Means, and Winona LaDuke. Dunbar-Ortiz, *Blood on the Border*, 38.

74. The Yanomami, an indigenous group living in the Amazon rain forests of Venezuela and Brazil, were threatened by violent gold prospectors who were encroaching on their territories in the mid-1970s. The case was taken up by indigenous rights organizations like Survival International. One leader of the Indigenous Peoples' Documentation Center had worked on the Yanomami case before joining the DoCip volunteers. Author's interview with an administrator at the Indigenous People's Documentation Center, June 2010.

75. Ibid.

76. Ibid.

77. Ibid.

78. Ibid.

79. Dunbar-Ortiz, *Blood on the Border*, 38. Also see Dunbar-Ortiz, "What Brought Evo Morales to Power?," xiii.

80. Siegfried Wiessner, "Introduction." United Nations Declaration on the Rights of Indigenous Peoples. Audiovisual Library of International Law. Online: http://legal.un.org/avl/ha/ga_61-295/ga_61-295.html. Accessed May 30, 2015.

81. Author's research and interview with an administrator at the Indigenous People's Documentation Center. June 2010.

82. Diana Taylor, *The Archive and the Repertoire* (Durham, NC: Duke University Press, 2003), 19, 20, 28.

83. Dunbar-Ortiz, *Blood on the Border*, 38. Also see Dunbar-Ortiz, "What Brought Evo Morales to Power?," viii.

84. Dunbar-Ortiz, *Blood on the Border*, 38.

85. Roach, 25–32.

86. Author's interview with an administrator at the Indigenous People's Documentation Center. June 2010.

87. This title was inspired by Russell Leslie Peterson, *Strange Bedfellows: How Late-Night Comedy Turns Democracy into a Joke* (New Brunswick, NJ: Rutgers University Press, 2008).

88. Dunbar-Ortiz, *Blood on the Border*, 68.

89. Ibid., 68.

90. Vernon J. Vavrina, "The Reagan Administration, The United Nations & Human Rights." Forum on Public Policy, 2006. Online: http://forumonpublicpolicy.com/archive07/vavrina.pdf. Accessed May 30, 2015. For a contemporary articulation of the "turnaround thesis," see Tamar Jacoby, "The Reagan Turnaround on Human Rights." In *Foreign Affairs* vol. 64, no. 5, summer 1986, (The Council on Foreign Relations, Inc., Washington, DC), 1066–1086.

91. Dunbar-Ortiz, *Blood on the Border*, 44–46.

92. Ibid., 232.

93. Ibid., 110–113.

94. UNCHR session February 21, March 7, 8, 1978. Bound volume "United Nations Economic and Social Council Commission on Human Rigths 1978–9, E/CN.4/SR.1441–1480. UNCHR session March 13 10 AM, 3 PM, 1979. Bound volume "United Nations Economic and Social Council Commission on Human Rights 1979–80, E/CN.4/SR.1481–1522. UNCHR session March 11, 12 10 AM, 3 PM, 1985. Bound volume "United Nations Economic and Social Council Commission on Human Rights 1985, E/CN.4/1985/SR 46–58. UNCHR session February 19, 27, 1990. Bound volume "United Nations Economic and Social Council Commission on Human Rights 1990, E/CN.4/1990/SR 20–40. United Nations Library, Palace of the Nations.

95. "United Nations Commission on Human Rights (thirty-seventh session)," *Oyate Wicaho* February–May 1981, 6. Underground Newspaper Collection. Also "Written statements" E/CN.4/NGO/299 February 4, 1981; E/CN.4/NGO/311 February 17, 1981; E/CN.4/NGO/319 March 2, 1981, United Nations Economic and Social Council, Commission on Human Rights, (thirty-seventh session, agenda item 13). United Nations Library.

96. UNCHR session February 10, 1989. Bound volume "United Nations Economic and Social Council Commission on Human Rights 1989–90, E/CN.4/1989/SR 1–20. UNCHR session February 21, March 1, 1989. Bound volume "United Nations Economic and Social Council Commission on Human Rights 1989–90, E/CN.4/1989/SR 21–36. UNCHR session March 6, 7, 1989. Bound volume "United Nations Economic and Social Council Commission on Human Rights 1989–90, E/CN.4/1989/SR 50–57. United Nations Library.

97. See L.26 draft resolution on human rights in Cuba by the U.S., and L.35 draft resolution on human rights in U.S. by Cuba. Bound volume "United Nations Economic and Social Council Commission on Human Rights 1985–88, E/CN.4/1988/L.12-104. Also UNCHR session March 10, 1988. Bound volume "United Nations Economic and Social Council Commission on Human Rights 1988, E/CN.4/1988/SR 42–57. United Nations Library.

98. Ibid, 38. Also see Dunbar-Ortiz, "What Brought Evo Morales to Power?," xiii.

99. Siegfried Wiessner, "Introduction." United Nations Declaration on the Rights of Indigenous Peoples.

100. Dunbar-Ortiz, "What Brought Evo Morales to Power?," xvii.

101. Special Rapporteur on the Rights of Indigenous Peoples website. Online: http://www.ohchr.org/EN/Issues/IPeoples/SRIndigenousPeoples/Pages/SRIPeoplesIndex.aspx. Accessed May 30, 2015.

102. Permanent Forum on Indigenous Issues website. Online: http://social.un.org/index/IndigenousPeoples.aspx. Accessed May 30, 2015.

103. The Expert Mechanism on the Rights of Indigenous Peoples website. Online: http://www.ohchr.org/EN/Issues/IPeoples/EMRIP/Pages/EMRIPIndex.aspx. Accessed May 30, 2015.

104. The United Nations Declaration on the Rights of Indigenous Peoples. March 2008. Online: http://www.un.org/esa/socdev/unpfii/documents/DRIPS_en.pdf. Accessed May 30, 2015.

Chapter 7

1. Smith and Warrior, 236.

2. Means with Wolf, 324–245.

3. See Kenneth S. Stern, *Loud Hawk: The United States versus the American Indian Movement* (Norman: University of Oklahoma Press, 1994); Peter Matthiessen, *In the Spirit of Crazy Horse* (New York: Viking Press, 1983); Ward Churchill, *Agents of Repression: The FBI's Secret War against the Black Panther Party and the American Indian Movement* (Boston: South End Press, 1988); and Smith and Warrior.

4. Means with Wolf, 328; Banks with Erdoes, 220.

5. Banks with Erdoes, 225.

6. See Stern; Matthiessen; Churchill, *Agents of Repression*; and Smith and Warrior.

7. In 1977 Peltier was convicted for killing the two FBI agents, and given two consecutive life sentences. Over the following three decades, one of the major campaigns of the International Indian Treaty Council was to raise international support for the release of Leonard Peltier as a political prisoner of the U.S. justice system.

8. "American Indian Movement." May 1976 telegram from the Director of the FBI to Deputy Attorney General's Analysis and Evaluation Unit, the Attorney General's sections of General Crimes and Internal Security, the U.S. Marshals Service, the U.S Secret Service, and the Department of the Interior, 1–3. Roger A. Finzel American Indian Movement Papers.

9. Ibid., 4.

10. Ibid., 3.

11. It may not be far-fetched to suggest that there is a continuity between Euro-American panics and policy about Indian gatherings such as those at Wounded Knee in 1890, 1973, 1976, and the fact that after the September

11, 2001, terrorist attacks, several U.S. government legal briefs were based on strategies used by the U.S. military against the Seminoles in Florida. "Andrew Jackson's Actions Model Anti-Speech, Perpetual War Legislation" by Gale Courey Toensing, *Indian Country Today Media Network*, June 7, 2011. Online: http://indiancountrytodaymedianetwork.com/2011/06/07/andrew-jacksons-actions-model-anti-speech-perpetual-war-legislation-37239. Accessed May 30, 2015. "Welcome to the United Police State of America" by Gale Courey Toensing, *Indian Country Today Media Network*, December 8, 2011. Online: http://indiancountrytodaymedianetwork.com/2011/12/08/welcome-united-police-state-america-66376. Accessed May 30, 2015.

12. "Statement of Charles Abourezk, Sam Moves Camp, Rene LeDeaux—In Response to FBI Memo . . . ," no date. 1. Also "Joint Statement by Charles Abourezk, Renee LeDeaux Sam Moves Camp." June 25, 1976, 1–2. Roger A. Finzel American Indian Movement Papers.

13. "FBI Continues COINTELPRO Tactics Against Native Americans." Press release by Native American Solidarity Committee, June 23, 1976, 1, 2. Roger A. Finzel American Indian Movement Papers.

14. Ibid., 2–3. Also "Statement of Charles Abourezk, Sam Moves Camp, Rene LeDeaux—In Response to FBI Memo . . . ," no date, 1. Also "Joint Statement by Charles Abourezk, Renee LeDeaux Sam Moves Camp," June 25, 1976, 1. Roger A. Finzel American Indian Movement Papers.

15. "Operation Bicent: The Latest Step in the Military's Plans to Take Over the Police" by Frank Browning and Jeff Stein, research by Tim Butz. *Washington Newsworks*, June 24–30, 1976, 8–9. Roger A. Finzel American Indian Movement Papers.

16. See *Book III: Final Report of the Select Committee to Study Governmental Operations with Respect to Intelligence Activities*, United States Senate, April 23, 1976, U.S. Government Printing Office, Washington, DC: 1976. Online at the Assassination Archive and Research Center: http://www.aarclibrary.org/publib/church/reports/book3/pdf/ChurchB3_0_Title.pdf. Accessed May 30, 2015.

17. For more on the federal government's responses to the transnational relations of the early black civil rights movement, see Von Eschen, *Race Against Empire*.

18. "Threats to the Peaceful Observance of the Bicentennial. Hearing before the Subcommittee to Investigate the Administration of the Internal Security Act and Other Internal Security Laws of the Committee on the Judiciary, United States Senate, Ninety-Fourth Congress, Second Session, June 18, 1976." U.S. Government Printing Office, Washington, 1976. Online: http://en.wikisource.org/wiki/Page:Threats_to_the_peaceful_observance_of_the_bicentennial.djvu/1. Accessed May 30, 2015.

19. Thurmond's sentences in the record are evidence that there was at least one performance aiming to counter the Subcommittee's performative branding of these organizations as risks to national security. Ibid., 1.

20. Ibid., ii, 1–2. Emphasis added.

21. Ibid., 16.

22. It is likely that in light of the recent scandal over the FBI "dog soldiers" memo, the Subcommittee toned down its rhetoric to appease South Dakota Senator James Abourezk, whose son Charles had been implicated, and who sat on the Senate Committee on the Judiciary. See Senator Thurmond as quoted above, and also Martha Roundtree's testimony. Ibid., 2, 3–4.

23. "Bomb Threat to Embassies from American Indian (Movement) Extremists," Secretary of State cable to posts in Western Europe, December 13, 1973 and January 31, 1974. State Department Records online database.

24. My claims here are more preliminary than conclusive, since much of the diplomatic materials of the period are still classified.

25. See Hixson, 29–87.

26. See Saunders.

27. See Arndt.

28. See Caute, 247–468, and Naima Prevots, *Dance for Export: Cultural Diplomacy and the Cold War* (Hanover and London: Wesleyan University Press, 1999).

29. Smith and Warrior, 236.

30. Photocopies of Wounded Knee press credentials. Records of the Wounded Knee Legal Defense/Offense Committee.

31. "The American Indians" undated booklet, United States Information Service, New Zealand. State Department Records. A more general description of *Dialogue* can be found in Hans N. Tuch, *Communicating with the World: U.S. Public Diplomacy Overseas* (New York: St. Martin's Press, 1990), 60–61.

32. These included "Introduction—the Art of the First Americans," Norman Feder's "The Art of the American Indian," "Pictures of Traditional Art," an exposé on "Contemporary Indian Artists" by Lloyd E. Oxendine, "Report to Crazy Horse" by William Stafford, and M. Scott Momaday's "A Vision Beyond Time and Place." "The American Indians" undated booklet, United States Information Service, New Zealand. State Department Records.

33. Ibid., 1–2.

34. Ibid., 19, 66.

35. Ibid., 19–29.

36. Deloria does not mention that Bruce was subsequently fired after he sided with the Native occupiers during the 1972 takeover of the BIA building in Washington, DC. Ibid., 19–20, 23–25.

37. Ibid., 26.

38. Ibid., 24, 26.

39. Ibid., 27.

40. Ibid., 27–28.

41. Ibid., 28.

42. "Transforming Token Integration into Good Faith: Martin Luther King Talks to Czechoslovak Radio." Radio Prague website. Online: http://www.

radio.cz/en/section/archives/transforming-token-integration-into-good-faith-martin-luther-king-talks-to-czechoslovak-radio-1. Accessed May 30, 2015.

43. Ibid., 25, 28.

44. Ibid., 67.

45. Ibid., 68.

46. Ibid., 68.

47. Ibid., 68.

48. See Arndt.

49. November 8, 1973; March 13, 29; April 18; May 7, 13; and June 6, 1974 cables between the U.S. Embassy in Warsaw and the Secretary of State, Washington, DC. State Department Records online database.

50. According to the cables, the exhibition met with unprecedented success also with Romanian standards. February 8; March 7, 25; and April 8, 1974 cables between the U.S. Embassy in Bucharest, Romania and the Secretary of State, Washington, DC. State Department Records online database.

51. September 24, October 8, 22, 1974; March 6, December 16, 1975 cables between the U.S. embassies in Bucharest, Romania, Manama, Bahrein, Cairo, Egypt, and the Secretary of State and USIA, Washington, DC. State Department Records online database.

52. October 2, 1975 cable from U.S. Embassy in Tokyo, Japan to Secretary of State, Washington, DC. State Department Records online database.

53. January 23, 1976 cable from U. S. Embassy, Rome, Italy to Secretary of State and USIA, Washington, DC. State Department Records online database.

54. June 5, 1975 cable from Secretary of State to Sidney, Australia; August 1, 1975 cable from Lisbon, Portugal to Secretary of State; April 19, 1976 cable from Khartoum, Sudan to Secretary of State; April 29, 1976 cable from U.S. Embassy in Manila, the Philippines to Secretary of State, Washington, DC. State Department Records online database.

55. September 27, 1976 cable from the U.S. Embassy in London, United Kingdom to Secretary of State, Washington, DC. State Department Records online database.

56. Sally Price, *Primitive Art in Civilized Places* (Chicago: University of Chicago Press, 1989), 90–91, 102, 121.

57. September 27, 1976 cable from the U.S. Embassy in London, United Kingdom to Secretary of State, Washington, DC. State Department Records online database.

58. See "Anonymity and Timelessness" in Price, 56–67.

59. September 27, 1976 cable from the U.S. Embassy in London, United Kingdom to Secretary of State, Washington, DC. State Department Records online database.

60. September 27, 1976 cable from the U.S. Embassy in London, United Kingdom to Secretary of State, Washington, DC. State Department Records online database.

61. See Dudziak; and Von Eschen, *Satchmo Blows Up the World*.

62. September 27, 1976 cable from the U.S. Embassy in London, United Kingdom to Secretary of State, Washington, DC. State Department Records online database.

63. December 18, 1975, April 16, May 7, 1976 cables from Moscow to Secretary of State, Washington, DC. State Department Records online database.

64. December 14, 1973 cable from Secretary of State, Washington, DC. to the U.S. Embassy in the Hague, Netherlands. State Department Records online database.

65. August 27, 1975 cable from Secretary of State, Washington, DC to the U.S. Embassy in Lisbon, Portugal. State Department Records online database.

66. October 31, 1975 cable from U.S. Embassy, Berlin, West Germany to Secretary of State, USIA, and other posts. State Department Records online database.

67. February 11, 1976 cable from the U.S. Embassy in Berlin to the Secretary of State, Washington, DC. State Department Records online database.

68. July 8, 1976 cable from U.S. embassy in Copenhagen, Denmark to State Department, Washington, DC. State Department Records online database.

69. July 8, 1976 cable from U.S. embassy in Copenhagen, Denmark to State Department, Washington, DC. State Department Records online database.

70. For more, see President Jimmy Carter's "First Inaugural Address." January 20, 1977. Online: http://teachingamericanhistory.org/library/index.asp?document=1194. Accessed May 30, 2015; also "Human Rights and Foreign Policy," Jimmy Carter's commencement speech at Notre Dame University, June 1977. Online: http://teachingamericanhistory.org/library/index.asp?document=727. Accessed May 30, 2015.

71. Jimmy Carter, *Public Papers of the Presidents of the United States: Jimmy Carter*, vol. 1 (1977), 954. Online: http://infousa.state.gov/government/overview/carter.html.

72. May 18, 1977 letter from Virginia Saurwein of the UN Committee on Non-Governmental Organizations to Jimmie of the International Indian Treaty Council. Consultative Arrangements and Relations with the International Indian Treaty Council-OR 340 (958), Pt. 1. S-0446-0264-0003, UN. Registry Section, Archive Series-Box S-0446-0264, Registry Archive Group—Organizational (OR). United Nations Archives.

73. January 22, 1975 cable from Secretary of State to all East Asian and Pacific diplomatic posts, Moscow, Budapest, etc. State Department Records online database.

74. November 9, 1976 cable from the U.S. Mission to the UN, Geneva, Switzerland to the Secretary of State, Washington, DC. State Department Records online database.

75. "Excerpts of Statements Made at Plenary Sessions & in Commissions." In "Report of International NGO Conference on Discrimination Against Indigenous Populations in the Americas—1977," 43–49. Records of the Indigenous Peoples' Information and Documentation Center.

76. Dunbar-Ortiz, *Blood on the Border*, 5.

77. "Appendix—Legal Commission Report." "Report of International NGO Conference on Discrimination Against Indigenous Populations in the Americas—1977," 19. Box "United Nations Conferences 1977." Records of the Indigenous Peoples' Information and Documentation Center.

78. "American Indians Accuse U.S." *The Washington Post*, September 23, 1977. Underground Newspaper Collection.

79. "Flap over Views at Indian Parley." *The Washington Post*, September 25, 1977. Underground Newspaper Collection.

80. "Statement Submitted by the Government of the United States of America." In "Report of International NGO Conference on Discrimination Against Indigenous Populations in the Americas—1977," 67–68. Records of the Indigenous Peoples' Information and Documentation Center.

81. Ibid., 67.

82. Andrew DeRoche, *Andrew Young: Civil Rights Ambassador* (Wilmington, DE: Scholarly Resources, 2003), 102.

83. Ibid., 103.

84. Dunbar-Ortiz, *Blood on the Border*, 51.

85. It is not clear how much the future Iranian revolutionary and religious leadership may have engaged with the Wild West-themed exhibitions and programming that the U.S. State Department had put on in Tehran in the years preceding the hostage crisis. These included, in September 1974, the Smithsonian's "George Catlin's American Indian Paintings" in 1974; the book exhibit titled "The American West"; and several other exhibitions, theater performances and film screenings. September 24, October 8, 22, 1974; March 6, December 16, 1975 cables between the U.S. embassies in Bucharest, Romania, Manama, Bahrein, Cairo, Egypt, and the Secretary of State and USIA, Washington, DC. State Department Records online database. "The American West" book exhibit catalog; "The American West" folding pamphlet; "The American West" booklet in English and Persian. State Department Records.

86. Memorandum 2873, for Hamilton Jordan from Ed Torres, May 22, 1980, the White House, 1–2. Jimmy Carter Presidential Library, Atlanta, Georgia.

87. David Patrick Houghton, *US Foreign Policy and the Iran Hostage Crisis* (Cambridge, UK, and New York, USA: Cambridge University Press, 2001), 107.

88. Means with Wolf, 399.

89. Untitled and undated (between January 25 and January 31, 1980) description of the Hostage Mail Exchange Service. "Troubled areas—terrorism—American Diplomats held hostage in Teheran, Iran. S-0904-0093-06. UN. Secretary-General (1972–1981: Waldheim), Political matters—country files." United Nations Archives and Records Management Section.

90. January 14, 1980 cable to Chef de Cabinet of the UN Secretary-General Rafeeuddin Ahmed from Yammin. In ibid.

91. Untitled and undated (between January 25 and January 31, 1980) description of the Hostage Mail Exchange Service. In ibid.

92. In Means with Wolf, photo section after page 430.

93. Untitled and undated (between January 25 and January 31, 1980) description of the Hostage Mail Exchange Service. "Troubled areas—terrorism—American Diplomats held hostage in Teheran, Iran. S-0904-0093-06. UN. Secretary-General (1972–1981: Waldheim), Political matters—country files." United Nations Archives and Records Management Section.

94. February 1, 1980 letter from John Adams of the United Methodist Church to UN Chef de Cabinet Rafeeuddin Ahmed. In ibid. Less than two weeks later, Native activist John Thomas disclosed American Indian involvement in the hostage mail service in a comment in a newspaper report. "Activist Says Rescue Endangered Mail Exchange." Associated Press. *The Lakeland Ledger*, 6A, February 12, 1980.

95. Memorandum 2873, for Hamilton Jordan from Ed Torres, May 22, 1980, the White House, 1. Jimmy Carter Presidential Library, Atlanta, Georgia.

96. By "triangulation" I mean the sovereignty movement's use of its UN status and ideological and political independence from the U.S. government to broker and facilitate the Hostage Mail Exchange Service. This was a move that leveraged their non-state actor transnational status and reputation to accomplish a task that neither the U.S. government, nor the United Nations itself, nor the various Iranian groups (government, religious leadership, or Student Council) would have been able to achieve.

97. DeRoche, 111–112.

98. This title was inspired by the title of von Eschen's *Race Against Empire*.

99. For more, see Means' speech "For America to Live, Europe must Die" at the Black Hills International Survival Gathering, South Dakota, July 1980. In Means with Wolf, 545–554.

100. For more about Dunbar-Ortiz's views, see her *Indians of the Americas*.

101. Means with Wolf, 461, 463, 466.

102. Dunbar Ortiz, *Blood on the Border*, 12.

103. "International Indian Treaty Council Report," *Oyate Wicaho* Nov 1980, 6–8; "Nicaragua's Literacy Crusade: A Revolutionary Priority," *Oyate Wicaho* June–Aug 1981, 5; "Liberated Indian Country: Free Nicaragua," *Treaty Council News* July 1981, 3. Underground Newspaper Collection.

104. "Liberated Indian Country: Free Nicaragua," *Treaty Council News* July 1981, 3. Underground Newspaper Collection.

105. "AIM and Treaty Council Visit Nicaragua," *Oyate Wicaho* Jan–March 1982, 6. Underground Newspaper Collection.

106. Ibid.

107. "Clarification of Treaty Council Position on the Miskito Indians of Nicaragua," *Oyate Wicaho* May–Aug 1982, 8–9. Underground Newspaper Collection.

108. Dunbar-Ortiz, *Blood on the Border*, 129, 135–136. Also Means with Wolf, 459–460

109. Ibid., 137.

110. "To the Editors of Akwesasne Notes," by Roxanne Dunbar-Ortiz, July 16, 1982, *Oyate Wicaho* May–August 1982, 9. Underground Newspaper Collection.

111. Dunbar-Ortiz, *Blood on the Border*, 137.

112. Means with Wolf, 463, 466; also "Leaders Decry Proposal to Have US Indians Fight Sandinistas" *The Daily Californian* April 3, 1985; AIM Governing Council press release April 4, 1985. Records of the International Indian Treaty Council; also Dunbar-Ortiz, *Blood on the Border*, 247.

113. For example, the IITC invited and hosted pro-Sandinista Miskito at a conference in Arizona. "Clarification of Treaty Council Position on the Miskito Indians of Nicaragua," *Oyate Wicaho* May–Aug 1982, 8–9. Underground Newspaper Collection.

114. "NCAI President Enters into an International Agreement with General Commander Brooklyn Rivera, of MISURATA, Nicaragua" Aug. 15, 1983. Records of the International Indian Treaty Council.

115. Letter from Armstrong Wiggins of the Indian Law Resource Center to William Means of IITC, June 25, 1984. Records of the International Indian Treaty Council's office. Accessed June 2010. Also see Dunbar-Ortiz, *Blood on the Border*, 113.

116. "Clarification of Treaty Council Position on the Miskito Indians of Nicaragua," *Oyate Wicaho* May–Aug 1982, 8–9. Underground Newspaper Collection.

117. Letter from Armstrong Wiggins of the Indian Law Resource Center to William Means of IITC, June 25, 1984. Records of the International Indian Treaty Council. Also see Dunbar-Ortiz, *Blood on the Border*, 113.

118. Letter from Glenn Morris of Colorado AIM to Bill Means and Bill Wahpepah of the IITC, Oct. 29, 1986. Records of the International Indian Treaty Council.

119. Dunbar-Ortiz, *Blood on the Border*, 257.

120. For more on the all-German solidarity with Nicaragua in the 1980s, see Erika Harzer, *Aufbruch nach Nicaragua: Deutsch-deutsche Solidarität im Systemwettstreit* [*Departure for Nicaragua: Inter-German Solidarity in the Battle of the Blocs*] (Berlin: Links, 2009).

121. Letter from Hank Adams of the Survival of the American Indians Association to President Ronald Reagan, November 30, 1985. Records of the International Indian Treaty Council. Also see Dunbar-Ortiz, *Blood on the Border*, 258–259.

122. Ibid., 199–200.

123. Ibid., *Blood on the Border*, 258, 259.

124. This formulation was inspired by the title of von Eschen's *Race Against Empire*.

125. Dunbar-Ortiz, *Blood on the Border*, 268.

Conclusion

1. "Statement of the United Nations Special Rapporteur on the Rights of Indigenous Peoples, James Anaya, upon conclusion of his visit to the United States." The University of Arizona Support Project for the United Nations Special Rapporteur on Indigenous Peoples. Online: http://www.unsr.jamesanaya.org/statements/statement-of-the-united-nations-special-rapporteur-on-the-rights-of-indigenous-peoples-james-anaya-upon-conclusion-of-his-visit-to-the-united-states. Accessed May 30, 2015. "UN Official's Comments on Indian Land Restoration Create Stir Around the Globe," *Indian Country Today*, Media Network, May 8, 2012. Online: http://indiancountrytodaymedianetwork.com/2012/05/08/un-officials-comments-indian-land-restoration-create-stir-around-globe-111885. Accessed May 30, 2015. "U.S. must heal native peoples' wounds, return lands: U.N." by Louis Charbonneau. Reuters, May 4, 2012. Online: http://www.reuters.com/article/2012/05/04/us-usa-indigenous-un-idUSBRE8431Q220120504. Accessed May 30, 2015.

2. Author's interviews with Claus Biegert, Munich, Germany, July and December 2011.

3. Visit to the office of the International Indian Treaty Council, San Francisco, May–June 2010.

4. Visit to the office of the Society for Endangered Peoples, Göttingen, Germany, summer 2011.

5. See Roxanne Dunbar-Ortiz, "What Brought Evo Morales to Power?"

6. "Statement of the United Nations Special Rapporteur on the Rights of Indigenous Peoples, James Anaya, upon conclusion of his visit to the United States." The University of Arizona Support Project for the United Nations Special Rapporteur on Indigenous Peoples. Online: http://www.unsr.jamesanaya.org/statements/statement-of-the-united-nations-special-rapporteur-on-the-rights-of-indigenous-peoples-james-anaya-upon-conclusion-of-his-visit-to-the-united-states. Accessed May 30, 2015. "UN Official's Comments on Indian Land Restoration Create Stir Around the Globe," *Indian Country Today*, Media Network, May 8, 2012. Online: http://indiancountrytodaymedianetwork.com/2012/05/08/un-officials-comments-on-indian-land-restoration-create-stir-around-the-globe-111885 Accessed May 30, 2015. "U.S. must heal native peoples' wounds, return lands: U.N." by Louis Charbonneau. Reuters, May 4, 2012. Online: http://www.reuters.com/article/2012/05/04/us-usa-indigenous-un-idUSBRE8431Q220120504. Accessed May 30, 2015.

7. While it is unlikely that the United Nations could do much without the collaboration of the United States government, see "Sale of the Sacred: How Pe' Sla may test the uncharted waters of the UNDRIP," by Lise Balk King, *LastRealIndians.com*. Online: http://indiancountrytodaymedianetwork.com/2012/08/24/sale-sacred-how-pe-sla-may-test-uncharted-waters-undrip. Accessed May 30, 2015.

8. On November 5, 2009 and December 16, 2010, President Barack Obama hosted a summit of the leaders of all federally recognized Native nations in the White House. On June 13, 2014 the president visited the Standing Rock Sioux Reservation. On November 24, 2012, the Department of the Interior approved a Land Buy-Back Program for Tribal Nations, estimated at $1.9 billion, to purchase "fractionated" land from current owners and put it into trusts for Indian nations. See Katie Zezima, "As Obama makes rare presidential visit to Indian reservation, past U.S. betrayals loom." *The Washington Post*, June 13, 2014. Online: http://www.washingtonpost.com/politics/obama-to-make-rare-presidential-visit-to-indian-reservation-past-betrayals-loom-over-meeting/2014/06/13/70046890-f26f-11e3-9ebc-2ee6f81ed217_story.html. Accessed May 25, 2015. Sunlen Miller, "Obama Hosts Conference for Native American Leaders." ABC News. Online: http://abcnews.go.com/Politics/president-obama-hosts-conference-native-american-leaders-white/story?id=8999579. Accessed May 25, 2015. "Interior Announces Steps Underway for Implementation of $1.9 Billion Land Buy-Back Program for Tribal Nations." Press release. Department of the Interior website. June 18, 2013. Online: http://www.doi.gov/news/pressreleases/interior-announces-steps-underway-for-implementation-of-land-buy-back-program-for-tribal-nations.cfm. Accessed May 25, 2015.

Bibliography

Ames, Eric. "Seeing the Imaginary: On the Popular Reception of Wild West Shows in Germany, 1885–1910." In Pamela Kort, Max Hollein, eds, *I Like America: Fictions of the Wild* West. München, New York: Prestel, 2006, 212–29.

Anderson, Benedict. *Imagined Communities: Reflections on the Origins and Spread of Nationalism.* London and New York: Verso, 1991.

Memorial website for "Stefania Antoniewicz—Indiańska Babcia." In Polish. Online: http://www.indianie.eco.pl/bylo/babcia.html.

Richard T. Arndt. *The First Resort of Kings: American Cultural Diplomacy in the Twentieth Century.* Washington, DC: Potomac Books Inc., 2005.

Banks, Dennis, and Richard Erdoes. *Ojibwa Warrior: Dennis Banks and the Rise of the American Indian Movement.* Norman, OK: University of Oklahoma Press, 2004.

Bánhegyi, Anna. "Where Marx Meets Osceola: Ideology and Mythology in the Eastern Bloc Western." Doctoral dissertation. Southern Methodist University, 2012.

Bender, Peter "Wyoming." Pete Wyoming Bender's public website. Online: http://www.pete-wyoming-bender.de/.

Bérczes, László, and Tamás Cseh. *Cseh Tamás: Bérczes László beszélgetőkönyve* [Conversations with Tamás Cseh by László Bérczes]. Budapest: Palatinus, 2007.

Biegert, Claus, and Bertram Verhaag, dirs. *Die Donnervogelfrau* [*Thunderbird Woman*] (1995).

Birraux, Pierrette, and Volkmar Ziegler, dirs. *Indian Summer in Geneva*, (Kisos Films and the Indigenous Peoples' Information and Documentation Center, 1986).

Bolz, Peter. "Indian Images for the King: George Catlin in Europe." In Pamela Kort, and Max Hollein, eds., *I Like America: Fictions of the Wild* West. München, New York: Prestel, 2006, 68–85.

———. "Life Among the "Hunkpapas": A Case Study of German Indian Lore." In Christian F. Feest, ed., *Indians and Europe: An Interdisciplinary Collection of Essays.* Aachen: Edition Herodot Rader-Verlag, 1987, 475–90.

Von Borries, Friedrich, and Jens-Uwe Fischer. *Sozialistische Cowboys: Der Wilde Westen Ostdeutschlands*. Frankfurt am Main: Suhrkamp Verlag, 2008.

Brave Bird, Mary, with Richard Erdoes. *Ohitika Woman*. New York: Grove Press, 1993.

Bruyneel, Kevin. *The Third Space of Sovereignty: The Postcolonial Politics of U.S.–Indigenous Relations*. Minneapolis, London: University of Minnesota Press, 2007.

Calloway, Colin G. "Historical Encounters across Five Centuries." In Colin G. Calloway, Gerd Gemünden and Suzanne Zantop, eds., *Germans and Indians: Fantasies, Encounters, Projections*. Lincoln, NE; London: University of Nebraska Press, 2002, 47–82.

Carter, Jimmy. *Public Papers of the Presidents of the United States: Jimmy Carter*, vol. 1 (1977). Online: http://infousa.state.gov/government/overview/carter.html.

Caute, David. *The Dancer Defects: The Struggle for Cultural Supremacy during the Cold War.* Oxford, New York: Oxford University Press, 2003.

Cherokee Nation v. Georgia. 30 U.S. 1 (1831), Online: http://www.mtholyoke.edu/acad/intrel/cherokee.htm.

Churchill, Ward. *Agents of Repression: The FBI's Secret War against the Black Panther Party and the American Indian Movement.* Boston: South End Press, 1988.

"The Civil Rights Struggle, African-American GIs, and Germany." Website. Online: http://www.aacvr-germany.org/AACVR.ORG/.

Cobb, Daniel. *Native Activism in Cold War America: The Struggle for Sovereignty.* Lawrence, KS: University Press of Kansas, 2008.

———. "Talking the Language of the Larger World: Politics in Cold War (Native) America." Daniel Cobb and Loretta Fowler, eds., *Beyond Red Power: American Indian Politics and Activism since 1900*. Santa Fe, NM: School for Advanced Research, 2007.

Conrad, Rudolf. "Mutual Fascination: Indians in Dresden and Leipzig." In Christian F. Feest, ed., *Indians and Europe: An Interdisciplinary Collection of Essays.* Aachen: Edition Herodot Rader-Verlag, 1987, 455–73.

Cowger, Thomas W. *The National Congress of the American Indians: The Founding Years.* Lincoln, London: The University of Nebraska Press, 1999

Crow Dog, Mary, and Richard Erdoes. *Lakota Woman*. New York: Grove Weidenfeld, 1990.

Cseh, Tamás. *Hadiösvény (1968–69)* [*War Path*]. Konkrét Könyvek, Budapest, 2008.

Deloria, Philip J. *Indians in Unexpected Places.* Lawrence, KS: University Press of Kansas, 2004.

———. *Playing Indian*. New Haven, CT; London: Yale University Press, 1998.

DeRoche, Andrew. *Andrew Young: Civil Rights Ambassador*. Wilmington, DE: Scholarly Resources, 2003.

Desmond, Jane C., and Virginia R. Dominguez. "Resituating American Studies in a Critical Internationalism." *American Quarterly* 48, no. 3 (1996): 475–90.

Donahue, Bill. "Ways and Means." *The Washington Post*, June 29, 2008, p. W08. Online: http://www.washingtonpost.com/wp-dyn/content/article/2008/06/24/AR2008062401162.html?hpid=topnews.

Dudziak, Mary L. *Cold War Civil Rights: Race and the Image of American Democracy*. Princeton, NJ; Oxford: Princeton University Press, 2000.

Dunbar-Ortiz, Roxanne. "What Brought Evo Morales to Power? The Role of the International Indigenous Movement and What the Left is Missing." *Counterpunch*, February 10, 2006. Online: http://74.125.93.132/search?q=cache:rmXpdqxoWrgJ:www.counterpunch.org/ortiz02102006.html+1977+Geneva+Indigenous&cd=2&hl=en&ct=clnk&gl=us.

———. *Blood on the Border: A Memoir of the Contra War*. Cambridge, MA: South End Press, 2005.

———. *Indians of the Americas: Human Rights and Self-Determination*. London: Zed Books Ltd, 1984.

The Expert Mechanism on the Rights of Indigenous Peoples website. Online: http://www.ohchr.org/EN/Issues/IPeoples/EMRIP/Pages/EMRIPIndex.aspx.

Fisher Fishkin, Shelley. "Crossroads of Cultures: The Transnational Turn in American Studies. Presidential Address to the American Studies Association, November 12, 2004." In *American Quarterly* 57, no. 1 (March 2005): 17–57.

Gemünden, Gerd. "Between Karl May and Karl Marx: The DEFA Indianerfilme." Colin G. Calloway, Gerd Gemünden, and Suzanne Zantop, eds., *Germans and Indians: Fantasies, Encounters, Projections* (Lincoln, NE; London: University of Nebraska Press, 2002), 243–56.

Gonzales, Yolanda Broyles. "Cheyennes in the Black Forest: A Social Drama." In Roger Rollin, ed., *The Americanization of the Global Village: Essays in Comparative Popular Culture.* (Bowling Green, KY: Bowling Green State University Popular Press, 1989), 70–86.

Hixson, Walter L. *Parting the Curtain: Propaganda, Culture, and the Cold War, 1945–1961*. New York: St. Martin's Press, 1997

Horváth, Kata. "A Borsányi név: A politikai és a tudományos megfigyelés határai" [The Name Borsányi: The Borders of Political and Scientific Observation] *AnBlokk* magazine special issue on Surveillance 3, (2009).

Houghton, David Patrick. *US Foreign Policy and the Iran Hostage Crisis*. Cambridge, MA; New York: Cambridge University Press, 2001.

Huhndorf, Shari M. "Picture Revolution: Transnationalism, American Studies, and the Politics of Contemporary Native Culture." *American Quarterly* 61, no. 2 (June 2009): 359–81.

———. *Mapping the Americas: The Transnational Politics of Contemporary Native Culture*. Ithaca, NY: Cornell University Press, 2009.

Jackson, Helen H. *A Century of Dishonor: A Sketch of the U. S. Government's Dealings with Some of the Indian Tribes*. New York: Harper and Brothers, 1881.

Jacoby, Tamar. "The Reagan Turnaround on Human Rights." *Foreign Affairs* 64, no. 5, (Summer 1986): 1066–86.

Johansen, Bruce Elliott, and Barbara Alice Mann, eds. *Encyclopedia of the Haudenosaunee (Iroquois Confederacy)*.Westport, CT; London: Greenwood Press, 2000.

Johnson, Troy R. *Red Power: The Native American Civil Rights Movement*. New York: Infobase Publishing, 2007.

Kalshoven, Petra Tjitske. *Crafting the Indian: Knowledge, Desire and Play in Indianist Reenactment*. New York and Oxford: Beghahn Books, 2012.

Kaplan, Thomas. "Iroquois Defeated by Passport dispute." *The New York Times*, July 17, 2010, p. D1. Online: http://www.nytimes.com/2010/07/17/sports/17lacrosse.html.

Kipp, Woody. *Viet Cong at Wounded Knee: The Trail of a Blackfeet Activist*. Lincoln, NE: University of Nebraska Press, 2004.

Klimke, Martin. *The Other Alliance: Student Protest in West Germany & the United States in the Global Sixties*. Princeton, NJ; Oxford: Princeton University Press, 2010.

Kovai, Melinda. "Az "Indiánok" fedőnevű ügy" [Operation "Indians"] In *AnBlokk* magazine special issue on Surveillance 3, (2009, Budapest and Pécs, Hungary).

Kowal, Rebekah J. "Staging the Greensboro Sit-Ins." *The Drama Review* 48, no. 4 (Winter 2004): 135–54.

Kreis, Karl Markus. "German Wild West: Karl May's Invention of the Definitive Indian." In Pamela Kort, Max Hollein, eds, *I Like America: Fictions of the Wild* West (München, New York: Prestel, 2006), 249–73.

Krupat, Arnold. *The Voice in the Margin: Native American Literature and the Canon*. Berkeley: University of California Press, 1989.

Kunze, Anja. "Die Indianistikszene der DDR" [The Indianistic Scene of the German Democratic Republic]. Master's Thesis in European Ethnography and Geography, Humbold University of Berlin, October 2006.

Kyrova, Lucie. "Native American International Activism and Political Thought during the Cold War, 1950–1989." Unpublished doctoral dissertation. Department of History, College of William and Mary, May 2016.

Matthiessen, Peter. *In the Spirit of Crazy Horse*. New York: Viking Press, 1983.

May, Karl *Winnetou*. Translated by Michael Shaw. New York: The Seabury Press, 1977.

Means, Russell, with Marvin J. Wolf. *Where White Men Fear to Tread: The Autobiography of Russell Means*. New York: St. Martin's Press, 1995.

Meland, Carter, Joseph Bauerkemper, LeAnne Howe, and Heidi Stark. "The Bases Are Loaded: American Indians and American Studies." Joint issue of *Indigenous Studies Today: An International Journal* and *American Studies* (incorporating *American Studies International*) (Fall 2005): 391–416.

Miccosukee Seminole Nation Department of Public Information. Online: http://www.miccosukeeseminolenation.com/.

Moses, L. G. *Wild West Shows and the Images of American Indians, 1883–1933*. Albuquerque, NM: University of New Mexico Press, 1996.

Muehlebach, Andrea. "'Making Place' at the United Nations: Indigenous Cultural Politics at the U.N. Working Group on Indigenous Populations." In *Cultural Anthropology* 16, no. 3, (2001): 415–48.

Mulvey, Christopher. "Among the Sag-a-noshes: Ojibwa and Iowa Indians with George Catlin in Europe, 1843–1848." In Christian F. Feest, ed., *Indians and Europe: an Interdisciplinary Collection of Essays*. Aachen: Edition Herodot, Rader Verlag, 1987, 253–75.

Nesper, Larry. *The Walleye War: The Struggle for Ojibwe Spearfishing and Treaty Rights*. Lincoln, NE: University of Nebraska Press, 2002.

Niezen, Ronald. *The Origins of Indigenism: Human Rights and the Politics of Identity*. Berkeley, CA; London: University of California Press, 2003.

Nowicka, Ewa. "The 'Polish Movement Friends of the American Indians.'" Christian F. Feest, ed., *Indians and Europe: An Interdisciplinary Collection of Essays*. Aachen: Edition Herodot Rader-Verlag, 1987, 606–7, 599–608.

Meg Devlin O'Sullivan. "'We Worry About Survival': American Indian Women, Sovereignty, and the Right to Bear and Raise Children in the 1970s." Doctoral dissertation. Department of History, the University of North Carolina at Chapel Hill, 2007.

Nesper, Larry. *The Walleye War: The Struggle for Ojibwe Spearfishing and Treaty Rights*. Lincoln, NE: University of Nebraska Press, 2002.

Paskievich, John, dir. *If Only I Were an Indian*. Winnipeg: National Film Board of Canada, 1995.

Penny, Glenn. "Red Power: Liselotte Welskopf-Henrich and Indian Activist Networks in East and West Germany," *Central European History* 41, (2008), 447–76.

———. "Elusive Authenticity: The Quest for the American Indian in German Public Culture." In *Comparative Studies in Society and History* 48, no. 4, (October 2006): 798–818.

———. *Kindred by Choice: Germans and American Indians since 1800*. Chapel Hill: The University of North Carolina Press, 2013.

Permanent Forum on Indigenous Issues website. Online: http://social.un.org/index/IndigenousPeoples.aspx.

Peyer, Bernd C. "Who is Afraid of AIM?" In Christian F. Feest, ed., *Indians and Europe: An Interdisciplinary Collection of Essays*. Aachen: Edition Herodt-Rader Verlag, 1987, 551–64.

Pratt, Mary Louise. *Imperial Eyes: Travel Writing and Transculturation*. London, New York: Routledge, 1992.

Price, Sally. *Primitive Art in Civilized Places*. Chicago: University of Chicago Press, 1989.

Radway, Janice. "What's in a Name? Presidential Address to the American Studies Association, 20 November 1998." *American Quarterly* 51, no. 1 (1999): 1–32.

Roach, Joseph R. *Cities of the Dead: Circum-Atlantic Performance*. New York: Columbia University Press, 1996.

Rosier, Paul C. *Serving Their Country: American Indian Politics and Patriotism in the Twentieth Century*. Cambridge, MA: Harvard University Press, 2009.

Saunders, Frances Stonor. *The Cultural Cold War: The CIA and the World of Arts and Letters*. New York: New Press, 2000.

Sayer, John William. *Ghost Dancing the Law: The Wounded Knee Trials*. Cambridge, MA: Harvard University Press, 1997.

Schechner, Richard. *Performance Studies: An Introduction*. New York, London: Routledge, 2002.

Schroeder, Aribert. " 'They Lived Together with Their Dogs and Horses:' 'Indian Copy' in West German Newspapers 1968–1982." In Christian F. Feest, ed., *Indians and Europe: an Interdisciplinary Collection of Essays*. Aachen: Edition Herodot, Rader Verlag, 1987, 527–50.

Shull, Tad. *Redefining Red and Green: Ideology and Strategy in European Political* Ecology. Albany, NY: State University of New York Press, 1999.

Sieg, Katrin. *Ethnic Drag: Performing Race, Nation, Sexuality in West Germany.* Ann Arbor MI: The University of Michigan Press, 2002.

Sieg, Katrin. "Indian Impersonation as Historical Surrogation." Colin G. Calloway, Gerd Gemünden, and Suzanne Zantop, eds., *Germans and Indians: Fantasies, Encounters, Projections*. Lincoln, NE; London: University of Nebraska Press, 2002, 217–42.

Smith, Paul Chaat, and Robert Allen Warrior. *Like a Hurricane: The Indian Movement from Alcatraz to Wounded Knee*. New York: The New Press, 1996.

Special Rapporteur on the Rights of Indigenous Peoples website. Online: http://www.ohchr.org/EN/Issues/IPeoples/SRIndigenousPeoples/Pages/SRIPeoplesIndex.aspx.

Stern, Kenneth S. *Loud Hawk: The United States versus the American Indian Movement*. Norman, OK: University of Oklahoma Press, 1994.

Storr, Mel. *Latex and Lingerie: Shopping for Pleasure at Ann Summers Parties*. New York: Berg Publishers, 2003.

Taylor, Diana. *The Archive and the Repertoire*. Durham, NC: Duke University Press, 2003.

———. "Performance and/as History," *The Drama Review* 50, no. 1 (Spring 2006): 67–86.

"Threats to the Peaceful Observance of the Bicentennial. Hearing before the Subcommittee to Investigate the Administration of the Internal Security Act and Other Internal Security Laws of the Committee on the Judiciary,

United States Senate, Ninety-Fourth Congress, Second Session, June 18, 1976." U.S. Government Printing Office, Washington, 1976. Online: http://en.wikisource.org/wiki/Page:Threats_to_the_peaceful_observance_of_the_bicentennial.djvu/1.

Threlkeld, Megan. "The Pan-American Conference of Women, 1922: Successful Suffragists Turn to International Relations." *Diplomatic History* 31, no. 5 (November 2007): 801–28.

Tuch, Hans N. *Communicating with the World: U.S. Public Diplomacy Overseas.* New York: St. Martin's Press, 1990.

Turski, Birgit. *Die Indianistikgruppen in der DDR: Entwicklung, Probleme, Aussichten.* Idstein: Baum, 1994.

Tyeeme Clark, D. Anthony, and Norman R. Yetman, " 'To Feel the Drumming Earth Come Upward': Indigenizing the American Studies Discipline, Field Movement." Joint issue of *Indigenous Studies Today: An International Journal* and *American Studies* (incorporating *American Studies International*) (Fall 2005): 7–22.

The United Nations Declaration on the Rights of Indigenous Peoples. March 2008. Online: http://www.un.org/esa/socdev/unpfii/documents/DRIPS_en.pdf.

Von Eschen, Penny M. *Satchmo Blows Up the World: Jazz Ambassadors Play the Cold War.* Cambridge, MA: Harvard University Press, 2004.

———. *Race Against Empire: Black Americans and Anticolonialism, 1937–1957.* Ithaca, NY; London: Cornell University Press, 1997.

Weaver, Jace. *The Red Atlantic: American Indigenes and the Making of the Modern World, 1000–1927.* Chapel Hill: University of North Carolina Press, 2014.

Wilkinson Charles. *Blood Struggle: The Rise of Modern Indian Nations.* New York: Norton, 2005.

Williams, Jr., Robert A. "Treaties as Sacred Texts." In *Linking Arms Together: American Indian Treaty Visions of Law and Peace, 1600–1800*, New York: Oxford University Press, 1997, 40–61.

Wise, Gene. "Some Elementary Axioms for an American Culture Studies." *Prospects: An Annual of American Cultural Studies*, 4 (1979): 517–47.

Wood, Molly. " 'Commanding Beauty' and 'Gentle Charm': American Women and Gender in the Early Twentieth-Century Foreign Service," *Diplomatic History* 31, no. 3 (June 2007): 505–30.

Yearbook of the United Nations. Online: http://unyearbook.un.org/index.html.

Archival and Record Collections

Audiovisual Library of International Law. Online: http://untreaty.un.org/cod/avl/ha/ga_61-295/ga_61-295.html.

Wounded Knee Legal Defense/Offense Committee Records. Minnesota Historical Society, St. Paul, MN.

"Wounded Knee Legal Defense/Offense Committee: An Inventory of Its Records at the Minnesota Historical Society." Online finding aid: http://www.mnhs.org/library/findaids/00229.xml.

Underground Newspaper Collection, Center for Southwest Research, University of New Mexico, Albuquerque, NM.

Roger A. Finzel American Indian Movement Papers. Center for Southwest Research, University of New Mexico, Albuquerque, NM.

Carol Sullivan Papers, Center for Southwest Research, Zimmerman Library, The University of New Mexico, Albuquerque, NM.

State Department Records. National Archives II, College Park, MD.

State Department Papers. National Archives II. College Park, MD. Online database: http://aad.archives.gov/aad/series-description.jsp?s=4073&cat=all&bc=sl.

Smithsonian National Portrait Gallery. Online database: http://npgportraits.si.edu/emuseumCAP/code/emuseum.asp.

The Richard Erdoes Papers. Yale Collection of Western Americana, Beinecke Rare Book and Manuscript Library, Yale University, New Haven, CT.

Guide to the Richard Erdoes Papers. Online: http://drs.library.yale.edu:8083/saxon/SaxonServlet?style=http://drs.library.yale.edu:8083/saxon/EAD/yul.ead2002.xhtml.xsl&source=http://drs.library.yale.edu:8083/fedora/get/beinecke:erdoes/EAD&query=inca&filter=&hitPageStart=1.

Records of the International Indian Treaty Council office in San Francisco.

United Nations Archives and Records Management Section, New York City, NY.

Minutes of the United Nations Commission on Human Rights, 1977–1990. United Nations Library, Palace of the Nations, Geneva, Switzerland.

Records of the UN Working Group on Indigenous Populations, 1982–1990. United Nations UNOG Registry, Records and Archives Sub-Unit, Palace of the Nations, Geneva, Switzerland.

League of Nations Museum, United Nations Palace of the Nations, Geneva, Switzerland.

Records of the Indigenous Peoples' Information and Documentation Center, Geneva, Switzerland.

Fővárosi Szabó Ervin Library, Budapest, Hungary.

Baktay Ervin Memorial House and Museum of Western Games/Cowboys and Indians, Kisoroszi, Hungary.

Records of the Gesellschaft für bedrohte Völker (Society for Endangered Peoples), Göttingen, Germany.

Records of the office of Incomindios Schweiz, Zürich, Switzerland.

Federal Archive, Reich and GDR Department, Archive of the Parties and Mass Organizations of the GDR, Berlin, Germany.

Federal Commissioner for the files of the State Security Service of the former German Democratic Republic, Berlin, Germany.

Abkürzungsverzeichnis [List of Acronyms] Federal Commissioner for the files of the State Security Service of the former German Democratic Republic,

Berlin. Online: http://www.bstu.bund.de/DE/Wissen/Publikationen/Publikationen/E_abkuerzungsverzeichnis.pdf?__blob=publicationFile.

Yearbook of the United Nations. Online: http://unyearbook.un.org/index.html.

Interviews and Personal Communication

Interview with long-time member and leader of the Bakony group of Hungarian Indian hobbyists, Budapest, June 2011. Source kept anonymous due to research ethics regulations.

The author's interview with anonymous Hungarian hobbyist of the Danube valley group, Kisoroszi, Hungary, July 2011. Source kept anonymous due to research ethics regulations.

Personal interviews with Claus Biegert, Munich, Germany, July and December 2011.

Martin Klimke. Personal communication, Chicago, January 6, 2012.

Roxanne Dunbar-Ortiz. Personal communication via electronic mail, March 30, 2012.

Personal communication with staff of Incomindios Schweiz, Zürich, Switzerland.

Personal communication with staff of the Indigenous Peoples' Information and Documentation Center, Geneva, Switzerland.

Personal communication with staff of the Gesellschaft für bedrohte Völker (Society for Endangered Peoples), Göttingen, Germany.

Personal communication with staff of the International Indian Treaty Council office in San Francisco.

Index